EMBODIED

CHRISTOPHER ECCLESTON

EMBODIED

The psychology of physical sensation

OXFORD
UNIVERSITY PRESS

OXFORD

UNIVERSITY PRESS

Great Clarendon Street, Oxford, OX2 6DP,
United Kingdom

Oxford University Press is a department of the University of Oxford.
It furthers the University's objective of excellence in research, scholarship,
and education by publishing worldwide. Oxford is a registered trade mark of
Oxford University Press in the UK and in certain other countries

© Oxford University Press 2016

The moral rights of the author have been asserted

First Edition published in 2016

Impression: 4

Published in the United States of America by Oxford University Press
198 Madison Avenue, New York, NY 10016, United States of America

British Library Cataloguing in Publication Data
Data available

Library of Congress Control Number: 2015951251

ISBN 978–0–19–872790–3

Printed and bound by
CPI Group (UK) Ltd, Croydon, CR0 4YY

For Zoe

ACKNOWLEDGMENTS

Many people helped me find my way on this journey. Particular thanks go to those who allowed me to peer into their lives and ask them questions about how they live with their bodies and their sensory worlds. I am grateful to all of those striving to push themselves to their limits. Hopefully their voices will speak for many people. In the order they appear, thank you to Luna Othnin Girard, Debbie Hollingsworth, Luke Rendell, Jeremy Clark, Emma Roy, Marni Elder, Sam Kirby, Ian Taylor, Kerry Sutton, Sarah Prior, Ilana and Crispin Wigfield, Rupert Fingest, James Reynolds, Neil Carrier, Alex Coode, Euphemia Graham, Jean Christophe Slowik, Tom Strawson, Arthur Smith, and Connie Webber.

I am also grateful for the help of many colleagues and friends. Thank you to Anna Broderick who invited me to the Central Ballet School in London. She has a wonderful energy and enthusiasm for helping people achieve their dreams. Resmi Malko allowed me to observe his dancers. His quiet authority and connection with their movement was inspiring. Anna Hobson suggested I talk with Debbie Hollingsworth and made the introductions. Richard Tite encouraged me to think about acrobatics when thinking about movement, and introduced me to Luke Rendell. Jeremy is an old friend. Amanda Williams suggested I talk with Sam Kirby as a fellow champion freediver, and Mike Osborn and Jackie McCallum were very kind in introducing me to the amazing Ian and Pat Taylor. Caro Taraskevics suggested I talk with Emma Roy, and Isabelle Sully encouraged the remarkable Marni Elder that it might be fun to talk to me. Zoe Eccleston suggested I talk to Kerry Sutton who trains in Bath and had just completed her jungle run. Thank you to Anne Johnson from the Chronic Fatigue Service at the Royal National Hospital for Rheumatic Diseases NHS Trust in Bath. Their service is second-to-none internationally; their understanding of the needs of people with chronic fatigue is remarkable. Mike Osborn suggested to the Wigfields that a psychological approach to the marathon might add an interesting aspect. Rupert Fingest I have known for a very long time. Thanks to Nicolette Craig from the education department of the Cotswold Wildlife Park for being interested in the idea and suggesting I talk to James Reynolds. And Janet Bultitude introduced me to Neil Carrier. I am grateful to her for thinking so carefully about the book and who might be able to help. Euphemia Graham is a family friend, and Will Hawking gave me the idea of forge working that led to the fascinating Alex Coode. Dawn Hawking was kind in tracking down Jean Christophe and for the ice-cream ideas. And I am very grateful to Emma Fisher for persuading Tom Strawson that talking to a psychologist was not so weird a thing to do. Arthur Smith I cold-called. I am grateful he could not resist talking about flatulence. And, finally, Sarah Dalrymple took me seriously when I wanted to talk about vomiting and introduced me to Connie Webber.

Many other people made connections and suggestions, and so helped me ask the right questions. From OUP, Charlotte Green, Martin Baum, and Matthias Butler were patient with my bombarding them with drafts. There were many conversations with friends and colleagues along the way, in particular Geert Crombez, Amanda Williams, Nina Attridge, and Emma Fisher, who read unpolished versions. I am also grateful for the individual chapter reviews from the busiest of experts: Andrea Evers, Omer Van den Bergh, Kim Delbaere, Bob Hockey, and Martin Burton. I corresponded with many of the authors of the papers referred to. I am repeatedly amazed at how generous people are in sharing their work and discussing ideas within the papers. It would not be possible without their primary research. Ulrike Bingel and Thomas Tölle gave me invaluable advice in exploring the ideas of *das unkörperliche*.

Finally, thank you to Zoe for living with *The Body*, as it was known, for more than a year, for journeying with these chapters, for the home experimentation, for editing, and for staying positive as it emerged out of its shell.

CONTENTS

List of Figures   *xv*
List of Tables   *xvi*
List of Boxes   *xvii*

1. The ten neglected senses   1
   The big five senses   2
   Methods of inquiry   4
   Personal stories   5
   The physical senses   5
   References   6

2. Balance   8
   Learning to stand on your own two feet   9
   A psychology of falling   9
   Deliberate falling   10
   Fear of falling   11
   Accidental falling   14
   Achieving balance (equilibrium)   15
   Natural balance awareness   16
   Interview: Luna, the dancer: "when you are on balance you can
     grow, almost out of the ground"   17
   Losing balance (disequilibrium)   19
   Dizziness   19
   Vertigo   22
   Interview: Debbie, living with vertigo: "your mind can play amazingly
     cruel tricks on you"   23
   Height intolerance   25
   Height intolerance autoscopy   26
   Summary   29
   References   29

3. Movement   33
   Proprioception   34
   Developing movement control   34

Embodied cognition   35
Clumsiness   36
Improving motor performance   37
Personal theory of movement   39
Interview: Luke, the acrobat: "it is more about focus than thinking" 40
Personal space   43
Posing and strutting   44
Disorders of movement   46
Anosognosia   47
Tremor   47
Start and stop   48
Fine motor control   48
Interview: Jeremy, recovering from stroke: "you take things for granted" 49
Summary   51
Notes   51
References   51

4. Pressure   55
Flexibility   56
Stiffness   56
Flexibility-stiffness continuum   57
Interview: Emma, the Yoga teacher: "I am aware of my body all the time" 60
Strength   62
Weakness   62
Strength-weakness continuum   63
Heaviness   64
Lightness   66
Heaviness-lightness continuum   67
Swollen   68
Reduced   69
Swollen-reduced continuum   71
Interview: Marni, living with lupus: "it feels like every inch of your
    body weighs too much"   72
Summary   75
Notes   75
References   75

5. Breathing   79
Catching your breath   80
Taking control of breathing   81
Breathing to achieve   82
Breathing at height and depth   84

CONTENTS

Interview: Sam, the freediver: "it is massively a mental game"   86
Respiratory awareness   88
Respiratory variability   89
A focus on rumination   90
Relearning to breathe   91
Panic   92
Dyspnea   95
Terror management   100
Interview: Ian, living with dyspnea: "it is about feeling vulnerable"   101
Summary   103
Notes   103
References   103

6. Fatigue   107
Being tired   107
The fallacy of resource depletion   109
Fatigue as motivation to change   110
The urge to sleep   112
Vitality, energy, and perseverance   112
Brain training   113
Indefatigable   115
Interview: Kerry, the ultra runner: "when my body says
    stop I won't accept it"   116
Being tired all the time   118
Cognitive behavioral model   119
Attention to threat   120
Cognitive behavioral therapy   122
Interview: Sarah, living with fatigue: "everything is planned"   123
Summary   125
Note   125
References   125

7. Pain   129
The problem of pain   130
Pain mechanisms   130
Motivated interruption   131
Religion   132
Rites of passage   134
Self-injury   134
Goal pursuit   135
Interview: The Wigfields, running a marathon together: "what I
    often do is think 'one more mile'"   137

CONTENTS

Paying attention to pain   139
Living in an analgesic culture   140
Pain that won't go away   141
Trying to cope alone   141
Vigilance   142
Worry   143
Courageous engagement   144
Interview: Rupert, living with chronic pain: "I will always push
    through if what I am doing is worth it"   145
Helping people to cope   146
Summary   148
Notes   148
References   148

8. Itch   152
From itch to scratch   153
Function of itch   153
Grooming   154
Social contagion of itch and scratch   155
A hygiene paradox   157
On the pleasure of itch   158
Interview: James, working with itch: "it is the horrible looking
    creatures that I see a beauty in"   159
Chronic itch   161
Attending to itch   162
If you have an itch, don't scratch   163
Social emotions   164
Shame and disgust   165
Formication   168
Psychodermatology   169
Interview: Neil, living with itch: "it is hard for me to imagine
    what it is like not to itch"   170
Summary   172
Note   173
References   173

9. Temperature   176
Thermoregulation   177
Blowing hot and cold: judging others' character   179
Please hold my coffee   179
Cold and lonely: a Bridget Jones effect   180
Protecting ourselves from the elements: secondary regulation   181

CONTENTS

Mad dogs and Englishmen   181
"The apparel oft proclaims the man"   182
Entering the extremes   183
Interview: Alex, the heritage blacksmith: "you have a holiday
    from your body"   184
The paradox of sweating   186
Hot flushes   189
The psychological ambiguity of heat   189
Being cold   190
Raynaud's phenomenon   191
Cold comfort   192
Interview: Euphemia, living with Reynaud's: "I guess I am
    learning all of the time"   194
Summary   196
Notes   196
References   197

10. Appetite   201
Appetite regulation   201
Power   203
Setting priorities   204
The pleasures of desire   205
Eat your greens   206
Lipsmackinthirstquenchinacetastinmotivatingoodbuzzincool
    talkinhighwalkinfastlivinevergivincoolfizzin Pepsi   208
What's on the menu?   209
Interview: Jean Christophe, the restaurateur: "I love what we serve
    and we serve what I love"   212
Personal responsibility   214
"I'm on a diet"   215
Hungry behavior   216
Craving   217
Interview: Tom, the jockey: "the discipline comes
    from an ambition to succeed"   220
Summary   222
Notes   222
References   222

11. Expulsion   225
Human jets   226
"Coughs and sneezes spread diseases"   227
Common and public   227

CONTENTS

Hiccup   229
Releasing gases   230
Burping   230
Farting   232
Why is farting funny?   234
Interview: Arthur, the comedian: "we are hardwired to laugh at farting"   234
Continence psychology   236
Toilet training   236
Managing incontinence   237
Emotion and incontinence   238
Vomiting   238
Voluntary vomiting   240
Interview: Connie, on modern vomiting: "we are putting more
    alcohol in so we need to take it out."   241
Reproductive removal   242
Ejaculation   244
Tell no one   245
Summary   246
Notes   246
References   247

12. Embodied and embedded   251
Transitive and intransitive   252
Attending   252
Vigilance   253
Urge   254
Corporeal derealization   256
Aging   258
Hands up   259
A psychology of the body   260
References   260

Index   261

LIST OF FIGURES

Figure 2.1:   Cartoon of two extreme experimental conditions: well lit and walking on the ground, and dimly lit and walking on an elevated platform.

Figure 3.1:   Three sitting poses, two expansive and one constricted.

Figure 4.1:   Shrinking waist and hips study. The design of the study and position of the hands to the body.

Figure 5.1:   The relationship between the pressure of inspired oxygen at different altitudes.

Figure 5.2:   Equipment for 24-hour monitoring of breathing and ambulation.

Figure 8.1:   The distribution of scratching episodes in widespread (scattered) areas, in patients with atopic dermatitis (AD) and healthy subjects. (Plate 1)

Figure 8.2:   Stimuli used in the paired disgust sensitivity task. (Plate 2)

Figure 9.1:   Average daily deaths and monthly temperatures in England and Wales in 2012/13 and a five-year average. (Plate 3)

Figure 10.1:   Rated characteristics of salmon-flavored food presented as either "ice-cream" or "frozen savory mousse."

Figure 10.2:   Body modifications student and professional actors would undertake to achieve their "dream job."

Figure 11.1:   Coughs and sneezes spread diseases. Circa 1960. (Plate 4)

Figure 11.2:   Domains of Quality of Life judged by women with normal menstrual bleeding and heavy menstrual bleeding (HMB).

LIST OF TABLES

Table 2.1: The phenomenology of four autoscopic illusions
Table 4.1: Yoga poses and descriptions used in clinical trial
Table 5.1: Language used to describe breathlessness by those with and without a Chronic Obstructive Pulmonary Disorder
Table 7.1: The benefits of pain and associated processes
Table 12.1: The functions of physical senses

LIST OF BOXES

Box 2.1.   Luna, the dancer: *"when you are on balance you can grow, almost out of the ground"*
Box 2.2.   Debbie, living with vertigo: *"your mind can play amazingly cruel tricks on you"*
Box 3.1.   Luke, the acrobat: *"it is more about focus than thinking"*
Box 3.2.   Jeremy, recovering from stroke: *"you take things for granted"*
Box 4.1.   Emma, the yoga teacher: *"I am aware of my body all the time"*
Box 4.2.   Marni, living with lupus: *"it feels like every inch of your body weighs too much"*
Box 5.1.   Sam, the freediver: *"it is massively a mental game"*
Box 5.2.   Ian, living with dyspnea: *"it is about feeling vulnerable"*
Box 6.1.   Kerry, the ultra runner: *"when my body says stop I won't accept it"*
Box 6.2.   Sarah, living with fatigue: *"everything is planned"*
Box 7.1.   The Wigfields, running a marathon together: *"what I often do is think 'one more mile'"*
Box 7.2.   Rupert, living with chronic pain: *"I will always push through if what I am doing is worth it"*
Box 8.1.   James, working with itch: *"it is the horrible looking creatures that I see a beauty in"*
Box 8.2.   Neil, living with itch: *"it is hard for me to imagine what it is like not to itch"*
Box 9.1.   Alex, the heritage blacksmith: *"you have a holiday from your body"*
Box 9.2.   Euphemia, living with Raynaud's: *"I guess I am learning all of the time"*
Box 10.1   Jean Christophe, the restaurateur: *"I love what we serve and we serve what I love"*
Box 10.2.   Tom, the jockey: *"the discipline comes from an ambition to succeed"*
Box 11.1.   Arthur, the comedian: *"we are hardwired to laugh at farting"*
Box 11.2.   Connie, on modern vomiting: *"we are putting more alcohol in so we need to take it out"*

CHAPTER 1

THE TEN NEGLECTED SENSES

This book is about how we experience our bodies and how our bodies experience the world; it is about physical sensation. For the most part the body has been neglected and ignored in psychology, thought of merely as a taxi for the mind, dwarfed by the study of observable behavior, action and agency, motivation and performance, cognition and emotion. We take for granted the obvious truth that the objects of our study (personality, motivation, emotion, cognition, and behavior) are quite literally embodied. We are encased by flesh in a physical being that defines the limits of our ability to act upon the world, and provides the medium by which the world acts upon us.

All of the human sciences are interested in bodies, in their biological, physiological, chemical, and biomechanical functions. The collective application of these sciences as medicine is comprehensively invested in understanding the disordered body and its effects on human function, including the opportunity for repair. The experience of the bodily senses, and of having a body, is much less investigated. As Rom Harré (1991) noted, being embodied means to be instantiated, to be definable, observable, and accountable. Ultimately it also means to have one's limits defined. It is the limits that are partly of interest here. It is only when forced to our limits that we come to understand the possibilities of being. And in each of the ten individual sense chapters that follow, extreme physical experiences provide one important source of evidence.

Psychology was not always uninterested in bodily sensations. At its birth, German structural psychology, borne from physiology and philosophy, was greatly concerned with the phenomenology of physical experience and with the close observation and detailed report of sensation. Much of Wilhelm Wundt's early innovation in laboratory science came in the form of improved instrumentation to measure the speed of perception and the integration of sensory information (Rieber and Robinson, 2001). Methods of close introspection were an early casualty of the turn to observable behavior as the new subject of psychology (Danziger, 1990). How we actually experience our senses came to be seen with suspicion, often removed as a source of experimental noise from otherwise perfect behavioral experiments (Leary, 1995). Phenomenology was sent back to philosophy. In this book, however, the feel of one's own body is an important source of evidence for a psychology of physical sensation, and is brought back out of the shadows.

1

The big five senses

Open any general textbook of psychology and perception will be covered in detail. However, much of it will be about the big five senses, the senses we grew up learning about as children: sight, sound, smell, taste, and touch. The primacy of these sensations in our thinking and learning is reflected in their cultural dominance. The big five dominate across cultures, religions, and histories, starting perhaps with Aristotle's conjecture in *De anima* that five senses were philosophically sufficient.

Vision, of course, is hugely important to the coherence of our behavior and to learning and development. To a great extent we live in a world that reflects the dominance of vision, with a built environment dependent upon and determined by visual capabilities. Culturally, vision also dominates and can be seen in our everyday language with the use of visual metaphors and references—as I just did with "can be seen" (Duncum, 2001). Psychologically, vision achieves quite astonishing computational challenges in returning coherence of experience from the physical barrage of light energy. Perhaps the challenge of vision science is not to map the complexity of what our visual system can achieve, but to address a fundamental conundrum of consciousness. Simply put: how close to reality is our visual experience? What is real to us as perception is largely an approximation, augmented by computational rules, finessed to achieve efficiency and to infer a good-enough version of reality, one that allows decision making and coherent behavior (Knill and Richards, 1996). What you see is not what you get. Where the scientific study of vision goes we will just have to "wait and see."

Vision is fascinating but is a scientific sponge. It soaks up attention and resources. Audition comes a close second in the perception popularity stakes. The science of hearing is wide-ranging, from physics through engineering and mathematics, to architecture and the social study of sound. Acoustic psychology is interested largely in how perceptual rules govern heard experience, in particular how we achieve discrimination in the amount, location, character, and quantity of sound, and how we segment signals from noise. A major research interest is in how meaning is identified in otherwise disordered sound, in what distinguishes noise from music, or one musical tone from another (Lotto and Holt, 2011). What distinguishes the distressed cry from the contented gurgle of a child is hard to explain by reference to the signal alone. Explaining the emotional content and the personal recognition of sound as meaningful is where much of the interesting psychological investigation of auditory perception lies.

The other two senses with biological organs front-loaded in the head also attract some attention. Smell (olfaction) and taste (gustation) use different sensory apparatuses but operate around the same functions of exploring the properties of food or potential food, and by providing critical information regarding toxicity or danger. For example, Daniel Kelly explores the evolutionarily quite ancient ability of our midbrain to use the sensory input from taste and smell to trigger an extreme affective experience of disgust (Kelly, 2011). Smell, of course, provides the material for psychological functions that go beyond self-protection or the provision of food. Smell provides information on environmental danger, on health status, and on preferences. Fragrance can affect everything from one's judgments about liking (both people and things) to one's consumer choices, and even mate selection.

Taste, however, occupies an interesting cultural position in this battle for the hierarchy of senses. There is a cultural ambiguity around taste, which is best understood by the desire to rescue taste from base consumption; a desire that can be traced to the sixth century (Jütte, 2005). To taste means to consume, but to "have taste" means to be especially discriminating, to be able unfalteringly to identify quality, to be attuned to fine differences, and of course to reject the ugly, the common, and the familiar. Confusingly, *taste* is applied across the realm of aesthetic judgments: one can have (or be lacking in) taste in music, visual art, dance, and, of course, in judgments about food and drink. The sensory apparatus of taste allows discrimination and is complexly organized around categories of experience, with a particular reference to emotion and memory, but its discriminatory ability is minimal in comparison to vision and audition. In the world of the big five senses, it should be more flattering to be described as having *sight* or *smell* than it would to be described as having good *taste*.

The co-location of sensory apparatuses in the head to enable the four primary senses of sight, sound, smell, and taste is no evolutionary accident. The head provides an efficient guidance system enabling us to move at speed away from danger and toward safety, comfort, and reward. In addition, having duplicated organs of detection allows for location and motion detection. More than a simple system of detecting change, the environment can now afford action specific to the needs of its context: a delicate play of sense and context defining possible action (Gibson, 1979/1986; Stoffregen, 2003).

Sight, hearing, smell, and taste have also promoted *social* scientific debate. Lisa Blackman argues for a hierarchy of civilized sensation: vision and sound are the primary civilized sensations, with smell and taste relegated to the animalistic, the base, and the primal (Blackman, 2008). Sight and sound are senses primarily of discrimination, of discernment, of clarification, and of precision, both practically and culturally. The gustatory sensations of taste and smell are less precise and more personal. Sight and sound can be achieved distally, and often covertly, whereas taste and smell require proximity and intimacy. In other words, you can watch someone undiscovered at a distance, but to smell and taste someone you need to be up close and personal. A primary feature of the passage to adulthood is the negotiation of the space between senses in a socializing process. Children are encouraged that licking, biting, spitting, and overtly smelling others are going to be unwelcome in public adult society. Adolescent and adult transgressions of these rules are socially troublesome and demand explanation, explanations that are often pathologically framed. Taste and smell are the most private and intimate of the big five.

Finally, touch, like taste and smell, involves proximity because it requires contact with what is outside the body in a way that leaves the integrity of the body intact, its boundaries unbroken. Central to touch is a discrimination of what is inside and outside. Touch is also the only one of the big five senses to have extended its sensory apparatus away from the head. Sensory nerve endings capable of discriminating change in their environment through contact with the outside world are distributed throughout the skin and so around the entire body. They are the principal methods of embodiment. Most of the touch apparatus however is digital: located in and referring to fingers. To manipulate and explore the world through touch, and to extend personal space to the peripersonal arc of our physical reach is a critical part of defining personal and embodied being (Patterson, 2007).

The big five senses of seeing, hearing, smelling, tasting, and touching are undoubtedly interesting and a major part of embodiment. But they are not everything. Perhaps our fascination with these dominant senses has come at the cost of a lack of investigation of the neglected other ten bodily senses that form a core part of the intertwined experiences of the body: being physically embodied and environmentally embedded (Haugeland, 1998).

Methods of inquiry

I adopt a transdisciplinary approach for this investigation of the physical senses. Any one source of evidence is not going to be enough. For each sense it will be important to review the biological structure and function of each system, with enough anatomy and physiology to understand when and why structural limits of experience arise. Relevant also will be the sciences of medicine as they apply to each case. And equally important are the cultural and humanity studies, especially of historicized personal accounting of experience, and narrative representations of extreme cases.

Steve Brown and colleagues neatly summarize traditions of enquiry in embodiment (Brown et al., 2011). Sociologists have been interested in how specific bodily practices such as cosmetic or adornment rituals (e.g., tattooing) operate within cultures, made more interesting by the modern challenges of robotics, miniaturization, and the blurring between what is manufactured and what is natural in new bodies (Crossley, 2005). But much social theory has also grappled with the body as a site of contested power and governance, most notably in cultural methods of objectification and display (Turner, 1992). Feminist theory has perhaps done most to traverse disciplinary boundaries with a specific focus on the gendered experience of bodies as a site of argumentation over identity, control, and possibility (Ussher, 1997). Also relevant are philosophical investigations on embodied cognition, which promote a cognitive version of direct perception. In its strongest form, embodied cognition holds that bodies not only constrain cognition but also shape and regulate it. Bodies create minds (Foglia and Wilson, 2013).

4

The psychology of the physical senses I explore is strongly influenced by a tradition of enquiry that can be broadly defined as *functionalist*, one that focuses on the experience of behavior in context. However, I have tried to extend this functionalism to make space for personal experience. Examining personal experience has roots in phenomenology, in existential philosophy, and in the structuralism of early perceptual physiology. Existential psychology, as it was originally known in the German tradition, focused on the precise description of the structure of private experience; self-observation of that experience was the primary source of scientific evidence (Titchener, 1912). Scattered across the subdisciplines of psychology, you can find calls to return experience to its place at the center of psychological enquiry (Stenner, 2008). I develop here, following Andy Clark, a form of *extended functionalism* (Clark, 2008). Under investigation is environmentally embedded experience that is constrained and made possible by both having and being a body. Missing for me from these analyses is the empiricism of private experience, and in this sense I extend functionalism with a phenomenological consideration of the personal.

Personal stories

For each of the ten physical senses I asked people to talk with me about their experience of the sensation being investigated. There are twenty-one personal stories appearing throughout. Their stories are idiosyncratic. They are not case summaries and are not meant to be typical. They are specific. My aim is to exemplify, sometimes to investigate, but always to humanize. Psychology can lose itself in method sometimes, and it is important to come back to real people and their experiences with their bodies.

The stories are written as brief sections of interview. I don't pretend to have captured the complexity of people's lives. Reported are stripped-down versions of experience focused specifically on the sense being discussed. Importantly, they are edited. Natural speech is less accessible when reproduced verbatim. In editing, though, I have always attempted to keep the meanings intact. I also offered everyone the opportunity to be anonymous. Some people took up that offer, so some of the names have been changed. The people I met were, without exception, intriguing, beguiling, and, above all, generous.

The physical senses

My choice of ten will be contentious to some. There has been no shortage of attempts to draw a hierarchy of the senses (see Robert Jütte's helpful 2005 history of the senses). Some attempts focus on a philosophical distinction of felt experience. David Armstrong, for example, argued for the importance of a difference between *transitive* sensations, whose existence can occur without the sensing person, such as balance, and *intransitive* senses, which can exist only in and of the person, such as itch (Armstrong, 1962). Others are pragmatic. For example, both Mark Patterson (2007) and Mark Hollins (2010) extend touching to do the work of many interoceptive (bodily) sensations. Although the philosophical arguments are instructive, and the biological psychology of levels of perception and cognition interesting, the experience of each sensory category is equal across the ten, and so their treatment here is equal. I am deliberately attempting a complete psychology of the body.

Each chapter focuses on a neglected physical sense. They are not neglected in real life. We are only too happy to talk about how our bodies feel. But they are neglected from the point of view of serious psychological enquiry. Of course some are more studied than others, but compared to the big five, the ten bodily senses have been neglected for too long.

I start with *balance* and *movement*, the proprioceptive senses that position us in relation to space. Next, I investigate a category of experiences of working with force as *pressure* senses. Within *pressure* I deliberately wanted to explore the common human experiences of flexibility and stiffness, strength and weakness, heaviness and lightness, and the feelings of being swollen or in some way reduced. *Breathing* is given a whole chapter because the perception of breathing and its absence are unique. Next come three chapters on the interoceptive domains of *fatigue, pain*, and *itch*, which are followed by chapter-length considerations of *temperature* and *appetite*. Finally, I introduce perhaps the most neglected of all bodily senses, the physical experiences that accompany the *expulsion* of matter from the body. They include, in the order in which they are treated, the air-removal senses of sneeze, cough, hiccup, burp, and fart; and the fluid-removal senses of defecation, urination, vomiting, menstruation, and ejaculation.

Each of the ten senses is explored as if it were isolated. This is a deliberate methodological choice. It is so rare to have a focus on a specific physical sense that I tried to avoid distraction. It might seem odd to explore appetite without taste, for example, or motion without sight—but these senses deserve to be foregrounded, dragged into the spotlight. In the final chapter I look across the physical senses for what is common, at what we can learn for a more encompassing, more complete psychology of embodiment.

References

Armstrong, D.M. (1962). Bodily sensations. London: Routledge and Kegan Paul.
Blackman, L. (2008). The body. Oxford: Berg.
Brown, S.D., Cromby, J., Harper, D.J., Johnson, K. and Reavey, P. (2011). Researching "experience": embodiment, methodology, process. *Theory and Psychology*, 21, 493–515.
Clark, A. (2008). Pressing the flesh: a tension in the study of the embodied, embedded mind. *Philosophy and Phenomenological Research*, 76, 37–59.
Crossley, N. (2005). Mapping reflexive body techniques: on body modification and maintenance. *Body and Society*, 11, 1–35.

Danziger, K. (1990). Constructing the subject: historical origins of psychological research. Cambridge: Cambridge University Press.

Duncum, P. (2001). Visual culture: developments, definitions and directions for art education. *Studies in Art Education*, 2001, 42, 103–112.

Foglia, L. and Wilson, R. (2013). Embodied cognition. *WIREs Cognitive Science*, 4, 319–325.

Gibson, J.J. (1986). The ecological approach to visual perception. New York: Taylor and Francis. (Originally published 1979)

Harré, R. (1991). Physical being: a theory of corporeal psychology. Oxford: Blackwell Publishers.

Haugeland, J. (1998). Mind embodied and embedded. In J. Haugeland (Ed.), Having thought: essays in the metaphysics of mind (pp. 207–240). Cambridge: Harvard University Press.

Hollins, M. (2010). Somesthetic senses. *Annual Review of Psychology*, 61, 243–271.

Jütte, R. (2005). A history of the senses: from antiquity to cyberspace. Cambridge: Polity Press.

Kelly, D. (2011). Yuck! the nature and moral significance of disgust. London: Bradford Press.

Knill, D.C. and Richards, W. (Eds.). (1996). Perception as Bayesian inference. Cambridge: Cambridge University Press.

Leary, D. (Ed.). (1995). Metaphors in the history of psychology. Cambridge: Cambridge University Press.

Lotto, A. and Holt, R. (2011). Psychology of auditory perception. *Wires Cognitive Science*, 2, 479–489.

Patterson, M. (2007). The senses of touch: haptics, affects and technologies. New York: Berg.

Rieber, R.W. and Robinson, D.K. (Eds.). (2001). Wilhelm Wundt in history: the making of a scientific psychology. New York: Kluwer.

Stenner, P. (2008). A.N. Whitehead and subjectivity. *Subjectivity*, 22, 90–109.

Stoffregen, T.A. (2003). Affordances as properties of the animal-environment system. *Ecological Psychology*, 15, 115–134.

Titchener, E.B. (1912). Prolegomena to a study of introspection. *American Journal of Psychology*, 23, 427–448.

Turner, B.S. (1992). Regulating bodies: essays in medical sociology. London: Routledge.

Ussher, J. (Ed.). (1997). Body talk: material and discursive regulation of madness, politics and reproduction. London: Routledge.

CHAPTER 2

BALANCE

Staying upright is a remarkable feat of human biology that we rarely if ever consider; until, that is, we are confronted with its failure. Adopting and maintaining a stable position in a direct relationship with gravity is a basic requirement. Literally, one must take a stand in relation to the world. The perception of imbalance and its removal to create balance (also known as being in disequilibrium or equilibrium) is achieved by the convergence of sensory input from the visual, vestibular, and proprioceptive systems, and their cortical integration. I have chosen here to focus exclusively on balance and imbalance. From a neuroanatomical point of view, balance is only one specific function of integrated sensory systems controlling bodily position; it is a core part of many physical experiences. Running, walking, jumping, and even lying all involve balance. From a psychological perspective, however, the phenomenological experiences of being in or out of balance have a unique character. We know what being unbalanced feels like.

I am interested in the plasticity of balance perception, from the excitement of the infant achieving standing unsupported to how balance can be trained, controlled, or improved. I explore normal balance, with a focus on applied attempts to train people to overcome or control the perception of imbalance in the context of skill development and falls prevention. I then turn to a clinical focus on the disorders of imbalance, both primary and those secondary to disease or injury. Finally, I offer a functional view that places balance in a cognitive and motivational context, in which one's beliefs about how the world should be are perhaps as important as one's perception of the world.

Extreme experiences are an important source of evidence. There are people who have trained and trained until they can achieve remarkable feats of balance, often for public performance or just private pleasure. At the other extreme, there are many people who live with one of the challenging disorders of balance; they are often hidden from public view, unable to stand without dizziness, vertigo, and a feeling of falling. I explore both of these extremes with the help of two people who live with the experience of extreme balance or imbalance. I talked with Luna who is a classically trained professional dancer; understanding balance during complex movements is central to her art. And I met Debbie who has had vertigo for the last two years and is learning to live with an impermanent physical world.

Learning to stand on your own two feet

The human ear enables the perception of sound, balance, and positioning of the head in concert with visual feedback. The vestibular system contains in each inner ear three semicircular canals ending in ampullae, and two orthogonally positioned otolithic organs, the saccule and the utricle. The latter contain areas of hair-shaped cells (cilia) in membranous folds with, suspended above them in endolymphatic fluid, crystals of calcium carbonate that add mass to allow movement of the cilia giving critical positioning information (Van De Water, 2012). All sensory information passes through the vestibular nuclei to the thalamus, to the cerebellum, and to various cortical areas of the brain (Lopez and Blanke, 2011). This vestibular system works with information from the visual system, from touch, from proprioceptive transducers in muscle, joint, and skeleton, interoceptive feedback, and from memory, to produce balance. Balance in this psychological sense refers to more than just equilibrium: balance is the stable gravitational position in relation to the world, an egocentric sense of position within the world (where I am in relation to other objects), and a sense of agency (control over that position).

The lack of specificity and failure to reliably identify a unique vestibular cortex is part of the intriguing neuroscience of vestibular function. Its cortical projections spread widely across the brain, and interact with other sensory systems, including touch and pain (Ferrè et al., 2013). The primary function of the system in giving critical information about the self in relation to the world is now thought to go beyond the provision of information on agency, position, and object relations. Vestibular information appears to contribute to body schemata in general (Lopez et al., 2012), and specifically to one's sense of ownership over all or part of one's body (Lopez et al., 2008).

We learn to stand by training our intact vestibular system through goal-directed movement. It is because we are inherently curious that we need to quickly train our sensory apparatus to help us explore. Unsupported bipedal postural control, or *standing* as we call it, is critical to the development of point and reach, which are themselves critical determinants of social development in infants. We learn to stand, typically at the end of the first year, partly because of physical maturation, and in part due to the richness of the context we are learning to explore. Controlling postural sway and reducing the randomness (or *entropy*) of that sway while positioning for point or reach are helped by repeated reaching (Claxton et al., 2012). Even at ten years of age children are adopting alternative balancing strategies to achieve a stable position to allow reach and grasp (Haddad et al., 2012).

A psychology of falling

Balance, of course, relies on more than vestibular function; it involves contributory postural information from muscle and skeleton. Proprioception and movement perception are explored in Chapter 3. But maintaining postural equilibrium—centering and main-taining the body's mass in relation to gravity—is a critical and automatic human sen-sorimotor activity that goes on all the time, without us noticing. I propose a psychology of falling. We can learn a lot from both deliberate and accidental falling. A relatively modern human invention is the pursuit of safe deliberate falling: think about free-running (parkour), parachuting, or the roller coaster ride. What can we learn from these newly engineered experiences? I examine the experience of those attempting to master and control balance: those who work or play at heights, or who take part in activities that require high levels of balance control, such as gymnastics or ballet. Also interesting are the trips, slips, and collapses of accidental falling. Finally, I focus on the disorders of balance, in particular those suffering from dizziness, vertigo, and height intolerance.

Deliberate falling

Falling involves both the loss of equilibrium (imbalance) and a loss of control to gravity. A fall can be of a short duration (e.g., collapse to the floor from standing) or a long dur-ation (e.g., a parachute jump). Deliberate falling is associated with the momentary sacri-fice of control to gravity. But this sacrifice is only partial. Those who engage in deliberate falling trust in a set of control procedures, tactics, equipment, or agents that limit any damage from the fall, such as the parachute, a bungee rope, or the fairground engineer.

One might think that extreme sports people are likely to be risk takers, but the opposite appears to be true. For example, in a large sample of free-runners, worry and anxiety about action were related to risk taking but were mediated by self-control and self-ability beliefs (Merrit and Tharp, 2013). In other words, believing you are in con-trol when planning to lose control seems to be an important part of the experience of deliberate falling. Further, the pursuit of freedom to live as you choose, expressed in extreme and unusual sport, is paradoxically characterized by high levels of com-mitment, discipline, and skills development. For example, Eric Brymer and Robert Schweitzer interviewed 15 extreme athletes, including base jumpers, waterfall kayak-ers, and big wave surfers. The athletes they found "revealed a consciousness of choos-ing a way of being-in-the-world in which predictability was subjugated in preference to letting go of control." They noted also that there was

a paradox to participants' experience in that they develop skills to engage in activities "at the extreme" and develop the skill and flexibility to experience some degree of control and mastery of the techniques which enable them to engage in the activities. (Brymer and Schweitzer, 2013, p. 871)

They were interested in fear and motivations. All reported fear but judged this as healthy and necessary. Mastering fear was a prime motivation (Brymer and Schweitzer, 2012).

A less extreme example of the transformative power of overcoming fear is the fairground ride. Many roller coaster rides include a fall or a *drop*. The drop rides are marketed to youth and are relatively common (Gothelf et al., 2010). They provide a modern cultural mechanism for the safe exploration of fear. Imagine that before the advent of mechanized safe fear it was impossible to experience the long-duration fall and live to explain the feeling. Kathryn Woodcock (2007) gives us an intriguing glimpse into the world of those attempting to improve the safety of fairground rides, when by their nature people are seeking to experience the illusion of serious risk. Posting warnings, for example, are unlikely to be effective. She observed over 5,000 journeys on 103 different rides, at three carnivals in Canada. She recognized that raising awareness to situational danger was difficult to achieve:

> Situation awareness is an unusual challenge in this domain. During the ride, the rider will be immersed in the illusory physical sensation contrived by the ride designer, be it unpredictable changes of direction, flying, or free falling or the illusion of a ride narrative, such as travelling to distant lands or other worlds. To the investigator, the real-world limits are apparent, thus the rider's behaviour may be interpreted as a loss of situation awareness, in the failure to be aware of the danger of an action, or a mode error, where the action taken is appropriate in another mode but not the current one. Unlike most other human error circumstances, in this domain the requisite consciousness of the real-world situation would cause failure to achieve the ride's other mission, which requires immersion in the illusory world. (Woodcock, 2007, pp. 394–395)

This is perhaps why people put themselves at risk by attempting to increase the thrill (e.g., standing out of harness).

The context of the deliberate fall is crucially important. Whether it is in pursuit of a hedonic thrill, the safe testing of fear, or an experience narrated as transformative, the meaning of the fall is important. We know that when standing on a precipice, fear of falling over the edge is directly related to one's perception of height (Proffitt, 2006; Teachman et al., 2008). What is missing from this literature is any phenomenological sampling of the experience during the fall.

Deliberate falling is a modern invention. Exposure to terror with new technology like the bungee rope or the fairground drop provides novel opportunities to sample the perception of prolonged imbalance. Just as visual illusions and altered mirrors taught us much about visual perception, so perhaps the mechanisms of deliberate falling used to thrill could teach us about balance perception.

Fear of falling

Some researchers have asked people what it is like to fall. I could find no studies of people reporting the experience of deliberate falling, no speak-aloud studies during an actual fall: that would be interesting. But we know that the meaning of the fall, how it came about and its consequences, are what matters. To older people the meaning of falling is the challenge to independence, a possible signal of a new stage of decline, and a threat to one's identity as competent (Dollard et al., 2012). A common feature of accidental falling is the experience of shock. For example, in one interview with 27 older people who had fallen suddenly, finding oneself on the floor emerged as the most disturbing aspect of falling. One participant, for example, said:

> Well, it came as a shock. It's a shock to me, very much. I really didn't think anything like this would ever happen to me. Nothing ever has of all the years . . . and it came as a terrible shock. (Roe et al., 2008, p. 592).

As with deliberate falling in the sportsperson, accidental falling in the older person can also be a transformative experience, but the transformation is to a life of everyday fear. Falling as an older person is not useful or edifying; it is unpleasant and disruptive. Unplanned and unwelcome falling is experienced as a loss of autonomy and control over a basic human function (staying upright): it is immediate discomfort along with a more reflexive fearful concern of an altered future. When one has had a fall, one becomes vigilant for possible future falls. A primary goal for assistive devices and treatments is not only to stop the fall, but also to reduce the burden of feeling constantly vigilant to the possibility of a fall (Williams et al., 2013).

Fear of further falling is a common consequence of a fall, and in an extreme form is sometimes referred to as a post-fall syndrome. More than just a further source of distress, fear of falling has emerged as a predictor of future falling. For example, in an interesting longitudinal study of over 2,000 people, "fear of falling at baseline was an independent predictor of being a faller at follow-up" (Friedman et al., 2002, p. 1333). Is it likely that adjusting one's sense of risk, typically through activity restrictions and over-cautiousness, paradoxically increases the likelihood of falling? Perhaps being cautious becomes self-fulfilling, confirming an unhelpful belief in personal vulnerability and frailty.

Thomas Hadjistavropoulos and colleagues have argued for a re-examination of this popular view of avoidance. They do not doubt that people are fearful following a fall, and that this can lead to avoidance of activity associated with the fall, but the cause may be due to the effect of anxiety on balance perception (Hadjistavropoulos et al., 2011). Kim Delbaere is one of the few scientists to explore fear of falling with experimental paradigms that offer closer examination of the interplay of physiological and psychological factors in balance adjustment. For example, in a walking study she and her colleagues used an elevated walkway and measured the physical changes produced by increased fear of falling (Delbaere et al., 2009). They asked their participants to walk in two different light intensities (dim and bright) and at two different heights

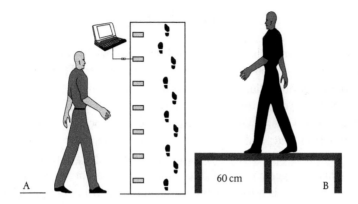

Fig. 2.1. Cartoon of two extreme experimental conditions: well lit and walking on the ground, and dimly lit and walking on an elevated platform.

Reproduced from Kim Delbaere, Daina L. Sturnieks, Geert Crombez, and Stephen R. Lord, Concern about falls elicits changes in gait parameters in conditions of postural threat in older people. *Journal of Gerontology A: Biological Sciences and Medical Sciences*, 64(2), pp. 237–242, Figure 1 © 2009, Oxford University Press.

(ground and elevated). Figure 2.1 depicts their apparatus. They found evidence for a paradoxical effect of fear on balance, increasing a risk of postural instability. We might think that being concerned or fearful makes us more careful which should decrease the risk of falling. The opposite was true in this experiment: the greater the concern of falling the larger the alterations in speed and type of walking. A fear of falling may paradoxically increase the risk of falling.

Fear of falling may arise due to largely unconscious sensorimotor adjustments leading to overcompensation and hence a sensation of frailty, which in turn can exacerbate a belief in poor balance control and increase fear of falling. Perhaps paradoxically, fear following a growing belief in lack of balance can increase the risk of postural instability, and an overall self-confirming belief of increasing frailty, inevitable decline, and the surrender of control. Undermining this surrender of control and the belief in the inevitability of falling is at the heart of falls prevention strategies.

These modern interpretations of the psychology of falling are just making their way into treatments, (e.g., the iStoppFalls program funded in Europe; http://www.istoppfalls.eu/). However, we don't know how to interpret patients' initial reports of frailty and fear of falling. If we rush too soon to a primarily behavioral treatment of fear we might miss its potential role as a useful early warning system. More investigation is needed into the possibly primary role of aging sensory and motor systems in falling, the emergence of a fear of falling, and falls efficacy interventions (Pasma et al., 2014).

Accidental falling

Falling when it is not one's choice, through roll, trip, slip, or collapse, is common, with the incidence peaking at both ends of the age spectrum. We tend to think of falling as a problem of old age but falling is also the primary cause of injury in infants attending the emergency room, either through being dropped or rolling off beds and furniture (Pickett et al., 2003). Older children's falling is typically associated with play or sport. For example, Glenn Keays and Robin Skinner compared injury from falling between home and public play equipment from a database of over 39,000 children, ages three to eleven. Eighty-four percent of all falls occurred in public, outside of the home, but severe injury was more likely to occur with home equipment; for example, falling from a garden slide onto a hard yard surface (Keays and Skinner, 2012). Also common are falls from sports, either sports at height (e.g., rock climbing) or sports in which balance can be compromised—for example, the barge in basketball or soccer, a trip running to field a cricket ball, or the poor control of the novice snowboarder. Most of these falls are from a short height. Falling from buildings (windows, balconies, roofs, fire escapes), high trees, or walls also occurs (Keogh et al., 1996), and is a particular issue of growing urbanization, high-rise building, and multigenerational dwelling (Pressley and Barlow, 2005). The epidemiology of childhood falling comes largely from the study of injury and its prevention, caused either through trauma from the fall, or often from attempts to minimize the effects of a fall through reaching, causing shoulder, arm, or hand injury. We know very little about the everyday, clinically uninteresting falls, as children stumble and bounce their way into adulthood, learning about gravity as they go along.

Nonclinical information on adult falling is available from occupational settings. In young adults, falling arises from slips or trips when there are unexpected changes in ground surface, from poor or impaired hazard perception, or from distraction (Nenonen, 2014). Although falling is associated with working at heights, in truth accidental falling is possible anywhere and everywhere, in fact wherever there are trip hazards, or wherever we bring distractions with us, such as mobile phones (Schabrun et al., 2014), or increase risks, as with the destabilizing effects of fashionable footwear (Kilby and Newell, 2012).

Perhaps the largest concern with falling is at the other end of the age spectrum. Falling is a common feature of older age, although its incidence in many countries is in decline (Finland; Korhonen et al., 2012). In the elderly, the likelihood of falling is greatly increased by multimorbidity, by the experiences of illness and treatment, and by general physical frailty with specific regard to musculoskeletal dysfunction. Alan Morrison and colleagues looked at the incidence of fracture from falls. In the United States they found that

> 1.4% of the community-dwelling elderly experience a fracture annually due to a low-impact fall.... Extrapolating to the 39 million US population ≥ 65 years living outside of skilled nursing facilities in 2010 yields a total of 0.53 million such fractures per year. (Morrison et al., 2013, p. 15)

In a comprehensive systematic review of 22 studies of falling and its consequences, in China, Hong Kong, Macau, Singapore, and Taiwan, the "reported annual rate of falls in older Chinese community-dwelling people ranged from 11% to 34% in retrospective studies and 15% to 26% in prospective studies" (Kwan et al., 2011, p. 537). However, what was particularly interesting in this study was the high incidence of fear of falling as a direct consequence of a fall: "Fear of falling [reported in four studies] as a result of a fall ranged from 42% to 70%" (Kwan et al., 2011, p. 540). Fear of falling is emerging as a crucial feature of the experience of falling, suggesting that it is one characterized by feelings of being out of control and of being at high risk of future danger.

Achieving balance (equilibrium)

The clinical literature on balance is focused on people's belief that they cannot maintain their balance and so must be cautious. But belief in one's ability to be balanced is not always associated with fear. Context matters.

Consider the world of the ballet dancer. When standing, one is swaying and correcting movements unconsciously within a fixed perimeter. The size of the area of acceptable sway is determined in part by the base of support one has. Ballet dancers often reduce that base of support to the smallest possible amount; for example, when standing *en pointe*. In an intriguing study, Roger Simmons from San Diego investigated professional dancers' neuromuscular control, and found "a superior postural control mechanism in trained dancers [which] may explain the ability of dancers to maintain static balances over a small base of support" (Simmons, 2005, p. 1193). A recent review of the balance abilities of ballet dancers found it likely that they have increased postural control. However, these authors argued the opposite to Simmons: namely, that when highly experienced dancers compromise vestibular and proprioceptive feedback, in the dance, they instead rely heavily on visual cues (Silva da Silveira Costa et al., 2013).

Visual feedback is certainly used in dance training, with a reliance on mirrors and techniques of distancing and anchoring to fixed points in space. Kimberley Hutt and Emma Redding explored a novel method of training that relies on nonvisual information. Working with 18 elite ballet dancers, they compared an eyes-closed group with a standard group on a training intervention over four weeks. The dancers who put more reliance on vestibular and proprioceptive adjustments were much better on a range of objective balance tests (Hutt and Redding, 2014). Training with eyes closed is one technique for improving balance. Another might be training in complex environments, with an understanding of the multiple and interacting demands on balance.

In normal life balance is rarely a sole goal; it is normally just part of what we are trying to do (Huxham et al., 2001). Elite sports, however, often require greater balance control and so greater training and awareness. Equestrian sports are particularly interesting in regard to the study of recreational and nonclinical balance. Comparatively little is known about the biomechanical performance of rider and horse working together, although there is evidence that expertise is predicted by better balance control (Douglas et al., 2012). Balance in this context is not always about postural adjustments in response to the horse changing position, but is about merging movements into a singular flow of rider and horse. In dressage riding, for example, maintaining balance and constant contact with the horse not only through the use of reins and legs, but also principally with the pelvis, is important. In a study of 20 novice and professional riders, all wearing accelerometers to measure the movement of their pelvis, professional riders were more adept at making micro-adjustments in the pelvis, micro-adjustments that could be the difference between winning and losing (Münz, et al., 2014).

Natural balance awareness

The biomechanical and physiological study of normal balance and balance in elite activities are relatively well studied in comparison to the study of people's awareness of their balance abilities. In specific communities, be it ballet, riding, gymnastics, or judo, there is a narrative of balance as part of performance and training. But there are very few studies taking as their point of interest people's beliefs about their balance performance.

In our dressage example, pre-performance fear is a well-documented challenge for riders. In a small study of riders before a competition, the experienced and elite riders showed more vigor and clarity or purpose than novice riders, who were more confused. The authors interpreted this confusion as a sign of low rider confidence (Wolframm et al., 2010). Although speculative, we can transfer learning from the study of balance in older age. We do not know whether the lack of confidence displayed by athletes before competition can profitably be framed as performance anxiety, or whether it is a sign of skill insufficiency: overconfidence is being corrected with information about lack of precision.

There is one area of human activity in which an awareness of and learning about balance is a requirement: high-wire walking (funambulism). Perhaps the most famous example was the spectacle of Philippe Petit walking a high wire, and lying on it, and bouncing on it; the wire was suspended between the almost-built twin towers of the World Trade Center in New York, in 1974. This performance was more than a simple high-wire act. It is explored now in a range of texts as the ultimate form of social transgression. It crosses the boundaries of entertainment and danger, of spectacle and horror, and of order and disorder. Chloe Johnston explores the added poignancy of that act of defiance and art in the context of the now-destroyed twin towers (Johnston, 2013).

Philippe Petit has talked about his experience. In his book, first called *To Reach the Clouds* and later, after the success of the film, reissued as *Man on a Wire*, he explains the planning and execution of the feat in some detail (Petit, 2003). He is particularly forthcoming about how he understands the physical challenge. As with athletes of extreme sports involving a deliberate fall, acrobatic athletes who are working hard not to fall are planful, self-disciplined, organized, and extremely aware of what they are doing and its risks. On stepping out onto the 400-meter high tower for the first time, to test the conditions, Petit recalls the inner battle he had with feeling drawn into the depths, struggling with a natural vertigo. The small steps are important as one seeks to tame the challenge, to fight the urge to control. After six years of planning and training for this event he finally makes it onto the wire. It is here that the training is tested. We witness the mind of the athlete who knows that true mastery of this balancing involves not control but the surrender of control, and a trust in one's body—a body trained for the task. For Petit, the path to success is very clear: the funambulist has to be expert in not fighting, he has to abandon his desire to take charge of every step and observe his trained feet finding their own way. In part, for Petite, this is an aesthetic and sensual experience; he talks of allowing the beauty of movement to be unencumbered by a clumsy body, and an even clumsier mind. There is a necessary abandonment.

Achieving more than the normal level of skill in balance, in whatever sphere of life, requires training of the vestibular and sensorimotor system over hours of repeated practice. In addition, letting go of the urge to control, not attending to vestibular and proprioceptive information, but trusting in the training, appear to be important for elite performance. Natural balance awareness may be crucial to the acquisition of balance, but at some level natural balance ignorance appears to be important to its expert performance.

To explore these ideas of being in balance further, I talked to Luna Othnin Girard (see Box 2.1).

Box 2.1. Luna, the dancer: *"when you are on balance you can grow, almost out of the ground"*

Luna is eighteen, comes from France, but lives and works in the UK. She describes herself as "a passionate fighter." We talked about the work and discipline involved in achieving the mix of being an athlete, an artist, and a work of art, all at the same time. We also discussed what it means to be in balance, or as dancers call it, being *on your leg*.

Chris: What is it like to be *on your leg*?

Luna: For balance it is weird. There are days when you feel that you are just on balance. You don't have to think about it. Your body just puts you in the right place. But there are days when you are more tired, when you have to fight for the balance. When you take balance at the bar you wouldn't find it. It wouldn't be quite right. So you have to start again. And again. Until you find your balance. There are days when you really need to fight because it is hard. The more you find your balance everyday, the more reliable you are. I know that when I am not on my leg, it can be someone else's good day on their leg. When

(Continued)

Box 2.1. *Continued*

you get tired and you have to stay on balance, it is your muscle memory that will put you on your leg rather than just luck. It is really training to find your center all the time.

Chris: What does it feel like? Do you have a sense of being perfectly balanced?

Luna: You know when you are not on it. There is always a time when you feel perfectly on balance, but those times are so rare. You will need adrenalin to feel exquisitely on your leg. You would feel it because the whole combination of steps would work as perfectly as your whole body can manage. The feeling of that is incredible. But when you are training every day you are not going to be able to have that.

When you do a movement and you put feeling into it, it works. But in everyday life we need to work on the technical aspects. So one day I will focus on my turn-out. Another week I will work on my upper body, and will think that my arms need to be placed right every time. When you are on balance you grow and you can expand onto that axis but when you are not on it you work around it. When you are on balance you can grow, almost out of the ground through the axis.

Chris: Is it a search for the perfect balance so you avoid imbalance?

Luna: No, it is not avoiding it. It's working to get it perfect every time. So being off-balance is going to happen. Every day there is going to be a point where I know it didn't work. But then it's the way you work within that that's going to make you more consistent in getting toward that point of balance.

Chris: As a dancer are you in balance or are you always moving toward and away from it?

Luna: It is more moving through my balance. Because dancing is movement, movement is not static, therefore we can't be on balance all the time. What makes us on balance or not is how we move to get to the balance—moving through the balance out onto another movement. We would work, using our balance, to be on our legs all the time; to be able to hit the balance; to carry on without wobbling.

Dancing is about *plié-ing*, stretching, and movement from one leg to the other. So it is about being up and down and all the way around. Moving. And that gets more complicated when you use different levels. In contemporary dance you use the ground a lot. It is not the same axis you would find when you are on your feet. But you still have to move through. Sometimes you are on your back and do a backward roll, then the axis is in the middle of your body rather than just your feet. It becomes a 360-degree middle, so not just one spot. It moves with you.

What is great about contemporary dance is that you use your axis and being off-balance to make your movements even bigger. Because you can be low to the ground you can really move from one side through yourself—up from being off-balance to catch yourself again and then fall and catch it again.

Chris: Does confidence in the move matter?

Luna: It changes the movement itself. If you believe you can do it you are halfway to doing it. If you believe you are never going to make it, it is never going to happen. It just

> **Box 2.1.** *Continued*
>
> won't happen. If you think there might be a chance and you are going to go for it, you are already halfway to doing it right.
>
> *Chris*: And what is the experience like when it works as you wish?
>
> *Luna*: When you let go, your body will just do the steps. You will feel your body moving but your mind will be free; sometimes it is not on the physical part but on the emotional part.
>
> You feel light. It feels like it is part of you. When you do a step that you know you can do, nearly 100 percent of the time, good every time, it is really fluid when it comes out. It brings you happiness. It is quite amazing when you know you can do that one thing and when it works when you are on stage. It makes the hours of training worthwhile.
>
> ---
>
> For Luna balance has come to mean something specific to her dance. It is not the stout planting of feet we do on the subway to avoid falling, or to pick up a box. It is a perfect moment, captured fleetingly, in passing from one position to another. It is a celebration. Being out of balance is also different. It is not the lack of control that we might feel in falling, but a controlled and artful imbalance that is always moving one toward balance. Confidence in disequilibrium, a sense of one's body in space as potentially beautiful, and hours of training, can tame imbalance into an artful path to balance.

Losing balance (disequilibrium)

For many people, working to achieve and sustain balance is a struggle fought not in the context of artistic improvement but in a context of fear of damage. For those living with a balance disorder the most basic of human biomechanical functions such as standing can be challenging. There are many causes of balance disorder—infection, trauma, or disease. Whatever the cause, the main symptoms of the balance disorders are similar, and include postural instability, increased risk of falling, dizziness, and vertigo.

Dizziness

Feeling light-headed when standing (orthostatic dizziness) is a common complaint and comes with a risk of fainting (syncope). For some, dizziness it is a constant menace. Jacquelien Dros and colleagues call it a geriatric "giant" because it is a common and debilitating symptom experienced in older age. In a large study of people attending primary care, they explored the impact that dizziness has on people's lives. They defined dizziness as "a giddy or rotational sensation, a feeling of imbalance, lightheadedness, and/or a sensation of impending faint" (Dros et al., 2011, p. 2), and found that "almost 60% of dizzy older primary care patients experience moderate or severe impact on everyday life due to dizziness" (p. 6).

That dizziness is disabling is not surprising, but patients with chronic dizziness experience great distress. Strangely, the distress of dizziness is often talked about in the clinical literature as an abnormal and puzzling presentation. A small thought experiment, imagining the experience, might be enough to convince one of how easily it can unsettle and threaten. Consider the potential loss of function, social restriction, and health anxiety. Sarah Kirby and Lucy Yardley, who have done much to explore the meaning of dizziness to patients, and how to improve function, reviewed the studies on psychological distress for those with Ménière's disease (Kirby and Yardley, 2008). Dizziness is only one symptom of Ménière's disease, which includes tinnitus and hearing loss, but it is associated with anxiety about health; in particular, worry about the future and uncertainty over both diagnosis and cause.

Qualitative studies of living with chronic dizziness reveal confusion over cause and diagnosis, uncertainty over course, and worry about the future. In a qualitative study, one could see the lack of understanding of the biology of balance. One patient, for example, said:

> The Ear-doctor did nothing but a hearing test. Finally, to me, this seems absurd, very absurd.... If I have different arguments, this has nothing to do with hearing, and I have always said, hearing is not the problem. (Kruschinski et al., 2010, p. 8)

Confusion and the need for clearer communication are at the heart of the experiences of people with dizziness.

As we will see with both pain and itch, and with fatigue, the chronic experience and complaint of some sensory experiences attract confusion and fear. This fear is exacerbated by diagnostic uncertainty and the stigmatizing implication of an implied psychosomatic cause (Yardley, 1994). Much of the psychology of dizziness is mired in an unhelpful language of patient psychopathology. Patients are often described as expressing inappropriately high anxiety, symptom reporting, or a psychosomatic disease (Orji, 2014). There seems to have been a collapse of theory or knowledge translation in this field. Lucy Yardley's early theoretically rich direction has not been built upon.

An extended functionalist account of dizziness requires an understanding of the phenomenology of the experience, of its social meaning, and of its function in prioritizing behavior. Disequilibrium, or the threat that one is about to lose control of one's gravitational position, is a threat to coherence and to complete action. Feeling light-headed and expecting to faint is a threat that is hard to ignore. Attending to that threat may be relevant in chronic dizziness (Asmundson et al., 2000). Older people worried about falling are often preoccupied with perceived risks of further falling. It is a reasonable hypothesis that those with chronic dizziness may also show a bias of attention to possible cues of dizziness, an increase in behaviors (often ineffective) that patients think will postpone the onset or exacerbation of dizziness, and altered behavioral patterns of postural adjustment.

Gerhard Andersson and colleagues reported a rare experimental study of patients with dizziness. They compared 20 patients, all of whom met the criteria for vestibular disorder (including ten with Ménière's disease), with 20 people free from such problems. The study required everyone to close their eyes while they received vibration delivered to the calf, a procedure designed to induce a cue of impending postural instability: it feels like you are going to fall. This all happened while participants were standing on a force platform measuring body sway. People were also asked about their perceptions of body sway and their perception of risk of losing balance, both before and after stimulation. This unique experimental setup was to test an intriguing hypothesis of the function of beliefs about balance. They predicted, first, that patients would overestimate the threat of the vibratory stimulation, thinking it more damaging than it was. Second, they thought that these fears would be resistant to correction through experience, so that overestimation and anxiety would be maintained. The opposite of what was expected occurred: "Contrary to what we expected the control group overpredicted sway to a greater extent than the patients did." Further, "regarding the predictions of 'risk of losing balance,' rather similar results were obtained with the difference that the groups did not differ significantly across trials" (Andersson et al., 2008, p. 180).

Putting the behavior of patients with dizziness in the context of threat shows that attempting to control balance, and vigilance for signs of imbalance, is to be expected. A normal psychology of balance would expect patients to attend to the threat of imbalance, attend quickly to that threat, and adjust posture to maintain balance.

The patient with vestibular dysfunction might usefully be compared to the ballet dancer. They both inhabit an environment of persistent challenge to balance. They are both trained to recognize, and are continually training to recognize, the cues for threat to balance so as to adjust efficiently to that threat. Unlike the patients at risk of fall who may be accurately reflecting their physical frailty in their avoidance behavior, the person with Ménière's disease might usefully be thought of as an expert in achieving equilibrium. Andersson and colleagues hint at this idea when they say, "One interesting possibility, following the findings of this study, is the notion that dizzy patients are more correct than incorrect in monitoring their balance." (Andersson et al., 2008, p. 181).

21

From a treatment perspective, the extent to which people with chronic dizziness are accurate in their perceptions of threat to equilibrium is crucially important. If inaccurate—given to overestimating threat, leading to avoidance—one might adopt a cognitive behavioral approach to improving balance confidence, correcting inaccurate beliefs (Schmid et al., 2011). If accurate, one might encourage vestibular rehabilitation with the repeated practice of movements or the training of positioning (Hillier and McDonnell, 2011). Perhaps when it comes to disorders of balance perception, training (and yet more training) of perception is more important than altering belief.

If psychology is going to be relevant in helping people balance, it will be in devising methods to motivate and encourage persistent engagement with repetitive physical therapy, or inventing more accessible ways to deliver treatments to patients, such as community education or the use of virtual reality (Yardley and Kirby, 2006). Of course beliefs and the content of fear matter, but understanding those beliefs as rational and sensible in the context of dizziness will be important when considered in rehabilitation (Staab, 2011).

Vertigo

Vertigo was recently defined by consensus as "the sensation of self-motion when no self-motion is occurring or the sensation of distorted self-motion during an otherwise normal head movement" (Bisdorff et al., 2009, p. 1). The different types of vertigo are classified largely by presumed cause, starting with a distinction of spontaneous versus triggered vertigo; the symptoms of vertigo are described in terms of their specific phenomenological quality. For example, a distinction is made between vestibulo-visual symptoms, such as the feeling that the world is oscillating (oscillopsia), and visual lag, in which the perceived environment lags behind real movement. Similarly, a distinction is made between postural symptoms, such as a near-fall steadied with an outstretched hand or lean, and unsteadiness.

The phenomenological focus of vertigo in diagnostic discourse is on a perception of a body moving (or being moved) out of one's control, and it overlaps with experiences of dizziness, as they often occur together. What is common across different presentations of vertigo is the experience of spatial impermanence and the threat to balance. In one sense the fundamental belief in a physically stable world is challenged, often without warning. Indeed, the very earth beneath one's feet appears to be moving.

To learn more about the experience of vertigo, of living in an unstable impermanent world, I talked to Debbie Hollingsworth (see Box 2.2).

Box 2.2. Debbie, living with vertigo: *"your mind can play amazingly cruel tricks on you"*

Debbie is a support worker for a charity helping those in housing crises. She describes herself as "an activist," someone who is engaged in social justice and equality campaigns. She likes to challenge both herself and the status quo. For the last three years she has had episodes of spasmodic episodic vertigo. She can spend months without an episode but has had some weeks where the symptoms were daily. I was interested to learn what feeling unbalanced was like, and how she made sense of it.

Chris: When did you first know something was wrong?

Debbie: About two years ago. It came on quite suddenly and the doctor did not really know what kick-started it. But I just kept getting this sensation that I wasn't comfortable with. And then you start imagining all sorts of things like blood clots and things like that on your brain. Your mind can play amazingly cruel tricks on you. You can imagine all sorts of things going wrong. And I think it is the unknown that is more frightening. Once you have a diagnosis you can deal with it.

Chris: What are the feelings like when you have an attack?

Debbie: Your head is just swimming. That is the only way of explaining it. It just swims. It feels as though you are going backward and forward but you are not actually moving. And it doesn't matter if you are lying flat or sitting up or if you are moving quickly or slowly, it is just this continual swimming, and it comes in waves in your head. It is mainly your head. It is just the sensation that your head is swimming inside. It is also a feeling of going left to right. So you can lie down and at first you think that will sort it out, but your head keeps going left to right. It is like a crescendo; it goes up and down and back up again. It just makes you feel really sick. Yes, very nauseous. And if you are standing up you are likely to stagger.

Chris: Is it just your head or do the room and floor move also?

Debbie: There are times when the whole room is orbiting. And there are times when you are stuck in places. I have had that a handful of times. Not often. But that is when you are more likely to lose your balance. It is the two. It is your head and your environment that are moving against each other. It is just very disorientating. Your head is going one way and the room is moving around but it won't just spin but it will be a disjointed moving backward and toward you. So you get a sensation that the wall is just much closer than it actually is. Or it is further away. So you start to lose perception of your surroundings, and that can be quite frightening. And that is when I am more likely to lose my balance and I will have to grab something to right myself.

Chris: Do you ever feel like your body is being left behind?

(Continued)

Box 2.2. *Continued*

Debbie: I have woken up sometimes and moved over, and my head feels like it is coming after me. It is like a delayed reaction of your head catching up: your insides catching up with your physical head. That is quite strange as well. It is like a different feeling altogether of everything catching up after you. But that only happens when you are lying down. That has never happened when I am standing up.

Chris: Have you ever felt that the world is starting to control you rather than you control it?

Debbie: No. I have not had that. That would be frightening. The closest I have had is that things are not where they should be. When everything is moving around you, you can never be sure that the table you reach for is still there. Because you can't always judge whether you have moved. You can't be sure whether you have moved away because everything is moving. Your legs do feel a bit weird. If I have been standing I am not sure if my legs have moved somewhat or if I am standing still. I am not sure if my body has moved or I am standing still. It is hard to judge. You are not quite sure because the floor could be feeling like it is moving as well, and is it the floor or is it you?

Chris: Is there anything pleasant or intriguing about these feelings?

Debbie: No. There is nothing pleasurable. It is unpleasant. That is the word. You can't say it is painful; it is just unpleasant. Not nice. And the longer it goes on, then that is when you start feeling more nauseous. And that in itself is uncomfortable.

Chris: When does it start to become frightening?

Debbie: It is just that you don't know what is going to happen. If you are at the top of stairs and it goes, there is the instant thought of falling so you just grab whatever is there to steady yourself. The fear comes afterward. If you have ever had a near collision in a car where you have almost knocked into something and afterward you get butterflies, anxiety in your stomach, and your heart is racing. It is that sort of near-miss feeling when you realize that you are OK. For me it is afterward. I don't worry about it in advance, it comes afterward.

Chris: Do you plan differently now?

Debbie: No. You can't. I can't just sit at home waiting for it to happen. I need to earn a living. I think I am a fairly positive person anyway and you just get on with things. It if happens it happens. There is not much I can do. I think it is not worth stressing or worrying over something I can't control. I have no control over it so I might as well just get on with life. When it happens I think it is not going to go on forever. It will stop at some point. I suppose I look at it that there are people far worse off than me, so it is something you put up with. It is better than having a lot of other things wrong with you.

Box 2.2. *Continued*

Debbie captures perfectly the extent to which imbalance and the fear of falling are risks, but they are not what dominate her story. The altered reality, the loss of control, the confusion, and the challenge of how to respond are core parts of vertigo. In the same way that Luna experienced near-perfect balance and control over the relative position of her body in space, so Debbie describes having to experience being in a world in which the physical certainties have been altered, the coordinates have been scrambled: keeping you own body coherent and attempting to act on the world takes effort.

Height intolerance

One form of vertigo is particularly interesting in terms of its prevalence and the experience of a changed physical reality. Vertigo often occurs in those with a fear of heights (acrophobia), with visual height intolerance, and is a common symptom of panic disorders. Thomas Brandt has worked hard to separate height intolerance and subsequent vertigo from a psychiatric discourse in which the expressed fear of heights is used to identify a primary anxiety disorder (Brandt et al., 2012). Almost 30 percent of us report height intolerance, which includes the distortion of perception of body and space, postural sway, a perception of postural instability, and a fear of falling. In essence, height vertigo can usefully be considered a primary balance disorder.

In an acute attack, typically occurring when climbing a tower, crossing a bridge, or mountain hiking, people are often able to discuss their experiences. Doreen Huppert and colleagues report that as many as 50 percent of people report frequent avoidance of actions (e.g., climbing a ladder) that will induce height vertigo, and as many as a quarter engage in avoidance or help-seeking when an attack begins (Huppert et al., 2013). In an interesting qualitative study, this same research group interviewed 18 adult members of the German Alpine Association living in Munich who had identified themselves as experiencing height intolerance to the extent that they had sought help (Schäffler et al., 2014). In addition to the experience of vertigo, participants were forthcoming about the experiences of falling, fear of falling, physical arrest, and of being drawn to an edge. One participant described actually falling: "And then you could really look down five floors vertically into the lobby. And then I fell over. Actually it was really the case . . . that my knees turned to jelly" (p. 704).

Another described not a real fall but a fear of falling:

During height intolerance I have the additional feeling that I could fall down somewhere, into a, for me, bottomless abyss, even if it's only 50 cm deep, that is still for me at the time into a bottomless abyss. (p. 704)

Another described the unusual phenomenon of physical arrest or paralysis, of an inability to move. This is beyond a fear of falling, as people describe almost being an observer of their body, ignoring or denying instructions to move: "Yeah and when it gets really bad, then I can't even lift my foot. It's like my feet are glued to the ground. I'd probably remain standing there forever, for I can't move my legs" (p. 702). Going beyond the perception of physical disobedience, in which agency is intact but one is fixed to the ground, is the report of being drawn: "The funny thing is that whenever I look down anywhere, I automatically feel this pulling sensation, as if I had almost already fallen down" (p. 702).

Disturbance in the sense of body ownership, witnessed here in the failure of agency in not being able to move, and a separation of agency in the feeling of being controlled, is similar to those described by Yen Pik Sang and colleagues who described experiences of derealization and depersonalization in a matched sample of 50 patients with a primary vestibular disease (Sang et al., 2006). They found that after dizziness, imbalance, and difficulty attending, a "feeling of not being in control of oneself" (p. 762, Table 3) was the most common symptom. They argue:

> Derealisation occurs in vestibular patients because their distorted vestibular signals create a misleading frame of spatial reference which mismatches with the other senses, giving rise to illusory, "unreal" perceptions of the patient's transactions with the physical world. (Sang et al., 2006, pp. 765–766).

Feeling paralyzed, helpless, and incapable of action—or feeling drawn toward an undesirable and dangerous act, exactly toward the danger one rationally wants to avoid—brings the sensation of balance into the realm of strong belief, urge, and autoscopic phenomena. Depersonalization in observing one's body collapsing, loss of agency in being able to move (rooted to the spot), together with the feeling of being urged or drawn to danger, could usefully be considered a form of autoscopic illusion. Autoscopic illusions range from the out-of-body phenomenon of experiencing yourself as separate, typically floating above your supine body, to a heautoscopic illusion of seeing yourself and being seen by yourself, to a vague feeling of a presence (Lopez et al., 2008). Olaf Blanke and colleagues, for example, in their case studies of brain-injured patients reporting out-of-body experiences, report their first patient who "felt as if she would be elevated vertically and effortlessly from her actual position associated with vertigo and fear" (Blanke et al., 2004, p. 245). Table 2.1 summarizes well the different possible autoscopic illusions.

Height intolerance autoscopy

What makes this form of autoscopic illusion different to those from a known neurological trauma is its high prevalence. It may be a common feature of height intolerance,

Table 2.1: The phenomenology of four autoscopic illusions

Phenomenology	out-of-body experience	heautoscopy	autoscopic hallucination	feeling-of-a-presence	room tilt illusion
Vestibular disturbance	+++	++	-	+	+++
Disintegration in personal space	+++	+++	+++	+++	-
Disintegration between personal and extrapersonal space	+++	++	-	+	+++
Disorder	embodiment body ownership	embodiment body ownership	-	body ownership	-
Brain mechanisms	right TPJ	left TPJ	occipito-parietal	posterior parietal/TPJ premotor	PVC

(*Continued*)

Table 2.1 (*Continued*)

"Phenomenology and physiopathology of the autoscopic phenomena and the room tilt illusion. For each paroxysmal illusion, the actual position of the patient's body is schematically represented by black lines and that of the parasomatic body by dashed lines. The direction of the visuospatial perspective is indicated by an arrow pointing away from the location where the patient has the impression he is located. The patient has the impression to see the environment from the physical body in the case of autoscopic hallucination, feeling-of-a-presence and room tilt illusion, alternatively from the physical and the parasomatic body in the case of heautoscopy; and from the parasomatic body in the case of out-of-body experience. The paroxysmal illusions are characterized by a different pattern of vestibular disturbance and of disintegration in personal space and between personal and extrapersonal space. The lower part represents the hypothetical involvement of the different multisensory vestibular regions in the different form of paroxysmal illusion (TP): temporoparietal junction; PIVC: parieto–insular vestibular cortex)." Reproduced from Clinical Neuropsychology, 38 (3), C. Lopez, P. Halje, and O. Blanke, Body ownership and embodiment: Vestibular and multisensory mechanisms, p. 151, doi:10.1016/j.neucli.2007.12.006 Copyright (2008), with permission from Elsevier.

Reproduced from *Clinical Neurophysiology*, 38(3), C. Lopez, P. Halje, and O. Blanke, Body ownership and embodiment: Vestibular and multisensory mechanisms, pp. 149–161. Figure 1, doi:10.1016/j.neucli.2007.12.006 Copyright (2008), with permission from Elsevier.

although its incidence is unknown. Height intolerance autoscopy, if discussed at all, is discussed only in the context of derealization that occurs in panic. However, under-standing it as a feature of a primary balance disorder may help to both normalize the frightening illusory experience and direct research into treatments for height intoler-ance that do not rely solely on challenging beliefs during exposure. There has been no research on this specific form of autoscopy. If it exists in any stable form, it should have two primary features: first, the loss of agency, or paralysis, of part or all of one's body; and second, the perception of being under the control of an external force in being drawn toward danger. Extending the boundaries of study away from the idea of an intact agent experiencing confusing perception, to an altered agent out of control of perception is necessary. Height intolerance may be less about an altered perception of heights and more about an altered perception of self.

Summary

Balance is a prerequisite for action. From birth we train our balance system by the force of creativity, reaching for the world and learning about the consequences of instability. Intriguingly, it seems that the allure of falling, the curious thrill of "the drop" never goes away. Now it is possible to explore it safely, and so the deliberate fall is used as a form of entertainment. I argue that technologies of the deliberate fall offer possibilities for research that have yet to be exploited. At the extremes of balance, there are those who have trained repeatedly in the micro-adjustment of posture, as with the dressage rider, or in the art of falling away from and returning through bal-ance in the flow of dance. But at the other extreme are people suffering with the fear of falling, with dizziness, with vertigo, and with height intolerance. Their experience shows how a disorder of imbalance is much more than falling: it can challenge one's perception of reality and of agency, whether you can act independently in the world.

References

Andersson, G., Ljunggren, J. and Larsen, H.C. (2008). Prediction of balance among patients with vestibular disturbance: application of the match/mismatch model. *Audiological Medi-cine*, 6, 176–183.

Asmundson, G.J.G., Wright, K.D. and Hadjistavropoulos, H. (2000). Anxiety sensitivity and disabling chronic health conditions: state of the art and future directions. *Scandinavian Jour-nal of Behaviour Therapy*, 29, 100–117.

Bisdorff, A., Von Brevern, M., Lempert, T. and Newman-Toker, D.E. (2009). Classification of vestibular symptoms: towards an international classification of vestibular disorders: first consensus document of the Committee for the Classification of Vestibular Disorders of the Bárány Society. *Journal of Vestibular Research*, 19, 1–13.

Blanke, O., Landis, T., Spinelli, L. and Seeck, M. (2004). Out-of-body experience and autoscopy of neurological origin. *Brain*, 127, 243–258.

Brandt, T., Strupp, M. and Huppert, D. (2012). Height intolerance: an underrated threat. *Journal of Neurology*, 259, 759–760.

Brymer, E. and Schweitzer, R. (2012). Extreme sports are good for your health: a phenomenological understanding of fear and anxiety in extreme sport. *Journal of Health Psychology*, 18, 477–487.

Brymer, E. and Schweitzer, R. (2013). The search for freedom in extreme sports: a phenomenological exploration. *Psychology of Sport and Exercise*, 14, 865–873.

Claxton, L.J., Melzer, D., Hyun Ryu, J. and Haddad, J.M. (2012). The control of posture in newly standing infants is task dependent. *Journal of Experimental Child Psychology*, 113, 159–165.

Delbaere, K., Sturnieks, D.L., Crombez, G. and Lord, S.R. (2009). Concern about falls elicits changes in gait parameters in conditions of postural threat in older people. *Journal of Gerontology A: Biological Sciences and Medical Sciences*, 64, 237–242.

Dollard, J., Barton, C., Newbury, J. and Turnball, D. (2012). Falls in older age: a threat to identity. *Journal of Clinical Nursing*, 21, 2617–2625.

Douglas, J.-L., Price, M. and Peters, D.M. (2012). A systematic review of physical fitness, physiological demands and biomechanical performance in equestrian athletes. *Comparative Exercise Physiology*, 8, 53–62.

Dros, J., Maarsingh, O.R., Beem, L., van der Horst, H., ter Riet, G., Schellevis, F.G. and van Weert, H.C.P.M. (2011). Impact of dizziness on everyday life in older primary care patients: a cross-sectional study. *Health and Quality of Life Outcomes*, 9, 2–7.

Ferrè, E.R., Bottini, G., Iannetti, G.D. and Haggard, P. (2013). The balance of feelings: vestibular modulation of bodily sensations. *Cortex*, 49, 748–758.

Friedman, S.M., Munoz, B., West, S.K., Rubin, G.S. and Fried, L.P. (2002). Falls and fear of falling: which comes first? A longitudinal prediction model suggests strategies for primary and secondary prevention. *Journal of the American Geriatrics Society*, 50, 1329–1335.

Gothelf, N., Herbaux, D. and Verardi, V. (2010). Do theme parks deserve their success? *Innovative Marketing*, 6, 48–61.

Haddad, J.M., Claxton, L.J., Keen, R., Berthier, N.E., Riccio, G.E., Hamill, J. and Van Emmerik, R.E.A. (2012). Development of the coordination between posture and manual control. *Journal of Experimental Child Psychology*, 111, 286–298.

Hadjistavropoulos, T., Delbaere, K. and Fitzgerald, T.D. (2011). Reconceptualizing the role of fear of falling and balance confidence in fall risk. *Journal of Aging and Health*, 23, 3–23.

Hillier, S.L. and McDonnell, M. (2011). Vestibular rehabilitation for unilateral peripheral vestibular dysfunction. *Cochrane Database of Systematic Reviews*, Issue 2, CD005397. doi:10.1002/14651858.CD005397.pub3

Huppert, D., Grill, E. and Brandt, T. (2013). Down on heights? One in three has visual height intolerance. *Journal of Neurology*, 260, 597–604.

Hutt, K. and Redding, E. (2014). The effect of an eyes-closed dance-specific training program on dynamic balance in elite pre-professional ballet dancers: a randomized controlled pilot study. *Journal of Dance Medicine and Science*, 1, 3–11.

Huxham, F.E., Goldie, P.A. and Patla, A.E. (2001). Theoretical considerations in balance assessment. *Australian Journal of Physiotherapy*, 47, 89–100.

Johnston, C. (2013). On not falling: Philippe Petit and his walk between the Twin Towers. *Performance Research: A Journal of the Performance Arts*, 18, 37–41.

Keays, G. and Skinner, R. (2012). Playground equipment injuries at home versus those in public settings: differences in severity. *Injury Prevention*, 18, 138–141.

Keogh, S., Gray, J.S., Kirk, C.J.C., Coats, T.J. and Wilson, A.W. (1996). Children falling from a height in London. *Injury Prevention*, 2, 188–191.

Kilby, M.C. and Newell, K.M. (2012). Intra- and inter-foot coordination in quiet standing: footwear and posture effects. *Gait and Posture*, 35, 511–516.

Kirby, S.E. and Yardley, L. (2008). Understanding psychological distress in Ménière's disease: a systematic review. *Psychology, Health and Medicine*, 13, 257–273.

Korhonen, N., Niemi, S., Palvanen, M., Pakkari, J., Sievänen, H. and Kannus, P. (2012). Declining age-adjusted incidence of fall-induced injuries among elderly Finns. *Age and Ageing*, 41, 75–79.

Kruschinski, C., Theile, G., Dreier, S.D. and Hummers-Pradier, E. (2010). The priorities of elderly patients suffering from dizziness: a qualitative study. *European Journal of General Practice*, 16, 6–11.

Kwan, M.M.-S., Close, J.C.T., Wong, A.K.W. and Lord, S.L. (2011). Falls incidence, risk factors, and consequences in Chinese older people: a systematic review. *Journal of the American Geriatrics Society*, 59, 536–543.

Lopez, C. and Blanke, O. (2011). The thalamocortical vestibular system in animals and humans. *Brain Research Reviews*, 67, 119–146.

Lopez, C., Halje, P. and Blanke, O. (2008). Body ownership and embodiment: vestibular and multisensory mechanisms. *Neurophysiologie Clinique/Clinical Neurophysiology*, 38, 149–161.

Lopez, C., Schreyer, H.-M., Preuss, N. and Mast FW. (2012). Vestibular stimulation modifies the body schema. *Neuropsychologia*, 50, 1830–1837.

Merrit, C.J. and Tharp, I.J. (2013). Personality, self-efficacy and risk-taking in parkour (free-running). *Psychology of Sport and Exercise*, 14, 608–611.

Morrison, A., Fan, T., Sen, S.S. and Weisenfluh, L. (2013). Epidemiology of falls and osteoporotic fractures: a systematic review. *ClinicoEconomics and Outcomes Research*, 5, 9–18.

Münz, A., Eckardt, F. and Witte, K. (2014). Horse-rider interaction in dressage riding. *Human Movement Science*, 33, 227–237.

Nenonen, N. (2014). Analysing factors related to slipping, stumbling, and falling accidents at work: application of data mining methods to Finnish occupational accidents and diseases statistics database. *Applied Ergonomics*, 44, 215–224.

Orji, F.T. (2014). The influence of psychological factors in Ménière's Disease. *Annals of Medical and Health Science Research*, 4, 3–7.

Pasma, J.H., Engelhart, D., Schouten, A.C., van der Koolj, H., Maier, A.B. and Meskers, C.G. (2014). Impaired standing balance: the clinical need for closing the loop. *Neuroscience*, 267, 157–165.

Petit, P. (2003). To reach the clouds: my high-wire walk between the Twin Towers. London: Faber and Faber.

Pickett, W., Streight, S., Simpson, K. and Brison, R.J. (2003). Injuries experienced by infant children: a population-based epidemiological analysis. *Pediatrics*, 111, 365–370.

Pressley, J.C. and Barlow, B. (2005). Child and adolescent injury as a result of falls from buildings and structures. *Injury Prevention*, 11, 267–273.

Proffitt, D.R. (2006). Embodied perception and the economy of action. *Perspectives on Psychological Science*, 1, 110–122.

Roe, B., Howell, F., Riniotis, K., Beech, R., Crome, P. and Ong, B.N. (2008). Older people's experience of falls: understanding, interpretation and autonomy. *Journal of Advanced Nursing*, 63, 586–596.

Sang, F.Y.P., Jáuregui-Renaud, K., Green, D.A., Bronstein, A.M. and Gresty, M.A. (2006). Depersonalisation/derealisation symptoms in vestibular disease. *Journal of Neurology, Neurosurgery and Psychiatry*, 77, 760–766.

Schabrun, S.M., van den Hoorn, W., Moorcroft, A., Greenland, C. and Hodges, P.W. (2014). Texting and walking: strategies for postural control and implications for safety. *PloS one*, 9, e84312.

Schäffler, F., Müller, M., Huppert, D., Brandt, T., Tiffe, T. and Grill, E. (2014). Consequences of visual height intolerance for quality of life: a qualitative study. *Quality of Life Research*, 23, 699–707.

Schmid, G., Henningsen, P., Dieterich, M., Sattel, H. and Lahmann, C. (2011). Psychotherapy in dizziness: a systematic review. *Journal of Neurology, Neurosurgery and Psychiatry*, 82, 601–606.

Silva da Silveira Costa, M., de Sá Ferreira, A. and Ramiro Felicio, L. (2013). Static and dynamic balance in ballet dancers: a literature review. *Fisioterapia e Pesquisa*, 20, 292–298.

Simmons, R.W. (2005). Neuromuscular responses of trained ballet dancers to postural perturbations. *International Journal of Neuroscience*, 114, 1193–1203.

Staab, J.P. (2011). Behavioral aspects of vestibular rehabilitation. *Neurorehabilitation*, 29, 179–183.

Teachman, B.A., Stefanucci, J.K., Cherkin, E.M., Cody, M.W. and Proffitt, D.R. (2008). A new mode of fear expression: perceptual bias in height fear. *Emotion*, 8, 296–301.

Van de Water, T.R. (2012). Historical aspects of inner ear anatomy and biology that underlie the design of hearing and balance prosthetic devices. *The Anatomical Record*, 295, 1741–1759.

Williams, V., Victor, C.R. and McCrindle, R. (2013). It is always on your mind: experiences and perceptions of falling of older people and their carers and the potential of a mobile falls detection device. *Current Gerontology and Geriatrics Research*, Article ID 295073, 7 pp.

Wolframm, I.A., Shearman, J. and Micklewright, D. (2010). A preliminary investigation into pre-competitive mood states of advanced and novice equestrian dressage riders. *Journal of Applied Sports Psychology*, 22, 333–342.

Woodcock, K. (2007). Rider errors and amusement ride safety: observation at three carnival midways. *Accident Analysis and Prevention*, **39**, 390–397.

Yardley, L. (1994). Prediction of handicap and emotional distress in patients with recurrent vertigo: symptoms, coping strategies, control beliefs, and reciprocal causation. *Social Science and Medicine*, 39, 573–581.

Yardley, L. and Kirby, S. (2006). Evaluation of booklet-based self-management of symptoms in Ménière disease: a randomized controlled trial. *Psychosomatic Medicine*, 68, 762–769.

CHAPTER 3

MOVEMENT

Engaging with the world requires more than balance. We are constantly in motion, moving toward or away from objects in a shared environment. To act upon the world we need to know where we are in space relative to everything else. Knowing the position of one's body in space is achieved through the integration of information from the vestibular system, from muscles and joints, from touch, and from vision. As I write this, I can see now my fingers moving in my peripheral vision, feel the touch of the keys as I type, but I also know that my whole body is in gravitational equilibrium, and the joints and muscles of my fingers are giving detailed information about specific position and about movement. Thankfully, all of this goes on without my knowing, largely out of awareness.

I am interested in these experiences of moving bodies. What does it feel like to move through space? To be totally aware of your own body in space would perhaps be distracting, at least if you attempted it all of the time. But an acute or momentary awareness of the moving body is common. This experience of bodily awareness is most commonly discussed either in the context of learning or relearning a motor skill (e.g., juggling or playing an instrument), or in rehabilitation after injury or disease (e.g., physical therapy). We know how it feels to be clumsy, when reach and grasp start to fail, and we know what precision can feel like, when a finessed movement you have practiced so many times runs exactly as planned.

I begin at the beginning, with infants learning to move, and then explore the experience of fine motor control and its failure as *clumsiness*. The opposite of clumsiness is also interesting, especially about what matters when we come to talk of someone as an expert. I then examine the role of peripersonal space; in particular, one's perception of personal boundary maintenance: where I end and another person begins, and the acceptable space between. Finally, I examine the experiences of those with far-reaching disorders of proprioception and movement for what they teach us about bodily perception.

Two people offered to share their experiences of proprioception at its limits. Luke is an acrobat. He works with a human circus in Las Vegas. Precision movement is crucial to the success of his art and to his survival. I also talked with Jeremy just after he experienced a stroke. He struggles both to initiate and conclude movement, and describes himself as "frustrated," having lost precision control of his limbs and his body.

Proprioception

Proprioception was a term introduced by Charles Sherrington in his published lecture series *The Integrative Action of the Nervous System*; it refers to the position of the body in space and the limbs of the body in relation to the rest of the body (Sherrington, 1906). Mechano-receptors are found in skin, skeleton, muscle, and connective tissue, which, in concert with vestibular information, inform the central nervous system of movement. Of course, input from the periphery does not occur in isolation. The central nervous system is constantly modulating and adapting local sensory environments with top-down interactive control. Motor control involves multiple brain structures, not only the cerebellum and the motor cortex. Felt experience typically emerges from a mismatch between what is expected and what occurs. But this mismatch rarely occurs between expected and real limb position, making a sudden awareness of proprioception unusual (Proske and Gandevia, 2012). The general idea—that proprioception functions largely out of awareness—is intriguing. As we saw with balance in Chapter 2 and will see for breathing in Chapter 5 and temperature in Chapter 9, knowing when and when not to attend to bodily information is crucial to embodied action.

Developing movement control

Humans are not born with intact proprioceptive abilities. Unlike species able to immediately self-propel, as with the standing foal or calf, controlled human movement takes time to develop. As Esther Thelen said:

> Human infants are born with very little control over their bodies. Yet within a year or so, they are able to sit, stand, walk, reach, manipulate objects, feed themselves, gesture, and even speak a few words. A year later, toddlers are adept at running, climbing, scribbling, riding a tricycle, and talking in simple sentences.[1]

The developmental study of movement has focused on postural control, the direct shaping of perception and cognition by the environment, and on the adoption and mastery of specific motor skills.

At birth, humans have intact basic movement reflexes, but learned movements quickly overtake them. Francesco Lacquaniti and colleagues neatly summarized the development of postnatal movement, showing how very young children explore their environment with everything that is available to them, using all limbs:

> Toddlers often place a foot on the obstacle or on the edges of the stairs, presumably as part of an exploratory strategy of the environment. . . . Most toddlers spontaneously carry objects while walking, combining locomotor and manual skills. Despite the

additional biomechanical constraints, carrying an object is actually associated with improved upright balance, as demonstrated by smaller probabilities of falling with the object than without.[2]

Here, the authors refer to an intriguing naturalistic study of 13-month-old children in their home environments. In a similar study of spontaneous carrying behaviors, 26 infants who were crawling and 24 who were walking were observed. The prevailing view is that carrying behavior occurs only after movement control is established, but the opposite was found: infants appear to spontaneously carry as a way of self-training their movement control (Karasik et al., 2012).

What emerges from the contemporary study of postural control and motor development is the idea of the infant as an active participant in the self-development of locomotion. Many of the carrying episodes observed appeared to be without obvious motivational purpose: "with no apparent object-related or mother-related destination" (Karasik et al., 2012, p. 394). Pushing or carrying objects in hand, under one's arm, or in one's mouth, for no purpose might appear biomechanically inefficient, but may actually be part of locomotor self-training. Even before walking or crawling, we are feet-reaching toward intrinsically attractive objects, using the environment for locomotor development (Galloway and Thelen, 2012). From the very beginning of rudimentary motor control, we are driven to engage with the environment.

Embodied cognition

This functional view of human movement extends beyond motor learning. For example, a popular movement in cognitive science, which has come to be known as *embodied cognition*, views movement as central not only to the development of proprioception, but also for cognition. In its purest form, this view is of all cognition as situated: of movement that is always of and for action. Rather than viewing the body as simply a receptacle for the mind, as a means of moving a thinking machine around, the mind is a product of physical being in interaction with the world. In 2002, Margaret Wilson recognized the popularity of this emerging set of ideas and mapped out six versions of it as she saw them developing. She is troubled by the most extreme of these ideas, which essentially positions the mind as one enmeshed part of a continuous, highly integrated information flow (Wilson, 2002). For a deeper analysis of this position it is worth visiting Thomas Stoffregren and Benoît Bardy's important discussion piece, "On Specification and the Senses" (Stoffregren and Benoît, 2001).

Movement creates the possibilities for thought. It is only in exploration that intelligence can emerge. Another way of thinking about this comes from computer science. How do we train an artificial intelligence? In "Six Lessons from Babies," Linda Smith and Michael Gasser asked what we can learn about embodied cognition from the developing child. For our purposes, lesson four is the most important: "Babies explore—they move and act in highly variable and playful ways that are not goal-oriented and are seemingly random. In doing so, they discover new problems and new solutions. Exploration makes intelligence open-ended and inventive."[3] Smith and Gasser conclude:

> Young mammals, including children, spend a lot of time in behavior with no apparent goal. They move, they jiggle, they run around, they bounce things and throw them, and generally abuse them in ways that seem, to mature minds, to have no good use. However, this behavior, commonly called play, is essential to building inventive forms of intelligence that are open to new solutions.[4]

Exploring space, and exploring one's manipulation of space, functions to train proprioception, and through that training create the possibilities of cognitive development.

This training of and by locomotion continues throughout infancy into adolescence. Walking patterns are still in development well into adolescence. Movement skills are crucially important to master in childhood because competency at walking, hopping, throwing, and catching are associated with a lower risk of obesity and the associated health benefits that accrue from exercise, potentially across the lifespan (Lubans et al., 2010). The finding that low competency in fundamental motor skills is associated with low physical activity is not unusual (Hardy et al., 2012) and perhaps to be expected, interrelated as they are.

Only now emerging, however, is information to suggest that lower competence in fundamental motor skills increases the risk of obesity and exercise avoidance. For example, in one study of 5- to 13-year-olds, poor motor control, measured objectively with tasks such as walking backward on a narrowing beam and one-legged hopping over an obstacle, significantly predict an increase in body mass index two years later (D'Hont et al., 2014). It is too soon to tell whether difficulty in catching and throwing in childhood can be used as an indicator of increased risk of morbidity. If the lessons of babies are true for adolescents, then we might expect that any reduction in opportunities for exploratory play or movement in the world will limit proprioceptive development and possibly cognitive development.

Clumsiness

How good are you at throwing and catching a ball? When Mark LeGear and his colleagues asked 260 children in kindergarten (aged about five years old) this question, the average answer was very positive. In fact, it was a lot more positive than their actual abilities, which were quite poor. Girls were more positive than boys (LeGear et al., 2012). So what happens to this confident start on our view of our own motor abilities? Unfortunately, it does not last very long. Jacqueline Eccles and colleagues show that older children are more accurate, or perhaps more pessimistic, in their perception of how competent they are at throwing (Eccles et al., 1993). In a synthesis of 22 meta-analyses of studies assessing people's perception of their own abilities, it becomes quite clear that we are pretty bad at judging our own abilities (Zell and Krizan, 2014). We witness our abilities all of the time, but somehow still have a biased perception of them. This perception failure is an interesting puzzle. For example, it is not clear whether the biases in our self-perception are general across domains (from mathematics to throwing and catching) or whether they are domain-specific. Also unclear is how stable or open to influence these biases are.

Daniela Rigoli and her colleagues have argued that this self-perception is more than just an abstract puzzle. A sample of 93 adolescents with poor motor coordination showed elevated emotional problems, principally anxiety. However, this study had a measure of self-perception of ability. The relationship between motor coordination and emotional state was mediated by the *self-perception* of poor ability. In other words, believing you have poor motor control is what makes it possible for poor motor performance to be linked to anxiety (Rigoli et al., 2012).

Some people have motor problems that are severe enough to attract a label of dyspraxia, also described as a motor coordination disorder. Although commonly thought of as a developmental disorder, many people continue to have problems into adulthood. Amanda Kirby and colleagues found that adult coordination problems were characterized by items such as "have difficulty playing team games, such as football, volleyball, catching or throwing balls accurately" (p. 135), with 75.5 percent of the sample agreeing that this was usual. Fine motor movements such as writing, captured with the item "have difficulty writing neatly when having to write fast" (p. 136), were endorsed as usual by 71.4 percent (Kirby et al., 2010).

Part of Kirby and colleagues' interest in adult motor control problems was the extent to which one is able to compensate for and work around coordination problems. They found that avoidance of group activities, such as team sports and socializing (when it included dancing), was common, as were difficulties in the mastery of social skills such as driving, reading, self-care, and financial management. Although such motor disorders are common, there is little research into people's perceptions of their motor abilities, except in diagnostic interviews or in accounts of a specific experience of dyspraxia resulting from developmental disorder or brain injury. Casey Edmonds argues that for children, at least, this lack of research into their experience leaves them at risk of poor education and social exclusion (Edmonds, 2013).

Improving motor performance

Psychology has long been interested in the improvement of motor performance; in particular, as it relates to skill development. Most of us, even as adults, are visited by the idea of learning a new skill, such as playing a musical instrument or improving performance in a sport: in my case, learning piano as an adult novice and trying to run a faster marathon.

We have seen already that perhaps more than any other sensory system, propriception needs training. Interaction through locomotion, play, or object manipulation is how one learns about the world and how one sharpens sensory systems to allow learning about the world. Specific skills, however, require repetition of movement. Whether one is learning to shape a ceramic pot (Gandon et al., 2013), returning a beach volleyball serve (Cañal-Bruland et al., 2011), or mastering the Chopin's Ballade No.1 in G Minor (Rusbridger, 2013), skill acquisition is dependent on repetition. Practice is undeniably crucial.

Anders Ericsson has busily worked on expert performance and the psychology of experts for over 20 years. He introduced the idea that skills take at least ten years of effortful practice. This seems to be true of academic, physical, sporting, and musical expertise. The idea is now more commonly accepted, but it is worth reflecting that he and his colleagues were presenting these ideas against a backdrop of the lingering Victorian belief in the inheritability of limits to ability. Of course, many people work away at physical skills for more than ten years and appear to plateau or go backward. In their authoritative summary, Ericsson and his colleagues Ralf Krampe and Clemens Tesch-Römer addressed the important question of what we mean by practice. They were particularly interested in deliberate, goal-directed practice. In two studies, one of violinists and one of pianists, they conclude:

> People believe that because expert performance is qualitatively different from normal performance the expert performer must be endowed with characteristics qualitatively different from those of normal adults. This view has discouraged scientists from systematically examining expert performers and accounting for their performance in terms of the laws and principles of general psychology. We agree that expert performance is qualitatively different from normal performance and even that expert performers have characteristics and abilities that are qualitatively different from or at least outside the range of those of normal adults. However, we deny that these differences are immutable, that is, due to innate talent.[5]

They also make an intriguing suggestion for future research that has not been well developed; namely, that we should view experts not only as expert in their skills, but also experts at practice, experts at summoning and maintaining motivation to practice, and experts at resisting distraction.

In some ways the idea that one can, with enough grit and determination, and with ten years, or over 10,000 hours of deliberate practice, achieve expertise is now as popular as the biological determinism Ericsson and colleagues were reacting against. David Hambrick and colleagues comment that this idea has been popularized in journalism, most prominently in Malcom Gladwell's book *Outliers* (Gladwell, 2008), and they describe the ideas as a popular myth. They argue:

Deliberate practice does not explain all, nearly all, or even most of the variance in perform-ance in chess and music, the two most widely studied domains in expertise research. Put another way, deliberate practice explains a considerable amount of the variance in per-formance in these domains, but leaves a much larger amount of the variance unexplained.[6]

The extent of expertise is, however, to some extent a personal value judgment. Anders Ericsson has made the point repeatedly that what counts as success in skilled movement changes each year, whether it is Olympic records being re-made or once famously unplayable musical pieces like the Chopin Ballade now in the repertoire of the amateur. The 10,000 hours is a contextual idea—it is about the time invested in adjusting to environmental restrictions. But when we come to look at the experience of the expert, there are two aspects that are not commonly discussed, but are pertin-ent to our functional exploration of the physical senses. The first extends Ericsson and colleagues' interesting idea that perhaps as important to understand as the amount of practice undertaken is its psychology. Is practice more than just movement repeti-tion? The second relates to the experience of experts in the act of their expertise. What is the role of awareness in relation to limb and body position, or bodily movement and locomotion, during skilled performance?

The acquisition of motor skills is typically thought to happen without awareness or central monitoring. But practice in the pursuit of skills acquisition is at least delib-erate in its initiation: we decide to practice a task. But are one's beliefs about practice and its effects relevant to performance? In one study, 45 male Gaelic football players were asked to make two kicks toward goalposts, one from their hands and one from the ground. The footballers were either experts or at an intermediate level. In addition to measuring performance at different stages of practice, the researchers investigated the footballers' subjective physical exertion, mental effort, and enjoyment of phys-ical activity. The results were that the expert group "invested greater physical effort, greater mental effort, and rated practice activity as being less enjoyable than did the intermediate group" (Coughlan et al., 2014, p. 457).

At one level this is perhaps not surprising. That could be a good summary of what makes an expert. But what is surprising is the self-report. Developing Ericsson's idea, what may be as important as practice for motor performance is a personal *theory of movement*, a reflexive account of what one is engaging in, why, and exactly how.

Personal theory of movement

There are two schools of thought when it comes to the idea of a personal *theory of movement*, which are opposed. The first can be called *mindful*. A number of authors have argued, as with Coughlan and colleagues and their Gaelic football players, that if you ask people directly they will tell you about their bodies in motion. Perhaps it is just that psychology has not traditionally been a part of the study of motor performance, which is dominated by interests in physiology, biomechanics, and the applied practice of training. We don't have a research habit of investigating experience, and seem to avoid self-report data. Rebecca Lewthwaite and Gabriele Wulf have argued that a grand challenge in movement science will be to embrace a broader cognitive and emotional perspective (Lewthwaite and Wulf, 2010).

The second school of thought can be called *mindless*, not meant pejoratively. Gunner Breivik calls the state of lack of awareness of motor control "zombie-like" (Breivik, 2013). The extreme form of a mindless view is that highly automatized expert behavior does not need conscious control; in fact close attention to expert skills might actually be disastrous to performance. If I ask the concert pianist to think carefully and in detail about where she places her fingers on the keys and their touch and feel, such executive control of action will slow performance. Andrew Greeves and colleagues reported an analysis including interviews with expert concert musicians who were emphatically of this opinion (Greeves et al., 2014). Not everyone agrees, of course, and there is a movement for exploring what *mindful* playing could add to performance (Montero, 2010).

Skill and practice awareness are likely to be individual to the context of the skill, but there is an intriguing gap in our knowledge. The developmental model suggests that children engage in a great deal of self-exploration. When an infant sits and watches her hands manipulating an object, she is actively creating connections across motion sensing systems; it is neurological development in action. When the expert pianist makes decisions about whether to practice more, and what to practice, she is applying a theory of what needs to improve, based in part on proprioceptive feedback. An acrobat planning to fly through the air to catch a moving swing would not do it without first planning and practicing the required moves. But as to whether individuals in the very act of performance are partially or wholly controlling actions, or are relegated to the status of observer of those actions, we do not know.

To explore these ideas further, I talked with Luke Rendell (see Box 3.1).

Box 3.1. Luke, the acrobat: *"it is more about focus than thinking"*

Luke is an acrobat with Cirque du Soleil. He competed as an athlete in trampoline with the Great Britain team. He also trained in dance. When we talked he was on a break from performing ten shows a week in the Michael Jackson One extravaganza. Luke described himself, and his fellow athletes, as adrenalin connoisseurs. He is someone who enjoys being expert, and admires people who can transfer expertise and excel across domains. I was particularly interested in his experience of precision and flight, of understanding a body in motion.

Box 3.1. *Continued*

Chris: Do you know with any precision your position in the air as you fly?

Luke: Yes, I do. It comes from training. It is just like catching a ball. If you are somersaulting and you are short of rotation or you've travelled a little bit, you know exactly where you are because you have done it so many times. The trouble is that these skills are not in normal walks of life.

Chris: What does it mean to be aware of your body in flight?

Luke: You do learn aerial awareness and where you are in space when you are somersaulting or twisting, and you learn what is around you, but then you do get the odd talented person who can get in trouble in the air but know where she is and can get out of it and land on her feet, like a cat. These people have an extra talent. What you do in the air is such an unnatural thing. If you think you are going to mess it up, you will. You need to think more basically. People are extremely spatially aware and very quick on reactions. They will get lost and then find themselves again, in a split second. Transfer that from sport into an acrobatic act: you have ten people, three trampolines, people jumping over and under you, or running up the wall with someone at the top of the wall there to catch you. You have to learn this extra awareness. You have to be able to know your way around so well, and for it to be automatic. Your friends need to be "on it" also, because if he messes up I am in trouble, or if I mess up he is in trouble. You are dealing with life-or-death situations. You are 25 feet above the ground and you have to know exactly where you are.

Chris: How can one be aware, but at the same time not think too much?

Luke: It is an optimum thing. When you are on a trampoline you are thinking about parts of a skill, or you go into meditation. If you think about it too much it will mess up. However, when you are doing the move, you get into that zone of automaticity and you don't think—you just do it. When you mess it up it is like a blank part of your mind, the world collapses almost and then you think: "Oh no, I am in trouble now: I don't know how to get out of this." So when you are training hard you have to be in a balanced mind. You can't be concentrating too much on the skill and you can't be not concentrating. You have to be calm and ready to go. It is more about focus than thinking.

Chris: But does this awareness extend to personal space? Being aware of others' position in space relative to you?

Luke: It happens naturally. You find in a lifetime of trampolining that you start to know whether people are about to fall and whether you need to catch them, so transferring this to the circus, you know when you need to follow and what is safe. It is automatic. You have a sixth sense of being safe or unsafe, distance-wise—as long as you are not going to hit me in the face and knock me out, then you are good. Some, like trapeze artists, are catching less than a foot away. When they come round from a triple and reach for their catcher, his arms may have to be bent. Not catching is not an option, it is black or

(Continued)

41

Box 3.1. *Continued*

white. You have to catch— you have to know that you are going to save that man and he is going to save you.

Chris: Do you need to give verbal instructions or is it unspoken?

Luke: Any extra sound distracts some members, and they worry. Sometimes you communicate to motivate. I might say, "I have you" or "Watch out." We try not to communicate with new artists, but when you know people well you know when to speak and when not to speak. Sometimes they say, "Shut up: don't say anything to me. I know when I am in trouble." It is a pride thing.

Chris: You mention worry. Is there fear when you are flying high up?

Luke: It is situational. If you are standing in a cage that someone says is safe, even if it is 60 feet up, it is safe. Take away that cage and put a solid platform there. Stand on the edge of that and look down—you will get vertigo. I would have done that before Cirque. But you go into that environment and you train and train, and it becomes automatic. Then you add a handloop. Hang from that. Now I am 60 feet up and relying on just my grip. It becomes even more dangerous. Then you rely on yourself and your own anxiety. If you get too anxious, too nervous, it could go the other way. This is what I have learned. Don't concentrate too hard, but concentrate; don't get too nervous, but nerves are good. You have to have both and you have to make sure it is at its peak. We need to have explosive power to get where we want to be, but can't be too anxious because then the nerves and the adrenalin go too far.

Chris: Is peak performance about a balance of fear and attention?

Luke: I know what I am going to do before I have done it. I know what will happen before it happens. In my mind I am watching myself, and watching myself through my eyes.

Luke expresses beautifully the tension between awareness and automaticity. He has a complex personal theory of movement that does not fit the simplistic dualism of mindful or mindless. Knowing exactly where you and others are in shared space, being scared but not too scared, aware but not too aware, and ultimately being able to act and observe oneself at the same time, are all unusual perceptual achievements. Luke shows how the self-report of expert behavior can enrich psychology and be a useful theoretical tool. We need to develop a language for these experiences of the expert, because our current concepts are inadequate to the task of explanation.

Personal space

You know when someone is in your space. We don't own the space around us, but it feels like we do. How uncomfortable do you feel when strangers enter that space? Biological psychology has defined this as *peripersonal* space, the reachable distance immediately outside of the space you occupy. This definition, although a useful summary, has been expanded to account for some anomalies. For example, you can extend your space by tool use: if you carry a bag this is now in your space. We have found that that space is not dependent on intact limbs; it remains in place after loss of limb. Interestingly, although one cannot reach very far with one's head or by extending your tongue, peripersonal space around the head is much larger than one's reach. And, finally, this space is fundamentally malleable, dependent on a variety of environmental and interpersonal factors (Cardinali et al., 2009). Your perception of being and moving in space is dynamic, action-oriented, and environmentally contingent. For a good summary, Dorothée Legrand and her colleagues argue that what we make possible relates constantly to our fixed location as perceivers, and that multisensory input about personal space is integrated to allow us to act on the world (Legrand et al., 2007).

Often this peripersonal space is described as an invisible bubble that defines the limits of reach and of comfort. When two bubbles of egocentric interpersonal space approach each other, or collide, how we move to re-establish acceptable distance becomes an interesting focus of study. The management of interpersonal space, or of the maintenance of your own peripersonal space, is known as the study of *proxemics*; that is, the study of what is proximal (Bruno and Muzzolini, 2013). Proxemic control or awareness is variable and dependent upon gender, age, status, attraction, and environmental influences such as light.

Marco Costa, from the University of Bologna in Italy, recognized that most studies of proxemics have been undertaken with only static stimuli. He decided to study how people manage their interpersonal space when they are moving. He observed 1,002 groups (of between two and five people) walking in the daytime in an urban setting. He found that women are more likely to walk abreast, whereas groups of men will more often adopt a forward and backward position. Costa interprets this to be a consequence of social dominance effects. He also found that groups of three most often walk in a "<" formation with the central person receded. This may be only an acoustically efficient strategy to facilitate communication, but is more likely a specific effect of ensuring that one's personal space, even in a group, is maintained for all members (Costa, 2010). Taking this idea further, personal proximity may also predict walking speed and changes in direction: the more crowded a space is, the more one jostles (speeds up and changes direction) to maintain one's space (Frohnwieser et al., 2013).

Posing and strutting

What happens when one deliberately takes control of posture and movement? Can we reverse the influence of social factors? Can we influence other people and their perceptions of us by deliberately adopting different positions in space (posing) and deliberately adopting different gait patterns (strutting)?

The first of these questions was examined experimentally with a focus on space-taking *expansive* postures and space-limiting *constricted* postures. In one experiment, 93 young people engaged with actors who were secret confederates in the experiment. These confederates adopted one of three postures: expansive, neutral, and constricted. The postures adopted by the participants in response were recorded and analyzed. The interest was in whether adopting expansive postures would evoke mimicry in observers or whether it would evoke a complementary, opposite response. There was no evidence for mimicry. In fact,

> When the confederate displayed a dominant or submissive posture, participants were likely to respond with the opposite kind of display. Dominance appears to invite submissiveness and submissiveness appears to invite dominance. Dominant and submissive behaviors do not just affect perceptions of the actor, as has been shown in previous research, but also the behavior of people around that actor.[7]

In a second study, Tiedens and Fragale explored people's sense of comfort and their awareness of the posture they had adopted in response. Did they know they were doing it? They did not. It seems that we are generally unaware of the posture we adopt, which, given what we know about proprioception, is not surprising. More surprising was the finding of this study that people report being more comfortable when adopting a complementary posture. In other words, we seem to like a vertical social order to be observed, and posture is an immediate, nonverbal, and easy to communicate means of establishing that order.

There is an emerging view that the social dominance encoded in postures may be universal, and biologically mediated (Carney et al., 2010). But Lora Park and colleagues have argued that dominance postures are culturally constructed. They examined three expansive sitting postures and compared them to a constricted sitting posture. Figure 3.1 shows the postures. They compared student perceptions of those born in the United States, and those born in East Asia, on these three different *power poses*, using a variety of methods. Contrary to their general hypotheses, they found evidence that expansive postures do indeed seem to communicate power and dominance across cultures. However, more specific dominant poses, such as one that involved putting one's feet on the desk and displaying the soles of one's shoes, vary across cultures (Park et al., 2013). This shoe effect is perhaps unsurprising, as the display of shoes and feet vary in meaning across cultures. In Middle Eastern cultures,

Expansive-Upright-Sitting-Pose

Expansive-Hands-Spread-on-Desk-Pose

Expansive-Feet-on-Desk-Pose

Constricted-Sitting-Pose

Fig. 3.1. Three sitting poses, two expansive and one constricted.

Reprinted from *Journal of Experimental Social Psychology*, 49 (6), Lora E. Park, Lindsey Streamer, Li Huang, and Adam D. Galinsky, Stand tall, but don't put your feet up: Universal and culturally-specific effects of expansive postures on power, pp. 965–971, Appendix A, doi:10.1016/j.jesp.2013.06.001 Copyright (2013), with permission from Elsevier.

for example, shoes are unwelcome or banned in religious building (Ibrahim, 2009, p. 219). Being sensitive to the local cultural meaning of posture is important, but nonetheless it appears that using more of your peripersonal space—seeking to fill it rather than reduce it—could have far-reaching effects on both your own experience of feeling empowered and your influence on others.

If some postures are universally constructed as dominant, are some gait patterns also encoded differently to others? There is interest in whether emotion is communicated in the way people walk, in their gait and posture (Gross et al., 2010). In particular, there is a growing applied interest in whether we can identify furtive, aggressive, or threatening behavior through observation alone; research driven by a concern with security and threat identification. Unfortunately, there is no mature research interest in how gait might shape the behavior of others, either in proxemic control or in approach or avoidance of activity. One might start with an approach similar to Lora Park and colleagues, and try to identify emotional or intentional states universally encoded in bodily movement, such as pain, aggression, or love.

Disorders of movement

There are many neurological disorders that alter one's perception of position in space. Incoherence from conflicting sensory input can cause perceptual illusion, inaction, or compulsion, all of which invoke cognitive involvement in the form of attention and executive control of action. Simply put, when proprioception and kinesthesia fail to deliver the expected action, then the control of that action becomes a task. There are acute movement and spatial awareness problems, such as motion sickness; there are primary movement disorders that arise from nervous system disease, such as Parkinson's disease; and there are movement disorders arising from brain injury, such as cerebrovascular insult, or stroke. From a functional psychological perspective, I am interested in the experience of movement disorders, grossly defined, not from within their biological categories but from their phenomenological categories. Christine Klein defines movement disorders as a

> clinically, pathologically and genetically heterogeneous group of neurological conditions. Despite this variability, there is considerable overlap between different forms of movement disorders, as they all share the common features of impaired planning, control or execution of movement. (Klein, 2005, p. 426).

Three broad categories of altered experience can be explored across different conditions: tremor, start and stop, and fine motor control. However, there is one extreme case that is interesting because it involves a failure in belief rather than perception.

Anosognosia

Anosognosia is a disorder characterized by a denial of a deficit (Coslett, 2005). It is a useful concept that is rarely used because of its breadth and confusion with over-lapping constructs, such as denial. But in spatial awareness anosognosia can be described as a form of neglect with or without extinction. Typically the patient with neglect will, as the name suggests, neglect information placed in the contralateral side of the brain damage. Hence a right hemisphere stroke might induce a distortion of perception in the left side of one's personal space. This can be true for information in any perceptual domain, although it is most commonly identified in visual-spatial tasks. Extinction, a subtler observation, can occur in all perceptual systems "whereby patients can detect a single stimulus in either hemispace, but fail when another identical stimulus is presented simultaneously in the other hemispace" (Cocchini et al., 1999, p. 286). These symptoms are not of movement but of spatial awareness and belief. The co-occurrence of a neglect of all information in a particular quadrant or location in our peripersonal space—together with a strong, often emotionally dominant belief that one is *not* ignoring that space: the ignored stimuli cannot possibly exist—show how perception and belief can co-occur.

The case of brain injury is often quite specific and allows for the observation of a disorder, but there is less interest and exploration in anosognosia in the broader category of normal movement disorders. For example, there may be interest in extending the findings reviewed above on the common bias to a misjudgment of perception of action, to a natural case of denial of action (Zell and Kirzan, 2014). Todd Feinberg considers anosognosia as a part of a wider family of disorders of self (Feinberg, 2011). There is much to learn about how we come to deny experience in the space we occupy (as in denying the existence or loss of a limb), how we deny experience in our peripersonal space (as in neglect), and how we come to deny the existence in our extrapersonal space (as in the case of attentional blindness). By definition, however, any attempt to explore the phenomenology of denial will be brief.

Tremor

Tremor (trembling or rhythmic shaking) is a common experience of locomotor disorders and occurs either as the primary presenting problem in essential tremor or as a symptom, as in Parkinson's disease (Grimaldi and Manto, 2013). There are some studies of the experience of tremor, but they are focused largely on the disability associated with disease or the lack of awareness and understanding among communities of the disease. For example, Gerry Mshana and colleagues reported a study of people's experience of Parkinson's disease in rural Tanzania and the general lack of understanding that dominates. One 65-year-old woman said "I get tired ... the tremor is not only on the hands ... the whole body tremors ... even the intestines tremor ... and at night I get tired ... I become unhappy" (Mshana et al., 2011, p. 4).

Although in some ways it is difficult to disentangle one particular symptom from another in terms of its effects, the experience of tremor has not been adequately described or understood. The effects of tremor on quality of life, and the indirect effect on activities of daily living, are well mapped; but what it feels like to shake, and the role of beliefs about the cause, consequence, and controllability of the experience has hardly been explored. Given how close belief and perception can be, the absence of any understanding of the personal meaning of tremor is concerning. There is the beginning of a recognition of the importance of beliefs in movement disorders (Hurt et al., 2015), and it will be interesting to see whether it can extend to a neuroscientific study of the experience of tremor.

Start and stop

The specific experience of delay in the initiation of a behavior, freezing, or the inability to control the stopping of a behavior, is particularly challenging for patients with Parkinson's disease or dystonia. The regulation of desire and will and the obedience of our bodies in response to instruction are for many people distressing experiences. Consider the experience of musculoskeletal injury, such as fracture, that biomechanically denies movements, or of the experience of attempting to walk while dreaming. Typically one experiences the sending of an instruction and confusion over the delay or lack of response. As with tremor, there is no mature body of knowledge on the experience of having a disobedient body or of experiencing a delay in motor control. There are hints of concern. For example, Taku Hatano and colleagues interviewed patients and carers with Parkinson's disease and found that both patients and carers expressed a common concern of not being able to keep pace with the patient's movements, making the management of movement in peripersonal space an issue to address (Hatano et al., 2009). It is not clear the extent to which people with motion delay or freezing develop a pattern of excessive control in attending toward instruction, or whether further guided attempts at executive control of action could improve the coherence of motor experience.

Fine motor control

In movement disorders that affect global planning and delivery, such as Parkinson's disease or cerebral palsy, the combination of motor and nonmotor symptoms affect all aspects of function. But for some focal dystonias, especially peripheral dystonias, they are often related to a specific activity, making their psychology different. Often dystonias are specific to an occupation, such as arising from being a writer, a pianist, a golfer, or a hairdresser. The psychology of peripheral dystonias is one strangely dominated by old-fashioned ideas of psychologically generated disability, with investigations of psychological characteristics in samples of patients presenting with pain, anxiety, disability, and a threat to livelihood or career (Enders et al., 2011).

However, this old fashioned dualism of physical and psychological should be discarded because it is both irrelevant and unhelpful. At face value patients often do present anxiously, but the extent to which this anxiety reflects a premorbid tendency to anxiety is normally unexamined. Alternative nonpathologizing explanations may lie in the complexity of the environment of skilled performers, artists, or craft workers, in movement repetition and the demands of their production. For one example of this approach, Eckart Altenmüller and his colleagues explored the experience of 591 musicians with *musician's cramp*. They explored the relationship between demands for spatiotemporal precision from different instruments and showed that behavioral triggers were important to the onset of the dystonia (Altenmüller et al., 2012), in particular the demands of individual instruments on particular dystonias.

The psychology of movement disorders is struggling to move away from a clinical habit of framing patient experience as psychopathological. What is needed in the psychology of movement is an understanding of felt experience as an expression of a perceptual system driven to deliver phenomenological and behavioral coherence. Missing is the voice of the person struggling to make sense of changes in their embodied cognition.

To explore these ideas further I talked with Jeremy Clark (Box 3.2).

Box 3.2. Jeremy, recovering from stroke: *"you take things for granted"*

Jeremy had a stroke only 20 days before we talked. He had a right-sided cerebral infarct, leaving him with left-sided loss of sensation and motor control. He also had a right carotid endarterectomy to remove the offending plaque. He was active in early rehabilitation. We did not talk for long because he was easily fatigued, but he was keen to talk about his experience of movement and movement effort.

Chris: How sudden was the experience of stroke?

Jeremy: My feeling about a stroke before I had one was that it was something very dramatic. And instant. To me, although the end result was quite dramatic, the actual event itself didn't seem to be dramatic. It develops. There is constant monitoring as it is going on.

Chris: How would you describe the dominant feelings now?

(Continued)

Box 3.2. *Continued*

Jeremy: Absolute frustration. Very fatigued. Tired all the time. And I am constantly aware of an area of pain in the legs on the left hand side. Frustration is the biggest thing I am dealing with at the moment: of not being able to do simple things. You take things for granted. You put your hand on the table and the physical therapist says, "Tuck your fingers in," and you try and do it and it does not happen, and you don't know how to do it. It is so frustrating.

Chris: It must be hard when your body does not obey.

Jeremy: Yes. You then worry it is never going to. If movement does not happen when in a relaxed situation, will it ever? I will get there. You just have to believe that really.

Chris: Does it feel like you are sending messages that are not being received?

Jeremy: I suppose that is my problem. Technically I don't know how to send that message. When you think about it, it is rather amazing that the brain sends these messages. I am not aware of sending them, and in some instances I am not sending them. It is amazing that today my index finger is moving. How I am doing that I have no idea.

Chris: What are the major concerns now?

Jeremy: Where I go from here really. If I can get back to near where I was before the stroke I will be happy. It is the loss of mobility and independence that you take for granted without a stroke. Being able to get up and go somewhere, being able to drive. Even walking the dog. That is a fear. Getting back to some form of normality, to the same position as before.

Chris: Is this the focus of the treatment?

Jeremy: They have me up standing and walking which gives a sense of progress, because you can still have an element of control over that when you are doing it. You can still sense that you are doing things that affect the outcome. It is going through the mechanics of moving. How your feet fall in walking, putting your legs and feet in the right position. Quite intriguing really; I have never thought that much about walking. That is what you take for granted. When you walk somewhere you don't think about where to put your feet, you just do it. Hence the frustration.

Chris: Does belief that you can move matter?

Jeremy: You have to believe you can do it, be convinced, and trust in the professional. The longer I am being encouraged, and the more I practice and rethink everything about moving, the better the signs are. I believe it will come.

The simplest of movements become frustratingly difficult. The experience of movement disorders are of a disobedient body. But, as Jeremy discusses, the lack of control, of trying to experience the sending of messages, is more than a simple on/off switch. Belief in movement, practice, exploring the sensation of wanting and wishing to move, is part of the rehabilitation, or working to new limits.

Summary

We take our motor performance for granted. It is only when a child, when we are try-ing to learn or perfect a skill, or when we suffer disease or injury, that we come to appreciate the astonishing achievements of how our bodies move in space. Psychology has been relatively slow to embrace movement as perception, despite a growing inter-est in embodied cognition. A strong version of movement psychology is needed that embraces the phenomenology of position in space and how who we are can change through movement. Important will be to know how far practice is really important in skill development, not just for the expert, but for us all. Important will be to develop our concepts beyond the simple dichotomies of awareness. Alterations in movement perception are not simple biomechanical degrees of freedom. Movement is central to ego development, to intelligence, and to shaping the behavior of others.

Notes

1. Reproduced from *International Journal of Behavioral Development*, 24 (4), Esther Thelen, Motor development as foundation and future of developmental psychology, p. 385 doi:10.1080/01650250075037937 Copyright (2000), with permission from SAGE.
2. Reproduced from *Current Opinion in Neurobiology*, 22 (5), Francesco Lacquaniti, Yuri P Ivanenko, and Myrka Zago, Development of human locomotion, p. 825, doi:10.1016/j. conb.2012.03.012 Copyright (2012), with permission from Elsevier.
3. Reproduced from Linda Smith and Michael Gasser, The Development of Embodied Cog-nition: Six Lessons from Babies, *Artificial Life*, 11 (1–2), p. 13, doi:10.1162/1064546053278973 Copyright © 2005, Massachusetts Institute of Technology.
4. Reproduced from Linda Smith and Michael Gasser, The Development of Embodied Cog-nition: Six Lessons from Babies, *Artificial Life*, 11 (1–2), p. 13, doi:10.1162/1064546053278973 Copyright © 2005, Massachusetts Institute of Technology.
5. Reproduced from Anders K. Ericsson, Ralf T. Krampe, and Clemens Tesch-Römer, The role of deliberate practice in the acquisition of expert performance, *Psychological Review*, 100 (3), p. 400, doi:10.1037/0033-295X.100.3.363 © 1993, American Psychological Association.
6. Reprinted from *Intelligence*, 45, David Z. Hambrick, Frederick L. Oswald, Erik M. Altmann, Elizabeth J. Meinz, Fernand Gobet, and Guillermo Campitelli, Deliberate practice: Is that all it takes to become an expert?, p. 41, doi:10.1016/j.intell.2013.04.001, Copyright (2014), with permission from Elsevier.
7. Reproduced from Larissa Z. Tiedens and Alison R. Fragale, Power moves: Complementarity in dominant and submissive nonverbal behavior, *Journal of Personality and Social Psychology*, 84 (3), pp. 563–564, doi:10.1037/0022-3514.84.3.558 © 2003, American Psychological Association.

References

Altenmüller, E., Baur, V., Hofmann, A., Lim, V.K. and Jabusch, H.-C. (2012). Musician's cramp as manifestation of maladaptive brain plasticity: arguments from instrumental differences. *Annals of the New York Academy of Sciences*, 1252, 259–265.

Brevik, G. (2013). Zombie-like or superconscious? A phenomenological and conceptual analysis of consciousness in elite sport. *Journal of the Philosophy of Sport*, 40, 85–106.

Bruno, N. and Muzzolini, M. (2013). Proximics revisited: similar effects of arms length on men's and women's personal distances. *Universal Journal of Psychology*, 1, 46–52.

Cañal-Bruland, R., Mooren, M. and Savelsbergh, G.J.P. (2011). Differentiating experts' anticipatory skills in beach volleyball. *Quarterly Journal for Exercise and Sport*, 82, 667–674.

Cardinali, L., Brozzoli C. and Farnè, A. (2009). Peripersonal space and body schema: two labels for the Same Concept? Brain Topography, 21: 252–260.

Carney, D.R., Cuddy, A.J.C. and Yap, A.J. (2010). Power posing: brief nonverbal displays affect neuroendocrine levels and risk tolerance. *Psychological Science*, 21, 1363–1368.

Cocchini, G., Cubelli, R., Della Sala, S. and Beschin, N. (1999). Neglect without extinction. *Cortex*, 35, 285–313.

Coslett, H.B. (2005). Anosognosia and body representations forty years later. *Cortex*, 41, 263–270.

Costa, M. (2010). Interpersonal distances in group walking. *Journal of Nonverbal Behavior*, 34, 15–26,

Coughlan, E.K., Williams, M.A., McRobert, A.P. and Ford, P.R. (2014). How experts practice: a novel test of deliberate practice theory. *Journal of Experimental Psychology: Learning, Memory and Cognition*, 40, 449–458.

D'Hont, E., Deforche, B., Gentier, I., Verstuyf, J., Vaeyens, R., de Bourdeaudhuij, I., Philippaerts, R. and Lenior, M.A. (2014). Longitudinal study of gross motor coordination and weight status in children. *Obesity*, 22, 1505–1511.

Eccles, J., Wigfield, A., Harold, R.D. and Blumenfeld, P. (1993). Age and gender differences in children's self- and task perceptions during elementary school. *Child Development*, 64, 830–847.

Edmonds, C. (2013). Why teachers need to hear the voice and experience of the child with dyspraxia. *Research in Teacher Education*, 3, 5–10.

Enders, L., Spector, J.T., Altenmüller, E., Schmidt, A., Klein, C. and Jabusch, H.-C. (2011). Musician's dystonia and co-morbid anxiety: two sides of the same coin? *Movement Disorders*, 26, 539–556.

Ericsson, K.A., Krampe, R.T. and Tesch-Römer, R. (1993). The role of deliberate practice in the acquisition of expert performance. *Psychological Review*, 100, 363–406.

Feinberg, T.E. (2011). Neuropathologies of the self: clinical and anatomical features. *Consciousness and Cognition*, 20, 75–81.

Frohnwieser, A., Hopf, R. and Oberzaucher, E. (2013). Human walking behavior—the effect of pedestrian flow and personal space invasions on walking speed and direction. *Human Ethology Bulletin*, 28, 20–28.

Galloway, J.C. and Thelen, E. (2012). Feet first: object exploration in young infants. *Infant Behavior and Development*, 27, 107–112.

Gandon, E., Bootsma, R.J., Endler, J.A. and Grosman, L. (2013). How can ten fingers shape a pot? Evidence for equivalent function in culturally distinct motor skills. *PLoS One*, 11, e81614 1–11.

Gladwell, M. (2008). Outliers: the story of success. New York: Little, Brown and Company.

Greeves, A., McIlwain, D.J.F., Sutton, J. and Christensen, W. (2014). To think or not to think: the apparent paradox of expert skill in music performance. *Educational Philosophy and Theory*, 46, 674–691.

Grimaldi, G. and Manto, M. (Eds.). (2013). Mechanisms and emerging therapies in tremor disorders. New York: Springer.

Gross, M.M., Crane, E.A. and Fredrickson, B.L. (2010). Methodology for assessing bodily expression of emotion. *Journal of Nonverbal Behavior*, 34, 223–248.

Hambrick, D.Z., Oswald, F.L., Altmann, E.M., Meinz, E.J., Gobet, F. and Campitelli, G. (2014). Deliberate practice: is that all it takes to become an expert? *Intelligence*, 45, 34–45.

Hardy, L.L., Reinten-Reynolds, T., Espinel, P., Zask, A. and Okely, D. (2012). Prevalence and correlates of low fundamental movement skill competency in children. *Pediatrics*, 130, e390–e398.

Hatano, T., Kubo, S.-I., Shimo, Y., Nishioka, K. and Hattori, N. (2009). Unmet needs of patients with Parkinson's Disease: interview survey of patients and caregivers. *Journal of International Medical Research*, 37, 717–726.

Hurt, C.S., Julien, C.L. and Brown, R.G. (2015). Measuring illness beliefs in neurodegenerative disease: why we need to be specific? *Journal of Health Psychology*, 20, 69–79.

Ibrahim, Y. (2009). The art of shoe-throwing: shoes as a symbol of protest and popular imagination. *Media, War and Conflict*, 2, 213–226.

Karasik, L.B., Adolph, K.E., Tamis-LeMonda, C.S. and Zuckerman, A.L. (2012). Carry on: spontaneous object carrying in 13-month-old crawling and walking infants. *Developmental Psychology*, 48, 389–397.

Kirby, A., Edwards, L., Sugden, D. and Rosenblum, S. (2010). The development and standardization of the Adult Developmental Co-ordination Disorders/Dyspraxia Checklist (ADC). *Research in Developmental Disabilities*, 31, 131–139.

Klein, C, (2005). Movement disorders: classifications. *Journal of Inherited Metabolic Disease*, 28, 425–439.

Lacquaniti, F., Ivanenko, Y.P. and Zago, M. (2012). Development of human locomotion. *Current Opinion in Neurobiology*, 22, 822–828.

LeGear, M., Greyling, L., Sloan, E., Bell, R.I., Williams, B.-L., Naylor, P.-J. and Temple, V.A. (2012). A window of opportunity? Motor skills and perceptions of confidence in children in kindergarten. *International Journal of Behavioral Nutrition and Physical Activity*, 9, 29 1–5.

Legrand, D., Brozzoli, C., Rossetti, Y. and Farnè, A. (2007). A. Close to me: multisensory space representations for action and pre-reflexive consciousness of oneself-in-the-world. *Consciousness and Cognition*, 16, 687–699.

Lewthwaite, R. and Wulf, G. (2010). Grand challenge for movement science and sport psychology: embracing the social-cognitive-affective-motor nature of motor behavior. *Frontiers in Psychology*, 1, 1–3.

Lubans, D.R., Morgan, P.J., Cliff, D.P., Barnett, L.M. and Okely, A.D. (2010). Fundamental movements skills in children and adolescents: review of associated health benefits. *Sports Medicine*, 40, 1019–1035.

Montero, B. (2010). Does bodily awareness interfere with highly skilled movement? *Inquiry*, 53. 105–122.

Mshana, G., Dotchin, C.L. and Walker, R.W. (2011). "We call it the shaking illness": perceptions and experiences of Parkinson's disease in rural northern Tanzania. *BMC Public Health*, 11, 219 1–8.

Park, L.E., Streamer, L., Huang, L. and Galinsky, A.D. (2013). Stand tall, but don't put your feet up: universal and culturally-specific effects of expansive postures on power. *Journal of Experimental Social Psychology*, 49, 965–971.

Proske, U. and Gandevia, S.C. (2012). The proprioceptive senses: their roles in signaling body shape, body position and movement, and muscle force. *Physiological Review*, 92, 1651–1697.

Rigoli, D., Piek, J.P. and Kane, R. (2012). Motor coordination and psychosocial correlates in a normative adolescent sample. *Pediatrics*, 129, e892–e900.

Rusbridger, A. (2013). Play it again. London: Jonathon Cape.

Sherrington, C.S. (1906). The integrative action of the nervous system. London: Yale University Press.

Smith, L. and Gasser, M. (2005). The development of embodied cognition: six lessons from babies. *Artificial Life*, 11, 13–29.

Stoffregren, T.A. and Benoît, B.G. (2001). On specification and the senses. *Behavioral and Brain Sciences*, 24, 195–261.

Thelen, E. (2000). Motor development as foundation and future of developmental psychology. *International Journal of Behavioral Development*, 24, 385–397.

Tiedens, L.Z. and Fragale, A.R. (2003). Power moves: complementarity in dominant and submissive nonverbal behavior. *Journal of Personality and Social Psychology*, 84, 558–568.

Wilson, M. (2002). Six views of embodied cognition. *Psychonomic Bulletin and Review*, 9, 625–636.

Zell, E. and Krizan, Z. (2014). Do people have insight into their abilities? A metasynthesis. *Perspectives on Psychological Science*, 9, 111–125.

CHAPTER 4

PRESSURE

There is a class of experience that comes when forces are applied to our bodies, when we attempt to move the whole body or parts of our bodies, or when the outside world resists force. I call these senses, the senses of *pressure*. I am interested in those experiences that we often discuss as the action of a braking system that allows or restricts movement. *Pressure* is not the most exact noun, but it is the closest in English I could find. It captures the sense of force against resistance. There are eight sensations of pressure narrated as four sets of opposing pairs. I am interested in the experiences of being flexible or stiff, strong or weak, heavy or light, and swollen or reduced.

Action is limited by a number of interrelated physical, biomechanical, and sensorimotor features. The simplest perhaps is the case of a physical barrier caused by an enlarged limb or organ denying free range of motion. Imagine an arm so swollen that you cannot move it freely without it colliding with one's chest, or a stomach and chest so large that an arm is restricted in its range of motion. Mechanoreceptors are distributed throughout peripheral structures and are in some ways the most complex of all sensory receptors (Delmas et al., 2011). The cortical fate of position and force information is partly dependent on the origin and function of the sensory information. The perception of pressure is broadly represented across multiple cortical, subcortical, and brainstem structures.

Emerging is an architectural idea of a *tensegral* living system of interrelated, often opposing, pressures—a perfect interdependent system in which live physical structures operate with and against each other to produce a unified system. The structures are in part elastic, and can change their elasticity in response to force. In the language of ecological perception, the environment affords the perception of pressure through the medium of interacting muscle, skeletal, and connective tissues that envelop us (Turvey and Finseca, 2014).

Many people could have helped me in exploring these pressure sensations. But two had particularly relevant experience of working with or against their brakes. First, I interviewed Emma. Emma is a yoga teacher. Every day she works to extend her limbs into full stretch. Freedom of movement is important to her; removing restrictions to the extent and fluidity of movement are key to the practice of yoga. Second, I interviewed Marni, who was diagnosed with lupus in 2008. Feeling restricted in her movement because of stiffness, swollen joints, and heaviness are all part of her life.

Flexibility

How flexible you are is normally defined by a test of your range of motion on a particular movement. But as anyone who has ever attempted to take part in an organized sport will know, there is a popular view that stretching—extending a movement to the extent of the range of motion and holding it—has beneficial effects, either immediately in extending range as part of a pre-exertion, warming-up exercise aimed at improving performance, or in reducing the risk of injury (Behm and Chaouachi, 2011).

Changing the range of motion of joints before exertion seems like a good idea. However, the idea that static stretching—the short-term extension and hold of a position—is beneficial has been hotly debated. Indeed, some studies have found no benefit at all. Katie Small and her colleagues reported an early meta-analysis of the effects of static stretching as part of warming up but found no real benefit (Small et al., 2008); a finding repeated by Mari Leppänen and her colleagues (2014).

Perhaps as important as whether stretching is effective, is whether people *believe* it to be effective (Beckett et al., 2009). In one study, Sandra O'Brien Cousins surveyed 143 women aged over 70 about what they thought the likely benefits or risks might be of different exercises. She included six categories: walking, cycling, water exercise, arm curls, push-ups, and stretching. Two thirds of the women believed that stretching would likely be of benefit. However, of all of the exercises suggested, including push-ups, the largest number of responses about fear of risk came for stretching. Twenty percent of the women expressed a concern that it would "hurt my neck/back"; 8 percent said simply that they did not believe they could do it (O'Brien Cousins, 2000). Often conversations and instructions to exercise as a way to increase flexibility imply that static stretching is a relatively low-level, easy, and simple method of warming up. However, what little data there are give the opposite impression: the experience of stretching is, for some at least, unwelcome or feared, and is believed to be injury-inducing, not injury-preventing.

Stiffness

Avoiding stretching for fear of injury or because it is judged unpleasant raises the question as to how the opposite state is experienced: what it feels like to be stiff, either in terms of a limited range of motion or a lack of fluidity of movement. Stiffness is a symptom common to many diseases, but it has probably been most studied in rheumatology. Stiffness, especially morning stiffness, is part of the diagnostic criteria for various rheumatologic conditions, such as rheumatoid arthritis, fibromyalgia, and ankylosing spondylitis. Even so, it has traditionally been less investigated than the other major symptoms of pain and fatigue.

Rheumatology has led the way in the quiet revolution in medicine of promoting a greater understanding and prominence of patient experience, and measuring that experience as part of the outcome of treatments. If asked, patients report that stiffness is a major source of concern. But you have to ask them. In one study, for example, severe morning stiffness was a prominent reason for early retirement in a large sample of German patients with early onset rheumatoid arthritis, although it has not traditionally been discussed as a risk factor of occupational change (Westhoff et al., 2008). In another study, stiffness was reported as part of the hard-to-manage flare in symptoms often experienced as uncontrollable (Hewlett et al., 2012; Flurey et al., 2014).

Ana-Maria Orbai was interested in what stiffness meant to different people who were living with the condition. She and her colleagues ran four focus groups with 20 adults, and asked them in some detail about their experiences. Patients discussed their experiences of stiffness as highly variable and thought that stiffness was related to other symptoms of pain and swelling. They discussed the factors that exacerbate it, including weather and inactivity, and activities that might relieve it. They also shared their thoughts on when and where it was most likely to occur, and the limitations that stiffness causes. One specific theme they identified as particularly interesting. They labeled this theme *individual context and meaning*. Routinely, people rely on mechanical metaphors to describe what it feels like to be stiff. For example:

> In 2 groups ... the experience of stiffness was described using imagery of the "Tin Man" from L. Frank Baum's *The Wonderful Wizard of Oz*. This description was spontaneously produced in each group and elicited considerable acknowledgement from other group members. In a third group a participant similarly described the effect of warm water on the joints, as "greasing the joints ... oiling what needs to be oiled".[1]

Similar were the comments from Sarah Hewlett's study. One patient said, "I feel I am stuck together with superglue, everything is so stiff and won't move"; another said, "I'm locked in a box" (Hewlett et al., 2012, p. 71). Being restricted, held, fixed, or stuck is at the center of this experience, but it is a feeling of restriction from within. It is not about being held back by an external force, but a feeling of the whole machine—your whole body—seizing up.

Flexibility-stiffness continuum

If we ask people about the experience of being either flexible or stiff, they can eloquently describe the sensations and their meaning as part of their lives. However, I have presented them here as unique states. They are perhaps better represented as part of a continuum: as one becomes more flexible, one feels less stiff, and vice versa. Flexibility is something one is constantly moving toward or away from in time. This temporal aspect is not often discussed in the scientific or medical literature, but is an intrinsic part of how we approach managing the demands of pressure on joint structures.

To flex or not to flex, that is the question. Professional dancers, for example, have a good understanding that flexibility is not a state to be achieved once, but something to repeatedly work toward. Ballet training involves long periods of warming up with and without a bar, and dancers have few rest periods (Twitchett, 2010). Professional dancers have a sense of flexibility as inherently temporary, something to be achieved and lost every day.

Yoga offers an interesting case. The general belief about yoga is that it is good for flexibility. For example, the Beliefs About Yoga Scale has as an item that practicing yoga means "I would become more flexible" (Sohl et al., 2011, p. 91). People who may never have tried yoga believed it to have properties that improve flexibility. Further, people practicing yoga often report that they do feel more flexible, and that this feeling is welcome. For example, in a study of 42 older adults taking part in a clinical trial of yoga, flexibility was high on their list of benefits:

> Participants noted an improved capacity for stretching and renewed flexibility. As one participant described, practicing yoga was instrumental in "learning how to stretch properly." For others, yoga practice restored function or enhanced baseline physical fitness. One participant wrote, "I enjoyed the flexibility that had returned to my body. I have noticed the difference."[2]

Despite the perhaps anecdotal evidence about the real or perceived benefits of yoga in improving flexibility there is little research. Research on this core part of the experience has not developed (Field, 2011).

Yoga is used in a range of different clinical areas, from primary mental health problems such as depression, to disease prevention, and to rehabilitation for many chronic problems. In part the problem of the study of yoga is that it means different things to different people. To some it is a whole approach to life; to others it is a set of specific practices involving both mental and physical repetition with physical postures that are achieved slowly and held. In the context of an investigation of flexibility, the narrower consideration of yoga—a set of postures that extend one's normal range of motion—is relevant. For example, Zahra Rakhshaee conducted a study of just three specific postures: the cobra, the cat, and the fish (see Table 4.1).

All three postures involve trunk movement. She was interested primarily in the analgesic effects of these postures for adolescents with dysmenorrhea, but unfortunately did not measure other outcomes, such as flexibility or strength, or beliefs about the effectiveness of the postures. Although limited, this study does show how it might be possible to focus on specific aspects of the practice of yoga for specific outcomes (Rakhshaee, 2011). Other researchers are following this approach of working on specific postures by mapping their mechanical demands, with a view to advising how one can become more specific in their application for specific problems (Wang et al., 2013). I suspect that the next generation of studies of yoga, at least as applied in clinical medicine and rehabilitation, will adopt this focused approach.

Table 4.1: Yoga poses and descriptions used in clinical trial

Poses	Performing	Descriptions
Cobra		1. Lie down with your legs together and your hands palms down under your shoulders. Rest your forehead on the floor.
		2. Inhaling, bring your head up, brushing first your nose, then your chin against the floor. Now lift up your hands and use your back muscles to raise your chest as high as possible. Hold for a few deep breaths then. Exhaling, slowly return to position 1, keeping your chin up until last.
		3. Inhaling, come up as before, but this time use your hands to push the trunk up. Continue up until you are bending from the middle of the spine. Hold for two or three deep breaths, then exhale and come slowly down.
		4. Inhaling, raise the trunk as before, but this time continue up and back until you can feel your back bending all the way down from the neck to the base of the spine. Breathe normally. Hold the position for as long as you feel comfortable, then slowly come down and relax.
Cat		1. Start on your hands and knees. Position your hands directly beneath your shoulders and your knees directly beneath the hips. Make your back horizontal and flat. Your spine will be at full extension, with both the front and back sides equally long.
		2. When you are ready to begin, breathe in deeply. Do this by gently pulling the abdominal muscles backward toward the spine, tucking the tailbone (coccyx) down and under, and gently contracting the buttocks. Press firmly downward with your hands in order to stay lifted out of the shoulders, and press the middle of your back toward the ceiling, rounding your spine upward. Curl your head inward. Gaze at the floor between your knees.
Fish		1. Lie down on your back with your legs straight and your feet together. Place your hands, palms down, underneath your thighs.
		2. Pressing down on your elbows, inhale and arch your back. Drop your head back so that the top of your head is on the floor, but your weight should rest on your elbows. Exhale. Breathe deeply while in the position, keeping your legs and lower torso relaxed. To come out of the pose, first lift your head and place it gently back down, then release the arms.

Yoga is typically undertaken as an activity in and of itself. In its Westernized forms, at least, yoga is seen as a lifestyle intervention: a personal exercise and health choice. It often involves a narrative of personal growth and development. In this context it is different from the invitation to consider stretching as part of a seniors' exercise class, as a part of warm-up routine, or as a way to respond to morning stiffness from rheumatoid arthritis.

Perhaps the meaning of stiffness and flexibility is different for those who choose to live some of every day at the extremes of their joint ranges of motion. What does flexibility and stiffness mean to the dancer or the yoga teacher?

To explore the idea of the flexibility-stiffness continuum further I talked to Emma Roy (Box 4.1).

Box 4.1. Emma, the yoga teacher: "*I am aware of my body all the time*"

Emma lives in Wiltshire. After many years running a successful restaurant, she turned to yoga, first for herself and then as a teacher. She describes herself as highly sensitive to her environment and aware of herself in relation to the environment. I asked her to help me understand what being flexible can feel like.

Chris: What does flexibility feel like? Is it just the absence of stiffness?

Emma: When I first started, there were many things I could not do. The feeling of being flexible is fluidity, it is flow, it feels like there is nothing there to hinder. It feels like open space. So just as I can sweep my hand in front of me, that is how it feels on the inside and so then I can choose where I am going to move. It is actually something I am working more with now: allowing the body to move me, allowing my body to move where it wants to move. If my arm wants to move to a certain position it moves and it feels right. Then it is right.

Chris: So the feeling of fluid movement is important.

Emma: It is about not jerking. Because if you move quickly it will feel tight, but when you move with gentleness, the body is being allowed to investigate and go where it wants in its own way. And I think this is where taking the mind out of it is important. I will often talk about playing with not being in control. I will work with a movement. Often it is how people have already decided to think about a movement, and when they try it and they can do it, it is a surprise to them. Then it opens the mind to thinking of things as possible. For me, when I want to play with something I go into an inquisitive approach. I will deal with whatever comes. It is about being willing to investigate, to play the game, to have a go.

Chris: Does having a heightened awareness matter—what is often called mindfulness?

Emma: I think what others call mindfulness I would call creative awareness. We take so much for granted. We don't think about our physical movements. Creating an awareness of movement, of feeling, of the emotions that might be attached to the movements:

Box 4.1. *Continued*

for some people sometimes it can be very shocking. I remember reaching one movement I did not think possible and I had an explosion of emotion that I did not understand and just accepted. I think mindfulness is the kindergarten, the first stage of reaching a level of creative awareness.

Chris: For many people that level of creative awareness might be frightening at first.

Emma: Yes, it is scary. First you feel a fool. Second, the brain has worked out what movements do what. So if you do something different and bizarre with a movement, that is going into the unknown. For me, it is going into a place of inquiry. When you allow the body to be in charge rather than the head, then you have a completely different experience of life.

Chris: Do you think people can gain from adopting the yoga postures just as postures?

Emma: Well, I am sure you can do that. But without being encouraged to move into other aspects of the experience, it feels a bit flat. But when you look at it in relation to gravity and the feeling of the movement, it is massively different. When you come out of a posture, what happens next? The counterposture is needed to relieve the body of the movement. It is a kind of dance, but a structured dance. But within that structure you can find your own personal experience—when you are given the opportunity, when you are safe to explore your body.

Chris: It sounds so very positive. Are there any negative aspects to the experience?

Emma: At the beginning perhaps. Yes. I used to be the kind of person who pushed myself to the absolute limit. And that included flexibility. An example of how flexibility can play against you is from when I had been in my yoga class with my first teacher and we were doing a position that is seated with feet flat together and knees spread to the floor bending forward. It puts a lot of pressure on the abductor muscles. I am working away, really going for it. Of course, that is not the way to do yoga, and I felt them go *ping*. It took three years for them to recover: they just felt really tight. A lot of the time it was because I was allowing my flexibility to go beyond its safe range because there was this feeling I had of wanting to do more. Now I understand that it is OK to stay within my safe limit.

Chris: And now? Are you aware of your limits now?

Emma: Yes, but now I am also aware of my body all the time. My feeling of being complete is all the time. As I sit here now, I am very aware of how my bottom is feeling on the cushions. I am very aware of what I am seeing and how I am feeling. It is going on all the time. It is tiring sometimes, I will admit that, but the growth that has come from it is phenomenal.

Emma lives on this flexibility-stiffness continuum. She has trained over many years to understand the limits of what is possible, of how far she can go before being stopped. But her experience shows that the overcoming the limits is effortful and requires investment in a whole understanding of how to live. These are not exercises but a choice to gain and sustain an awareness of being embodied, and so living within and against, physical limits.

Strength

How strong are you? Or, in other words: how much weight can you bear, and for how long? These are complex judgments that inevitably involve the interplay and integration of other interoceptive sensations, such as fatigue and pain. However, as with our other neglected senses, there is a language of strength. When we refer to feeling strong it has both a physiological reference and a cultural relevance.

In many societies, feeling and appearing to be strong are highly valued. Doug McCreary and Doris Sasse recognized early that the once-marginalized idea of building muscle was transferring into mainstream culture. They established a measure of what they called a *drive to muscularity* that included items about satisfaction with body shape and size, and behaviors people adopt that will change muscle mass, but it also included beliefs about physical strength, such as "I think I would feel stronger if I gained a little more muscle mass" (McCreary and Sasse, 2000, p. 299). Although this aspect of a drive to muscularity is more prominent in men than women (McCreary et al., 2004), being muscular is also discussed by women, and in some specific cultures, such as women's bodybuilding, muscle definition is constructed as core to their feminine ideal. In this subculture, however, feeling physically strong is often exactly what is at stake in bodybuilding (Grogan et al., 2004).

There is a view emerging in the social science literature that the building of muscle through exercise or through food supplements is driven by a concern, especially by men, to match a stereotypical body image (Daniel and Bridges, 2010). Although body image is part of the reason to build muscle, much less investigated is a concern with strength. For many people, strength does not equate with muscle mass. Feeling strong is particularly important for many practices such as yoga, dance, or acrobatics: strength is valued highly but the appearance of muscle bulk is not.

There is little direct perceptual research on what the experience of strength is like. Tim Henwood and colleagues explored older adults' perceptions of a resistance training program. In a qualitative study with 18 seniors, they identified the now-common themes of benefits to body image and health, and the social aspects of engaging in a program (Henwood et al., 2011). Missing, however, is a concern for the felt experience. Do people enjoy resistance training? There is evidence that training for strength has a positive effect on anxiety (Asmundson et al., 2013), but there is no study of a possibly positive psychological effect of feeling competent in returning resistance to physical force. What is needed is an exploration of the experience of being and feeling strong in general and in specific situations.

Weakness

Feeling weak, however, is more discussed in the study of adjustment to physically debilitating illness, and in rehabilitation. Weakness is typically thought of as the failure to carry or endure load, the inability to match a previously possible requirement ("I used to be able to carry this"), or the inability to match one's own or others' expectations ("I/we thought I was strong enough to lift this"). Of course, weakness is also closely tied to the judgment of external force, such that one might complain equally of being weak or of the force being too great. Weakness can be specific and temporary, sometimes associated with injury, or can be discussed in narratives of age or illness-related decline as frailty. Often weakness is closely related to fatigue as the judgment of tiredness (see Chapter 6); failure to recruit energy to counter force may be discussed as performance loss.

Weakness is a common complaint of known neurological and muscular disorders, of malignant disease, and from iatrogenic complications of treatments such as radiation therapy. Rehabilitation focuses on strength and conditioning, largely with a goal of return to occupational activity. Qualitative studies tend to stay at the important but relatively macro-analytic level of identity, quality of life, relationships, and loss (Salter et al., 2008). There is little interest in the specific experience of being unable to meet force with resistance. These micro experiences are, however, potentially important. How one comes to judge whether one is too weak to open a door or take the lid from a jar could be a crucial part of everyday life.

In an interesting natural observation study of how humans manage in their built environment, Chang and Drury (2007) recorded 1,600 "human/door interactions" with a focus on hand position and the recruitment of whole-body force (e.g., leaning into or pivoting away from a door). That most common of human devices, the door, affords information to the operator on how heavy one might expect it to be, and so what force to match to it, by the position of handles and door mechanisms. Whether we are likely to feel weak in attempting to open a door is signaled far in advance of operating the door.

Susan Rodiek in Texas made the study of doors more real to the experience of the people behind them. Simply put, doors have multiple functions. They provide safety, protection from the elements, definition of boundaries, and access points between spaces. However, depending on their properties, they can also function as barriers. Rodiek and her colleagues assessed the properties of doors in different senior living facilities in the United States, and ran focus groups discussing these properties with residents. Lurking among the various features was a concern with forces. One participant said of the doors in the residential home, "I mean, it's hard. I have learned, but then sometimes I have to go through the living room because these doors are heavy." Another agreed: "You're right. I have trouble with my shoulder to open, push, and pull the doors. I find that I have difficulties going through the doors."[3]

Understanding the psychology of weakness, therefore, is not trivial. How we make decisions about force and about what we are capable of has real practical concerns.

Strength-weakness continuum

As with flexibility and strength, strength and weakness lie on a continuum. They are opposing features of the same physical experience and move together. When the perception of strength increases, the perception of weakness subsides, and vice versa. Knowing when to improve one's strength, perhaps by a program of exercise, or whether one should reduce the environmental pressure, perhaps by altering the task demand, is an interesting design question. When one is designing a task that requires force, one needs a sense of what is a reasonable requirement in lifting, carrying, pushing, and pulling (Garg et al., 2014). Outside of the world that can be controlled via design, when one is trying to encourage participation in the often immutable outside world, how much strength can one encourage people to achieve in order to promote participation? For example, a self-closing gate needs to be sprung to close automatically, and at the same time it needs to be able to be opened with human strength.

The extremes are easy to understand. If a door is so heavy that it is beyond the ability of 99 percent of people, then there is a strong argument for redesign. Similarly, if 1 percent of people cannot open it due to reversible muscle weakness, then there is a good argument for strengthening exercises. The problems come when these two ideas meet in the gray middle. As we age, how much should we work on building and maintaining strength? Or should we accept weakness as a consequence of aging and adjust our homes and environment accordingly? These are, of course, questions without easy answers. One might be tempted to argue that all strengthening exercise is good exercise; however, the data on both effectiveness and possible adverse effects are at worst unclear (Latham et al., 2004), and at best partial (Peterson et al., 2010).

The picture becomes even more complex when we remember that, like all subjective judgments, the decision of what is possible—how much force one can extend in manipulating the objective world—is sensitive to one's belief in one's ability to change the world, and its ability to be changed. Understanding the biases in our perception of personal strength and weakness is going to be important if we are to understand how people behave when faced with physical resistance. To date, there is no guidance on how to incorporate people's perception of their weakness or strength into either the design of strength training or the design of the built environment. That does not mean, of course, that architects, designers, ergonomists, and various therapists are not making such considerations. Experts make decisions. But there is an opportunity for the development of a more scientifically informed psychology of physical strength to contribute to decisions on what is possible and desirable to change.

Heaviness

Most studies of weight perception in psychology are concerned with the question of how we judge the weight of external objects or people. There is also a large literature on the self-perception of being large; in particular, of being overweight and its psychological causes and consequences. Here I am interested simply in the basic question of what does it feel like to be heavy; to experience the weight of your own body or of a body part; to be both a body that experiences and is experienced.

Heaviness is often discussed only in specific contexts. For example, the experience of heavy legs is common to post-exercise fatigue and to wearing high-heeled shoes. It is also commonly reported in venous insufficiency, often occupationally related, or emerges as "restless legs", or is hidden behind a more dominant sensation of pain (Jawein, 2009). Such vascular involvement in the judgment of heavy legs gave Emmanuele Varlet-Marie and her colleagues the idea of exploring cardiorespiratory function—in particular, blood flow—among athletes who had overtrained. They studied 37 French national-level football, volleyball, and basketball players, as well as triathletes. Fourteen reported being overtrained. The researchers found that compared to athletes matched for age and body mass index, the overtrained group had higher plasma viscosity; moreover, their red cells aggregated faster (Varlet-Marie et al., 2003, pp. 154–155). It was argued that overtraining leads to higher blood viscosity, which in turn causes circulatory slowness. Investigating venous return highlights the importance of cardiovascular function in general when one is making a judgment about heaviness in limbs.

In this study of athletes, changes in blood viscosity emerged as a marker of overtraining, probably caused by local inflammation and general dehydration. But it is interesting that heavy legs are discussed as a cardiovascular phenomenon—a specific sensation, before fatigue or pain sets in. People who have suffered a cardiovascular accident or injury also report this sense of heaviness. For example, in their analysis of transition from hospital to home following a stroke, the expression of a "heavy" body often appears. In an interview study, one woman said: "My body feels so heavy. Have I been like this all the time or have I become worse?" (Eilertsen et al., 2010, p. 2009). This almost ethereal sense of distancing from a body is part of the experience of heaviness. It is not clear whether in stroke the experience of heaviness is mediated by aspects of cardiac and vascular function, or if it reflects a more central process of personal weight perception.

Radically life-altering changes in physical health status caused by neurological disease or accident, such as stroke, do bring with them a new vigilance for how one's body feels. Carla Ruis and her colleagues, in establishing norms for a commonly used questionnaire about psychological symptoms, the Symptom Checklist 90, found that the subscale somatic symptoms (which includes the item "heavy feelings in your arms") is highly elevated compared to those without disorder (Ruis et al., 2014). Attention to all aspects of physical being, including the perception of heaviness, is often invoked in illness.

Normal changes in body weight also cause changes in the perception of heaviness. For example, pregnant women can discuss the experience of being heavier than normal, and there is a language of feeling heavy in the literature on obesity and weight management. However, the discussion of heaviness is largely lost in these literatures in the much broader and less exact discussion of "feeling fat" and its social consequences. For example, in one qualitative study of 76 women and their experience of trying to lose weight, one participant said:

The amazing thing is, in the past if I'd been 9 and a half stone I'd be disgusted with my-self, I'd be really heavy, and now I was jubilant because I felt I was really light. It's all relative. (Byrne et al., 2003, p. 958).

In this example, the perception of heaviness may be specific or simply a general marker of weight-related changes in both perception and self-perception.

Lightness

Susan Byrne's just-mentioned qualitative study showed that people when dieting can make judgments about feeling heavy and also about feeling light. Feeling light in this case is a pleasant experience of weight loss achieved. But again, is the report of light-ness a specific sensation, or is it a general term for freedom of movement or lack of fatigue—or a composite of both? What do people mean when they report feeling light?

An artificial method of creating weightlessness is to propel a body into zero gravity in space, or create a microgravity environment on earth. The effects of long-term weightlessness can be debilitating. Our musculoskeletal, respiratory, and motion systems are shaped under pressure, exist in their shape largely in response to that pressure. To remove it completely leaves those pressure-sensitive systems unsup-ported. The long-term effects are typically discussed as *deconditioning*, but, really, they are caused by a locomotion and physical control system cut loose from its context and all its dependencies: it is perhaps better thought of as *decontextualized*. Elizabeth Blaber and her colleagues have summarized the effects of changes to the body under prolonged zero or altered gravity. They conclude that the changes in muscle function on exposure to weightlessness is the principal physiological barrier to a successful Mars landing (Blaber et al., 2010). Given the many challenges of space flight and the extreme demands of this peculiar working and living environment, a concern for the felt experience of lightness is not high on anyone's agenda, although, paradoxically, heaviness after re-entry often is.

Unwanted lightness after loss of body mass is, however, discussed more frequently in specific discourses, often of illness or older age. For example, a common occurrence in advanced cancer is *cachexia*, a form of generalized metabolic dysfunction (Fearon et al., 2011). The primary feature of cachexia is marked weight loss and the inabil-ity to maintain or increase weight. It is normally associated with other symptoms, such as weakness, loss of appetite, and fatigue, and is experienced often with extreme distress by both patients and carers. Joanna Reid believes it to be one of the most distressing symptoms of the cancer experience. In Belfast, Reid and her colleagues interviewed 15 patients with advanced and incurable cancer and cachexia. There were interesting themes in these interviews, many of which revolved around strategies for dealing with weight loss, such as coping through distraction, as well as strategies for increasing weight (Reid et al., 2009). However, the felt experience of weight loss in the context of end of life is rarely discussed. Instead, it is a signal of a larger source of distress in the collective fear of imminent death, expressed as denial of weight loss or conflict over appetite, food, and social control (Oberholzer et al., 2013).

Heaviness-lightness continuum

There is, across multiple literatures, and in different fields of study, a lack of investigation into the experience of feeling heavy, and even less on the direct experience of feeling light or lighter. As discussed in previous chapters with the sensations of balance and motion, to attend to somatic sensations and make complex judgments about one's body weight, without the aid of a set of scales, is perhaps too clumsy, difficult, and, frankly, unnecessary. It perhaps has no function. Unless one is faced with an unusual technical challenge, such as propelling the weightless body into space, maybe there is simply no advantage to self-weight perception.

Or is there? Nicholas Edwards and his colleagues in Minnesota reported an interesting finding concerning the biased judgment of adolescents. Using a representative longitudinal survey of over 14,000 adolescents, they were able to compare adolescent absolute weight at different time points with a self-perception measure of how they would describe their weight. Approximately 30 percent of youth underestimated their bodyweight. This misperception would be just interesting if it were only a guess-my-weight parlor game. But what also emerged from this study was the role of misperception on subsequent behavior. The more accurate young people were in estimating their own weight, the more likely they were to eat less and exercise more (Edwards et al., 2010, p. 456). It seems that the advantage of accuracy in deciding whether one is over- or underweight is that it is more likely to come with adaptive attempts to manage weight. In the context of Western nations reporting high and rising levels of overweight and obese populations, the ability to make an accurate judgment about a crucial aspect of identity and embodiment may be exactly the advantage one needs to develop.

How you decide if you are heavy or light, and under what circumstances, are not often investigated. In summary, it appears that we rarely make the judgment of how heavy or light we are. But we can do it if asked. However, when we do, we are not particularly good at making such judgments, typically underestimating rather than overestimating. To develop these ideas further, we need a better understanding of what it feels like to be heavy or light,

In addition, we need to better understand the feelings of heaviness and lightness in relation to feelings of pain, strength, and fatigue, and as judgments of external load. Is there a bias toward not judging (ignoring) or underrepresenting (diminishing) one's own weight? If so, does the relative ignorance of one's own weight allow for a better judgment of the weight of an external object lifted or carried? Can we learn to accurately perceive bodyweight through training, as we do strength and flexibility?

And, finally, is there any phenomenologically distinct character to judgments on the heaviness-lightness continuum?

Developing a psychology of the perception of bodyweight may help us achieve a better understanding of when and how we act to *change* body shape and body size, regardless of whether the context is cosmetic, astronautical, illness preventive, or palliative.

Swollen

The final pressure sensation that is closely related to the senses of flexibility, weight, and strength is the sense of being physically extended in a limb, head, or torso, or of being systemically swollen. There are multiple causes of swelling. The most common are vascular, either in normal erectile tissue, from a failure in lymphatic carriage of interstitial fluid normally removed from tissue, or from the arrival of fluid to tissue as part of an inflammatory response to injury. The feeling of being swollen or extended can also come from the over-filling, or failing to void, body spaces such as bladder, colon, stomach, or lungs.

Like balance, the sensation of pressure is largely unattended to—until it reaches a salience. How that salience is interpreted is interesting, and is in part dependent upon the functional context of what is swollen, when, and for what purpose (if any). The pressure of overeating after a meal, for example, has a totally different meaning to the unwanted bloating from opioid-induced constipation as an adverse effect of a treatment for cancer. Two specific cases of feeling swollen can help to exemplify this effect of context: the first is breast surgery, which causes lymphedema in approximately 5 percent of patients. The second is of constipation, which is both a common nuisance for some and a severe problem for others.

Over three million women in the United States are living with a diagnosis of breast cancer, and 232, 670 further women were diagnosed in 2014 (DeSantis et al., 2014). Approximately 38 percent will undergo a partial or total mastectomy (Mahmood et al., 2013). Of these, approximately 5 percent will go on to suffer lymphedema. By conservative estimates, this means that each year in the United States alone, 45,000 women will start on a post-cancer survivorship trajectory, one dominated by living with edema.

There are many unwelcome changes from such a challenging intervention, including how to manage a broad array of symptoms. But a swollen limb brings significant problems of its own. Women often report emotional challenges such as embarrassment or shame, and practical problems with clothing, especially in warm weather, which can increase the edema (Taghian et al., 2014)

Mei Fu and Mary Rosedale attempted to understand the symptom experience of women with lymphedema following breast surgery. They interviewed 34 women and deliberately went beyond the broader experiences of changes in body image, confidence, and fractured life course, with an attempt to capture the felt experience of being or feeling swollen. Women do talk about unpredictability, the fear of cancer recurrence, and handicap, but they also use interesting language about the actual experience of distension or swelling as a pressure building to capacity. One said, "Whenever I take a look at my ugly arm, it's just like a giant bomb to me" (Fu and Rosedale, 2009, p. 853). Another reported that her boss described it as "bursting." Although there are many aversive sensations (pain, fatigue, weakness, inflexibility) that accompany postsurgical lymphedema, the experience of pressure and a limb close to bursting is one that deserves further investigation.

Patients who are constipated also report this unique sensation of potential explosion. Claire Ervin and her colleagues, who are working to highlight a consideration of patient-reported outcomes as a worthwhile primary goal of clinical trials in constipation, found this concern raised frequently. In their study of 28 participants, interviewed to augment a larger survey of trial reports, people typically reported two feelings. One was of general discomfort; the other was of abdominal distention: "huge . . . about to pop," and "about six-months pregnant" (Ervin et al., 2014, p. 195). Feeling swollen, distended, full, bloated, or tumescent comes with many sensations, but perhaps unique to them is the experience of being *close to bursting*.

Reduced

Less common is the experience of being in some way reduced, diminished, smaller, slighter, or of being empty. Being under normal pressure, or the return to normal size following pressure, does not have any specific phenomenological quality, other than a sense of returning to normal or an awareness of pressure lifting. However, there is one sense in which people discuss a more abstract idea of being physically reduced or physically less.

In a large observational study, a sample of 8,610 women was tested. The average age was 71. Their height was measured and on average the women had lost 4.5 centimeters since their recorded tallest height. It is true that we become literally less as we age. In this study, however, the investigators went one step further and asked the women to estimate their own height. They found that women routinely underestimated this height loss as much as by two centimeters (Briot et al., 2010). Such bias in estimation is perhaps not unusual, but it raises the question of whether there is any perception of being reduced, or of being physically less. Aside from the visual inspection of weight loss or change in body shape, and the proprioceptive changes in feeling lighter, is there any sense of being shrunken or reduced?

Clearly changes in mass take time. Those changes usually fall outside of perception, and the norm can fail to be updated. But there is some direct evidence that a perception of sudden change might be possible. For example, in neurology it is possible to induce somatosensory cortical changes through visual-tactile illusions and produce

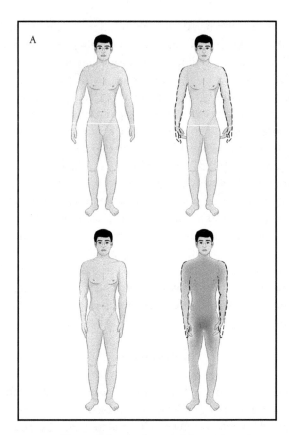

Fig. 4.1. Shrinking waist and hips study. The design of the study and position of the hands to the body.

When the palms of the hands were in contact with the body, the vibration of the two wrists elicited the illusion that the wrists were passively flexing and the waist and hips were shrinking (A, lower right). When the hands were not in contact with the body, the vibration of the wrists only elicited the illusion that the hands were flexing (A, top right). In two additional conditions, we vibrated the skin over the styloid bone beside the tendon, which does not elicit any illusions (A, top left and lower left). The neural effect of the shrinking-body illusion can be modeled as the interaction term between hand position and site of vibration in a 2×3×2 factorial design (see [B], [TENDON CONTACT—SKIN CONTACT]—[TENDON FREE—SKIN FREE]).

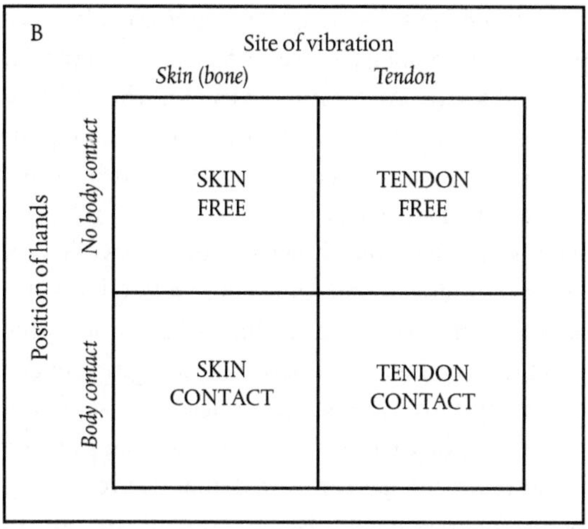

B	Site of vibration	
	Skin (bone)	Tendon
No body contact	SKIN FREE	TENDON FREE
Body contact	SKIN CONTACT	TENDON CONTACT

(Left axis label: Position of hands)

Fig. 4.1. Continued

a noticeable change in body schema. One can manufacture altered positioning, size, and number of limbs. But also possible is the peripheral manufacture of the *illusion* of reduction, as in, for example, the "shrinking waist illusion" (Ehrsson et al., 2005). In this study the researchers were actually able to induce the experience of both hips and waist getting slimmer. Figure 4.1 shows the procedure in which a vibration device is fixed to the wrist with contact points extending to the palms of the hand. This produces a sensation of a shrinking waist.

And, perhaps equally bizarre, is one naturally occurring abnormal example. In cultural psychiatry there are reports—although they have yet to be independently corroborated—of localized outbreaks of an epidemic of genital shrinking. In West Africa and South East Asia, men have reported the sudden loss (or theft) of their genitals. Vivian Dzokoto and Glenn Adams report epidemics of genital theft as a form of culture-bound mass psychogenesis (Dzokoto and Adams, 2005).

Perhaps the idea of being reduced or shrunk is both socially rare, and neurologically indistinct, such that it will be difficult to explore it in isolation. It is always experienced in the immediate context of what is lost or reduced, and in the broader social context of the meaning of that loss.

Swollen-reduced continuum

Perception abhors a vacuum. More than any other of the pairs of pressure senses, being swollen dominates. Being less, or experiencing the loss of mass, is rare. It is possible to produce artificially in the laboratory, and when isolated it is experienced

71

as vivid, but when spontaneously discussed it is vague and often no more than a general background phenomenon open to psychological and cultural influence, and discussed in the broadest of terms. At its other extreme, when a full stomach becomes swollen, or an arthritic joint becomes inflamed, or a postsurgical edema feels ready to explode, then the action of pressure is felt acutely; then it functions, as do many other of the hidden senses, to alarm and to motivate.

From a functionalist perspective, however, being swollen offers an unusual challenge. Like pain and fatigue, it can function as a low-level alarm giving critical information about one's state that one can address (e.g., stop eating now, or visit the toilet). But it also has the capacity to function as a high-level alarm, imposing an immediate priority on a system. Like our other neglected senses, at their limits they function to return us from the extreme to a more normal state. Often a sense at its limits demands a clear course of action: pain demands avoidance, fatigue demands switch of attention, imbalance demands postural adjustment, etc. It is not clear, however, what the experience of being swollen, and the distressing extent of feeling like one will burst, demands. Perhaps this particular form of "putting on the brakes" operates at a whole system-wide level, demanding interpretation. Unlike the other physical senses, it functions to invoke conscious investigation and a high level of interpretation.

To explore this phenomenon better, I talked to Marni Elder (Box 4.2).

Box 4.2. Marni, living with lupus: *"it feels like every inch of your body weighs too much"*

We know so little about the experience of feeling heavy, swollen, or stiff. Marni is 21. She describes herself as "thoughtful" and "interested in how other people feel." She is someone who is "never knowingly boring." Marni has had lupus since she was 16. I was interested in particular in her experience of the pressure senses.

———————————————————

Chris: Tell me about when you first knew something was wrong.

Marni: I first presented symptoms when I was 16 but was not diagnosed until I was 17. It started in Jan 2010. My hair started thinning. Slowly but surely the problems rotated around my body. Each of my joints would become inflamed, hot, itchy, and really sore. Initially it was in one joint at a time. My wrist would hurt, my elbow would hurt, and next day my knee, my ankle. But then over time it became all of them at once. Then came the fevers and complete lack of appetite, nausea, severe migraines, and tiredness. At the time I was just concerned about my lovely locks falling out. But as the reality became clearer and I realized it was more serious, I became less concerned with the hair loss.

Box 4.2. *Continued*

Chris: Is being tired with lupus a different sensation than before the lupus?

Marni: Yes, I can't remember what it is like to not be tired. So in a way I am really used to it and I can manage it, but I am also hyperaware of it being there all of the time. It is the same with joint pain. There is a strange way of being able to forget about it and carry on, but also staying very aware of it, of any changes in it.

My fatigue now is so different than how it was before. When you're a teenager you get tired and don't want to get out of bed. But now it is so hard a task that it becomes such a physical challenge. I feel that when I am really tired in the morning it is almost like there is literally a weight sitting on all of my limbs that can't be moved. And lifting yourself up is so tasking that sometimes you are not sure whether to just push through it. Sometimes it is fine and I can carry on, but sometimes I think maybe I should listen to it and just lie here. It literally feels like I am being weighted down. But from the inside it's like my muscles have become solid and dense, too dense for my body to take the weight.

Chris: It does not sound like fatigue as we think of it: as an urge to stop.

Marni: No, that is right. It is different because it is not the mental lethargic fatigue with a fuzzy head. It is not a full body tired that I need to go to bed and sleep. It is something you have when you wake up. It feels like every inch of your body weighs too much. Like it has been filled with something that should not be there, that shouldn't be carried around with you.

Chris: What other sensations are there?

Marni: The symptom I suffer the worse with is joint pain. That is the one I find disappears the quickest as soon as I have immediate treatment. The lupus pain is about joints swelling up and being hot to the touch. You can always feel my joints as hot. They go red hot. Sometimes before they swell up. But that is a separate pain to being in a flare because when I flare I have the swelling and the heat. Then comes the stiffness: they do always get really stiff. But I am unsure whether they are stiff because of the huge amount of swelling around the joints, or if they are stiff because it hurts so much to move them. But I tend to keep any joint that is swollen as immobile as possible because it is the least painful option.

Chris: Does the swelling and stiffness change how your move?

Marni: I have always been reasonably accident-prone. But I feel like it has made me a lot less dexterous. It probably affects my hands the most. It obviously swells up and makes them look strange. I do feel off-balance with it sometimes, clumsy. It is very normal for me to walk into doorframes and lamp-posts when there are not really any obstacles in the way.

Chris: how has the experience changed how you think about your body?

(Continued)

Box 4.2. *Continued*

Marni: I don't like it quite so much as I used to. Sounds like a weird thing to say but I suppose in some ways I am more precious about it with everyday things I do. I tend to think of my body as something more fragile now. I never used to think of it in that way. I am definitely more aware of it being something that can break or be broken. But I'm also less fazed by injuries. It does not shock me as much. But in day-to-day things like bumping into things and knocking things, I am aware now that I am fragile. It is not a nice feeling, really.

Chris: Do you feel you have control over the symptoms?

Marni: Sometimes. I am definitely better with it now. It has taken me a really long time to understand my limits, as to where I can push myself and when I can take a back seat. I prefer not to plan things. I obviously try as much as I can not to cancel, but if I am planning a couple of weeks in advance I always feel like I am already potentially double-booking, because I never really know how I am going to feel, so I tend to hold back on planning.

When I was first ill I missed two terms of school and everything I wanted to do socially, which, when you are 16 and 17, felt like the end of the world. I felt I missed out on so much. So after that I decided I would try and do everything that I could, within reason—which I maybe did too much of when I was recovering. So when I went to university I thought, I need to pace myself more. But I don't want any of the symptoms to be something people notice about me. I don't want people to think of me as weary, boring, or tired.

Chris: Has there been anything positive about the experience?

Marni: Yes, there is self-improvement. I think I am definitely more sympathetic toward other people. I understand other people who are feeling unwell. My friends and family came through and continue to a lot. That is definitely positive. Also I always think that if I had not been ill I would not have ended up studying English literature. I had no indication what I wanted to do academically. I always found biology and chemistry easy and I was going down a route of medicine. But if the lupus had not happened I would not be studying English now. I would have just carried on. And English is definitely the right choice for me. It is definitely, definitely, what I should be doing.

It is not an expertise she ever wanted, but Marni is an expert on the pressure senses. She cleaves apart the specific sense of having a body that feels too heavy from the general senses of pain and fatigue. It has its own quality. So does the challenge of being swollen. Like Emma earlier, Marni has had an education on the limits of her body, of what is possible and when and how to adapt in response to pressure. But at stake is also an ever-changing relationship with a body that is challenged and challenging. Impressive is her strength of character in focusing on what is positive and what is possible.

Summary

We live in resistance. Every movement is against force. I have called the senses that emerge the "pressure" senses because for me *pressure* captures the movement against force. Constantly under negotiation in all four pairs of sensations is what is the limit of the experience and what is its meaning. Although there is a rich psychology of pain and of fatigue, as two examples, there is little to say about how best to support people who are stiff, reduced, weighed down, or feeling like they are going to explode. There is little advice for designers of our built environment about how we judge our own strength, flexibility, or weight decisions. And there is yet to be any study of how one's relationship with core aspects of embodiment affects the normal subjects of psychological study, such as motivation, affect, and cognition. We have some work to do.

Notes

1. Reproduced from Ana-Maria Orbai, Katherine C. Smith, Susan J. Bartlett, Elaine Leon, and Clifton O. Bingham, "Stiffness Has Different Meanings, I Think, to Everyone": Examining Stiffness From the Perspective of People Living With Rheumatoid Arthritis, *Arthritis Care and Research*, 66 (11), p. 1669 (c) 2014, John Wiley and Sons.
2. Reprinted from *Complementary Therapies in Medicine*, 21 (1), Gina K. Alexander, Kim E. Innes, Terry K. Selfe, and Cynthia J. Brown, "More than I expected": Perceived benefits of yoga practice among older adults at risk for cardiovascular disease, p. 17, Copyright (2013), with permission from Elsevier.
3. Reproduced from You Can't Get There From Here: Reaching the Outdoors in Senior Housing, Susan Rodiek, Chanam Lee, and Adeleh Nejati, *Journal Of Housing For The Elderly*, 28 (1), p. 74, doi:10.1080/02763893.2013.858093 (c) 2014, Taylor and Francis. Reprinted by permission of the publisher (Taylor & Francis Ltd, http://www.tandfonline.com).

References

Alexander, G.K., Innes, K.E., Selfe, T.K. and Brown, C.J. (2013). "More than I expected": perceived benefits of yoga practice among older adults at risk for cardiovascular disease. *Complementary Therapies in Medicine*, 21, 14–28.
Asmundson, G.J.G., Fetzner, M.G., DeBoer, L.B., Powers, M.B., Otto, M.W. and Smits, J.A.J. (2013). Let's get physical: a contemporary review of the anxiolytic effects of exercise for anxiety and its disorders. *Depression and Anxiety*, 30, 362–373.
Beckett, J.R.J., Schneiker, K.T., Wallman, K.E., Dawson, B.T. and Guelfi, K.J. (2009). Effects of static stretching on repeated sprint and change of direction performance. *Medicine and Science in Sports and Exercise*, 41, 444–450.
Behm, D.G. and Chaouachi, A. (2011). A review of the acute effects of static and dynamic stretching on performance. *European Journal of Applied Physiology*, 111, 2633–2651.
Blaber, E., Marçal, H. and Burns, B.P. (2010). Bioastronautics: the influence of microgravity on astronaut health. *Astrobiology*, 10: 463–473.

Briot, K., Legrand, E., Pouchain, D., Monnier, S. and Roux, C. (2010). Accuracy of patient-reported height loss and risk factors for height loss among postmenopausal women. *Canadian Medical Association Journal*, 182, 558–562.

Byrne S., Cooper Z. and Fairburn C. (2003) Weight maintenance and relapse in obesity: a qualitative study. *International Journal of Obesity*, 27, 955–962.

Chang, S.-K. and Drury, C.G. (2007). Task demands and human capabilities in door use. *Applied Ergonomics*, 38, 325–335.

Daniel, S., Bridges, S.K. (2010). The drive for muscularity in men: media influences and objectification theory. *Body Image*, 7, 32–38.

Delmas, P., Hao, J. and Rodat-Despoix, L. (2011). Molecular mechanisms of mechotransduction in mammalian sensory neurons. *Nature Reviews Neuroscience*, 12, 139–153.

DeSantis, C.E., Chun Chieh, L., Mariotto, A.B., Siegel, R.L., Stein, K.D., Kramer, J.L., Alteri, R., Robbins, A.S. and Jemal, A. (2014). Cancer treatment and survivorship statistics 2014. *CA: A Cancer Journal for Clinicians*, 64, 252–271.

Dzokoto, V.A. and Adams, G. (2005). Understanding genital-shrinking epidemics in West Africa: *koro, juju*, or mass psychogenic illness? *Culture, Medicine and Psychiatry*, 29, 53–78.

Edwards, N.M., Pettingell, S. and Borowsky, I.W. (2010). Where perception meets reality: self-perception of weight in overweight adolescents. *Pediatrics*, 125, e452–e458.

Ehrsson, H.H., Kito, T., Sadato, N., Passingham, R. and Naito, E. (2005). Neural substrate of body size: illusory feeling of shrinking of the waist. *PLOS Biology*, 3, 2200–2207.

Eilertsen, G., Kirkevold, G. and Bjørk, I.T. (2010). Recovering from a stroke: a longitudinal, qualitative study of older Norwegian women. *Journal of Clinical Nursing*, 19, 2004–2013.

Ervin, C.M., Fehnel, S.E., Baird, M.J., Carson, R.T., Johnston, J.M., Shiff, S.J., Kurtz, C.B. and Mangel, A.W. (2014). Assessment of treatment response in chronic constipation clinical trials. *Clinical and Experimental Gastroenterology*, 7, 191–198.

Fearon, K., Strasser, F., Anker, S.D., Bosaeus, I., Bruera, E., Fainsinger, R.L., . . . and Baracos, V.E. (2011). Definition and classification of cancer cachexia: an international consensus. *Lancet Oncology*, 12, 489–495.

Field, T. (2011). Yoga clinical research review. *Complementary Therapies in Clinical Practice*, 17, 1–8.

Flurey, C.A., Morris, M., Richards, P., Hughes, R. and Hewlett, S. (2014). It's like a juggling act: rheumatoid arthritis patient perspectives on daily life and flare while on current treatment regimes. *Rheumatology*, 53, 696–703.

Fu, M.R. and Rosedale M. (2009). Breast cancer survivor's experiences of lymphedema-related symptoms. *Journal of Pain and Symptom Management*, 38, 849–859.

Garg, A., Waters, T., Kapellusch, J. and Karwowski, W. (2014). Psychophysical basis for maximum pushing and pulling forces: a review and recommendations. *International Journal of Industrial Ergonomics*, 44, 281–291.

Grogan, S., Evans, R., Wright, S. and Hunter, G. (2004). Femininity and muscularity: accounts of seven women body builders. *Journal of Gender Studies*, 13, 49–61.

Henwood, T., Tuckett, A., Edelstein, O. and Bartlett, H. (2011). Exercise in later life: the older adults' perspective about resistance training. *Ageing and Society*, 31, 1330–1349.

Hewlett, S., Sanderson, T., May, J., Alten, R., Bingham III, C.O., Cross, M., March, L., Pohl, C., Woodworth, T. and Bartlett, S.J. (2012). "I'm hurting, I want to kill myself": rheumatoid arthritis flare is more than a high joint count—an international patient perspective on flare where medical help is sought. *Rheumatology*, 51, 69–76.

Jawein, A. (2009). Unmet needs in the assessment of symptoms and signs related to chronic venous disease. *Phlebolymphology*, 16, 331–339.

Latham, N.K., Bennett, D.A., Stretton, C.M. and Anderson, C.S. (2004). Systematic review of progressive resistance strength training in older adults. *Journal of Gerontology: Medical Sciences*, 59A, 44–61.

Leppänen, M., Aaltonen, S., Parkkari, J., Heinonen, A. and Kujala, U.M. (2014). Interventions to prevent sports related injuries: a systematic review and meta-analysis of randomised controlled trials. *Sports Medicine*, 44, 473–486.

Mahmood, U., Hanlon, A.L., Koshy, M., Buras, R., Chumsri, S., Tkaczuk, K.H., Cheston, S.B., Regine, W.F. and Feigenberg, S.J. (2013). Increasing national mastectomy rates for the treatment of early stage breast cancer. *Annals of Surgical Oncology*, 20, 1436–1443.

McCreary, D.R. and Sasse, D.K. (2000). An exploration of the drive for muscularity in adolescent boys and girls. *Journal of American College Health*, 48, 297–304.

McCreary, D.R., Sasse, D.K., Saucier, D.M. and Dorsch, K.D. (2004). Measuring the drive for muscularity: factorial validity of the Drive for Muscularity Scale in men and women. *Psychology of Men and Masculinity*, 5, 49–58.

O'Brien Cousins, S. (2000). "My heart couldn't take it": older women's beliefs about exercise benefits and risks. *Journal of Gerontology: Psychological Sciences*, 55B, 283–294.

Oberholzer, R., Hopkinson, J.B., Baumann, K., Omlin, A., Kaasa, S., Fearon, K.C. and Strasser, F. (2013). Psychosocial effects of cancer cachexia: a systematic literature search and qualitative analysis. *Journal of Pain and Symptom Management*, **46**, 77–95

Orbai, A.-M., Smith, K.C., Bartlett, S.J., de Leon, E. and Bingham III, C.O. (2014). "Stiffness has different meanings, I think, to everyone": examining stiffness from the perspective of people living with rheumatoid arthritis. *Arthritis Care and Research*, 66, 1662–1672.

Peterson, M.D., Rhea, M.R., Sen, A. and Gordon, P.M. (2010). Resistance exercise for muscular strength in older adults: a meta-analysis. *Ageing Research Reviews*, 9, 226–237.

Rakhshaee, Z. (2011). Effect of three yoga poses (cobra, cat and fish poses) in women with primary dysmenorrhea: a randomized clinical trial. *Journal of Pediatric and Adolescent Gynecology*, 24, 192–196.

Reid, J., McKenna, H., Fitzsimons, D. and McCance, T. (2009). The experience of cancer cachexia: a qualitative study of advanced cancer patients and their family members. *International Journal of Nursing Studies*, 46, 606–616.

Rodiek, S., Lee, C. and Nejati, A. (2014). You can't get there from here: reaching the outdoors in senior housing. *Journal of Housing for the Elderly*, 28, 63–84.

Ruis, C., van den Berg, E., van Stralen, H.E., Huenges Wajer, I.M.C., Biessels, G.J., Kapelle, J., Postma, A. and van Zandvoort, J.E. (2014). Symptom Checklist 90–Revised in neurological outpatients. *Journal of Clinical and Experimental Neuropsychology*, 36, 170–177.

Salter, K., Hellings, C., Foley, N. and Teasell, R. (2008). The experience of living with stroke: a qualitative meta-synthesis. *Journal of Rehabilitative Medicine*, 40, 595–602.

Small, K., McNaughton, L. and Matthews, M. (2008). A systematic review into the efficacy of static stretching as part of a warm-up for the prevention of exercise-related injury. *Research in Sports Medicine*, 16, 213–231.

Sohl, S.J., Schnur, J.B., Daly, L., Suslov, K. and Montgomery, G.H. (2011). Development of the beliefs about yoga scale. *International Journal of Yoga Therapy*, 21, 85–91.

Taghian, N.R., Miller, C.L., Jammallo, S.L., O'Toole, J. and Skolny, M.N. (2014). Lymphedema following breast cancer treatment and impact on quality of life: a review. *Critical Reviews in Oncology/Hematology*, 92, 227–234.

Turvey, M.T. and Fonsecca, S.T. (2014). The medium of haptic perception: a tensegrity hypothesis. *Journal of Motor Behavior*, 46, 143–187.

Twitchett, E., Angio, i M., Koutedakis, Y. and Wyon, M. (2010). The demands of a working day among female professional ballet dancers. *Journal of Dance Medicine and Science*, 14, 127–132.

Varlet-Marie, E., Gaudard, A., Mercier, J., Bressolle, F. and Brun, J.-F. (2003). Is the feeling of heavy legs in overtrained athletes related to impaired hemorheology? *Clinical Hemorheology and Microcirculation*, 28, 151–159.

Wang, M.-Y., Yu, S. S.-Y., Hashish, R., Samarawickrame, S.D., Kazadi, L., Greendale, G.A. and Salem, G. (2013). The biomechanical demands of standing yoga poses in seniors: the Yoga Empowers Seniors Study (YESS). *BMC Complementary and Alternative Medicine*, 13, 1–11.

Westhoff, G., Buttgereit, E., Gromnica-Ihle. and Zink, A. (2008). Morning stiffness and its influence on early retirement in patients with recent onset rheumatoid arthritis. *Rheumatology*, 47, 980–984.

CHAPTER 5

BREATHING

Breathing, or, strictly speaking, ventilation, is the process of inhaling air from the atmosphere (inspiration) and exhaling air from the lungs (expiration). It is one part of a respiratory system that all aerobic organisms use to maintain a supply of oxygen and manage the acid base in the body. For us, that means taking oxygen from the air into the lungs and expelling carbon dioxide and water vapor. It happens continuously, automatically, rhythmically, and largely out of awareness, even when asleep. Breathing is also associated with narratives of emotion, especially surprise, horror, fear, and romantic love. It is even enjoying a revival in the West as a focus for the training of awareness and control over internal sensations, often in the pursuit of anxiety management. It is so fundamental to life, however, that it goes unremarked upon, except when we experience it in its extremes. Culturally, for example, there are narratives of the first breath taken in the cry of the newborn baby, and of the last breath taken at death. The millions of breaths in-between attract less attention.

Breathing has unique qualities that make it a suitable focus of attention as a neglected sense. From biomechanical and physiological perspectives, ventilation is similar to movement and balance. Innervated muscle and connective tissue provide specific position, capacity, and force feedback, and receptors identify the pressure of respiratory gases. It can be thought of as a special case of a pressure sense (see Chapter 4) in its reliance on the partial pressure of oxygen. Breathing has similarities, also, to the expulsion experiences discussed in Chapter 11, in that it operates largely out of awareness and is an experience that happens to one as much as it happens with one. But from a psychological perspective, breathing has a quality all of its own. Breathing is recognizable as a specific sensation, understood and discussed as a phenomenon, and we know what it feels like when it stops.

This chapter is devoted to the experience of ventilation as *breathing*. I review the peripheral and central mechanisms of inspiration and expiration, and what is considered normal. But human breathing is flexible, shown by those who deliberately attempt to control their breathing, either occupationally, in the management of a lifestyle, or in exercise. Finally, I examine how awareness of respiration is central to a psychology of immediate action, with a closer look at the case for relearning how to breathe. Some people have no choice, so particular attention is given to the special cases of panic and cardiopulmonary diseases for which air hunger (dyspnea) is the primary complaint.

Two people with very different experiences agreed to help me explore breathing at its limits. First, there are people who train for many hours to increase their breath-hold ability. I talked with Sam who is an experienced freediver and now a teacher of freediving. She is an expert at breathing and at breathhold. Second, there are many people who suffer from a range of cardiorespiratory disorders, the principal feature of which is dyspnea, or what used be known as air hunger. I talked with Ian who has an obstructive lung disease called bronchiectasis and has lived with dyspnea for the last five years.

Catching your breath

Breathing often feels like one is actively forcing air into or out of the lungs. However, counterintuitively, we do not expand our lungs by filling them with air. Instead our lungs expand, creating a partial vacuum, into which air must rush. For inspiration, both intercostal muscles (expanding the chest wall) and the diaphragm (contracting and flattening) act to expand the lungs. For expiration, the diaphragm and intercostal muscles return to their original position, reducing the volume of the lungs and hence the pressure. This cycle is under central autonomic control, which is also governed by a central brainstem concern for timing and rhythm (Feldman and Del Negro, 2006). Core to the experience of breathing is the experience of agency, a feeling of whether one is in or out of control of breathing, and the experience of rhythm, whether one's breathing follows a replicable and steady timing. These two characteristics of normal breathing (agency and rhythm) become important when one seeks to override the automaticity of breathing, and control or change one's breathing pattern.

Before the air reaches the lungs it needs to pass through the upper respiratory tract. The passage of air through the nasal cavity and into the trachea also has specific sensory characteristics. The function of the nasal pathway is first to protect the subsequent respiratory path from air particulates, which are extracted into the mucous blanket that through motion of its cilia can remove unwanted debris, swallowed mostly into the stomach (Reznik, 1990). At the same time, air is moistened by the action of the turbinates and warmed to body temperature.

These remarkable functions of the nose and nasal passage also create specific experiences. Sniffing, for example (brief forced nasal inspiration), may function for immediate olfaction, but it also breaks down particulates in the nasal vestibule (Sahin-Yilmaz and Naclerio, 2011). The experiences of forced expulsion of debris or mucus in sneeze or cough are investigated in Chapter 11. But the general experience of the flow of air is part of the experience of breathing; for example, in the extent one is spatially aware of the nasal cycle in which one switches the channel of air from side to side, allowing turbinates to replenish. This is the experience one has of the freer passage of air through one nostril rather than the other, switching rhythmically throughout the day, or of changes in its pattern during an upper respiratory tract infection (common cold).

Proprioceptively, the experience of the movement and position of the chest also form part of the experience of breathing. As we saw in Chapter 4, information about force on the body and about its position give a specific sensation of being enlarged or full at maximal inspiration, and, by extension, on expiration of being smaller and feeling spent. In the abnormal case these feelings of inadequate inspiration or expiration form a major part of the experience, described as feelings of tightness, restriction, or ventilation inadequacy (Courtney and Greenwood, 2009).

Stretch receptors, known as baroreceptors, monitor changes in extension of the blood vessels and associated changes in blood flow. Chemoreceptors in perhaps one of the most unusual and mysterious of our peripheral sense organs, the carotid bodies, sense change in blood oxygen in the arteries, in particular responding to a deficit in oxygen (*hypoxia*) or a surfeit of carbon dioxide (*hypercapnia*) These chemoreceptors project to the brainstem, which is responsible for autonomic responses, most critically here, respiration and blood pressure. It is not clear how far the peripheral detection of oxygen and carbon dioxide is necessary for awareness of a change in respiration, or whether awareness of respiration is merely a late product of a largely autonomous system perfected for cardiorespiratory control.

Taking control of breathing

How long can you hold your breath? Thirty seconds, ten minutes? When was the last time you tried? We don't often investigate our own breathing—perhaps only when panting from sudden exertion, inflating a balloon, running for a bus, or climbing a flight of stairs. Indeed, why would we seek to attend to our breathing? The phenomenology of respiration is kept out of conscious awareness because attention to breathing or its consequences are at best unnecessary and at worst disastrous to coherent and consistent behavior. However, there are times when attending to and taking control over the rate, flow, rhythm, extent, and capacity of breathing are necessary or desirable.

Control over breathing and its meaning are discussed in a number of different contexts. Typically, we discuss taking control of breathing when there is an immediate goal, as in holding your breath because of an unwelcome smell, or shouting to try to make yourself heard in a crowd. Or we take control when a long-term goal requires it, as in learning to sing, play a wind instrument, or excel at sport. Perhaps the most extreme case is when the goal is an overarching one of survival: when one attempts control over breathing because to do otherwise risks suffocation, such as when breath control might allow one to stay longer in an environment where it is hard (e.g., at altitude) or impossible (e.g., underwater) to ventilate.

So far I have discussed respiration as an unconsciously controlled process. Expiration, however, is particularly important for humans, serving multiple functions. In resting respiration, we might exhale in a regular rhythmical flow, but the passage of air over the vocal chords allows for speech and so is subject to tracheal, intercostal, and diaphragmatic neuromuscular control. We control the pulses of expiration in both speech and song, and in the playing of wind instruments. This interplay between voice and respiration starts very early in our development, and there is evidence that respiratory control and vocalization develop together. In one study, the breathing and vocalization of 40 infants were observed: 1,864 vocalizations were grouped into 21 categories, with the most common being syllable utterances, followed by whimpers and grunts. In this exhaustive study, body mechanics were also assessed, including body size, length, and lung volume. Tremendous variability in function was found, with numerous mechanical degrees of freedom at play, as if the vocalization and breathing control develop together, developmentally intertwined, and linked as much to speech as to motor development (Boliek et al., 1996). This is a pattern that continues to develop in early years. Taking control over breathing, typically in the pursuit of speech development, happens from before the first vocalization, and develops alongside speech and voice.

Breathing to achieve

Three areas of human practice are of particular interest, all characterized by people's attempts to improve skills that involve breathing. The first is professional singing; the second is sport, particularly sports that involve extreme cardiopulmonary challenge, such as swimming and rowing; and the third is breathing to enable sustained conscious activity at altitude or underwater.

Collen Skull undertook an interesting qualitative study. She was intrigued by how elite vocal performers manage a consistently high level of excellence. Five professional opera singers shared their experience. As you would expect, practice and preparation were key findings, but these singers were keen to stress the importance of physical training of their vocal and breathing anatomy. She says:

> In the area of fundamentals of vocal production from a physical perspective, the most pervasive theme was the importance of breathing as the cornerstone from which all advanced vocal production is based. Participants articulated the importance of practicing breathing and a sense of connectedness to the body as a necessity for sustaining performance excellence. (Skull, 2011, p. 271)

This is a rare study of expert vocal performers and it is interesting that the management and training of breathing was high on their list of experiences to share. The importance of breathing for musicians extends beyond the direct use of the voice. Lori Buma and colleagues explored the verbal reports of 44 elite musicians on what they thought and what they did when under pressure during an exacting musical performance. The most frequently endorsed statement, thought also to be the most important strategy, was "I focus on my breathing" (Buma et al., 2015, p. 463). This is discussed as a strategy for controlling anxiety and worry by focusing on the physical aspects of performance. However, it is also possible that when faced with a complex and demanding performance, a focus on breathing is part of an attempt to maintain the timing of the music (Dogantan-Dack, 2006).

The training of breathing is an integral part of endurance sports such as swimming, cycling, and rowing. Take distance swimming. Typically, distance swimmers using a crawl stroke breathe after numerous (sometimes seven-plus) strokes rather than every third stroke, which is more common in the amateur. Low-frequency breathing means developing a tolerance for the urge to breathe. One investigation of a program of mental training was undertaken with a group of adolescent, club-level swimmers who had all competed at a national level. The program included a focus on swimmers' physical state, including a relaxation component, but also including a specific component of "thought stopping" to interfere with the automatic interruption of performance-denying thoughts— thoughts such as "I can't do this" or "I have to breathe more." Overall the program was successful (Sheard and Golby, 2006). For my purposes what is most interesting in this study is the choice of psychological technique. Although the frame of the study is multiple treatment components for general performance and well-being outcomes, the specific components address the respiratory reality of a sport that demands close management of breathing efficiency. Tackled head-on is the experience of aversive sensation, and, as we will see with fatigue in the distance athletes in Chapter 6, challenging the belief and automaticity of the thought intrusion is important.

Roger Couture and his colleagues originally investigated these strategies with recreational swimmers. They compared swimmers who were either instructed to distract themselves from their bodily information by working on a mental task or focusing on the end of the pool (which they call dissociative strategies), or were instructed to focus on their breathing and the word *air* (which they call an associative strategy). The associative strategy produced better swimming times than those achieved with dissociative strategies (Couture et al., 1999).

The use of attentional focus is now common practice in sports training and performance, but there is still little consensus as to the role of awareness in breathing. Take running, for example. For students on a short-duration run, a dissociative strategy of focusing on distance already travelled was found to be superior to a focus on breathing when mean respiration rate was the outcome of interest (Neumann and

Piercy, 2013). There is a lack of consensus of whether the direction of attention or its content is what matters in altering performance. The exact strategy is likely to be determined by a combination of factors, including the sport, skill level of the athlete, and the parameter under investigation (e.g., pace, accuracy, etc.) (Brick et al., 2014). I suspect that what works as a strategy of distraction from discomfort or exertion in a short-duration activity is likely to be different to those in long-duration endurance sports, and subject to individual differences. Further, I predict that regardless of sport and individual training, a switch from dissociative to associative strategies will take place as respiratory demand—and performance-destructive thoughts—start to intrude and dominate.

Breathing at height and depth

Both expert musicians and elite endurance athletes are attempting to control respiration and attention to the experience of breathing in normal environments, typically at or near sea level, with normal atmospheric pressure. At high altitude, the oxygen available for respiration remains constant but the partial pressure of oxygen falls with the drop in atmospheric pressure; this makes gaseous exchange in the lungs inefficient, leading to *hypoxia* (oxygen deprivation). The carotid bodies will identify the change in oxygen and carbon dioxide and inform respiration rate. Ventilation will increase, with hypoxia occurring for most people who elevate to about 3,000 meters above sea level (Peacock, 1998).

To put this altitude into perspective, the tallest building in the world is Burj Khalifa in Dubai, at 829 meters, and the highest city in the United States is Leadville, Colorado, at 3,000 meters. Mountaineers, however, need to learn to breathe at heights beyond this. Mt. Everest base camp, for example, is at 5,500 meters, and its summit at 8,848 meters. Figure 5.1 shows the relationship between the pressure of inspired oxygen at different altitudes.

The deleterious effects of high altitude on cognition, night vision, decision making, and mood are relatively well documented (Bahrke and Shukitt-Hale, 1993), but less investigated is the experience of deliberate and purposeful climbing. Geoff Wilson reviewed various narratives of climbing and being in mountain spaces about 8,000 meters, and found there was a preoccupation with the physical challenge of moving in a hypoxic environment: "Narratives of pain, discomfort and suffering, for example, permeate all accounts, especially with regard to the effects of high altitude and lack of oxygen in the death zone" (Wilson, 2012, p. 31). Climbers suffered not only the discomfort of labored and inefficient ventilation, but also cognitive decline. The reliance on artificial breathing apparatuses changed the experience of flow and connection with the environment that is highly valued by climbers.

The sense of distancing and disconnection from the environment with assisted breathing apparatus is also one of the reasons given by freedivers for choosing to

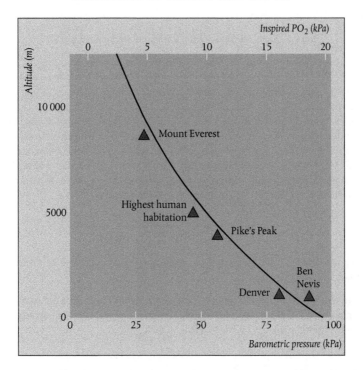

Fig. 5.1. The relationship between the pressure of inspired oxygen at different altitudes.

Reproduced from *British Medical Journal*, Andrew J Peacock, 317 pp. 1063–1066, Figure 2, doi:http://dx.doi.org/10.1136/bmj.317.7165.1063 Copyright © 1998, BMJ Publishing Group Ltd. With permission from BMJ Publishing Group Ltd.

dive without self-contained underwater breathing apparatuses (SCUBA). Emma Farell describes freediving as "not a quest for depth or endurance, but rather an experience of communion with our bodies, our breath, and our world" (Farell, 2006, p. 15). Freediving, also known as breathhold or apnea diving, is different things to different people. For some, like Farell, it is close to a spiritual experience of engagement and flow. For others, it is a sport, technical and scientific, in which one is constantly pushing physiological and psychological limits defined by apnea. The current world record for static apnea is over 11 minutes, and for diving to depth without assistance is over 200 meters. These are far outside of the range of normal human experience. Although there is interest in the physiological response to practiced apnea, and some psychology of the extreme, high-performing athlete, there has been very little interest in the phenomenology of deliberate apnea.

To learn more I talked to Samantha Kirby (Box 5.1).

Box 5.1. Sam, the freediver: *"it is massively a mental game"*

Samantha was captain of the UK freediving team, and now helps others to learn to freedive in her school *SaltFree*. She competes in two disciplines: *static apnea* and *constant weight*. Static apnea is described as when "the freediver holds his breath for as long as possible with his respiratory tracts immerged, his body either in the water or at the surface" (http://www.aidainternational.org/). Constant weight is described as when "the freediver descends and ascends using his fins/monofin and/or with the use of his arms without pulling on the rope or changing his ballast; only a single hold of the rope to stop the descent and start the ascent is allowed" (http://www.aidainternational.org/). Sam describes herself as taking a scientific approach to the sport—someone who is realistic about the demands she is placing on her body and on her mind.

Chris: Tell me about the static apnea. Does it matter if you believe you can do it, if you are confident?

Sam: Confidence is really important. It is massively a mental game. I think you obviously have to have a level of physical fitness and ability. People can be overconfident and over-stretch what they can do.

Chris: If it is a mental game, what are the thoughts that people have?

Sam: People might say, "I just had to breathe," "It was in my head," or they will say, "I had contractions in my diaphragm" or "I couldn't stop swallowing" or "I panicked." The psychological you can fend off and you can delay most of that feeling of "I need to breathe" until you get the physiological signs, and then you can use the physiological signs to pace how long you have got.

Chris: Do the thoughts come first, before the physiological signs?

Sam: Yes. I think, definitely. Even at a high level they do. Obviously they come later when you have trained for it. I have had occasions when I think that I know my breathhold pattern really well, I do a preparation, and then the clock will start. I will be fine and then nothing will happen for a minute. Then at a minute and a half I'll get contractions in my diaphragm and I'll fight them for another minute. I'll have all that in my head about what my body has done. Then on the day maybe I have prepared better and it does not happen like that, and I'll think, "It's a minute and a half, why is my body not reacting?" and then that will start me panicking. So, yes, it is hard to get rid of the psychological part. The thoughts are everywhere.

Chris: So, is it about managing breathhold or is it about managing panic?

Sam: A very good question, because they are interlinked. And actually you can have the best breathe-up procedure in the world planned in your head and every time you dive you do the same preparation. Everyone does something different, which for me says there is no perfect breathe-up. Freediving. It is bizarre, the differences in preparation. I am pretty convinced that all breathe-up preparation is mental, not physical. It is about following your own ritual.

Box 5.1. *Continued*

Chris: Tell me more about the thoughts that occur during a constant weight dive.

Sam: For me, I get very focused on the weight of the water above me. I can work out how much this column of water above me weighs and it's pushing on me and I can visualize it and I think I have got to get all the way up through that. As you get deeper the pressure is very obvious. Your mask pretty much collapses against your face and that makes you panic. That is a suffocation response. Because you've generally got a space between your nose and your mask and as you get deeper that space gets less and less. It is like somebody putting their hand around your face and trying to squash you, and you have to curl your body in to overcome that, which is again squashing your lungs, so it is a bit like suffocation.

You know you can't breathe until you get back up to the top. You know that if you have a problem below about 15 meters you are on your own. Someone will meet you at 15–20 meters and swim up the last bit with you, but if you have a blackout or a wobble or a panic before that, then you are totally on your own.

Chris: Do you have mental techniques to manage the thoughts?

Sam: Yes. I have what some people call mantras. I narrow my perception to the stages of the dive and what I'm doing. And not letting those negative thoughts in because you just can't afford to. You are down at that depth. There is no point in panicking; it is only going to make things worse. You've got to control that. I think that is what I like about the sport, actually, in that you narrow so much, that you get so focused and in the flow of what you are doing, that you can't be down at 20 meters, let alone 40 meters, worrying about how much money you've got in the bank, or what you've got to do tonight—you've just go to think about the dive . . . the dive is all you can think about.

Chris: Perhaps we are being too negative. Are their positive experiences also?

Sam: Oh, yes. There are. Obviously, or we wouldn't do it. There are immensely positive feelings of achievement, and of beauty and peace and tranquillity underwater. All the things about being on your own are also positive. It is me doing this; it is my body doing this. It is not anybody else helping me. It's about following your own ritual and achieving for yourself.

The mental is never far from the experience of breathhold for the freediver. The dissociative strategies are unlikely to work for long when a suffocation response is being triggered, but Sam describes the control she exercises over associative strategies of identifying her thoughts as thoughts, decoupled from knowledge of what her body can achieve when hypoxic. The sense is almost of a private battle in which apnea is motivationally driving a single behavior—to breathe—but the sport demands mastery over desire.

Respiratory awareness

Athletes such as Sam achieve remarkable feats that help us define human limits. To the nonathlete they can inspire awe and pique interest in our own physical limits. For the athlete who deliberately invites huge levels of cardiopulmonary challenge, awareness and control of respiration are a part of the sport, as important as muscle training. But is there any benefit in respiratory awareness and control for the nonathlete? Why should we attend to respiratory function, especially when it is so difficult? Or, put differently, what happens if you are rarely aware of your breathing, if you never give it a second thought?

For all of us, a lack of awareness of respiratory state can lead to adverse physical experiences that are often misinterpreted as symptoms of a major physical health problem. Hypoventilation leads to an increase in carbon dioxide concentration known as *hypercapnia*, and hyperventilation leads to a reduction in carbon dioxide concentration known as *hypocapnia*. Hypercapnia can be experienced as fatigue, pain, and air hunger (dyspnea), which are easily misinterpreted as symptoms of other complaints. Similarly, hyperventilation-induced hypocapnia is strongly associated with arousal and anxiety, and with cardiac symptoms, which can also be interpreted as frightening and serious. Panic is often misinterpreted as cardiac arrest.

Omer Van den Bergh and his research team at the University of Leuven in Belgium have perhaps done more than any other group to explore the role of awareness of respiratory function. He directs one of the only research laboratories able to experimentally examine the effects of ventilation patterns on cognitive and behavioral performance. For example, using a technique in which participants are asked to "over-breathe," Ilse Van Diest and colleagues compared performance on a numerical Stroop task. Stroop tasks are tests of executive control over attention in which one is presented with conflicting information from the same stimulus. To give the right answer one has to overcome the urge to give the incorrect dominant response. They found that induced hypocapnia slowed responding and increased errors on this test of attention (Van Diest et al., 2000). Hyperventilation, they were able to show, does lead to impaired cognitive performance.

Hyperventilation technically refers to an excess of air introduced to the lung alveoli in relation to metabolic requirements. But it can be self-induced by two related behaviors: increasing the volume of inspired air from each breath (deep breathing), and increasing the rate of respiration (rapid breathing). When we talk of hyperventilation, it is often not the technical definition we refer to but the observable behavior of seeking more air by breathing deeply or quickly. Voluntary hyperventilation is a common method for inducing hypocapnia and is relatively well understood as a method of inducing biological stress (Zvolensky and Eifert, 2001). However, involuntary hyperventilation—or hyperventilation without awareness, when you start to breathe more quickly and deeply but do not notice—is closely associated with fear, panic, and safety behaviors such as avoidance and escape. In fact, respiration is thought to map closely onto emotional state, and is directly susceptible to changes in emotional state.

Elke Vlemincx and her colleagues from the Leuven laboratory were interested in exploring the relationship between everyday emotion and respiration. They chose the natural variability in how we breathe as their focus of study. Of course, the rate at which we breathe and the tidal volume achieved with each breath varies within an individual, between individuals, and is sensitive to context. Intraindividual respiratory variability, they argued, is particularly important for emotion. If breathing is so closely tied to emotional state, it should perhaps change when emotion changes, but the exact nature of the change was unclear. The emotional stressor Vlemincx and colleagues chose was *worry*. Worry is an index of general anxiety, referring to perseverative verbal rumination about negative events that might occur in the future—events that are threatening to self or relationships. They chose participants who were free from anxiety disorder, and induced worry by asking them to think about their concerns over social relationships, money, or health. In another condition, the same people undertook a mindfulness procedure focused on breathing. Worry was associated with a loss of variability in patterns of breathing, variability countered by practicing mindfulness during worry. This rare study of normal worry and respiration gives us a hint of why respiratory awareness may be important: simple worry, the kind that occurs on a daily basis for many people, can be powerful enough to reduce respiratory variability, to make our responses rigid and slow to change.

Respiratory variability

Variability in respiratory function, like variability in heart rate, may be an accessible marker of the healthy switching between physiological control systems. Heart rate variability has been championed as an index of general health (Thayer et al., 2012), whereas invariability or rigidity is thought to be a major risk factor for cardiovascular disease and early aging (Thayer et al., 2010). The problem with heart rate variability is that heart rate perception is poor. We are unaware of heart rate, and its variability is impossible to monitor unassisted. Monitoring of an objective cardiovascular feature through biofeedback is needed. On closer examination, most attempts at improving heart rate variability involve relaxation or mindfulness protocols that teach breathing awareness and control. Omer Van den Burgh and colleagues at Leuven have perhaps identified a more specific, accessible, and readily translatable target for psychological and psychophysiological interventions (Vlemincx et al., 2013).

A rigidity or lack of variability in both respiration and heart rate may serve a useful primary function. In particular, hyperventilation behavior is initiated in response to threat and is a feature of physiological arousal. In an interesting experiment, the question of whether aspects of breathing could be conditioned by fear was investigated. Faces were selected as conditioned stimuli; these were then paired with an unconditioned stimulus, a loud human scream. Detailed respiration and heart rate parameters were collected. In a unique finding, the rate of inspiration was observed to increase as a learned response to fear (Van Diest et al., 2009). Perhaps increased speed of breathing is part of a learned mechanism to promote escape and avoidance from danger. In the laboratory, at least—and I suspect the same is true of everyday life—it is possible to induce hyperventilation by linking it to fear. In particular, one can increase the rate of inspiration. Outside of the laboratory, increases and decreases in respiration vary unconsciously by how one feels, and can become paired with specific anxious behaviors. In this study, the aversive stimulus of a human scream was both unrelated and introduced. Consider, for example, how cues can easily be established in those surviving suffocation or asphyxiation.

A focus on rumination

The role of worry has been more comprehensively investigated in cardiovascular activity. Jos Brosschot has argued repeatedly that the primary culprit of the prolonged and inflexible physiological activity we call *stress* is emotion (Brosschot, 2010). This cardiorespiratory inflexibility response is thought to be adaptive in acute threat, as it prepares one to flee, but it is potentially damaging in the context of chronic threat. The behavioral expression of this stress, Brosschot argues, is worry, or more specifically the ruminative aspect of worry, which he calls "perseverative cognition." These are the thoughts about bad things that might happen that just won't go away. This cognitive ability of ours to reflect on the causes and consequences of events, and to plot possible avoidance of danger, leaves us exposed to the risk of persistent, aversive worry, a learned respiratory response, and the chronic state of reduced flexibility in both respiration and heart function. A focus on both conscious and unconscious worry as a mediator of the stress and its effects on respiratory involvement in disease may be fruitful. Indeed, Brosschot suggests that a modern consideration of stress can now abandon its unhelpful restrictive duality between physiology and psychology. What cardiopulmonary reactivity shows us is that emotional and interoceptive experience are inextricably linked.

Hypoventilation is less investigated. Awareness of reduced breathing rate is rarely discussed and could be a useful target for future investigation. There are studies in which special populations, such as pilots, are trained to identify hypoxia (Malle et al., 2013). But in everyday life, causes of nonspecific hypoxia are typically through accidental or deliberate self-poisoning by tobacco smoke inhalation, opioid use, and from airway obstruction due to obesity or physical restriction. The emotional association of hypoventilation is discussed in depression as a consequence of hypoactivity and loss of motivation, because of a sedentary behavioral pattern (Lin et al., 2011). It would be helpful to know if, just as worry increases inspiration rate, induced emotions can also lead to decreases in inspiration or expiration rate.

Relearning to breathe

The idea of spending time learning to breathe again might seem at best inefficient, and at worst noncredible as a health-promoting or recreational activity. Surely we know how to breathe! After all, we have been doing it, on average, 15 times a minute our entire lives. But relearning how to breathe is exactly what is advised in a range of popular health-promotion or stress-reduction programs. Perhaps the most popular is known as mindfulness-based stress reduction, or just mindfulness training. Mindfulness is a form of meditation that attempts to raise awareness of presence. It promotes a form of "open" attention that allows one to be receptive, nonjudgmental, and accepting of current experience, free from the distal preoccupations characteristic of worry, of what might have caused an event, what its consequences might be, and what could or should be done. A nonreactive focus on the present may have benefits to general health in nonpatient populations, although it is fair to say that the evidence is to date underwhelming (Chiesa and Serretti, 2009; Khoury et al., 2013).

Most mindfulness techniques, like relaxation protocols before them, make use of breathing exercises, and often involve interoceptive, proprioceptive, or haptic awareness. They focus, for example, on the experience of breathing, moving in space, or being in contact with the ground. Mindfulness is most developed in mental health domains; in particular, in disorders characterized by experiential avoidance, when thinking about something is painful, and so trying not to think about or acting to change the experience is the norm, as in depression and anxiety disorders. But its value has not been established in physical disorders in which somatic awareness is a given and the *interpretation* of physical experiences is important. For example, in a randomized controlled trial of a mindfulness and breathing therapy, Richard Mularski and colleagues found no effect of the therapy in improving breathing characteristics of patients with a chronic obstructive pulmonary disorder (Mularski et al., 2009).

Perhaps the attentional redirection and meditative aspects of mindfulness are not crucial for people with conditions in which somatic awareness or preoccupation is already established. What might be fruitful is the development of protocols aimed directly at key features of the respiratory response to stress discussed here, with content explicitly focused on improving respiratory variability, or on the extinction through exposure of learned increases in the rate of inspiration, and to interoceptive awareness of arousal more generally.

Finally, it is clear that it is entirely possible to manipulate aspects of the breathing cycle in the short term. It can be altered: whether one is singing a difficult aria, diving underwater, or, as a subject in an experiment, listening to a loud human scream. What we don't know, however, is whether one can meaningfully alter a pattern of breathing over the long term without an immediate goal (such as exercise or meditation) to provide purpose and motivation. Daily practice of breathing exercises as part of a program aimed at improving emotional regulation can improve cardiovascular health and the self-report of well-being, but there is no evidence that one can improve respiratory variability in the long term without continual conscious interference. One normally needs to have a strong reason to engage in what would need to be a daily activity of learning to breathe again.

There are two populations of people who have just such a reason to relearn to breathe. The first are those who experience panic disorder in which hyperventilation is a principal feature. The second are those with a primary cardiovascular or respiratory disease in which difficulty breathing (dyspnea) is a primary complaint.

Panic

The relatively sudden, unbidden, unpleasant, and rapid escalation of anxiety is called *panic*. A panic attack is accompanied by a range of experiences, including autonomic arousal such as a pounding heart and temperature changes; feelings of ego separation such as derealization; fear of death; and dyspnea extending to a belief of being suffocated by smothering or choking (Craske et al., 2010). An attack must have a rise-and-fall pattern, peaking within ten minutes, to separate it from the experience of a more constant terror. Panic attacks occur with other anxiety disorders and phobias. Think about how some of us react on seeing a spider or when entering a large, windowless, crowded store with low ceilings. Many people have had a panic attack; one does not need to have an anxiety disorder to have a single or small number of episodes, if the context is right. The lifetime prevalence of a single panic attack is almost 25 percent— even higher when the triggers are known (Kessler et al., 2006).

Because of the social and emotional consequences of panic, feelings of shame, embarrassment, and low confidence can severely disable people. Panic is often treated together with *agoraphobia*, the fear of leaving a secure and familiar environment and going into the open. If it happens repeatedly, one might attract a diagnosis of *panic disorder*, which is defined pragmatically as the frequent experience of panic attacks in a range of contexts, together with disability, social isolation, and subsequent fear of future attacks. Although not common, panic disorder is socially and economically disastrous for individuals and their families (Skapinakis et al., 2011).

Despite respiratory function being one of the criteria for diagnosis—and a common feature occurring in 86 percent of cases in one illustrative sample (Cox et al., 1994), and 95 percent in another (Starcevic et al., 1993)—it attracts less interest than other features of autonomic arousal such as cardiac symptoms. Christiane Pané-Farré and her colleagues investigated patient reports of their first panic attack, and found cardiorespiratory symptoms to be the most distressing feature. Unfortunately they did not separate out these features and report respiratory features alone. They speculate that cardiorespiratory symptoms could trigger avoidance behavior, especially if linked to fear, and especially if this link occurs the first time one has a panic attack. (Pané-Farré et al., 2014).

Missing from the study of panic is a focus on the paradoxical presentation of an increased inspiration rate, accompanied by dyspnea; that is, people breathing in quickly but still feeling like it is just not enough. It is not clear if this respiratory pattern initiates, accompanies, or follows the cognitive and emotional peak of feeling morbidly threatened, urged to escape, and powerless. Meuret et al. (2010) attempted to look in some detail at the precipitating factors to a panic attack. Forty-three adults with a panic disorder were recruited from the community and asked to wear ambulatory physiological and respiratory monitors for a 24-hour period (see Figure 5.2). An event-sampling procedure was used in which the participant identified the onset

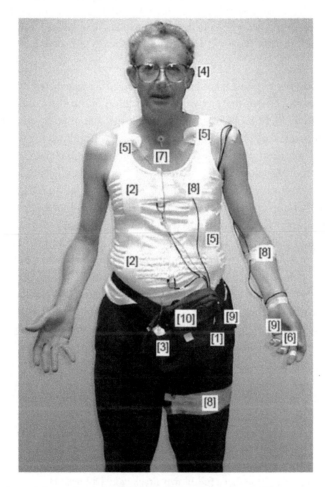

Fig. 5.2. Equipment for 24-hour monitoring of breathing and ambulation.

Reprinted from *International Journal of Psychophysiology*, 78 (1), Alicia E. Meuret and Thomas Ritz, Hyperventilation in panic disorder and asthma: Empirical evidence and clinical strategies, pp. 68–79, Copyright (2010), with permission from Elsevier.

of the panic attack manually, producing a time signature around which physiological recordings could be mapped, and triggering self-report of the experience. In all, 13 panic attacks were recorded. This remarkable study showed for the first time that the time before a panic attack is characterized by undetected respiratory changes. The researchers found

> that the hour preceding the onset of naturally occurring panic attacks was marked by significant cardiorespiratory instability. These changes were largely absent in the control periods. The physiological instabilities occurred in repeated bouts often initiated by HR [heart rate] accelerations. The period surrounding panic onset was dominated by respiratory changes. Before panic onset, VT [tidal volume or the depth of each breath] decreased and PCO_2 [carbon dioxide on expiration] increased, plateaued, and then decreased. At panic onset, HR and VT rose and then PCO_2 dropped.[1]

The common view of panic is that it is brought on, or exacerbated by, hyperventilation. This view is perhaps driven by our observation of the immediate surface features of a person in flight mode: breathing rapidly and scanning the environment for escape. The opposite may be true. Meuret and colleagues' findings suggest that hypoventilation may occur an hour before a panic attack, providing sufficient means for a panic response to develop. They tentatively support Donald Klein's ideas of panic as response to a suffocation false alarm in which hyperventilation is triggered interoceptively as either a hypersensitivity to carbon dioxide or, as here, in a precipitated suffocation reaction to hypoventilation (Preter and Klein, 2008).

Peter Lang and colleagues developed this further. They examined alarm caused by a suffocation challenge (an experimenter-controlled restricted airflow), showing heightened defensive responding to cues of suffocation. Taken together, there is a developing view of panic as a consequence, not the cause, of respiratory reaction (Lang et al., 2011). Breathing appears to be more than simply a passive reaction to threat. How we breathe may be critically important to the prevention of panic attacks and the development, for some, of a panic disorder (Pappens et al., 2012). As methods and technology develop, allowing more ethnographically sophisticated research, we will achieve a better understanding of exactly which aspects of breathing matter.

Although it is exciting to discover that breathing does matter in predicting suffocation reactions, including panic, Alicia Meuret and colleagues are not yet able to say whether people have any awareness of respiratory function prior to panic. They say:

> 'It is unclear whether patients sensed these events as an aura of the impending panic, giving them a premonition that a full-blown attack would follow.'[2]

It is not clear whether one's awareness of respiratory function is desirable, or even possible, as part of a strategy for managing suffocation anxiety or fear of panic attack.

Further, extending the ideas of Jos Brosschot, it would be interesting to discover whether the period of growing hypoventilation prior to panic is associated with perseverative cognition.

Currently, research in the field of panic is at an interesting respiratory crossroads. The study of breathing patterns, made more possible by technology miniaturized to allow constant physiological monitoring, provides the possibility for new applications of methods of restoring partial carbon dioxide, or in relearning to breathe. If there is a strong enough reason to relearn to breathe—as in reducing the incidence and severity of panic attacks—then how and when should one breathe differently, and what should one do? Alicia Meuret and her team reviewed all of the studies on breathing retraining and on exposure to feelings of restricted breathing, but were disappointingly unable to conclude whether retraining had any value (Meuret et al., 2005). The critical question remains unanswered: is primary prevention of panic attack a realistic possibility? Or can we only focus on secondary prevention, on recognizing and managing the symptoms when they occur, in part through changing one's breathing? Long-term changes in respiratory behavior by the deliberate conscious attempt to alter breathing, with or without meditative content, may simply be ineffective. More fruitful, applying the findings of aversive conditioning from the Leuven laboratory, might be to relearn the signals of altered breathing. The interpretation of respiratory signals, perhaps signals starting far outside of awareness, may be a more valuable target. One might usefully attempt to identify suffocation anxiety as a signal to alter one's breathing pattern, reset resting respiratory variability, and challenge the thoughts about what one's labored breathing might mean: perhaps not impending suffocation, but a signal to return control over respiratory variability (Sánchez-Meca et al., 2010).

Dyspnea

There are different experiences of being breathless. The exact experience is in part related to the physical cause. For example, an asthmatic attack can feel different to hypercapnia caused by respiratory depression from opioid consumption. One man, in an interesting psycho-biographical study reminiscent of twentieth-century neurology, shared his unusual experience. Michael Faulkner had the misfortune to experience three discrete forms of severe respiratory dysfunction in one lifetime: first from hypoxia caused at altitude, second from myasthenia gravis (a neuromuscular disease), and third from a pulmonary embolism (arterial blockage). Because he had undergone training in a decompression chamber during his time as an aeronautical research scientist, he was able to identify hypoxia. It was that training that helped him to survive. He teamed up with Clare Galtrey and Damian Wren from St. George's hospital in London to talk about the different experiences.

At altitude Michael Faulkner experienced hypoxia first as cognitive decay and then as increased respiratory rate. With myasthenia gravis, the breathlessness was specific to activity; in particular, exertion. He says:

> Swimming also provides an illustration, if I tried to use power the breathlessness cut in before my muscles had time to limit me. Provided I limited my swimming to low energy levels I would reach a state that I could sustain being mildly breathless and swim as long as I wanted. One length at my maximum strength would leave me gasping for air.[3]

The embolism, at this time undiagnosed, was a different sensation: "Over the following month my breathing deteriorated, at times it was so difficult it felt like near complete blockages, despite home oxygen I was still not coping. I realized that I was hypoxic which came in frightening waves."[4]

There are many people who live every day with exactly the feeling of activity restriction and feelings of suffocating. These people are not climbing at altitude or diving to the bottom of the sea; they are among the millions of people living with an obstructive lung disorder, with cardiovascular disease, with asthma, or dying of a late-stage malignant disease such as cancer. Chronic obstructive pulmonary disorder (COPD), for example, is a leading cause of death in many countries, ranking on average as the fifth most common, an incidence that is growing (Buist et al., 2007). COPD has a number of symptoms, including cough, increased sputum, pain, and fatigue—but its principal feature is dyspnea.

Although dyspnea is a common complaint in COPD and end of life, it is a highly intense and personal challenge (Akgün et al., 2012). It can be more than simply a hunger for air: "Dyspnea is not one experience, but encompasses a whole range of sensations (e.g. air hunger, feeling of increased effort, rapid breathing) that are highly subjective" (Hayen et al., 2013, p. 46). It encompasses feelings of urge to breathe, of obstruction, and of effort in breathing (De Peuter et al., 2004). In a qualitative study of people receiving palliative care at home, eight people who were receiving oxygen therapy were asked what dyspnea felt like. Some described it as a catastrophe: "Oh, it feels like it's the end of the world to me" said one, and "I might feel like dying" said another. Other people focussed on the sensations of restriction, dizziness, fatigue or air-hunger (Jaturapatporn et al., 2010, p. 766). Such dramatic and detailed descriptions are common. The sense of being on the edge of panic and living in fear of feeling suffocated appears to be the primary challenge.

In another study, 94 older people with COPD and 55 age-matched people without any history of respiratory disorder were asked to share the words they use about dyspnea (Williams et al., 2008, p. 490). If people reported never having been breathless, they were asked to think about when they were out of breath after a challenge such as walking upstairs. Table 5.1 shows the descriptors that people used and gives a flavor of their intensity. The most common descriptors were emotional. People with COPD

Table 5.1: Language used to describe breathlessness by those with and without a Chronic Obstructive Pulmonary Disorder

Volunteered Language Category	No. of Subjects Volunteering Descriptors		% of Total No. of Descriptors Volunteered	
	COPD (n = 94)	Non-COPD (n = 55)	COPD (n = 94)	Non-COPD (n = 55)
Frightening: "terrified, fear, panic, scared, bloody frightening"	42 (15)	1 (0)	12 (16)	1 (0)
Annoying: "bloody annoying, frustrating, nuisance, fed up with it all"	29 (11)	2 (1)	9 (12)	2 (2)
Awful: "horrible, terrible, bloody awful, think you're going to die"	27 (8)	0 (0)	8 (9)	0 (0)
Unique somatic: "sweat, painful, feel faint, headache and hot"	22 (4)	10 (4)	6 (4)	8 (8)
Difficulty breathing in: "can't take next breath, hard to breathe in, starved for air"	21 (8)	1 (1)	6 (9)	1 (2)
Uncomfortable: "discomfort, not good"	19 (5)	7 (5)	6 (5)	6 (10)
Tight: "tightness, constricted, chain around chest"	16 (3)	6 (3)	5 (3)	5 (6)
Strategies: "need to concentrate, find somewhere to lean, sit down and rest"	15 (3)	14 (5)	4 (3)	12 (10)
Helpless: "nothing you can do to stop it, nothing seems to help"	15 (4)	3 (2)	4 (4)	3 (4)
Suffocating: "suffocating, choke, like drowning, gasping"	15 (3)	2 (1)	4 (3)	2 (2)

(continued)

Table 5.1: (continued)

Volunteered Language Category	No. of Subjects Volunteering Descriptors		% of Total No. of Descriptors Volunteered	
	COPD (n = 94)	Non-COPD (n = 55)	COPD (n = 94)	Non-COPD (n = 55)
Hard to describe: "difficult to put into words, there is no word to explain it"	15 (1)	9 (2)	4 (1)	8 (4)
Can't breathe: "can't breathe, hard to breathe, can't get air in or out"	15 (2)	3 (0)	4 (2)	3 (0)
Worried: "anxious, apprehensive, nervous, stressful"	15 (2)	3 (0)	4 (2)	3 (0)
Short of breath: "short of breath, out of breath, can't catch breath"	15 (7)	22 (11)	4 (8)	18 (22)
Labor: "labored, heavy, hard, physical effort to get air"	14 (6)	6 (4)	4 (6)	5 (8)
Unique affective: "like a cow in a paddock, awareness of breathing"	12(1)	1(0)	4(1)	1 (0)
Regret: "not what I used to be like, can't do tasks I used to be able to"	10 (2)	1(0)	3 (2)	1 (0)
Depressed: "inept, you're not worth anything, wish you were dead"	8 (4)	0 (0)	2 (4)	0 (0)
Tired: "tired and weak, tiring, general exhaustion"	6 (3)	5 (2)	2 (3)	4 (4)
Deep: "can't take a deep breath, want to expand but lungs won't"	5(1)	1(1)	1(1)	1(2)

Descriptor				
Difficulty breathing out: "can get air in but can't get it out, can't get breath out"	2 (0)	0 (0)	1 (0)	0 (0)
Does not bother me: "doesn't hurt, what I expect to be, never alarming"	1 (0)	16 (7)	0.3 (0)	13 (14)
Unfit: "unfit, unconditioned, not as fit as I used to be"	0	3 (1)	0	3 (2)
Doesn't last long: "doesn't last long, recover quickly"	0	4 (0)	0	3 (0)

Reprinted from CHEST, 134 (3), Williams, Marie; Cafarella, Paul; Olds, Timothy et. al., The Language of Breathlessness Differentiates Between Patients With COPD and Age-Matched Adults, pp. 489–496, Table 2, doi:10.1378/chest.07-2916, (c) 2008 American College of Chest Physicians. Reproduced with permission from the American College of Chest Physicians.

*Numbers in parentheses are best volunteered descriptors.

report being terrified, frustrated, annoyed, scared, and frightened, and thought they were going to die.

Unusually for a study investigating people's experience, a sample *without* the experience followed the same protocol. What this revealed was intriguing: if you ask people to think about an experience they do not have, they will focus on the mechanics of the behavior, whereas what is really prominent in the experience is its emotional challenge. The authors of the study summarize:

> In general, only COPD subjects volunteered the descriptors "frightening," "worried," "helpless," "depressed," and "awful." However, only non-COPD subjects volunteered the descriptors "can't breathe out," "doesn't last long," "doesn't bother me," and "unfit." . . . When up to three statements of breathlessness were selected by subjects, 69% of subjects could be accurately classified within their original group. In general, only COPD subjects selected the descriptor statements "smothering," "constricted," "suffocating," and "cannot get enough air," while non-COPD subjects selected "breathing more" and "rapid."[5]

Terror management

Because breathing is such an omnipresent and emotionally immediate experience, it can be both common and unique: common to the population but unique to the individual. Marit Kvangarsnes and her colleagues interviewed ten people in depth about their experience. Unusual in this study was the report of extreme experiences leading up to acute exacerbations. Some people wanted to talk about changes in how unreal the world can seem when severely breathless, when nightmares are so vivid they are hard to ignore, or when, during an exacerbation, colors, furniture, and people seemed distorted (Kvangarsnes et al., 2013). This is the first hint that the extremes of derealization may play some part in the experience of dyspnea.

The psychological treatment of breathlessness is relatively underdeveloped, at least in comparison to pain and fatigue. The focus has been on primary prevention (e.g., smoking cessation), on secondary prevention of exacerbation, on comorbidities (e.g., anxiety, depression), and on the provision of simple techniques of relaxation or education (Baraniek and Sheffield, 2011; von Leupoldt et al., 2012). There is not yet an examination of how emotion can influence respiratory variability (and vice versa), and how the interpretation of breathing influences behavioral intentions, planning, and action. A focus on action in the context of the threat of suffocation might be an interesting avenue for investigation, as would the transfer of learning from normal respiration with its focus on variability and speed of recovery. Also important would be a focus on any perseverative cognition that might accompany the threat of suffocation.

For a functionalist account of breathing, what matters is the meaning of breathing and breathlessness, and their motivational significance. The phenomenology of breathlessness is intricately related to its meaning. For some it is a minor restriction, for others it is a constant reminder that taking away breath means taking away life, hope, and future. The emotional challenge of not being able to breathe can never be far away. I suspect that what is at the heart of the experience of dyspnea is a chronic form of terror management. Perhaps, as Michael Faulkner describes, there are "frightening waves" of breathlessness that sometimes threaten activity, and sometimes threaten suffocation, leading at the extreme of experience to dissociation. (Feinberg, 2011).

To explore these ideas further I talked with Ian Taylor (Box 5.2).

Box 5.2. Ian, living with dyspnea: *"it is about feeling vulnerable"*

Ian is a playwright, and has been a coal miner, builder, and an assistant to an accountant, among many other jobs in his life. Ian is a remarkable man with a rich personal history and many stories to tell. I met him with his wife in their home. He has severe bronchiectasis, a condition of expansion of lung tissue, and has repeated infections caused by chronic pseudomonas and stenotrophomonas. He suffers from chronic dyspnea, overproduction of sputum, fatigue, pain, and anxiety. Ian was happy to talk to me about the experience of finding it hard to breathe. Of course, what does not come across here is that our conversation was punctuated by frequent pauses for Ian to use breathing techniques, clear sputum, or to use the continuous positive airway pressure machine to help him breathe.

Chris: When did you first notice that breathing was becoming difficult?

Ian: The first time was about 15 years ago. The breathing started to bother me. I found that on occasion breathing normally had become a problem. I didn't make anything of it. It went on like that. And then about five years ago I could hardly do anything without being extremely beyond the point of breathing comfortably. I just could not breathe. I would then notice what is called a panic attack whereby you get to a point where you can't breathe and you're simply gasping, gasping for breath, and you can't find that breath. That is the most horrifying thing you can ever imagine because you feel as if you are, well, you feel as if you are dying.

Chris: Tell me about the first time you had one of these panic attacks.

Ian: When it first happens it is quite shocking. The first time it really happened I was on a trip to the cinema. I just stopped. I just could not breathe. I was in absolute agony and I mean real agony, not feeling a breath in my body, trying to find one. I waited and waited and then it passed. I sat there on my chair for about a quarter of an hour, and I was then fine. But it shocked me: that this had happened. And then it began to happen more. I remember going into a shop and all of a sudden—"woosh"—it happened. I had to hang on to the post. A young man came up and said, "You'd better come and sit down," and I was just sitting there gasping, gasping, gasping for every breath I could get. He wanted me to go to hospital and I said, No, no, no, no, this will pass. And after about half an hour

(Continued)

Box 5.2. *Continued*

it passed and I settled down. But this is what happens. Every now and again I get stuck. I am told it is a panic attack.

Chris: Does this idea of panic make sense to you?

Ian: I could never understand it. The first time someone told me it was a panic attack, it sounded a feeble thing. Considering what you are suffering. I mean, I know you will never stop breathing as such. The breath will always be there as long as you are not actually dying. But if you have one of the conditions I have, you will not die, your breathing will just be bad. But the shock it gives you. You don't know when it is going to happen. And I find the worst thing of all is the anxiety. It depletes me no end.

Chris: Are there ways you have found to cope with the attacks?

Ian: I have picked up ideas from here and there. Dorothy House [Hospice] have given me some tips. But they are only tips in the sense that you still have to go through with it. I have a way of coping with the attacks now. But it is surprising how sometimes you get caught out. For instance, I watched a violent film and it left such a mark on me. I was panting, ill, and everything. I am not sure why it bothered me so much. I worked out that it is about feeling vulnerable.

Chris: Do you every have a sense of things not being real?

Ian: Yes. I have had that. That happens.

Chris: Have you ever experienced overcoming the sense of panic?

Ian: Yes—when I had a cataract removal. I was lying down and all of a sudden I was thinking: "I am not going to be able to manage this"; "I am not going to be able to do it"; "All of this stuff is going to come up I am going to block myself off." And then all of a sudden something in my mind said: "You can do this"; "You can do it." And I did it.

Chris: Has there been anything remotely positive about the experience?

Ian: Yes; it makes me think more deeply. You think more about your own life. It teaches me tolerance. I was brought up in a tough town in the 40s and 50s. And I was not used to accepting. To think that I have to be careful now is hard for me.

Chris: Does confidence make a difference?

Ian: I think it must do. I mean, I know that if there was something wrong with my wife and she needed help I would throw everything off and do what I had to do. Nothing would stop me.

Ian describes the overwhelming sense of shock and terror that is a core part of the experience of dyspnea. For Ian the label of a panic attack was unhelpful. In part this is because of the phenomenology. The experience was always narrated as difficulty breathing that leads to high anxiety, not the reverse. Living with a severe and chronic breathing disorder is like living with the weight of water pressing down on one. Managing the terror and finding a way to resist the derealization is part of what it might mean to cope.

Summary

Breathing is the most functionally pure of the physical senses. Apnea urges breathing. When one is denied the ability to oxygenate—by illness, disease, or environment—the experience can bring one close to terror and provide an extreme drive to breathe. However, when difficulty breathing is chronic and explained, in chronic disease or in sport, people develop mental and physical techniques of managing the physiological and psychological consequences of apnea. Breathing is like funambulism (tightrope walking) in the sense that we are very close to death, seconds away. Unlike funambulism, we are born expert and do not need to think about it. When we do think about it we come closer to the terror. The psychology of breathing is surprisingly well developed. It has some of the best experimental science, the most creative of methods, and has real promise for developing new interventions. Understanding respiratory variability and its relationship with perseverative cognition offers real hope not only for depathologizing panic but also for helping people cope with chronic dyspnea.

Notes

1. Reprinted from *Biological Psychiatry*, 70 (10), Alicia E. Meuret, David Rosenfield, Frank H. Wilhelm, Enlu Zhou, Ansgar Conrad, Thomas Ritz, and Walton T. Roth, Do Unexpected Panic Attacks Occur Spontaneously?, p. 990, Copyright (2011), with permission from Elsevier.
2. Reprinted from *Biological Psychiatry*, 70 (10), Alicia E. Meuret, David Rosenfield, Frank H. Wilhelm, Enlu Zhou, Ansgar Conrad, Thomas Ritz, and Walton T. Roth, Do Unexpected Panic Attacks Occur Spontaneously?, p. 990, Copyright (2011), with permission from Elsevier.
3. Reproduced from *Practical Neurology*, Clare M. Galtrey, Michael Faulkner, and Damian R. Wren, 12 (1), p. 51, doi:10.1136/practneurol-2011-000116 © 2012, BMJ Publishing Group Ltd. With permission from BMJ Publishing Group Ltd.
4. Reproduced from *Practical Neurology*, Clare M. Galtrey, Michael Faulkner, and Damian R. Wren, 12 (1), p. 52, doi:10.1136/practneurol-2011-000116 © 2012, BMJ Publishing Group Ltd. With permission from BMJ Publishing Group Ltd.
5. Reproduced from Marie Williams, Paul Cafarella, Timothy Olds, John Petkov, and Peter Frith, The Language of Breathlessness Differentiates Between Patients With COPD and Age-Matched Adults, *CHEST Journal*, 134 (3), p. 494 doi:10.1378/chest.07-2916 © 2008, American College of Chest Physicians.

References

Akgün, K.M., Crothers, K. and Pisani, M. (2012). Epidemiology and the management of common pulmonary diseases in older persons. *Journal of Gerontology: Biological Sciences*, 67, 276–291.
Bahrke, M.S. and Shukitt-Hale, B. (1993). Effects of altitude on mood, behavior and cognitive functioning: a review. *Sports Medicine*, 16, 97–125.

Baraniek, A. and Sheffield, D. (2011). The efficacy of psychologically based interventions to improve anxiety, depression and quality of life in COPD: a systematic review and meta-analysis. *Patient Education and Counseling*, 83, 29–36.

Boliek, C.A., Hixon, T.J., Watson, P.J. and Morgan, W.J. (1996). Vocalization and breathing during the first year of life. *Journal of Voice*, 1, 1–22.

Brick, N., MacIntyre, T. and Campbell, M. (2014). Attentional focus in endurance activity: new paradigms and future directions. *International Review of Sport and Exercise Psychology*, 7, 106–134.

Brosschot, J.F. (2010). Markers of chronic stress: prolonged physiological activation and (un) conscious perseverative cognition. *Neuroscience & Biobehavioural Reviews*, 35, 46–50.

Buist, A.S., McBurnie, M.A., Vollmer, W.M., Gillespie, S., Burney, P., Mannino, D.M., . . . and Nizankowska-Mogilnicka, E., on behalf of the BOLD collaborative research group. (2007). International variation in the prevalence of COPD (the BOLD Study): a population-based prevalence study. *Lancet*, 370, 741–750.

Buma, L.A., Bakker, F.C. and Oudejans, R.R.D. (2015). Exploring the thoughts and focus of attention of elite musicians under pressure. *Psychology of Music*, 43, 459–472.

Chiesa, A. and Serretti, A. (2009). Mindfulness-based stress reduction for stress management in healthy people: a review and meta-analysis. *The Journal of Alternative and Complementary Medicine*, 15, 593–600.

Courtney, R. and Greenwood, K.M. (2009). Preliminary investigation of a measure of dysfunctional breathing symptoms: the Self Evaluation of Breathing Questionnaire (SEBQ). *International Journal of Osteopathic Medicine*, 12, 121–127.

Couture, R.T., Jerome, W. and Tihanyi, J. (1999). Can associative and dissociative strategies affect the swimming performance of recreational swimmers? *The Sports Psychologist*, 13, 334–343.

Cox, B.J., Swinson, R.P., Endler, N.S. and Norton, G.R. (1994). The symptom structure of panic attacks. *Comprehensive Psychiatry*, 35, 349–353.

Craske, M.G., Kircanski, K., Epstein, A., Wittchen, H.U., Pine, D.S., Lewis-Fernandez, R., Hinton, D. and the DSM V Anxiety, OC spectrum posttraumatic and dissociative disorder work group. (2010). Panic disorder: a review of DSM-IV panic disorder and proposals for DSM-V. *Depression and Anxiety*, 27, 93–112.

De Peuter, S., Van Diest, I., Lemaigre, V., Verleden, G., Demedts, M. and Van den Bergh, O. (2004). Dyspnea: the role of psychological processes. *Clinical Psychology Review*, 24, 557–581.

Dogantan-Dack, M. (2006). The body behind music: precedents and prospects. *Psychology of Music*, 34, 449–464.

Farell, E. (2006). One breath: a reflection on freediving. Devon: Pynto Press.

Feinberg, T.E. (2011). Neuropathologies of the self: clinical and anatomical features. *Consciousness and Cognition*, 20, 75–81.

Feldman, J.L. and Del Negro, C.A. (2006). Looking for inspiration: new perspectives on respiratory rhythm. *Nature Reviews Neuroscience*, 7, 232–242.

Galtrey, C.M., Faulkner, M. and Wren, D.R. (2012). How it feels to experience three different causes of respiratory failure. *Practical Neurology*, 12, 49–54.

Hayen, A., Herigstad, M. and Pattinson, K.T.S. (2013). Understanding dyspnea as a complex individual experience. *Maturitas*, 76, 45–50.

Jaturapatporn, D., Moran, E., Obwanga, C. and Husain, A. (2010). Patients' experience of oxygen therapy and dyspnea: a qualitative study in home palliative care. *Supportive Care and Cancer*, 18, 765–770.

Kessler, R.C., Chiu, W.T., Jin, R., Ruscio, A.M., Shear, K. and Walters, E.E. (2006). The epidemiology of panic attacks, panic disorder, and agoraphobia in the national comorbidity survey replication. *Archives of General Psychiatry*, 63, 415–424.

Khoury, B., Lecomte, T., Fortin, G., Masse, M., Therien, P., Bouchard, V., Chapleau, M.A., Paquin, K. and Hofmann, S.G. (2013). Mindfulness-based therapy: a comprehensive meta-analysis. *Clinical Psychology Review*, 33, 763–771.

Kvangarsnes, M., Torheim, H., Hole, T. and Öhlund, L.S (2013). Narratives of breathlessness in chronic obstructive pulmonary disease. *Journal of Clinical Nursing*, 22, 3062–3070.

Lang, P.J., Wangelin, B.C., Bradley, M., Versace, F., Davenport, P.W. and Costa, V.D. (2011). Threat of suffocation and defensive reflex activation. *Psychophysiology*, 48, 393–396.

Lin, H.-P., Lin, H.-Y. and Huang, A.C.-W. (2011). Effects of stress, depression, and their interaction on heart rate, skin conductance, finger temperature, and respiratory rate: sympathetic-parasympathetic hypothesis on stress and depression. *Journal of Clinical Psychology*, 67, 1080–1091.

Malle, C., Quinette, P., Laisney, M., Bourrilhon, C., Boissin, J., Desgranges, B., Eustache, F. and Piérard, C. (2013). Working memory impairment in pilots exposed to acute hypobaric hypoxia. *Aviation, Space, and Environmental Medicine*, 84, 773–779.

Meuret, A.E., Ritz, T., Wilhelm, F.H. and Roth, W.T. (2005). Voluntary hyperventilation in the treatment of panic disorder—functions of hyperventilation, their implications for breathing training, and recommendations for standardization. *Clinical Psychology Review*, 25, 285–306.

Meuret, A.E., Rosenfield, D., Wilhelm, F.H., Zhou, E., Conrad, A., Ritz, T. and Roth, W.T. (2011). Do unexpected panic attacks occur spontaneously? *Biological Psychiatry*, 70, 985–991.

Mularski, R.A., Munjas, B.A., Lorenz, K.A., Sun, S., Robertson, S.J., Schmelzer, W., Kim, A.C. and Shekelle, P. G. (2009). Randomized controlled trial of mindfulness-based therapy for dyspnea in chronic obstructive lung disease. *The Journal of Alternative and Complementary Medicine*, 10, 1083–1090.

Neumann, D.L. and Piercy, A. (2013). The effect of different attentional strategies on physiological and psychological states during running. *Australian Psychologist*, 48, 329–337.

Pané-Farré, C.A., Stender, J.P., Fenske, K., Deckert, J., Reif, A., John, U., . . . and Hamm, A.O. (2014). The phenomenology of the first panic attack in clinical and community-based samples. *Anxiety Disorders*, 28, 522–529.

Pappens, M., Smets, E., Vansteenwegen, D., Van den Bergh, O. and Van Diest, I. (2012). Learning to fear suffocation: a new paradigm for interoceptive fear conditioning. *Psychophysiology*, 49, 821–828.

Peacock, A. (1998). Oxygen at high altitude. *British Medical Journal*, 317, 1063–1066.

Preter, M. and Klein, D.F. (2008). Panic, suffocation false alarms, separation anxiety and endogenous opioids. *Progress in Neuro-Psychopharmacology and Biological Psychiatry*, 32, 603–612.

Reznik, G.K. (1990). Comparative anatomy, physiology, and function of the upper respiratory tract. *Environmental Health Perspectives*, 85, 171–176.

Sahin-Yilmaz, A. and Naclerio, R.M. (2011). Anatomy and physiology of the upper airway. *Proceedings of the American Thoracic Society*, 8, 31–39.

Sánchez-Meca, J., Rosa-Alcázar, A.I., Marín-Martínez, F. and Gómez-Conesa, A. (2010). Psychological treatment of panic disorder with or without agoraphobia: a meta-analysis. *Clinical Psychology Review*, 30, 37–50.

Sheard, M. and Golby, J. (2006). Effect of a psychological skills training program on swimming performance and positive psychological development. *International Journal of Sport and Exercise Psychology*, 4, 149–169.

Skapinakis, P., Lewis, G., Davies, S., Brugha, T., Prince, M. and Singleton, N. (2011). Panic disorder and subthreshold panic in the UK general population: epidemiology, comorbidity and functional limitation. *European Psychiatry*, 26, 354–362.

Skull, C. (2011). Sustained excellence: toward a model of factors sustaining elite performance in opera. In A. Williamson, D. Edwards, and L. Bartel (Eds.). Proceedings of the international symposium on performance science (pp. 267–273). Utrecht: European Association of Conservatoires, AEC.

Starcevic, V., Kellner, R., Uhlenhuth, E.H. and Pathak, D. (1993). The phenomenology of panic attacks in panic disorder with and without agoraphobia. *Comprehensive Psychiatry*, 34, 36–41.

Thayer, J.F., Åhs, F., Fredrikson, M., Sollers, J.J. and Wager, T.D. (2012). A meta-analysis of heart rate variability and neuroimaging studies: implications for heart rate variability as a marker of stress and health. *Neuroscience and Biobehavioral Reviews*, 36, 747–756.

Thayer, J.F., Yamamoto, S.S. and Brosschot, J.F. (2010). The relationship of autonomic imbalance, heart rate variability and cardiovascular disease risk factors. *International Journal of Cardiology*, 141, 122–131.

Van Diest, I., Bradley, M.M., Guerra, P., Van den Bergh, O. and Lang, P.J. (2009). Fear-conditioned respiration and its association to cardiac reactivity. *Biological Psychology*, 80, 212–217.

Van Diest, I., Stegen, K., Van de Woestijne, K.P. and Van Den Bergh, O. (2000). Hyperventilation and attention: effects of hypercapnia on performance in a Stroop task. *Biological Psychology*, 53, 233–252.

Vlemincx, E., Abelson, J.L., Lehrer, P.M., Davenport, P.W., Van Diest, I. and Van den Bergh, O. (2013). Respiratory variability and sighing: a psychophysiological reset model. *Biological Psychology*, 93, 24–32.

Vlemincx, E., Vigo, D., Vansteenwegen, D., Van den Bergh, O. and Van Diest, I. (2013). Do not worry, be mindful: effects of induced worry and mindfulness on respiratory variability in a nonanxious population. *International Journal of Psychophysiology*, 87, 147–151.

Von Leupoldt, A., Fritzsche, A., Trueba, A.F., Meuret, A.E., Ritz, T. (2012). Behavioral medicine approaches to chronic obstructive pulmonary disease. *Annals of Behavioural Medicine*, 44, 52–65.

Williams, M., Cafarella, P., Olds, T., Petkov, J. and Frith, P. (2008). The language of breathlessness differentiates between patients with COPD and age-matched adults. *Chest*, 134, 489–496.

Wilson, G.A. (2012). Climbers' narratives of mountain spaces above 8000 metres: a social constructivist perspective. *Area*, 44, 29–36.

Zvolensky, M.J. and Eifert, G.H. (2001). A review of psychological factors/processes affecting anxious responding during voluntary hyperventilation and inhalations of carbon dioxide-enriched air. *Clinical Psychology Review*, 21, 375–400.

CHAPTER 6

FATIGUE

Feeling spent, exhausted, tired, weary, lethargic, listless, or suffering from *fatigue*, are common complaints of everyday life. In fact, in a UK survey of 2,474 adults, a staggering 41.3 percent said they were feeling tired or run-down (McAteer et al., 2011). These were adults living in the community, going about their business—not clinical subjects seeking medical help for a fatigue problem. There is no reason to think of fatigue as a peculiarly British phenomenon, as similar data have been collected in the United States and Scandinavia (Loge et al., 1998; Ricci et al., 2007). The experience of being tired is extremely common, but for some people more than just an inconvenience: it is a major, limit-defining feature of life.

Fatigue has attracted a great deal of psychological debate. In this chapter I explore the different experiences we refer to when we describe ourselves as tired. There is a recurring metaphor of a limited "energy supply" that is never far from fatigue talk, and it is worth spending some time unpacking what the evidence is for fatigue as a depletion of resource.

There are other ways to think about fatigue, however. I contrast resource accounts with motivational accounts of fatigue as a general mechanism for switching away from unrewarding tasks that have minimal reward and high cost. Perhaps fatigue is less about energy depletion and more about energy optimization. Fatigue, viewed in this way, highlights two main problems, both of which we see clearly in extreme experiences. First, there are many people who experience severe, chronic, debilitating fatigue as unstoppable exhaustion. Second, there are people who operate with little rest, who rarely complain of feeling spent, and who instead boast vitality and energy. I explore both extremes with the help of two people whose lives are defined by these traits: Kerry, who is an endurance ultra runner (the thought of which is enough to tire most of us), and Sarah, who has had chronic fatigue syndrome for 16 years and who lives a life carefully balancing what she wants to do with what she judges to be possible.

Being tired

There are two traditions of fatigue research, which approach the problem from very different angles. First is the occupational study of fatigue in people engaged in work, sport, or leisure; second is the medical study of fatigue as a symptom of disease or disorder—as the primary presenting problem in clinical settings.

From almost the beginning of scientific psychology, the study of mental fatigue was a central concern, in part because it is a constant methodological problem in many experimental procedures. Measuring performance requires repetition over time, but repetition of simple tasks tends to induce fatigue, boredom, and the desire to alter behavior. Fatigue in the particular context of the experiment is a procedural nuisance to be controlled and managed, but it is much more than an artifact. In the early part of the twentieth century, fatigue was a major concern in the still industrializing West. Psychology was intimately involved in the social engineering of how to battle fatigue and thereby improve social, educational, and industrial performance.

From the very beginning of fatigue research, mental fatigue was recognized as an emotional and motivational construct. The problem was originally given as: why does continuous performance on a task lead to reduction in output, aversive feelings, and thoughts of wanting to stop? For a striking early example and definition of the problem, Tsuru Arai reported her now-famous experiments on repeatedly solving arithmetic sums, and the observation that in an experiment with herself as subject,

> the time taken to do a certain number of examples is almost doubled during twelve hours of mental multiplication. . . . In the case of the group of individuals (inexperienced subjects), the increase in the time taken to do a certain amount of work is 24 per cent during two hours of mental multiplication. (Arai, 1912, p. 114)

We might marvel at the dedication involved in this tradition of experimental introspection and at the twelve-hour marathon of arithmetic, but it does bring to life the problem of fatigue as a shorthand way of referring to the decrement in performance on repetition.

The classical and popular explanation for the problem of fatigue is that it is a sign of resource depletion, as a spluttering engine signals spent fuel. The modern view is that fatigue signals the need to change behavior. Although I have cast these as classical and modern, it would be wrong to think that one has replaced the other. Early studies of fatigue used a more phenomenological psychology and so very quickly became aware of the primacy of desire. It was recognized early that being tired is not an inability to concentrate, or an idle openness to random ideas, or even an unwillingness to engage in task demands, but rather the overwhelming desire to disengage from a task that is becoming aversive. As early as 1899 Thorndike observed that subjects in his cognitive experiments did less work when tired, "not because this stock of mental energy was running low, but because ideas of stopping, of 'taking it easy,' of working intermittently came in and were not inhibited" (Thorndike, 1899, p. 712).

Despite the early recognition that fatigue is not best characterized as a marker of spent energy, the more functional and phenomenologically rich view of fatigue was lost in the search for improved industrial performance.

The fallacy of resource depletion

Metaphors direct psychological thought and science. We become used to describing cognitive processes as limited by structural constraints such as "filters" and "spotlights" (Fernandez-Duqu and Johnson, 1999), or the dominant overarching metaphor of mind as computer. Cognitive functions as restricted to the limits of a finite resource is one of the more enduring and stubborn metaphors in psychology. David Navon (1984) laid bare the fallacy of resource depletion as a model of performance, largely due its lack of parsimony. Ideas in psychology that resort to resources can be described without reference to resources. Resources provide a shorthand way of referring to a range of observable phenomena for task performance, but divert scientific attention from alternate explanations for those phenomena.

Resource talk is difficult to eradicate, and has been recently rekindled in the modern return to the psychology of willpower, impulse regulation, and self-control. Roy Baumeister and colleagues promote a model of self- and motivated choice known first as the strength model of self-control (Baumeister et al., 1998), later as the ego depletion model. The principal observation across numerous studies is similar to the classical problem of fatigue: that the exercise of self-control in deliberately resisting automatic or desired choices is reported as effortful and detrimentally affects performance on the next task or choices. Muraven and Baumeister (2000) drop the reference to resource as a theoretical inference and reify it as a structural constraint, similar to energy expenditure in a muscle. This strong version promotes the idea of energy "conservation" in cognitive and motivational tasks, and the importance of "replenishment."

The idea of weakness through use and the need to replenish the spent resource of willpower provides a peculiar problem. How does one account for the return of performance? If the resource is unknown (and hypothetical), how does one replenish it? Ego repletion is suggested by a range of commonsense hypotheses, including doing something else, resting, sleeping, thinking positively, and—controversially—increasing blood glucose, thought to be in part a mechanism of depletion (Gailliot and Baumeister, 2007). This physiological turn is a sign of a metaphor in trouble, an idea being made to work too hard. The glucose hypothesis has been roundly criticized as overly simplistic and lacking in evidence. Indeed, the resource hypothesis as a whole has been described as "unlikely to be correct (in particular, the glucose version of a resource account)" (Kurzban et al., 2013, p. 715) and as a "sweet delusion" (Lange and Eggert, 2014).

The idea of fatigue as a sign of a depleted resource is a fallacy. Of course behavior is metabolically limited, but fatigue emerges before metabolic limits are met. The process by which this is governed is the subject of much research, especially in sports performance. Physical fatigue is subject to the subtle interplay of expectations of exertion, experience, and central nervous system control. The exact operation of any central control over exertion is not known, but there is wide acceptance that the experience of fatigue occurs long before biological homeostasis is threatened. This is true for both physical and mental performance.

Fatigue as motivation to change

The question persists, then, of why fatigue emerges if it is not a signal of a limit reached or a resource spent. Fatigue is an aversive emotional response to the demand of continuing a task, and a desire to stop or switch away from that task. Whether the primary task is a simple vigilance game or one of deliberate self-control, fatigue functions to motivate change. This motivational view of fatigue marks a return to Thorndike's original ideas, and now appears in different forms. There are at least four versions of a motivational view of fatigue that position it as (a) an intrinsic cost of mental control, (b) a method to promote awareness of the opportunity cost inherent in persisting with a task, (c) an aversion to the decoupling of attention, or (d) more simply, the "stop" emotion.

The first idea is that all tasks carry an *intrinsic cost*. This approach views the problem of fatigue from the perspective of studies on an economic long-term trade-off between competing demands. Task persistence is simply a way of achieving diminishing marginal returns. The longer you do something the less gain is possible: "In the context of prolonged, obligatory mental effort, the marginal cost of further effort is elevated, leading in some cases to a subsequent withdrawal from cognitively challenging activity" (Kool and Botvinick, 2014, p. 139). From this rational economic perspective, mechanism is irrelevant to the explanation of behavior. What is needed is simply an understanding of the utilities and their costs.

A similarly economic view is that subjective effort relies on selection, and where there is selection there is *opportunity cost*. One can attend only to a small number of tasks at the same time. Every selection means that other targets are not selected. The opportunities that could have come from selecting differently should also be thought of as costs. Hence the longer we continue with something, not only do the marginal returns diminish but the opportunity costs also increase. Robert Kurzban and colleagues argue that there is a calculation of exactly this cost-benefit trade-off, which is dynamically computed over the time of that task performance: "The crux of our argument is that the sensation of 'mental effort' is the output of mechanisms designed to measure the opportunity cost of engaging in the current mental task" (Kurzban et al.,

2013, p. 665). Fatigue grows as the opportunity costs of persisting with the same task grow. In this way fatigue functions to motivate people to switch to more profitable behaviors by reducing cognitive engagement.

A focus on disengagement is at the heart of fatigue for David Navon. He argues that the perception of effort arises from the disengagement, what he calls a *decoupling* from task: "Effort is not any scarce commodity. It is the aversive valence of the operation of decoupling. The more sustained decoupling is, the more aversive it is" (Navon, 1989, p. 203). This is an interesting idea subtly different in its suggestion that the negative feelings of fatigue are a by-product of the switch in attention, not the cause of the switch. A dynamic view of attending has signals preconciously vying for prioritization. Some signals may be strengthened over repeated failure and finally break through and capture attention in a forced decoupling that is felt aversively. Fatigue in this way is a symptom of an attentional system operating in a context of many competing demands. Again, there is no need here to postulate resources or any central unitary control (Navon, 2013).

Finally, fatigue has been called a *stop emotion*. Drawing on the distinction between liking and wanting currently of interest in the neurobiological study of reward and pleasure, fatigue does not affect a judgment of the valence of the reward, but affects the extent to which one is willing or able to extend effort to achieve a reward (Van der Linden, 2011). Fatigue shares properties of basic human emotions in its universality and specificity, but perhaps recasting it as an emotion is unnecessary. Nevertheless, this focus on the motivational properties of fatigue as an urge to disengage is valuable.

These different ways of thinking about fatigue share crucial properties. First, they are functional accounts: they are interested in how fatigue functions to change behavior in a context of multiple possible demands and rewards. Second, a consensus is emerging that tasks that are demanding of executive control (updating working memory, inhibiting automatic responses, decision making) are more susceptible to fatigue. Third, competing demands are at some level always linked, and perhaps in constant trade-off. And fourth, the felt experience of fatigue, whether it leads to a switch in behavior or follows a switch in behavior, is aversive even when the task one is persisting with is valued.

Bob Hockey captures the return to considering the function of fatigue in his excellent book *The Psychology of Fatigue*. In summary, he argues that "fatigue may be considered, like anxiety, to have an adaptive function, serving to protect the organism from over-commitment to specific goals, in the service of a balanced motivational strategy" (Hockey, 2013, p. 22). This motivational view of fatigue is essentially positive. Although the felt experience is unpleasant, its purpose is adaptive. This has practical considerations for the organization of work; for the design of tasks, especially simple and monotonous ones, for which the emergence of the desire to stop or avoid altogether is likely; and for the training of elite, highly skilled performance that requires one to control fatigue—to overcome the desire to stop.

The urge to sleep

Before considering the absence of fatigue, and our two extreme experiences of feeling energetic or tired all the time, it is worth mentioning briefly a specific case of fatigue, the urge to sleep. Horne (2010) notes the different ways we talk about *sleepiness* that include many of the features of fatigue, such as drowsiness, reduced environmental responsiveness, and the lack of motivation to engage in effort. Sleepiness is not always a need for sleep. Of interest for the motivational model of fatigue is the interruption of attention by the strong urge to sleep. In the case of sleep, fatigue is perhaps less a switch away from a task that offers only diminishing returns, but more a switch to a higher order goal of total cognitive disengagement. Sleep onset is associated with a range of physiological and behavioral changes, including loss of awareness and loss of control over thoughts, most of which are experienced as gradual (Yang et al., 2010). Resisting the urge to sleep is experienced as a battle, sometimes a battle that is lost very quickly and without warning (Herrmann et al., 2010). Fatigue urges disengagement from task, but not into sleep. We often confuse sleepiness and fatigue; the word *tired* in English refers to both. It is important in research, in clinical practice, and perhaps in life to distinguish the two.

Vitality, energy, and perseverance

I started this chapter with a UK finding that over 40 percent of people felt tired or run-down (McAteer et al., 2011). But that means nearly 60 percent were not tired. Maybe some of this majority felt not just the absence of fatigue but felt energetic or vital. Persuading people that they could feel more energized, or helping people to overcome fatigue is big business. Which of us would say no to the promise of feeling more energetic?

There are three main traditions of research into the question of how to improve a subjective sense of feeling energized and able to outperform the norm. First, there is a strong humanist tradition in psychology interested in vitality as a marker of personal growth and self-awareness. In contrast, there is a thoroughly nonhumanistic approach to performance enhancement, often by psychopharmacological means. Lastly, the experience of unusual individuals who achieve elite status in a chosen field can be instructive. People who have extreme abilities to persevere under duress may teach the rest of us about what is possible.

Vitality is captured by the report of feeling alive, alert, and bursting with energy (Bostic et al., 2000). Subjective vitality has been defined as "one's conscious experience of possessing energy and aliveness" (Ryan and Frederick, 1997, p. 530). This definition is circular and exchanges synonyms: *energy, vitality* and *aliveness*. It works well enough as a marker of a unique experience that is beyond the average. Modern psychology has not fully engaged with the study of positive experiences such as feeling energized. Research ranges from the study of energy and vitality as the absence of fatigue, to the more recent *positive psychology* that promotes a focus on happiness and personal growth. Vitality is linked with creativity, flow, positive distraction, and mindfulness (Hefferon, 2013). There is a mature clinical and counseling literature on personal growth, a literature on aging and late life development, and an educational and occupational psychology of engagement with work.

Casting vitality as the result of the active engagement of self in pursuit of meaning is in line with a functionalist account of fatigue. If fatigue is the motivational consequence of the diminishing returns of unrewarding behavioral selection, then one can understand why switching to a focus on the complexity of outdoor environments (Ryan et al., 2010) or the personal sharing of theories of self when investing in close relationships (Lambert et al., 2011) would counter fatigue or be potentially vitalizing. This is a motivational approach to vitality. We are motivated more than by the simple desire to increase pleasure and reduce or avoid discomfort.

Huta and Waterman (2014) summarize this approach to vitality as the study of *eudaimonia*—a concern with personal growth, with striving for value, authenticity, and meaning—in contrast to the study of *hedonia*: the pursuit of pleasure or avoidance of distress. The activities here thought to improve vitality are not passive; they are likely to involve complex cognitive activity. It is interesting that the study of vitality—with its roots in Gestalt and humanistic psychologies—seems to escape metaphors of resource, capacity, or limits. The theories and ideas are motivational and developmental, about human striving and growth (Maslow, 1971).

Brain training

In contrast, the study of how to improve performance by improving perseverance is more susceptible to the fallacy of resource depletion. There are many studies of how to improve performance on a task, whether by means of prescribed pharmacological stimulants, such as amphetamine and methylphenidate; commonly available substances, such as caffeine or nicotine; nonpharmacological interventions, such as exercise or physical training; or what is popularly known as "brain training."

The use of prescribed stimulants as a method of cognitive enhancement is common in some populations. In one review of studies with school or university students, between 2.5 and 35.5 percent reported using prescribed stimulants to enhance cognition (Smith and Farah, 2011). Despite the findings that the effects on decision making and working memory are relatively weak, there is a strong belief among the young that prescribed stimulants improve cognitive performance. Similarly, the nonprescription market for cognitive enhancement is now dominated by energy drinks (i.e., the sugar and caffeine industries), which are increasingly discussed as a public health hazard (Reissig et al., 2009). Both caffeine and nicotine have been found to improve aspects of cognitive performance in the laboratory, but as most are consumed with other substances—sugar and alcohol lead the list—research is now focusing on the interactive effects of multiple substance use. Most studies of cognitive performance do not measure subjective judgments of vitality or fatigue, so it is often not possible to tease apart short-term cognitive performance changes from the phenomenology of fatigue. Despite this shortcoming, there are some enthusiastic supporters of the caffeine stimulant market (Glade, 2010), but also some high-profile detractors. Kent Sepkowitz (2013), for one, discussed the harmful effects of high levels of caffeine, and pointed out that people who consume energy drinks may be unaware of just how much caffeine they are getting.

So if you can't reliably buy more energy in a drink, how else can you energize? Going to the gym may be a better way. Although exercise, being metabolically costly, is thought to reduce resources, in fact acute exercise is found to confer small improvements in cognitive performance (Chang et al., 2012). There is much debate about exactly what type of exercise matters, in whom, and for how long the benefits last, but at least there is consensus that exercise is mentally advantageous in the short term. Practices that combine physical movement with attention-control strategies such as Tai Chi can also improve cognitive performance (Wayne et al., 2014), as can strategies of attention management alone, such as mindfulness training (Chiesa et al., 2011).

Thus taking control of attending, however briefly, may well have benefits on cognitive performance, at least when measured in the shorter term and on the specific task. There is no compelling evidence, however, that these effects sustain or transfer. The lack of effects has not stopped the growth in the business of selling "brain-training" devices and instruction. At best we have rediscovered the findings from the early psychology of fatigue: repeated performance leads to practice effects. In what should be considered a landmark study of over 11,000 people undertaking online computerized brain training, Adrian Owen and colleagues could not find any evidence for the idea that using "brain-training" devices benefited cognition. Although people believe it is effective, there was no effect. (Owen et al., 2010).

Unfortunately, missing from most of these studies of nonpharmacological interventions is any concern with felt experience, with the onset or persistence of fatigue and with aversive thoughts of stopping. Meditation, mindfulness, and other strategies of cognitive control are typically studied only for the effect they may have on improving cognitive or motor performance, or for reducing the aversive effects of long-term illness. There are no studies of their effects on fatigue in a normal, everyday population. The earlier discussion of the history of fatigue research perhaps tells us why. Like any other cognitive activity, meditation is effortful. Taking control and directing one's attention is an active process. To choose to do it would need an overriding primary reason, such as the belief that it is leading to some long-term effect when framed in a narrative of training, or the belief that it will reduce a stronger aversive sensation associated with illness. Without a strong primary motivation, a nonpharmacological strategy for performance enhancement is just another form of task: it might improve performance momentarily, but will lead to fatigue and disengagement eventually.

Indefatigable

One last source of evidence for the study of vitality is to learn from those who consider themselves indefatigable. Successful people are often described, or describe themselves, as tireless, and such language normally operates to draw attention to socially valorized character traits such as being hard working, perseverant, or determined. However, the serious study of persistence without fatigue, or even despite fatigue, is sparse. There is a renewed interest in the study of both success and of successful people, whether in business, the military, academe, sport, the arts, or personal life.

A number of overlapping terms for positive characteristics are in use, and are being explored for their relationship with fatigue and performance. Terms such as *hardiness* (Bartone et al., 2013), *courage* (Rate et al., 2007), and *resilience* (Kitamura et al., 2013) are widely used. A favorite is the rhetorically colorful idea of *grit* (Duckworth and Gross, 2014). Angela Duckworth and colleagues define grit as the ability to persevere and work toward a long-term goal:

> Grit entails working strenuously toward challenges, maintaining effort and interest over years despite failure, adversity, and plateaus in progress. The gritty individual approaches achievement as a marathon; his or her advantage is stamina. Whereas disappointment or boredom signals to others that it is time to change trajectory and cut losses, the gritty individual stays the course.[1]

There are no accounts of how people who repeatedly demonstrate an ability to persist in challenging tasks experience fatigue, long past the time that the average person has responded to the stop signal. It is not even clear whether they *do* experience fatigue or are simply "bursting" with energy and vitality. In the absence of data, there are competing hypotheses. Perhaps the vital, high-performing, persevering person is pursuing a goal that is so important that they are able to be "single minded." Perhaps their skill is in diminishing the value of any possible competing tasks, in bolstering the value of their goal so it remains overwhelmingly important. Alternatively, the opposite may be true: high-achieving people may actually be in a permanent state of fatigue, living with the repeated aversive interruption by thoughts of quitting, but they have techniques to bat away the interruption with repeated switching back to their goal. Are endurance athletes less susceptible to fatigue when motivated to achieve, or more skilled at managing inevitable fatigue?

To explore these ideas further I talked with Kerry Sutton, an ultra-marathon runner (Box 6.1).

Box 6.1. Kerry, the ultra runner: *"when my body says stop I won't accept it"*

Kerry describes herself as "challenge driven." When I interviewed her, she was training for the 100-mile, 24-hour run from London to Oxford. We met in a university sports training facility where she took time out to "refuel" and talk about her experience of fatigue. She is an experienced athlete, having run the Marathon de Sables, a 250-kilometer cross-desert race, and the Jungle Ultra in Peru, a self-supported, five-day race with a marathon stage, a hill stage, an endurance 100-kilometer run, and a sprint stage. I asked her about her motivation, about how she experiences fatigue, and about how it has changed her.

Chris: I am interested in your motivation. Why extreme running?

Kerry: I don't know. I have theories. I think if I set a goal I will not give up because of my sense of failure. I don't want to fail. I am driven in some senses to compete: with myself. It is always pushing myself harder. I am trying to get *me* better. It is to do with my self-worth. I needed a massive challenge. I needed to pitch myself against myself. When I started, I didn't care about the result. I just wanted to push myself to my utter limits and see if I was as tough as I thought I was.

Chris: What is the feeling of fatigue like? How would you describe it?

Kerry: You mind is tired of thinking about it. I am tired of having to think about having to push myself on. But I interpret that as fatigue. I am physically tired and my body wants to stop, but I believe that it's not—that my body can keep going. My muscles will keep going. It is my mind that is my weakness, not my body. I don't believe there is anything my body can't do. It will all be in my head. I trust my body will hold up. I trust in my body.

Chris: What are the thoughts you have?

Kerry: "I don't want to do it." I am angry. I get the extremes of my emotions. "I am not good enough," "I haven't trained hard enough," "other people are better than me," "I feel heavy and cumbersome." In the ultra-running community it is known as "hitting the dark side." We all get it. We all know it is there. All my demons come out. It is my mental state that will stop me well before my body is ready to stop. Absolutely, I want to stop. I get bored of pushing myself. That is the wrong word maybe. Constantly running to a time over hours and hours and hours, I think my mind becomes fatigued. It is repetition and the constant push. "I don't want to push myself." Then I start to question why I am doing it. It is mental fatigue in terms of the repetition of the action.

Box 6.1. *Continued*

Chris: Is it like height vertigo, being drawn to danger, or the unshakable belief that to climb higher or go to the edge is irrational?

Kerry: It is not as strong as a fear of falling off an edge; it is a different thing. It's sort of more of an anger. "I don't want to do it anymore." "I don't want to do it." "I do not."

Chris: What does failure look like?

Kerry: There was a race I stopped. That was my mind thinking I was fatigued, and I wasn't, because I'd run too fast. I had gone out too fast. I was trying to keep up with the front-runners and after two hours I was just, I was exhausted. I thought: "I can't do this." Had I even just dropped a bit I would have won the battle with my mind. But I couldn't rationally figure that out at the time. And my mind won and I gave up.

Chris: Does fatigue affect your judgment?

Kerry: I am scared of that bit: the irrationality, when my judgment goes slightly awry. In the jungle when I was on my own, and I was fatigued, and I was feeling threatened, I was very aware of my surroundings. I was running but unaware of my running because I was on high alert and became super-aware. My judgment was OK. Spot on. But there are times when I'm really fatigued and I am struggling with this mental block and I am completely unaware of the running. There is no world around me. I am totally oblivious to what is happening. I can't have music; I can't have any distraction. I am just me. I am not even aware of my physical presence, just of that little bit of road in front of me.

Chris: Are you an expert on your body, or have you learned to ignore your body?

Kerry: When my body says stop I won't accept it. I listen to my body, but I can't trust it. I have to become an expert in it. It is trying to be wise in managing both mind and body. I will try to listen to my body, and understand it—the same with my mind. I will try to pick apart the thought patterns. It is a dogged determination. I might feel fatigue but I have no option. So I override it. I will override my senses.

Chris: Has the experience of being at the limits of fatigue been useful in the rest of life?

Kerry: It has given me the capacity to deal with things in life. It does give me confidence. I am sure that I employ things I have learned in my race in everyday life, in dealing with situations. I have a much more relaxed approach to things. If people are getting upset about something, I tend to listen and assimilate, which I would not have done. It is not a personality trait of mine. I have changed that now.

In this extract Kerry captures well the challenge of fatigue. I suggested two possibilities: that interruption from thoughts of stopping is reduced in being single minded, or that

(Continued)

Box 6.1. *Continued*

interruption happens all the time but is managed with repeated switching back to the goal. For Kerry it is the second. She is competing in severe and extreme fatigue. What is remarkable about her endurance is not only the physical but the mental ability to continue against the rage of interruption demanding switch. Unexpected, because not discussed in research, was the emotional aspect of that switching back: the angry determination and the objectifying of fatigue as an aggressor to battle against.

Being tired all the time

It is not only elite athletes who are learning how to endure. There are many people who suffer unbidden and unplanned fatigue, people who are quick to tire, who find everyday demands overwhelming, who experience fatigue all day and every day.

Persistent fatigue is often experienced with disease or its treatment. It is a common and disabling symptom associated with many problems, including depression (Arnold, 2008), stroke (Lerdal and Gay, 2013), and cancers (Wagner and Cella, 2004). Fatigue is frequently given as a primary symptom causing distress and disability, and can be confusing and challenging for people as they struggle to make sense of what is normally temporary. It is often hard to know whether the feelings of fatigue are relevant to the disease and its management, or an unfortunate side effect (Kirkevold et al., 2012). For example, when asked to share thoughts, 73 fatigued cancer patients used the opportunity to write about their struggle with the idea of being cancer survivors, and in particular how to think about fatigue after cancer. The dominant discourse of successful cancer treatment involves the idea of return to previous health. The common ways of thinking and talking about life after cancer rarely recognize that people feel fundamentally different. Many continue to experience disabling fatigue, which they struggle to make sense of (Pertl et al., 2014).

Perhaps the most challenging clinical presentation of fatigue is those with a primary complaint of persistent and unremitting fatigue that limits or stops mental, physical, and social engagement, captured popularly by the label chronic fatigue syndrome (CFS). Although recognized as a clinical problem in its own right for many years, it was only in the 1980s that research was reignited. Calls for better definitions, for clarity about comorbidities, and for consistent language and approach were everywhere in the 1980s. It was perhaps not until Keiji Fukuda and colleagues from the International Chronic Fatigue Study Group published a statement on preferred terminology and criteria for assessment that the field started to coalesce.

The use of the term *syndrome* in chronic fatigue syndrome draws attention to the multifaceted nature of many complaints. The definition includes ideas about causation; in particular, it excludes any cause due to overexertion. The definition also references the condition's resistance to treatment (it is not helped by rest) and by the presence of cognitive problems, especially with memory and concentration (Fukuda et al., 1994). Other case definitions exist, and most now define "chronic" as the persistence of symptoms for six months or longer. Although case definitions are important for science and medicine, the search for what is specific—for a "caseness"—can obscure what is general. Glyn Lewis and Simon Wessely, UK psychiatrists interested in common symptoms such as fatigue, pain, and anxiety, argued early on that most people with chronic fatigue could helpfully be thought of as at the extreme on a continuum of fatigue (Lewis and Wessely, 1992).

The idea that clinical fatigue is an extreme of general fatigue was not meant to diminish the clinical need of patients who present with serious and debilitating problems. On the contrary, these and other authors repeatedly stress that the way to conquer chronic fatigue is to understand how people behave when fatigued, and how fatigue functions to halt adaptive behavior (Holgate et al, 2011).

The causes of CFS are unknown, but are likely to be varied, unlikely to be psychological in origin, and very likely to involve both central nervous and immune system dysfunction. Dantzer et al. (2014), attempting to combine neurological, immunological, and psychological studies of fatigue, as well as research with nonhuman species, remind us of the impact of illness on motivation. Sickness in general, they argue, causes lack of interest, failure to explore, and habit failure, all of which are immune-system mediated—evolved responses that function to promote withdrawal. Although preliminary, this view is motivational in the recognition that the defining feature of human fatigue is the interruption of behavior by signals to halt and withdraw, which in humans is verbalized as the growing dominance of thoughts to stop and switch.

Cognitive behavioral model

Cognition, then—in particular, the thoughts about needing to stop a particular behavior and the inability to engage in other behavior, even when desired—is at the heart of a science of chronic fatigue. Cognition is also the target of treatments aimed at management, rehabilitation, and recovery. Broadly, this focus on thought and action is referred to as a cognitive behavioral model. Its focus is pragmatic. It is not concerned with what precipitates or causes chronic fatigue but with what maintains it and what hinders recovery. Hans Knoop and his team narratively reviewed the role of beliefs, attitudes, and illness attributions (beliefs about the causes of fatigue and recovery) in the maintenance of CFS. They focused first on the specific beliefs that people hold and their effect on behavior, and second on the treatment literature, which often reports beliefs as mediators of treatment outcome (Knoop et al., 2010). This is a useful division, but it is worth adding a third source of evidence: patients' report of their experience—the *phenomenology* of chronic fatigue.

The role of cognition in the maintenance of fatigue and disability has been known for some time. The early ideas focused on patient judgments and the presumed over-estimation of the debilitating effects of physical effort and fear of disability caused by that effort (Fry and Martin, 1996). This focus on a mismatch between patient belief and presumed ability with use of terms such as *overestimation* and *exaggeration* reinforced an unfortunate mind-body dualism that continues to pervade the literature. For academics this is a minor philosophical problem and an intellectual irritant, but for patients it can be devastating.

The dualistic habit of describing symptoms as explainable by objectively observable disease causes major problems for patients suffering with so-called medically unexplained symptoms. The implication that chronic fatigue syndrome is in some way a failure in individual judgment propels many patients into a battle to legitimize their suffering, exposing themselves to stigmatizing disbelief from professionals and the public. In short, fatigue has no objective measure. It is by definition subjective. The search for a method of removing the patient report of their experience in explaining the patient's experience is misguided. The idea of comparing patient report of fatigue with an observer judgment of what is normatively possible may be even more fraught with problems. We have seen from a number of studies the overwhelming evidence that the aversive cognitive demand to stop occurs long before any physiological limit has been reached.

In a thoughtful comment on medicine's formal attempts to make it possible to talk about cognition as important in the treatment of chronic fatigue, Wojtek Wojcik and colleagues discussed the beliefs of different medical professionals, principally neurologists, about how to classify CFS as a disease—a practice known as *nosology*. They conclude that chronic fatigue does not fit neatly into current ways of thinking about ill health and call it an "orphan illness". They call for better communication between medical professionals from different specialties about patient need, and less concern with nosology (Wojcik et al, 2011).

A functionalist account of chronic fatigue focuses on how fatigue functions to alter behavior through the establishment and maintenance of beliefs that stop recovery. It is useful to ask the question: what would be the consequence of the continual interruption of an unpleasant urge to stop? Framing the question in this way highlights the attention-demanding nature of the interruption.

Attention to threat

For a number of years, Rona Moss-Morris and her group have been investigating whether people with CFS show an attentional bias toward information that is threatening. The idea is a simple one. Being continually interrupted by a threatening stimulus can lead one to be vigilant for future interruption, paradoxically increasing the likelihood of interruption. In an early study, the researchers did not find bias toward threatening information in the form of words, such as *collapse, sick,* and *fatigue* (Moss-Morris and Petrie, 2003). This is now a fairly consistent general finding, although some researchers have demonstrated bias in some circumstances (Hou et al., 2014). There are questions about the methods of standard attentional bias research, in particular the relevance of words as a trigger of threat, and as to whether bias toward threatening words is relevant given that these words are common in the environment of the chronic fatigue patient. But, in summary, there is no good evidence for a clinically relevant and stable bias of chronic fatigue patients attending toward illness-related cues.

Also unclear is the extent to which there is a bias toward interpreting ambiguous but potentially threatening information as threatening. These studies typically present people with information that could be safe *or* threatening. The idea is that those with chronic fatigue will adopt an "if-in-doubt" strategy of assuming the worst: if it could be threatening, then safer to assume that it is. Although there were early demonstrations of this bias, they have not been easy to replicate (Martin and Alexeeva, 2010), and their clinical relevance remains questionable.

The evidence is missing that chronic fatigue patients habitually attend to the threat of illness and fatigue. It is unlikely to be true that people become vigilant to fatigue. What appears more compelling is the evidence on how people cognitively respond to fatigue. Chronic fatigue patients appear to demonstrate a high level of self-criticism and negative perfectionism (Luyten et al., 2011). People are highly critical and demanding in a self-defeating pattern that fuels ruminating thoughts of failure, and so depression. This pattern can be self-perpetuating as people fail to reach unrealistically high targets, which reinforces a belief of personal inadequacy. Specific beliefs are that the fatigue is uncontrollable, likely to lead to catastrophic outcomes, and that further activity will lead to physical damage. All appear to play a part in maintaining a lack of engagement with activity (Lukkahatai and Saligan, 2013).

Other strong beliefs, perhaps fuelled by the social context of CFS as a contested illness, are beliefs about the causes of the disease and what needs to be done. Simply put: if one believes strongly that exercising is not only going to be fatiguing but that it will cause damage, then one is unlikely to exercise. Further, one is likely to consider anyone who is suggesting exercise to be at least unwise and perhaps unkind. Ironically, the person with CFS can appear to observers to be passive and resting. The opposite is normally true. People with fatigue tend to be actively ruminating about possible solutions, and often desperate for change, but may be engaging in self-defeating attempts to achieve unachievable solutions.

Cognitive behavioral therapy

Some treatments attempt to work with these beliefs and help people make gradual and sustainable changes rather than sudden radical ones. Attempts at altering beliefs about fatigue, its causes, meaning, and consequences are part of cognitive behavioral therapy (CBT), which is increasingly offered as the most evidence-supported treatment approach. Typically these therapies are delivered as part of a program of rehabilitation that includes re-engagement with physical and social activity. A recent large trial published in *The Lancet* contrasted three different approaches to treatment based on different ways of thinking about fatigue. One treatment is based on the energy-resource model of fatigue I discussed earlier as a fallacy. Essentially, there is a dominant cultural view that fatigue is a signal of a depleted scarce resource, signaling that one should conserve energy and avoid exertion; instead one should use one's body as a guide. The alternative treatments do the opposite; they work on the assumption that for those with chronic fatigue one's body is an untrustworthy guide and should not be followed. The stop signals should be thought of as false alarms. CBT essentially seeks to shift people from fatigue-determined behavior to planful behavior in which one works toward meaningful valued goals according to how one has planned in advance, regardless of how one feels in the moment. This trial, the largest of its kind, showed that the treatments that are aimed at gradually increasing activity had better results overall than standard care, and were better than the treatment that proposed changing activity depending on how one felt (White et al., 2011). Part of the CBT approach is learning that the beliefs one has about fatigue, however sensible and internally coherent, may not be true, and, more importantly, may be unhelpful.

The beliefs one holds about fatigue do seem to be important in deciding how to behave and what is possible. Unfortunately, however, there is little guidance in research on what the experience of trying to ignore the strong and interruptive urge to stop is like for the person with chronic fatigue syndrome. There are many qualitative studies of what it is like to live with CFS but these tend to focus on the broader challenges. In a review of 34 qualitative studies of CFS, for example, the common themes that we would expect were found: of living a disrupted life, and of struggling with stigma and changes in identity (Anderson et al., 2012). Missing is any phenomenological study of what it feels like to live with this urge to stop. Is it the same or different as that experienced by the person continuing a repeated task with diminishing marginal returns? Is it the same as someone like Kerry, deliberately undertaking an extreme sport, working far beyond their limits, ignoring the desire to stop by focusing on a superordinate goal, and learning to reinterpret her body? Or is it nothing like those, but instead a constant base level of motivational drag, where the very thought of initiating action is quickly defeated?

To explore these ideas further I talked with Sarah Prior (Box 6.2).

Box 6.2. Sarah, living with fatigue: *"everything is planned"*

Sarah works part-time as a senior fundraiser for a charity. She was diagnosed with post-viral fatigue at 17, which was later diagnosed as chronic fatigue syndrome. When I interviewed her she described herself as "being in remission," having just recovered from a significant relapse. She has attended a rehabilitation program that teaches both energy management strategies and cognitive behavioral strategies, which she found very useful. I asked her about what the fatigue actually feels like, her relationship with her body and the information it gives her, and how she now lives her life.

Chris: What does the start of the day feel like?

Sarah: I wake up at seven. For the first hour after I have woken up I feel like I have the worst hangover. I feel like I haven't slept even though I know I have. I feel sick, have a pounding headache, and my brain feels like it is cotton wool. But I know it will die down so I listen to the radio. It takes about an hour to pass.

Chris: Are you tempted to sleep again?

Sarah: It is not that I am tired and need to sleep; it is a different type of tired. It feels like I haven't slept, but sleep will make no difference. I don't need to sleep. It is exhaustion; not a lack of sleep. I say that it feels like I have not slept because that is the closest I can get to the sensation. I use *hangover* because it is like that. It is like I have been poisoned. But it passes.

Chris: Tell me about the most recent time you overdid it?

Sarah: One Saturday I was reasonably careful in the morning. I did some housework. I had an event on in the afternoon. I felt it was important to go. There were a lot of people there I knew but hadn't seen for a long time so there was energy in talking to them. Then it got to four o'clock and I started to feel pain in my lower back, then a headache, then I started to feel slightly fluey. But I ended up leaving at five o'clock and I had a chore to do on the way home. And yes: I completely misjudged it and it was too much, unfortunately, and I then felt really poorly. So I got home and had to just lie down.

Chris: What are the thoughts when that happens?

Sarah: "Oh, my God, I am so stupid. Why have I done this? Oh, I can't believe it." I start planning. Yes planning, planning, which is not very restful. That is often how it goes when I have overdone it and I have been rather foolish about it. I should have been more careful.

The feeling is like a profound exhaustion. Like my battery has just died. It is flashing on 1 percent. That is how it feels. I think that "I need to lie down this second." I can't think straight. I can just about hold a conversation. But it probably does not make much sense. I feel shaky.

(Continued)

Box 6.2. *Continued*

Chris: What happens to your judgment?

Sarah: Oh, that is quite impaired. I say to myself: "This is not the time to make decisions about what you are going to do. Just leave that." But I have had to learn to do that, because the decisions are either too emotional, or just not reasoned. It's like making a decision when you are drunk. You can't rely on it. It is not reasoned, it's not thought through. It's not going to be a sensible decision when you are that tired.

Chris: Are you an expert on your body now?

Sarah: Yes, I am. So there is a judgment call about how much can you tolerate before you have to step in and take control. But, on the whole, my body is normally right. And I should listen to it. That has certainly helped me to improve. It is hard to listen to your body at first. It is partly cultural. You push on through. You go to work. You try harder. So at first I couldn't understand why it wasn't working. I was trying but was getting worse. I was pushing. So I just ignored it. I ignored all these symptoms and carried on anyway. But gradually I understood that I had to listen to my body.

Chris: Do you trust the information your body gives you?

Sarah: Yes, that was a hard lesson to learn. I did not want to accept it. I absolutely did not. This is not who I am. To do so little is wrong, I believe. I am only young. I should be working full-time, I should be doing all the sport I want to do, that I used to do. And I should be going out with my friends. So I have had to learn. I have tried to push through. I have absolutely tried that. But it doesn't work. I had to learn to listen to my body. If it is telling me that it is not just tired, that it is ill, then I had to stop. So now I am good at reading it.

Chris: It sounds like a life without spontaneity.

Sarah: There is almost no spontaneity. There can't be. Everything is planned. Which is sad. It is probably not how I would choose to be. But it works. You kind of weigh it up. And now I don't really worry about it too much. You know: it's a trade-off.

Sarah lives a planful life closely managing the boundaries of what is possible when there is the ever-present threat of severe fatigue. For her the idea of working through fatigue is something she tried that did not work. She has a close relationship with her body as a source of information that tells her what is achievable. Unlike Kerry, however, Sarah trusts the information her body gives her and tries to follow it. Like Kerry, Sarah is an expert on fatigue and motivation. The fatigue she describes is similar to Kerry's: a strong urge to stop. The thoughts are hard, if not impossible, to ignore. She knows not to make hasty decisions and that being active and achieving is an important part of who she is, but it must be done now in the context of the threat of relapse from forgetting hard lessons learned.

Summary

Feeling tired is a common physical complaint. We often talk about feeling tired. Surprisingly, however, as a perception it is still poorly understood. The idea that feeling tired is a reliable sign of depletion in energy resource can be rejected as a fallacy. Instead, fatigue seems to function as a signal of the growing costs of persisting in behavior for too long, as a motivation to change behavior. It functions to interrupt current engagement with a fairly well-formed and hard-to-ignore belief that one should stop. In this sense fatigue operates to limit performance or achievement, especially when that elite performance is dependent on persistence and repetitive practice. Attempts to remove or alter that limit by artificial or natural means have not proven successful, with the possible exception of physical exercise and attempts at self-actualization, both of which, paradoxically, are effortful. We can learn a lot, however, from those who live their lives in chronic and severe fatigue, whether deliberately by engaging in endurance sport, or non-deliberately in struggling with chronic fatigue syndrome. In the extreme cases, what is at stake is how far one can go in ignoring the urge, or, more accurately, the *demand* to stop and switch.

Note

1. Reproduced from Angela L. Duckworth, Christopher Peterson, Michael D. Matthews, and Dennis R. Kelly, Grit: Perseverance and passion for long-term goals, *Journal of Personality and Social Psychology*, 96 (6), pp. 1087–1088, doi:10.1037/0022-3514.92.6.1087 © 2007, American Psychological Association.

References

Anderson, V.R., Jason, L.A., Hlaverty, L.E., Porter, N. and Cudia, J. (2012). A review and meta-synthesis of qualitative studies on myalgic encephalomyelitis/chronic fatigue syndrome. *Patient Education and Counseling*, 86, 147–155.

Arai, T. (1912). Mental fatigue. New York: Teachers College, Columbia University.

Arnold, L.M. (2008). Understanding fatigue in major depressive disorder and other medical disorders. *Psychosomatics*, 49, 185–190.

Bartone, P.T., Kelly D.R., Mathews M.D. (2013). Psychological hardiness predicts adaptability in military leaders: a prospective study. *International Journal of Selection and Assessment*, 21, 200–210.

Baumeister, R.F., Bratslavsky, E., Muraven, M. and Tice, D.M. (1998). Ego depletion: is the active self a limited resource? *Journal of Personality and Social Psychology*, 74, 1252–1265.

Bostic, T.J., McGartland Rubio, D. and Hood, M. (2000). A validation of the subjective vitality scale using structural equation modeling. *Social Indicators Research*, 52, 313–324.

Chang, Y.K., Labban, J.D., Gapin, J.I. and Etnier, J.L. (2012). The effects of acute exercise on cognitive performance: a meta-analysis. *Brain Research*, 1453, 87–101.

Chiesa, A., Calati, R. and Serretti, A. (2011). Does mindfulness training improve cognitive abilities? A systematic review of neuropsychological findings. *Clinical Psychology Review*, 31, 449–464.

Dantzer, R., Heijnen, C.J., Kavelaars, A., Laye, S. and Capuron, L. (2014). The neuroimmune basis of fatigue. *Trends in Neurosciences*, 37, 39–46.

Duckworth, A. and Gross, J.J. (2014). Self-control and grit: related but separable determinants of success. *Current Directions in Psychological Science*, 23, 319–325.

Duckworth, A.L., Peterson, C., Mathews, M.D. and Kelly, D.R. (2007). Grit: perseverance and passion for long-term goals. *Journal of Personality and Social Psychology*, 92, 1087–1101.

Fernandez-Duqu, D. and Johnson, M.L. (1999). Attention metaphors: how metaphors guide the cognitive psychology of attention. *Cognitive Science*, 23, 83–116.

Fry, A.M. and Martin, M. (1996). Fatigue in the chronic fatigue syndrome: a cognitive phenomenon? *Journal of Psychosomatic Research*, 41, 415–426.

Fukuda, K., Straus, S.E., Hickie, I., Sharpe, M.C., Dobbins, J.G. and Komaroff, A. International Chronic Fatigue Syndrome Study Group. (1994). The chronic fatigue syndrome: a comprehensive approach to its definition and study. *Annals of Internal Medicine*, 121, 953–959.

Gailliot, M.T. and Baumeister, R.F. (2007). The physiology of willpower: linking blood glucose to self-control. *Personality and Social Psychology Review*, 11, 303–327.

Glade, M.J. (2010). Caffeine–not just a stimulant. *Nutrition*, 26, 932–938.

Hefferon, K. (2013). Positive psychology and the body: the somatopsychic side to flourishing. Maidenhead: Open University Press.

Herrmann, U.S., Hess, C.W., Guggisberg, A.G., Roth, C., Gugger, M. and Mathis, J. (2010). Sleepiness is not always perceived before falling asleep in healthy sleep-deprived subjects. *Sleep Medicine*, 11, 747–751.

Hockey, R. (2013). The psychology of fatigue: work, effort and control. Cambridge: Cambridge University Press.

Holgate, S.T., Komaroff, A.L., Mangan, D. and Wesseley, S. (2011). Chronic fatigue syndrome: understanding a complex illness. *Nature Reviews Neuroscience*, 12, 539–544.

Horne, J. (2010). Sleepiness as a need for sleep: when is enough enough? *Neuroscience and Biobehavioral Reviews*, 34, 108–118.

Hou, R., Moss-Morris, R., Risdale, A., Lynch, J., Jeevaratnam, P., Bradley, B.P. and Mogg, K. (2014). Attention processes in chronic fatigue syndrome: attentional bias for health-related threat and the role of attentional control. *Behavior Research and Therapy*, 52, 9–16.

Huta, V. and Waterman, A.S. (2014). Eudaimonia and its distinction from hedonia: developing a classification and terminology for understanding conceptual and operational definitions. *Journal of Happiness Studies*, 15, 1425–1456.

Kirkevold, M., Christensen, D., Anderson, G., Johansen, S.P. and Harder, I. (2012). Fatigue after stroke: manifestations and strategies. *Disability and Rehabilitation*, 34, 665–670.

Kitamura, H., Shindu, M., Tachibana, A., Honma, H. and Someya, T. (2013). Personality and resilience associated with perceived fatigue of local government employees responding to disasters. *Journal of Occupational Health*, 55, 1–5.

Knoop, H., Prins, J.B., Moss-Morris, R. and Bleijenberg, G. (2010). The central role of cognitive processes in the perpetuation of chronic fatigue syndrome. *Journal of Psychosomatic Research*, 68, 489–494.

Kool, W. and Botvinick, M. (2014). A labor/leisure trade-off in cognitive control. *Journal of Experimental Psychology: General*, 143, 131–141.

Kurzban, R., Duckworth, A., Kable, J.W. and Myers, J. (2013). An opportunity cost model of subjective effort and task performance. *Behavioral and Brain Sciences*, 36, 661–726.

Lambert, N.M., Gwinn, A.M., Fincham, F.D. and Stillman, T.F. (2011). Feeling tired? How sharing positive experiences can boost vitality. *International Journal of Wellbeing*, 1, 307–314.

Lange, F. and Eggert, F. (2014) Sweet delusion. Glucose drinks fail to counteract ego depletion. *Appetite*, 75, 54–63.

Lerdal, A. and Gay, C.L. (2013). Fatigue in the acute phase after first stroke predicts poorer physical health 18 months later. *Neurology*, 81, 1581–1587.

Lewis, G. and Wessely, S. (1992). The epidemiology of fatigue: more questions than answers. *Journal of Epidemiology and Community Health*, 46, 92–97.

Loge, J.H., Ekeberg, Ø. and Kaasa, S. (1998). Fatigue in the general Norwegian population: normative data and associations. *Journal of Psychosomatic Research*, 45, 53–65.

Lukkahatai, N. and Saligan, L.N. (2013). Association of catastrophizing and fatigue: a systematic review. *Journal of Psychosomatic Research*, 74, 100–109.

Luyten, P., Kempke, S., Van Wambeke, P., Claes, S., Blatt, S.J. and Van Houdenhove, B. (2011). Self-critical perfectionism, stress generation, and stress sensitivity in patients with chronic fatigue syndrome: relationship with severity of depression. *Psychiatry*, 74, 21–30.

Martin, M. and Alexeeva, I. (2010). Mood volatility with rumination but neither attentional nor interpretation biases in chronic fatigue syndrome. *British Journal of Health Psychology*, 15, 779–796.

Maslow, A.H. (1971). The farther reaches of human nature. London: Penguin.

McAteer, A., Elliott, A.M. and Hannaford, P.C. (2011). Ascertaining the size of the symptom iceberg in a UK-wide community-based survey. *British Journal of General Practice*, 61, e1–e11.

Moss-Morris, R. and Petrie, K.J. (2003). Experimental evidence for interpretive but not attention biases towards somatic information in patients with chronic fatigue syndrome. *British Journal of Health Psychology*, 8, 195–208.

Muraven, M. and Baumeister, R.F. (2000). Self-regulation and depletion of limited resources: does self-control resemble a muscle? *Psychological Bulletin*, 126, 247–259.

Navon, D. (1984). Resources—a theoretical soup stone? *Psychological Review*, 91, 216–234.

Navon, D. (1989). The importance of being visible: on the role of attention in a mind viewed as an anarchic intelligence system. I. Basic tenets. *European Journal of Cognitive Psychology*, 1, 191–213.

Navon, D. (2013). Effort aversiveness may be functional, but does it reflect opportunity cost? *Behavioral and Brain Sciences*, 36, 701.

Owen, A.M., Hampshire, A., Grahn, J.A., Stenton, R., Dajani, S., Burns, A.S., Howard, R.J. and Ballard, C.G. (2010). Putting brain training to the test. *Nature*, 465, 775–778.

Pertl, M.M., Quigley, J. and Hevey, D. (2014). "I'm not complaining because I'm alive": barriers to the emergence of a discourse of cancer-related fatigue. *Psychology and Health*, 29, 141–161.

Rate, C.R., Clarke, J.A., Lindsay, D.R. and Sternberg, R.J. (2007). Implicit theories of courage. *The Journal of Positive Psychology*, 2, 80–98.

Reissig, C.J., Strain, E.C. and Griffiths, R.R. (2009). Caffeinated energy drinks—a growing problem. *Drug and Alcohol Dependence*, 99, 1–10.

Ricci, J.A., Chee, E., Lorandeau, A.L. and Berger, J. (2007). Fatigue in the US workforce: prevalence and implications for lost productive work time. *Journal of Occupational and Environmental Medicine*, 49, 1–10.

Ryan, R.M. and Frederick, C. (1997). On energy, personality, and health: subjective vitality as a dynamic reflection of well-being. *Journal of Personality*, 65, 529–565.

Ryan, R.M., Weinstein, N., Berstein, J., Brown, K.W., Mistretta, L. and Gagne, M. (2010). Vitalizing effects of being outdoors and in nature. *Journal of Environmental Psychology*, 30, 159–168.

Sepkowitz, K. (2013). Energy drinks and caffeine-related adverse effects. *JAMA*, 309, 243–244.

Smith, M.E. and Farah, M.J. (2011). Are prescription stimulants "smart pills"? The epidemiology and cognitive neuroscience of prescription stimulant use by normal healthy individuals. *Psychological Bulletin*. 137, 717–741.

Thorndike, E. (1899). Mental fatigue. *Science*, 9, 712–713.

Van der Linden D. (2011) The urge to stop: the cognitive and biological nature of acute mental fatigue. In P.L. Ackerman (Ed.), Cognitive fatigue: multidisciplinary perspectives on current research and future applications (pp. 149–164). Washington: American Psychological Association.

Wagner, L.I. and Cella, D. (2004). Fatigue and cancer: causes, prevalence and treatment approaches. *British Journal of Cancer*, 91, 822–828.

Wayne, P.M., Walsh, J.N., Taylor-Piliae, R.E., Wells, R.E., Papp, K.V., Donovan, N.J. and Yeh, G.Y. (2014). Effect of Tai Chi on cognitive performance in older adults: systematic review and meta-analysis. *Journal of the American Geriatrics Society*, 62, 25–39.

White, P.D., Goldsmith, K.A., Johnson, A.L., Potts, L., Walwyn, R., DeCesare, J.C.... and Sharpe, M. (2011). Comparison of adaptive pacing therapy, cognitive behavior therapy, graded exercise therapy, and specialist medical care for chronic fatigue syndrome (PACE): a randomised trial. *The Lancet*, 377, 823–836.

Wojcik, W., Armstrong, D. and Kanaan, R. (2011). Chronic fatigue syndrome: labels, meanings and consequences. *Journal of Psychosomatic Research*, 70, 500–504.

Yang, C.-M., Han, H.-Y., Yang, M.-H., Su, W.-C. and Lane, T. (2010). What subjective experiences determine the perception of falling asleep during sleep onset period? *Consciousness and Cognition*, 19, 1084–1092.

CHAPTER 7

PAIN

We are born in pain, we will most likely die in pain, and many of the significant events that punctuate the story of our lives (such as childbirth, illness,
or injury) occur in the presence of pain. The good news, however, is that as a species
we have become quite skilled at the science and practice of pain relief, from the preparation of pharmacological analgesics to the management of incurable pain. Pain is
perhaps one of the most challenging of the physical senses in that, like fatigue, it functions to halt, limit, or change behavior, but in doing so can challenge our very sense of
who we are and what is possible in life.

Although common, pain is most often temporary. For example, in an early
observational study in Ontario daycare center, 56 children ages three to seven were
observed throughout a school day. On average a child complained of pain every
20 minutes. The pain "booboos," as this Canadian team called them, created distress
lasting approximately ten seconds (Fearon et al., 1996). These fleeting pain experiences are part of how we are shaped, how we grow, and how we learn about our
environment. There is no suggestion that they should be removed or treated as aber-
rant. But not all pain experiences are short-lived, and not all have any obvious value.

To give some idea of the numbers: in a recent study of adults from eight European
countries, 70 percent reported a major pain experience in the last month, and 77 percent of them thought it serious enough to seek analgesia (Vowles et al., 2014). The
experience is not a uniquely adult one, either. Sara King and colleagues reviewed
epidemiological studies on pain in childhood, and found high prevalence rates, with
headache being the most common, closely followed by abdominal and musculoskeletal pain (King et al., 2011). Although many of these individual experiences of pain are
clinically uncomplicated, and perhaps psychologically insignificant, some people go
on to have disabling chronic pain. In one large survey of over 46,000 adults in Europe,
as many as 19 percent of the sample reported their pain to have lasted longer than six
months, half of whom said it was constant (Breivik et al., 2006).

What do we mean when we say we are in pain? In this chapter I explore the way
we have come to think of pain as a problem to be fixed. I also take the opportunity to
discuss what little there is on the rather strange idea that pain might in some cases be
experienced as positive, or at least as a bearable cost in the pursuit of a greater gain.
Last I introduce the idea of a *normal psychology of pain* that extends a nonpathological
account of pain behavior. Adopting a normal psychological approach allows us to

make sense of how people behave when the pain becomes countercultural (cannot be fixed); how one adapts to a life lived against the backdrop of the constant interruption by the threat of pain.

Three people offered to share their experiences of pain in extremes. First, Ilana and Crispin are both amateur runners. They decided to run the New York City Marathon together and they agreed to think about their pain while doing it and share their experience with me. I also talked with Rupert who has had low back pain for over 20 years. He rarely talks about it, but agreed to help me make sense of how it has changed his life.

The problem of pain

The International Association for the Study of Pain defines pain as "an unpleasant sensory and emotional experience associated with actual or potential tissue damage, or described in terms of such damage" (Merskey and Bogduk, 1994; see http://www.iasp-pain.org/taxonomy). This definition recognizes three psychological realities of pain: first, that it is an immediately aversive emotional experience; second, that it is a subjective sensation that acts in reference to presumed physical trauma; and third, that it is social—pain communicates in a language of damage. In recent updates of the definition, the communication aspect has been developed to include nonverbal expressions of pain, primarily because of a concern that an emphasis on language allows for a denial of pain in those who are unable to verbalize.

This definition of pain, although successful in capturing pain as immediately aversive, physically referenced, and fundamentally social, is unsuccessful because it is silent about the function of pain. Pain functions primarily to alarm about a threat to physical integrity. It alarms to promote escape, avoidance, succor, or repair; by definition, it is threatening (Eccleston and Crombez, 1999). This threatening aspect of pain—or, for short, its *threat value*—is how it achieves interruption of current thought and action. When pain strikes, it starts a psychological chain reaction of first displacing whatever is in consciousness, such as thinking about your next meal or carrying on a conversation, and directs attention to the location of the pain, simultaneously promoting behavior that will remove the pain from your attention. It is this functional perspective that provides a springboard for a consideration of "the normal psychology of pain" explored here.

Pain mechanisms

There are different ways of classifying pain. One common system is by location (e.g., musculoskeletal vs. visceral vs. head pain). Another is by presumed mechanism. Fernando Cervero (2008) describes three types of pain based on the presumed mechanisms of inflammation (inflammatory), nerve damage (neuropathic), or the action of the peripheral nociceptors (nociceptive).

Pain can start in the periphery or can be centrally generated. Nociceptors—nerve cells specialized for the identification of damage or the threat of damage—have been mapped in most, although not all, tissue, are abundant in skin, in muscle and connective tissue, and are also present in specific structures such as the eye and the tooth. There are large gaps in nociceptor distribution and not all damage is identified; in particular, the changes in viscera. Nociceptors are often defined as "high-threshold" in that they respond at the higher levels of energy intensity (e.g., bright light, high pressure, high or low heat), and some are "polymodal" in that their free nerve endings will react to noxious input from a range of modalities (pressure, heat, chemical). They also operate at different transduction speeds through both slow unmyelinated C fibers and fast myelinated Aδ fibers, bearing some responsibility for the different qualia of throbbing dull pain and sharp stabbing pain, respectively. The idea, however, that pain can be explained fully by the function of peripheral sensory mechanisms has been long rejected. We have learned that pain experiences are dynamic, subject to change by both peripheral and central sensitization.

Spinal, brainstem, thalamic, and cortical systems are all involved in the further modulation of nociception. The brain has no "pain center." Pain is distributed across multiple structures, many of which are involved in non-pain activity such as orienting, attending, expecting, motor preparation, memory, interpretation, anxiety, and even higher-order emotional functions such as empathy, planning, and decision making. The involvement of multiple structures has led some to propose a "pain matrix" or interconnected pattern of structures involved in pain. This idea, has, however, been more recently cast aside, described by some as only a comforting myth (Canavero and Bonicalzi, 2014). Valery Legrain and colleagues argue that what we see in neuroimaging studies of pain may be better explained as the operation of a salience detection mechanism. They consider pain within the context of a larger defensive system (Legrain et al, 2011). Emerging is a dynamic view of pain operating within a broad salience detection system: not one mechanism, but multiple systems that select (and deselect) action in complex environments. Aaron Kucyi and Karen Davis from Toronto propose that we should think of pain as a "dynamic connectome": a mass of interrelated, constantly changing saliencies in response to environmental demands and individual differences (Kucyi and Davis, 2015).

Motivated interruption

Reframing pain as part of a salience detection system, functioning for the defense of the whole organism, is more radical than it first appears. A focus on the alarming qualities of pain suggests new targets for treatment development, both pharmacological and psychological, with a focus on altering attention rather than sensation. It also leads to novel explanations for why pain can become chronic, as we try to understand what maintains pain as a priority for selection over competing environmental priorities (Borsook et al., 2013).

Of course pain is more complex than a simple alarm system. But a focus on attention to threat allows us to view pain from the perspective of what it stops us from doing (Vlaeyen and Linton, 2000; Crombez, et al., 2012). To understand what makes pain salient, one needs to understand the motivational context in which pain emerges and is maintained, a context that is often changing, has multiple, competing, and sometimes contradictory goals, and a context that can change at the will of the person. Whether you accept, deny, distract, endure, catastrophize, or seek to change the meaning of pain, all make a difference. The context of interruption matters. Whether the pain is from an injury that can be fatal if not treated, or from complaining muscles as you are about to achieve a personal best in your sport, will fundamentally change the experience.

Pain that is not experienced as threatening is hard to achieve, but perhaps not impossible. There are communities of activity within which pain is constructed as either positive, necessary, or both. Three examples are instructive. The first is a religious view that constructs pain as a necessary part of suffering, which is itself an unavoidable consequence of humanity. The second is pain as a source of pleasure in activities described as transcendent or transgressive. And the third is a pragmatic view of pain as a useful source of information in the pursuit of a higher goal of excellence or survival.

Religion

C.S. Lewis, known to most as the writer of children's classics such as *The Chronicles of Narnia*, was also, in his later life, a committed Christian who chose to position pain as ultimately positive in dragging people back from worldly distraction. In *The Problem of Pain*—which might better have been called *A Defense of Suffering*—he argues that "pain insists on being attended to. God whispers to us in our pleasures, speaks in our conscience, but shouts in our pain: it is his megaphone to rouse a deaf world."[1] This Christian apologia, written during the Second World War, is an unusual defense of pain, and to the modern ear difficult to understand. However, although this particular form of the defense of suffering as a consequence of human shame (in the fall from grace) is far from most people's understanding of pain, it is interesting that it is possible to understand these ideas even in our modern cultures: it retains the power to resonate.

Elaine Scarry extends an analysis of the central place of pain and suffering in Jewish and Christian belief. In *The Body in Pain*, she explores the central aspect of embodiment. The Old Testament God is without form, and the corporeality of humanity is exactly a means to live in weakness and to suffer punishment. Indeed, in modern English *pain* takes the Latin form of *poena*; literally, punishment or penalty: the price that must be paid. Scarry describes this tension over physical form in the Old Testament:

> God's invisible presence is asserted, made visible, in the perceivable alterations He brings about in the human body: in the necessity of human labour and the pains of childbirth, in a flood that drowns, in a plague that descends on a house, in the brimstone and fire falling down on a city, in the transformation of a woman into a pillar of salt, in the leprous sores and rows of boils that alter the surface of the skin, in an invasion of insects and reptiles into the home of a population, in a massacre of babies, in a ghastly hunger that causes a people to so glut themselves on quail that meat comes out of their nostrils, in a mauling by bears, in an agonizing disease of the bowels, and so on, on and on.[2]

The fleshiness of mankind is, from an Old Testament view, both the cause and source of suffering. The Christian narrative extends this focus on pain with the emergence of God's son as embodied and so the focus of pain and suffering. Although there is a radical transformation from the God of anger and punishment of the Old Testament to a God of love and forgiveness in the New Testament, the place of pain as a bodily source of punishment for the weak, heinous, and unbelieving remains stubbornly in place.

The remnants of these ideas are still with us. Pain as a price to pay in necessary suffering can be found in measures of beliefs about pain. For example, Noreen Glover-Graf and her colleagues in Texas surveyed patients with pain, some of whom endorsed beliefs such as "I am grateful to God or a Spiritual Power that I have my painful condition" and "I believe that my painful condition is a punishment for wrongdoings that I have committed" (Glover-Graf et al., 2007, p. 29). In studies on general coping, one also finds religious beliefs and practices implicated in the attempts people make to cope with pain. Praying and relying on faith in God, for example, are commonly found in measures of adaptation to pain and disability (Robinson et al., 1997).

José Closs and her colleagues in the United Kingdom, experts in meta-synthesis of qualitative data, undertook a systematic review of studies investigating religious identity and chronic pain. They deliberately extended the search for studies beyond Christian beliefs to Muslim, Hindu, Jewish, and Sikh beliefs, but were frustrated in their search, finding virtually no studies in non-Christian populations. Within the studies of Christian communities, they could also find no consensus on the dominance of particular beliefs, although it is clear that in modern life people can and do construct pain as a redemptive price to pay, and are able at times to cast it as positive (Closs et al, 2013).

Rites of passage

Secular narratives also exist that structure pain as potentially positive. It is possible to talk about pain as educative, teaching one about one's strengths and weaknesses, or as transformative, altering one's perspective on life. Consider the *rite of passage*, the change in individual status within a collective. Often transitions in status are marked by public social practices, many of which involve an ordeal and a display of emotion, often in a trial of endurance to unpleasant events such as shame, embarrassment, and, surprisingly often, of pain. In her analysis of female initiation rites in 75 societies, Judith Brown finds that painful initiation rites, typically genital operations, are performed largely as form of coercion into gender-specific roles for both men and women (Brown, 1963). Alan Morinis explores pain as part of initiation rites for adolescents. It is perhaps better in his own words:

> Reports tell of initiands being beaten, bitten, starved, incised, scarified, pierced, tattooed, terrified, mutilated, circumcized, infibulated, cicatrized, bound, and subject to the removal of parts of their bodies (especially teeth and fingers). It will be unnecessary for present purposes to provide a full compendium of the tortures and mutilations humans have invented to try their young, as the practices are well documented. . . . The record clearly shows that the delivery of a consistent, deliberate, direct experience of pain to participants in the ritual is a remarkably recurrent aspect of adolescent initiations.[3]

The role of pain in such initiation, Morinis argues, is not punishment but a sacrifice of autonomy in transitioning to a larger group identity. The public submission to, and endurance of, pain operates as a sign of acceptance and readiness to conform—or perhaps just surrender. Further, it functions to promote self-awareness by removing innocence, safety, and security, forcing young people to experience what they fear. Morinis argues that the presence of pain in practices that mark transition have specific functions that are positively framed—if not for the individual, then for the group or society. He does not argue that the experience of pain as unpleasant is changed. On the contrary, in this context the pain should be hard to endure, endured in public, and even celebrated.

Self-injury

Not celebrated, and a more private experience of mutilation, is the pain that occurs with self-injurious, nonsuicidal behavior such as self-cutting, strangulation, or bruising. The study of the phenomenology of self-injury relies on self-report after the event, but it is often associated, as pain in ritual can be, with the *absence* of pain report, and a sense of depersonalization (Nock, 2010). The advent of event-sampling techniques, in which people report on what they are feeling remotely at the time of the event, is allowing us access to experiences previously hidden.

Edward Selby and colleagues reported such a study with a focus on motivations for harming. The two main reasons given for repeated self-injury are to distract from hurtful thoughts and feelings, and to attempt to feel something—anything—in those who report being emotionally numb. In their clinical study of 30 adolescents, Selby and colleagues found that many of the adolescents wanted to feel pain because it was a relief from an absence or emptiness of feeling, and a commonly reported source of "satisfaction" (Selby et al., 2014). In this very particular context of extreme emotional dysregulation, injury that is avoidable and deliberately self-inflicted is associated with complex positive experiences.

Brock Bastian and his colleagues have argued that the feelings of satisfaction and control associated with abnormal practices such as deliberate self-harm may have their origins in features of a pain experience normal to us all. They argue that *relief* from pain is a critical pleasure, indeed a necessary part of pleasure: pain has the ability not only to provide pleasure in its offset but also to enhance that pleasure. Table 7.1 summarizes the variety of ways they consider pain to be linked to pleasure. Further, they intriguingly extend the argument offered by Alan Morinis, that pain serves to mature an awareness of meaning, relevance, and social order. In its modern version, Bastian and colleagues suggest that one is immediately more self-rewarding (self-comforting) if one has pain that is judged to be unfairly inflicted. On a much broader level, they argue that pain educates—or, more accurately, perhaps—that it has the capacity to edify (Bastian et al., 2014). This challenge to our view of pain as uncomplicatedly negative is an interesting check on our cultural analgesic tendencies. We tend to think of pain as always aversive and unwelcome. Pain can function in different ways, some of which are in the promotion of pleasure.

Goal pursuit

Pain at your own hands, or hurting so much that you can feel pleasure when it stops, are philosophically interesting, but rare experiences. What is common is the experience of pain that we believe to be an unavoidable part of a process of attempting to attain a higher-order goal. There are many goals that supersede the avoidance of pain. They include the natural (e.g., childbirth), the protective (e.g., inoculation), the aesthetic (e.g., depilation, surgery, tattooing, piercing), and the emergency. In many cases, pain is endurable because it is considered safe and brief, as in wax depilation. However, for other activities, deciding whether the pain is endurable, or worth enduring, is an ongoing, personal, cost-benefit analysis.

Endurance sport provides an environment for exploring the trade-off between pain and achievement. In one study of 114 amateur marathon contestants, the runners reported their beliefs at different stages of the race. They remembered weighing up the costs of pain against the benefits of completing the race, and this analysis peaked at 30 kilometers into

Table 7.1: The benefits of pain and associated processes

Benefit	Process
1. Pain facilitates pleasure	
i. Pain enhances subsequent pleasure	Pain provides a contrast for pleasure, and this increases the relative pleasantness of subsequent experiences.
ii. Pain heightens sensory sensitivity	Pain heightens arousal and constrains attention on sensory experience, thereby increasing sensory receptivity.
iii. Pain facilitates pleasure seeking	Pain provides a justification for indulgence of pleasures that might otherwise arouse a sense of guilt.
2. Pain enables self-regulation and enhancement	
i. Pain increases cognitive-affective control	Pain captures attention and brings cognitive resources online for effective problem solving in response to the threat of pain.
ii. Pain enables identity management	Pain promotes a physical experience of the self, thereby reducing high-level self-awareness and enabling identity change.
iii. Pain demonstrates virtue	Pain may be interpreted as providing a symbolic test of a range of personal virtues.
3. Pain promotes affiliation	
i. Pain arouses empathy in others	The expression of pain increases empathy and arouses care concern in others.
ii. Pain increases relational focus	People seek social support in response to pain. Pain therefore provides a novel source of social connection with others.
iii. Pain increases solidarity	Pain may be used to increase the value of relational ties with others, and shared pain may increase interpersonal bonding.

Reproduced from Brock Bastian, Jolanda Jetten, Matthew J. Hornsey, and Siri Leknes, The Positive Consequences of Pain: A Biopsychosocial Approach, Personality and Social Psychology Review, 18 (3), pp. 256–279, Table 1, doi:10.1177/1088868314527831 Copyright © 2014 by SAGE Publications. Reprinted by Permission of SAGE Publications.

the 42.2 kilometer race (Brandstätter and Schüler, 2013). Interestingly, this peak point, what Brandstätter and Schüler call an *action crisis*, does not occur at the end of the race. The last phase of an amateur marathon appears to be marked, at least for those who finish, by an extreme motivational drive. In a study of why distance runners collapse at the finish line, and collapse in the same anatomical pattern, the question of why people persist in the last quarter and persist right to the line is not asked (St. Clair Gibson et al., 2013).

What is the place of the felt experience of pain in the dynamic trade-off of competing goals: finishing vs. stopping the pain? How does enduring pain retain its value of "a price worth paying"? To explore these ideas of the dynamic trade-off of pain as sometimes positive and worth enduring, I recruited the help of two amateur marathon runners who had just run the New York City Marathon together, Ilana and Crispin Wigfield (Box 7.1).

Box 7.1. The Wigfields, running a marathon together: *"what I often do is think 'one more mile'"*

Ilana entered as the experienced runner, having already finished eight marathons. For Crispin, this was his first. They had taken mental notes and tried to record their feelings on a digital recorder as they went along. We talked after the race, about how they had felt at each mile marker point. I was interested in what the pain felt like, what thoughts they were having, and how it affected their motivation. The race didn't go to plan. Which races ever do? Ilana was struggling with an injury and Crispin was in self-confessed "unknown territory."

Chris: Was it as you expected it to be?

Ilana: Well, it hurt. But you are expecting it to hurt. It is rather like childbirth. It is something you are anticipating and there is a positive outcome at the end of it. But it is not something you can't deal with. You just do. And you know it will end. It has a finite time. It depends on how much you are willing to put up with.

Crispin: It was my first marathon and I went in with the mindset that it might be the only marathon I do. I spent a lot of time researching and trying to anticipate what it would be like.

Chris: And what surprised you?

Crispin: Every now and again there was a rise in anxiety and a feeling of despair. The long avenues are a challenge. Nobody had talked about the long avenues in Brooklyn.

Chris: Tell me about the pain.

Crispin: My pain was very low at the beginning, 5 out of 100. For the first 10 miles or so the pain was never more than a slight ache. There was no ache anywhere else, no chest pain. It hardly registered as pain. I started to struggle at mile 21 going uphill again to another bridge. Just knowing it is a long way. And I think at that point that my feet were beginning to hurt a bit. It is farther than I have ever run before. That thought does come. Also, at that point you are starting to see a lot of people walking and stopping with cramp, which is anxiety provoking. I thought, "Is it going to be me next, is it going to happen?" So it was not just pain but it was a buzz of anxiety.

(Continued)

Box 7.1. *Continued*

Ilana: It was sore. At 12 miles it was 5 out of 10 and I felt desperate. At mile 20 I was thinking, "Gracious, this hurts." I felt I had to keep going. What I often do is think "one more mile." I can keep it going and see how it is after the mile. It got to a point and never got any worse, so I then thought, This is it, just one more mile. I did not hit a wall in terms of difficulties of cognition. It was just pain. It was probably at 17 miles and it carried on. At 22, 23 it was just pain.

Chris: Did you think of stopping?

Ilana: No. But I thought to myself frequently: "I don't need to do this anymore, I don't need to do more marathons, I don't enjoy this anymore. There is no point in doing more." And the disappointment was in not doing as well as I have done in previous marathons. "What is the point of carrying on?" There was a lot of that negativity going on at the time. And running on an injury, I thought, "Oh dear, what a stupid thing to do. This is really going to set me back. Whose idea was this? I am not going to be able to run for months." There was a lot of worry. It got less as I went on and the pain did not get worse. But yes, there was quite a lot of worry.

Crispin: At mile 22, on Fifth Avenue, any communication between us had just shut down. I contemplated getting the dictaphone out to make notes but it was just too hard. I concentrated on just running, not falling over, not doing something that would just hold me up. Not walking, because if I started walking I would not start running again. About then someone in front of me stopped abruptly to take a telephone call and I nearly ran into them! It was then I knew I was off the pace so I tried to put some extra effort in and nothing happened, which was slightly alarming, and at mile 23 it was unpleasant and I could see that my time was getting slower and slower and slower. At 23 it was disappointment not pain. There were a lot of people walking at that point and a lot of people looking at me. The thought I had was "I want to finish and I want to finish well." I was very aware that any little thing could just ruin it.

Chris: What motivated you to finish?

Crispin: The crowds are just fantastic. There is a motivation boost, an extra rush. It is exciting to see so many people raising money for good causes and to be a part of that. Motivation was hard and I started to think about the people who had sponsored me. At mile 24 you enter the park and I was drained. I had nothing left. The crowd was great at pushing you along. Round about mile 25 it was getting cold in the shade; I had had enough; I was ready for it to finish.

Ilana: The main motivation for keeping going is that I don't like giving up on anything. If I was going to give up I should not have done it in the first place. I should have given up early, not at 20 miles.

Chris: It sounds like a marathon is as much a motivational challenge as a physical one.

Ilana: Yes, you do think about other things like hoping the children are having a nice day, and the beautiful scenery, but as it goes on maybe 50 to 70 percent of my attention was spent thinking about my body and the pain.

Box 7.1. *Continued*

Crispin: Yes, by the end I was just aware of how I was feeling, and the finish line. It was hard work then. But we crossed the line together.

Pain in the context of a marathon is one part of multiple challenges. But sampling two people's very different experience across a long exposure to pain shows that the pain was always being judged against the possibility of success, of avoiding failure in withdrawal, and of drawing support from other motivations like the crowd and the scenery. As it goes on, however, pain takes up more space and comes to dominate. Unexplored is the social display of endurance in pain, which, although not a rite of passage, is a public ordeal. Pain as a private mental event is displayed in public, with one's response to it open to private and public judgment.

Paying attention to pain

Finding value in pain—either in overcoming it to achieve positive goals such as finishing a marathon, or in its public endurance in a rite of passage—are rare experiences. These positive frames take effort to create and sustain; they involve much personal and cultural work. By far the most dominant experience of pain is of the *intrusion* of an unwelcome, aversive, threatening, hard-to-ignore bodily event, one that increases anxiety and challenges our motivation to achieve other goals. In short: pain interrupts, worries, and disrupts.

The positive experiences of pain, although very different, share one feature: the meaning of the pain is known. However, the meaning of most pain is at first *not* known, and the extent to which it persists in interrupting, worrying, and disrupting is related to the search for meaning and for how long the search continues. David Morris captures this well when he says that humans have always approached pain as something to be explained, as a conundrum (Morris, 1991). Delia Cioffi extended a similar argument. All physical sensations start with attention, but then very quickly they demand interpretation. This interpretation begins with a simple verbal labeling and then leads quickly to an attribution, a belief about the cause. This labeling and interpretation are open to influence from prior experience, from anxiety, and from other people's beliefs (Cioffi, 1991). More simply put: we want to know what the pain means and what threat it poses. For example, imagine that as you are sitting reading when you have a sudden pain in your chest. Is it meaningless? Is it a cramp from not moving enough? Or are you having a heart attack? The interpretation you choose will lead to very different defensive behaviors (Eccleston and Crombez, 2007).

Psychologists have been busy developing ways to measure different forms of anxious responses when in pain. In one study, we asked 508 adults to complete the most popular nine measures of anxiety used in pain research, including the Pain Catastrophizing Scale (Sullivan et al., 1995). Collapsing across all measures, we showed a latent three-part structure that underpins the experience of threat when pain is attended to: we labeled the parts *cognitive intrusion, general distress,* and *fear of pain from injury/illness* (Mounce et al., 2010). These three interrelated constructs might account for how the context of pain determines the overall experience. For some, the intrusion upon our thinking is itself highly aversive and hard to disengage from. For others, pain promotes a general, global sense of distress. For others still, the interruption of pain is taken as evidence for exactly what was feared all along: a catastrophic illness or injury is causing the pain (Vlaeyen and Linton, 2000).

Living in an analgesic culture

The simplest example of pain, perhaps the pain experienced by children in the playground every 20 minutes, is when it is normative. By normative I mean that it is culturally typical and follows the tacit rules we have for pain. We live in an analgesic culture, defined by the dominant belief that pain should be short-lived, diagnostically meaningful, and denote a fixable problem (Morris, 1991).

Some people find casting pain aside harder than others. For example, we developed a measure of the experience of cognitive intrusion in those without a clinical pain problem called the Cognitive Intrusion Scale. As the name suggests, we were interested in the extent to which people experience pain interruption ("Pain easily captures my thinking"), persistence ("I keep thinking about pain"), and dominance ("It is hard to think about anything else but pain") (Attridge et al., in press). Those who have this pattern are indeed more disrupted in their daily lives. The repeated work of labeling sensations, interpreting them as nonthreatening, and returning to previously interrupted goals and tasks takes time and effort.

What keeps people focused on pain is the subject of much research. Fear of pain as a source of distress is thought to be the cause of both a risk of pain-related disability and of avoidance of activity. The fear can be of the pain itself (e.g., "having a muscle cramp") (McNeil et al., 1998, p. 407) or that pain will lead to damage (e.g., "physical activity might be harmful") (Buer and Linton, 2002, p. 487). These fears are common in the population and not specific to patients. Friends, family, carers, and health care professionals often believe that pain is a reason to withdraw and rest, when for many people with chronic musculoskeletal pain the opposite would be more helpful. (Simmonds et al., 2012). For example, in a study we undertook with mothers of adolescents with chronic pain, we saw exactly the dilemma that those who care for others can have. We created an experiment in which mothers could watch their children taking part in painful rehabilitation. Mothers seeing their children in pain during activity understandably wanted the therapy to stop, even when they knew that the pain was part a higher goal of rehabilitation, and their child had chosen to do it (Caes et al., 2011, Study 2). When we act protectively, for others and ourselves, we are acting normatively. Our analgesic culture prioritizes escape from pain first and always.

Pain that won't go away

What is surprising about this analgesic culture we inhabit, and the normative expectations of pain it promotes, is that it persists despite the overwhelming evidence that the rules of pain we hold are frequently inadequate, false, or damaging. Scientific and experiential data show repeatedly that often pain is not diagnostically helpful, often pain emerges without explanation, often pain cannot be fixed, and all too often pain does not go away.

The large study of the population prevalence of pain in Europe found that one in five adults reported chronic pain (Breivik et al., 2006). However, these are average rates; they are more than twice as high in the older population (Johannes et al., 2010). In fact, chronic pain has developed into a major public health problem in many societies. Winfried Häuser led an investigation of chronic pain prevalence in Germany and helpfully focused on the broader impact on disability and distress. Comorbid disease, depression, and social inequality, indexed by employment, housing and family status, all had a contributory role to play in exacerbating the consequences of pain (Häuser et al., 2014). There is no suggestion that these factors are causal for pain and disability; rather, they significantly accelerate the impact of chronic pain. Given that most postindustrialized populations are aging, we should expect the population burden of chronic pain to increase. In an interesting summary, Stephen Gibson and David Lussier commented that we are unprepared and unplanned. It looks like we will struggle to meet the needs of the expanding pain population (Gibson and Lussier, 2012).

Trying to cope alone

However unprepared we may be for pain, we still try to find a solution, try to cope. I prefer a broad definition of coping as any attempt made in response to the stress of pain (Tunks and Bellissimo, 1988). In this sense coping is always active. Even when people are avoiding, praying, accepting, or distracting, these are often effortful and mindful attempts to escape from pain or its consequences. Not all attempts to cope with pain fail, but we know little about how people with chronic pain who do not present to health care settings manage their pain. For many people with chronic pain, attempts at escaping its negative consequences can actually increase suffering. When faced with inexplicable pain, many people persevere with attempts to find meaning. Indeed, patients often find it difficult to accept pain that cannot be explained (Martin et al., 2014), and often experience the idea of acceptance as surrender (Risdon et al., 2003).

For many chronic pain patients, three distinct patterns of behavior emerge, all of which are extreme versions of normal defensive behavior. Paradoxically, these patterns often achieve the opposite of what they were intended to achieve, propelling people into further suffering. First, being vigilant for pain and signals of impending pain can become a problem all by itself. Second, worry over the possible causes and consequences of pain can cease to be useful and can become a further independent source of distress. And third, when attempts to solve the problem are not effective, knowing when to persevere with the same tactic or when to try something new can be very confusing: often those with chronic pain wait too long to disengage from strategies that are not working.

Vigilance

If pain demands your attention because it might signal damage, when is it OK to not pay attention to it? For many people who experience a lot of pain, it makes sense to become vigilant. It is like being in a dangerous environment. For example, if you are on a battlefield, vigilance to the shout of a confederate may be life-saving. You learn to be more aware, not to ignore the signals of danger. Many chronic pain patients show the same learned pattern of heightened vigilance, in which the threshold for being interrupted by signals of possible danger is lowered (Crombez et al., 2004). This vigilance effect has been examined as a form of stable *attentional bias* in experimental studies. A meta-analysis of 50 of these studies found evidence for altered attention as a mechanism of chronic pain. Interestingly, there were no effects in those with naturally occurring acute pain, or in pain-free participants subjected to pain—just those with chronic pain (Crombez et al., 2013). For people who live with the threat of pain, attending toward signals that the pain might increase becomes habitual. Whether this habit of chronic attending is helpful has not yet been properly explored. It may emerge that it is ultimately a helpful strategy, or might be a cognitive fault line that lies behind the unpleasant experience of intrusion and repair in attending.

Distraction, a common strategy for coping with acute pain, is the opposite of vigilance. When the pain is short-lived—for example, during an injection for inoculation—deliberately attending away from pain can be helpful. But when the pain is chronic, attempting to attend away from it all the time can be fatiguing, fuel helplessness, because it so often fails, and can obstruct the learning of other techniques. This is not an unconscious process: people are very often aware of this pattern of attending. For example, we followed 62 chronic pain patients over a two-week period and periodically asked them about their pain. Many patients report attempts at distracting themselves from the pain, with varying degrees of success. Distraction is often a failed strategy in the management of chronic illness, but it is one that people hold in high regard. Even though it does not work, we often believe it does. This is perhaps more to do with a belief about how one should be rather than how one is—a pain-coping stereotype, perhaps. All over the world there are people attempting not to think about pain and growing increasingly distressed when it cannot be banished but persists as a threat.

Worry

Where there is threat there is a plan to avoid it. For some chronic pain patients, however, the ever-present threat and planning to avoid it are experienced as *worry*, which can become an added problem. Talking about worry is always fraught with linguistic danger. *Worry* is a meager word that has connotations of an avoidable neuroticism, or moral judgment; it is rarely thought about positively. There is, however, a positive story to tell about worry as a fundamentally helpful aspect of human psychology. Worry should be thought of, in the context of pain, as a normal response to threat. Consider what problems would ensue if we did not worry about pain in ourselves or others. Worry is often purposeful, active, and adaptive. It helps us prioritize; it makes us take pain seriously (Aldrich et al., 2000).

We were interested in exactly what it was that pain patients spent time worrying about, and what the experience of that worry was like in comparison to other sources of worry. Again using a diary method, we asked 34 chronic pain patients, over a seven-day period, to record each time they realized they were worrying. They also recorded the content of that worry and qualitative aspects such as how intrusive, dismissible, or distressing it was. The patients reported 473 discrete episodes of worry in the week, of which 271 were about pain. The worries lasted approximately 20 minutes each. The most common cause of worry was medical uncertainty linked with uncertainty about the future and fear of disability. One person reported:

> My most common worry is: will the pain ever go or will it continue on and off for the rest of my life, possibly getting worse? It already stops me from doing major exercise and reduces the amount of effort I can put into playing with my children and gardening.[4]

Not only does the pain interrupt and persist, but so too does the worry about its cause and consequence. For many patients this pattern of rumination around pain exacerbates distress and makes one vulnerable to a more far-reaching depression (Linton et al., 2011). Letting go of this worry, however, is very hard to achieve without therapy. For many patients, stopping the planning for a cure feels like defeat. Clumsy suggestions of not worrying about pain or accepting it are typically experienced as punishing. We found that patients endorsed a strong belief that they had to battle for the legitimacy of their concerns and this strengthened the framing of their problem as curable (Eccleston et al., 1997); a findings that is repeatedly reported (Froud et al., 2014).

Courageous engagement

The fear avoidance model introduced by Johan Vlaeyen and Steven Linton in 2000 was enormously helpful in shifting research away from presumed patient psychopathology and onto the normal function of pain as threatening. It helped us put into context why people behave as they do when in pain. What seemed like unusual behaviors of people persevering with strategies that have brought only misery make sense when one realizes that pain urges action. Better to keep doing something that does not work than do nothing. A consequence, however, of the dominance of the fear-avoidance model has been the focus on persistence as nearly always negative. Even in our own model of worry and problem solving, perseverance is presented negatively (Eccleston and Crombez, 2007).

Stefaan Van Damme and Hanne Kindermans have attempted to redress the balance and ask us to think about persistence in its motivational context. They use a language of self-regulation, referring to how we constantly update multiple goals. For them, persistence or avoidance can only be made sense of within the context of meaningful goals (Van Damme and Kindermans, 2015)

What is needed perhaps is less a theory of fear avoidance, and more a theory of courageous engagement. What matters in chronic pain, as we saw with endurance athletes, is what the costs of approaching or avoiding pain might be. One also witnesses patients engaging bravely with pain in the pursuit of a valued goal, or in the belief that that pursuit will lead to lasting analgesia. Unfortunately, many attempts are misdirected or lead to further distress and disability. But not all. And the action of engagement can itself be rewarding (Hasenbring et al., 2009). Nicole Andrews and her colleagues recently reviewed studies of engaging and avoiding patterns of reacting to chronic pain. They attempted to tease apart the findings hiding within different studies on pacing, activity, and coping. They did find the expected result that avoidance of activity is related to greater pain and disability. However, they also found hints that endurance may not always bring negative outcomes (Andrews et al., 2012).

The person in chronic pain is like an endurance athlete. They make repeated trade-off decisions about how much pain is tolerable in the context of achieving other goals. Some people endure, persist, worry, and plan their lives to achieve what is meaningful for them despite the constant presence of pain. However, many do not. Trying to find the best method of solving the problem of chronic pain, of coping, either alone or within a family, is a challenging and equally chronic task.

To explore these ideas further, I talked to Rupert Fingest (Box 7.2).

Box 7.2. Rupert, living with chronic pain: *"I will always push through if what I am doing is worth it"*

Rupert is a journalist in his late 40s. When he was twenty he was in a road traffic accident in which the car he was travelling in was hit by a firetruck attending an incident. He has chronic low-back and hip pain. Despite multiple interventions, the pain never left. He stopped searching for a cure in his 20s. He is now 46. He describes himself as tenacious and uncompromising.

Chris: How would you describe the pain?

Rupert: It is mostly a dull ache that is always there. On bad days the volume goes up and starts to block everything else out, but normally it is like background noise. More irritating than anything else.

Chris: People often talk about pain as distracting. Is that true?

Rupert: Yes, that is true. But pain is a funny distractor. Sometimes it is hard to think about anything else, but most of the time it just lurks in the background and occasionally jumps out! So it is distracting when it pushes itself on me, but otherwise it is only distracting if I go looking for it.

Chris: Why did you stop looking for a cure?

Rupert: After a while you have to realize that you are searching in vain. I would go and see doctors and they would fidget and look away and in the end I realized that they were sort of telling me to get on with it. It was hard at first, but when you realize that it is not going to kill you, you have to decide where to put your energies. Keep searching for a holy grail or start to learn how to live with it.

Chris: Have you accepted that you will always have pain now?

Rupert: No. I don't like that word because to me that just means that I have given up just like everyone else. Pain is not something to accept. It is something to fight. But fighting does not have to be negative. Maybe *fight* is the wrong word. I think of pain as an annoying travelling companion. Wherever I go, it goes. Most of the time it adds nothing to the journey, often it distracts me from beautiful things going on outside, but sometimes it is helpful, like when it is time to change course. I would rather be travelling alone but you don't always get to choose.

Chris: How do you know when to listen to the pain and when to push through?

Rupert: Hindsight is great teacher. I am much wiser about what I should have done than what I should do next. I am not a great planner. I find that if I plan for pain then that gives it too much respect—planning gives pain a space to expand into. Best not to pay it any credence. In fact, I think I have talked more about pain in this interview than I have in years! I will always push through if what I am doing is worth it. And it is normally worth

(Continued)

Box 7.2. *Continued*

it. Pain would stop everything if it could, so I try to make sure what I am doing is mean-ingful. If I don't care what I am doing, then it is easier to get distracted and pain will come in. That does mean that I am not very good at trivia anymore. Small talk is an impossible chore for me. It is just inviting my body to distract me.

Chris: Some people have tried to say that pain can be positive. Does that make any sense to you?

Rupert: Not easily. You can make it make sense if you want to. I think I am more deter-mined to achieve than I would have been without it. But it is hard to say. The worst thing about pain is that it forces me to live within quite tight boundaries, physically and men-tally. I don't make plans, but I rarely go out of my comfort zone. I am never spontaneous. But on the positive side, my life is full of meaning. To keep pain in its box I make sure that I spend as much of my time with people I love, and put all of my energies into things that are valuable and will make a contribution.

If I had not been in pain I think I might have allowed myself to have more fun. Who knows?

Rupert offers a nuanced approach to the idea of courageous engagement. We are used to the patient account in which pain intrudes, is hard to control, and comes to dominate. We also have accounts of enduring short-lived pain in high motivational environments such as sport. Rupert, who by his own admission rarely speaks of pain, offers a differ-ent, unexplored view of the person coping in silence. Here is the idea of goal-directed activity bringing reward and being analgesic. High value and meaningful activities are prioritized repeatedly, and pain is positioned as a threat to those, or as a nuisance. Unex-plored in the research on pain and motivation is this more subtle idea of how one can live within the tighter boundaries created and policed by pain.

Helping people to cope

Some people do manage to live unaided with chronic pain, finding a balance in man-aging interruption. Rupert's account is one example. We know very little about how people who do not present for help cope. We really need to find out more. Many peo-ple, however, do not find ways to live with pain, often swinging from avoidance to overactivity, from denial to misery, from hope to despair. Unfortunately, living with pain that does not follow the rules of our analgesic culture can leave one cast adrift in a nightmarish battle for legitimacy as a patient whose status as needing help is always being challenged (Delvecchio Good et al., 1992). For those who reach a psychological treatment facility or who can access rehabilitation for chronic pain, the focus will inevitably return to function, not sensation.

There is a rich tradition of psychotherapeutic and rehabilitative approaches to helping people manage chronic pain. Mark Jensen described what he refers to as a "family" of cognitive behavioral approaches, meant to capture the relatedness and the distinctiveness of different approaches (Jensen, 2011). Some focus on the management of symptoms. Such approaches include biofeedback, habit reversal, hypnosis, attention focusing, and reinterpretation. Others focus on the specific motivational aspects discussed here: problem framing, skills training, altering beliefs about cause and consequence, and addressing avoidance and endurance. The most common approach is to develop a program that combines different treatments, often with physical and occupational therapy alongside.

Unlike other areas of health psychology, there has been, and continues to be, development and innovation in psychological treatments for chronic pain. Overall, the evidence for the effectiveness of interventions is at best promising. For the Cochrane systematic review of psychological interventions for adult chronic pain, last updated in 2012, we included 42 randomized controlled trials. Compared with doing nothing (by leaving patients on a waiting list) or treating them with usual care, the treatments were relatively effective in altering disability and mood (Williams et al., 2012). In short, there is a strong case for the development of psychological treatments for chronic pain. Nevertheless, the very complexity of the problem—reflected in the huge variety of treatment approaches, types, and characteristics for a wide variety of patients—make the coherence of an overall review challenging.

Psychological interventions for chronic pain are best considered as emerging from their troubled adolescence. They have definitely grown out of infancy. There are well-established treatments. We know that people who otherwise would be left in misery can be helped safely in treatment. However, we don't know what works best for whom, in what circumstance, and for how long. Both treatment development, and, by extension, evidence synthesis, are at an interesting crossroads in the psychology of chronic pain. There is now recognition that there is no such thing as an "average" chronic pain patient, that we need to move beyond a general (catchall) treatment approach, and that outcomes expressed as a population average are close to meaningless. These lessons have been learned in nonpsychological treatments for pain already (Moore et al., 2013).

The next generation of studies will focus on specific psychological treatments with specific outcomes for individuals. For example, we have reported the evidence for treatments of chronic pain in children (Eccleston et al., 2012a) and for their families (Eccleston et al., 2012b), finding value in working directly with adolescents and their parents. When one is able to be more specific, the relevance of the analyses and guidance for future treatments both improve.

There are also new treatments being developed that offer a bright hope for the future. Some adopt hybrid techniques but focus on specific settings like the workplace (Linton and Fruzzetti, 2014). Other treatments are designed for very specific purposes with selected populations; for example, those needing to reduce or stop their prescribed opioid medicine (Windmill et al., 2013). Trials are also underway with specific populations, such as those with neuropathic pain conditions (Eccleston et al., in press). Finally, there is an increasing focus on modern methods of delivery, such as the Internet (Eccleston et al., 2014).

Summary

Our analgesic culture teaches us that pain is bad, should be short-lived, is diagnostically relevant, and should be removed. Closer examination shows that there are many experiences of pain: most escape research attention; some are educative or edifying. Endurance of pain and suffering is a marker of personality, group membership, achievement, and maturity. Our marathon runners pounding through the streets of New York, increasingly consumed by pain, being cheered by a crowd of strangers, are an example of the public role pain and its endurance can play. Chronic pain that flouts the received wisdom of pain as temporary offers a specific challenge to psychology. Psychology has attempted to explain chronic pain behavior with ill-fitting psychopathological models. By thinking about the normal response to an abnormal event, one begins to understand how persistent pain behavior is maintained, and how many people who present for help find themselves stuck in self-defeating patterns of vigilance, fear, worry, and perseverative problem solving. There are, however, well-established and promising treatments for people struggling to cope alone. A remaining challenge is to understand more about how the majority of people who cope in silence live with pain.

Notes

1. THE PROBLEM OF PAIN by CS Lewis © copyright CS Lewis Pte Ltd 1940.
2. This material was originally published in *The Body in Pain* by Elaine Scarry and has been reproduced by permission of Oxford University Press http://ukcatalogue.oup.com/product/9780195049961.do. For permission to reuse this material, please visit http://www.oup.co.uk/academic/rights/permissions.
3. Reproduced from Alan Morinis, The ritual experience: pain and the transformation of consciousness in ordeals of initiation, *Ethos*, 13 (2), p. 151, doi: 10.1525/eth.1985.13.2.02a00040 © 1985, American Anthropological Association.
4. Reproduced from *European Journal of Pain*, 5 (3), Chris Eccleston, Geert Crombez, Sarah Aldrich, and Cathy Stannard, Worry and chronic pain patients: A description and analysis of individual differences, p. 312, doi:10.1053/eujp.2001.0252 Copyright (2001), with permission from Elsevier.

References

Aldrich, S., Eccleston, C. and Crombez, G. (2000). Worrying about chronic pain: vigilance to threat and misdirected problem solving. *Behavior Research and Therapy*, 38, 457–470.
Andrews, N., Strong, J. and Meredith, P.J. (2012). Activity pacing, avoidance, endurance, and associations with patient functioning in chronic pain: a systematic review and meta-analysis. *Archives of Physical Medicine and Rehabilitation*, 93, 2109–2120.

Attridge, N., Crombez, G., Keogh, E., Van Ryckeghem, D. and Eccleston, C. (in press). The Experience of Cognitive Intrusion of Pain: scale development and validation. *Pain*.

Bastian, B., Jetten, J., Hornsey, M.J. and Leknes, S. (2014). The positive consequences of pain: a biopsychosocial approach. *Personality and Social Psychology Review*, 18, 256–279.

Borsook, D., Edwards, R., Elman, I., Becerra, L. and Levine, J. (2013). Pain and analgesia: the value of salience circuits. *Progress in Neurobiology*, 14, 93–105.

Brandstätter, V. and Schüler, J. (2013). Action crisis and cost-benefit thinking: a cognitive analysis of a goal-disengagement phase. *Journal of Experimental Social Psychology*, 49, 543–553.

Breivik, H., Collett, B., Ventafridda, V., Cohen, R. and Gallacher, D. (2006). Survey of chronic pain in Europe: prevalence, impact on daily life, and treatment. *European Journal of Pain*, 10, 287–333.

Brown, J.K. (1963). A cross cultural study of female initiation rites. *American Anthropologist*, 65, 837–853.

Buer, N. and Linton, S.J. (2002). Fear-avoidance beliefs and catastrophizing: occurrence and risk factor in back pain and ADL in the general population. *Pain*, 99, 458–491.

Caes, L., Vervoort, T., Eccleston, C., Vandenhende, M. and Goubert, L. (2011). Parental catastrophizing about child's pain and its relationship with activity restriction: the mediating role of parental distress. *Pain*, 152, 212–222.

Canavero, S. and Bonicalzi, V. (2014). Pain myths and the genesis of central pain. *Pain Medicine*, 16, 240–248.

Cervero, F. (2008). Pain theories. In C. Bushnell and A.I. Basbaum (Eds.), The senses: a comprehensive reference, vol. 5: pain (pp. 5–10). Amsterdam: Elsevier.

Cioffi, D. (1991). Beyond attentional strategies: a cognitive-perceptual model of somatic interpretation. *Psychological Bulletin*, 109, 25–41.

Closs, J., Edwards, J., Swift, C. and Briggs, M. (2013). Religious identity and the experience and expression of chronic pain: a review. *Journal of Religion, Disability and Health*, 17, 91–124.

Crombez, G., Eccleston, C., Van Damme, S., Vlaeyen, J.W.S. and Karoly, P. (2012). Fear-avoidance model of chronic pain: the next generation. *The Clinical Journal of Pain*, 28, 475–483.

Crombez, G., Eccleston, C., Van Den Broeck, A., Goubert, L. and Van Houdenhove, B. (2004). Hypervigilance to pain in fibromyalgia: the mediating role of pain intensity and catastrophic thinking about pain. *The Clinical Journal of Pain*, 20, 98–102.

Crombez, G., Van Ryckeghem, D.M.L., Eccleston, C. and Van Damme, S. (2013). Attentional bias to pain-related information: a meta-analysis. *Pain*, 154, 497–510.

Delvecchio Good, M.-J., Brodwin, P.E., Good, B.J. and Kleinman, A. (1992). Pain as human experience: an anthropological perspective. Berkeley: University of California Press.

Eccleston, C. and Crombez, G. (1999). Pain demands attention: a cognitive-affective model of the interruptive function of pain. *Psychological Bulletin*, 125, 356–366.

Eccleston, C. and Crombez, G. (2007). Worry and chronic pain: a misdirected problem solving model. *Pain*, 132, 233–236.

Eccleston, C., Crombez, G., Aldrich, S. and Stannard, C. (2001). Worry and chronic pain patients: a description and analysis of individual differences. *European Journal of Pain*, 5, 309–318.

Eccleston, C., Fisher, E., Craig, L., Duggan, G., Rosser, B. and Keogh, E. (2014). Psychological therapies (Internet-delivered) for the management of chronic pain in adults. *Cochrane Database of Systematic Reviews*, Issue 2, CD010152. doi:10.1002/14651858.CD010152.pub2

Eccleston, C, Hearn, L. and Williams A.C. de C. (in press). Psychological therapies for the management of chronic neuropathic pain. *Cochrane Database of Systematic Reviews*.

Eccleston, C., Palermo, T.M., Fisher, E. and Law, E. (2012b). Psychological interventions for parents of children and adolescents with chronic illness. *Cochrane Database of Systematic Reviews*, Issue 8, CD009660. doi:10.1002/14651858.CD009660.pub2

Eccleston, C., Palermo, T.M., Williams, A.C. de C., Lewandowski, A., Morley, S., Fisher, E. and Law, E. (2012a). Psychological therapies for the management of chronic and recurrent pain in children and adolescents. *Cochrane Database of Systematic Reviews*, Issue 12, CD003968. doi:10.1002/14651858.CD003968.pub3

Eccleston, C., Williams, A.C. de C. and Stainton Rogers, W. (1997). Patients' and professionals' understandings of the causes of chronic pain: blame, responsibility and identity protection. *Social Science and Medicine*, 45, 699–709.

Fearon, I., McGrath, P.J. and Achat, H. (1996). "Booboos": the study of everyday pain among young children. *Pain*, 68, 55–62.

Froud, R., Patterson, S., Eldridge, S., Seale, C., Pincus, T., Rajendran, D., Fossum, C. and Underwood, M. (2014). A systematic review and meta-synthesis of the impact of low back pain on people's lives. *BMC Musculoskeletal Disorders*, 15, 50, 1–14.

Gibson, S.J. and Lussier, D. (2012). Prevalence and relevance of pain in older persons. *Pain Medicine*, 13, S23–S26.

Glover-Graf, N., Marini, I., Baker, J. and Buck, T. (2007). Religious and spiritual beliefs and practices of persons with chronic pain. *Rehabilitation Counseling Bulletin*, 51, 21–33.

Hasenbring, M., Hallner, D. and Rusu, A.C. (2009). Fear-avoidance and endurance related responses to pain: development and validation of the Avoidance Endurance Questionnaire (AEQ). *European Journal of Pain*, 13, 620–628.

Häuser, W., Wolfe, F., Henningsen, P., Schmutzer, G., Brähler, E. and Hinz, A. (2014). Untying chronic pain: prevalence and societal burden of chronic pain stages in the general population—a cross-sectional survey. *BMC Public Health*, 14, 352, 1–8.

Jensen, M.P. (2011). Psychosocial approaches to pain management: an organizational framework. *Pain*, 152, 717–725.

Johannes, C.B., Kim Le, T., Zhou, X., Johnston, J.A. and Dworkin, R.H. (2010). The prevalence of chronic pain in United States adults: results of an Internet-based survey. *The Journal of Pain*, 11, 1230–1239.

King, S., Chambers, C.T., Huguet, A., MacNevin, R.C., McGrath, P.J., Parker, L. and MacDonald, A.J. (2011). The epidemiology of chronic pain in children and adolescents revisited: a systematic review. Pain, 152, 2729–2738.

Kucyi, A. and Davis, K. (2015). The dynamic pain connectome. *Trends in Neuroscience*, 38, 86–95.

Legrain, V., Iannetti, G.D., Plaghki, L. and Mourax, A. (2011). The pain matrix reloaded: a salience detection system for the body. *Progress in Neurobiology*, 93, 111–124.

Lewis, C.S. (1940). The problem of pain. London: HarperCollins.

Linton, S.J. and Fruzzetti, A.E. (2014). A hybrid emotion-focused exposure treatment for chronic pain: a feasibility study. *Scandinavian Journal of Pain*, 5, 151–158.

Linton, S.J., Nicholas, M.K., MacDonald, S., Boersma, K. and Bergbom, S. (2011). The role of depression and catastrophizing in musculoskeletal pain. *European Journal of Pain*, 15, 416–422.

Martin, S., Daniel, C. and Williams, A.C. de C. (2014). How do people understand their neuropathic pain? A Q-study. *Pain*, 155, 349–355.

McNeil, D.W & Rainwater, A.J. (1998). Development of the Fear of Pain Questionnaire—III. *Journal of Behavioral Medicine*, 21, 389–410.

Merskey, H. and Bogduk, N. (Eds.) (1994). Classification of chronic pain (2nd ed.). Seattle: IASP Press.

Moore, R.A., Derry, S., Eccleston, C. and Kalso, E. (2013). Expect analgesic failure; pursue analgesic success. *British Medical Journal*, 346, f2690.

Morinis, A. (1985). The ritual experience: pain and the transformation of consciousness in ordeals of initiation. *Ethos*, 13, 150–174.

Morris, D.B. (1991). The culture of pain. Berkeley: University of California Press.

Mounce, C., Keogh, E. and Eccleston, C. (2010). A principal components analysis of negative affect-related constructs relevant to pain: evidence for a three component structure. *The Journal of Pain*, 11, 710–717.

Nock, M.K. (2010). Self-injury. *Annual Review of Clinical Psychology*, 6, 339–363.

Risdon, A., Eccleston, C., Crombez, G. and McCracken, L. (2003). How can we learn to live with pain? A Q-methodological analysis of the diverse understandings of acceptance of chronic pain. *Social Science and Medicine*, 56, 375–386.

Robinson, M.E., Riley III, J.L., Myers, C., Sadler, I.J.M.A., Kvaal, S.A., Geisser, M.E. and Keefe, F.J. (1997). The Coping Strategies Questionnaire: a large sample, item level factor analysis. *The Clinical Journal of Pain*, 13, 43–49.

Scarry, E. (1985). The body in pain: the making and unmaking of the world. New York: Oxford University Press.

Selby, E.A., Nock, M.K. and Kranzler, A. (2014). How does self-injury feel? Examining automatic positive reinforcement in adolescent self-injurers with experience sampling. *Psychiatry Research*, 214, 417–423.

Simmonds, M.J., Derghazarian, T. and Vlaeyen, J.W.S. (2012). Physiotherapists' knowledge, attitudes, and intolerance of uncertainty influence decision making in low back pain. *Clinical Journal of Pain*, 28, 467–474.

St Clair Gibson, A., de Koning, J., Thompson, K., Roberts, W., Micklewright, D., Raglin, J. and Foster, C. (2013). Crawling to the finish line: why do endurance runners collapse? Implications for understanding of mechanisms underlying pacing and fatigue. *Sports Medicine*, 43, 413–424.

Sullivan, M.J.L., Bishop, S.R. and Pivik, J. (1995). The Pain Catastrophizing Scale: development and validation. *Psychological Assessment*, 7, 524–532.

Tunks, E. and Bellissimo, A. (1988). Coping with the coping concept: a brief comment. *Pain*, 34, 171–174.

Van Damme, S. and Kindermans, H. (2015). A self-regulation perspective on avoidance and persistence behavior in chronic pain: new theories, new challenges? *The Clinical Journal of Pain*, 31, 115–122.

Vlaeyen, J.W.S. and Linton, S.J. (2000). Fear-avoidance and its consequences in chronic musculoskeletal pain: a state of the art. *Pain*, 85, 317–332.

Vowles, K.E., Rosser, B., Januszewicz, P., Morlion, B., Evers, S. and Eccleston, C. (2014). Everyday pain, analgesic beliefs and analgesic behaviors in Europe and Russia: an epidemiological survey and analysis. *European Journal of Hospital Pharmacy*, 21, 39–44.

Williams, A.C. de C., Eccleston, C. and Morley, S. (2012). Psychological therapies for the management of chronic pain (excluding headache) in adults. *Cochrane Database of Systematic Reviews*, Issue 11, CD007407. doi:10.1002/14651858.CD007407.pub3

Windmill, J., Fisher, E., Eccleston, C., Derry, S., Stannard, C., Knaggs, R. and Moore, R.A. (2013). Interventions for the reduction of prescribed opioid use in chronic non-cancer pain. *Cochrane Database of Systematic Reviews*, Issue 9, CD010323. doi:10.1002/14651858.CD010323.pub2

CHAPTER 8

ITCH

Itch functions to urge scratch. Of all of our ten neglected senses, itch, or *pruritus*, as it is known clinically, appears to be the most functionally straightforward. The psychology of itch emerges as both complex and intriguing. Traditionally, itch was thought of as a variant of pain. Although itch and pain feel different they were considered to be physiologically and behaviorally similar. This perception has been strong enough for the interest in itch to be subsumed for years under the broader canopy of the study of pain. Itch, however, deserves attention as a sensory experience in its own right.

As with all of our ten neglected senses, there is a unique sensory quality to itch; we know what it means to itch, and we know how the relief of itch feels when we scratch, rub, touch, or change temperatures. Culturally, itch is a marker of an urge that cannot be ignored; it is a primary and growing need that must be met, as in the idea of a "seven-year itch" in marriage, or the "itch" to purchase consumer goods, or as a general motivation when colloquially describing oneself "itching" to go. Its motivational character—an urgent quality—lies at the heart of its definition.

Similarly, scratch—the deliberate counterstimulation at the site of itch, including rubbing, pinching, or pushing skin—is inextricably linked to itch. Scratching without itch may be rare, normally accidental; when deliberate, it has a wholly different function of marking or sensation seeking. Why and how we scratch, and its consequences, are part of the enigma of itch and need to be examined together.

First, however, it is useful to review the mechanisms of itch, both peripheral and central, and especially how they promote self-stimulation and counterstimulation, such as scratching. Itching and scratching are considered within a context of personal and social hygiene. Finally, when itch becomes chronic it ceases to have any useful social or personal function. The experience of people with chronic pruritus is explored, with a focus on their attempts to live being constantly urged to scratch.

Itch is a part of almost everyone's life. But two people were particularly helpful in offering unusual insight into this neglected sense. First, I talked with James who works every day surrounded by plants and insects that most people avoid because they can cause itch; he inhabits a *pruritogenic* environment. James is the keeper of reptiles, arachnids, and insects in a wildlife park. I also talked with Neil who lives with chronic itch: his face itches constantly and has done so for as long as he can remember. He is an expert at making sure that he is never in a situation where it is not possible for him to scratch.

From itch to scratch

Itch is commonly defined as an unpleasant urge or desire:

> the unpleasant sensation that leads to the desire to scratch the skin. The terms "itch" and "pruritus" can be used interchangeably. Itch can be so severe that it causes insomnia, and scratching can be so intense that the skin is left raw and bleeding. (Hanfield-Jones, 2009, p. 273)

This pragmatic definition can be criticized for its lack of precision (Savin, 1998), in part because of its insistence on the unpleasant quality of itch and on scratch as inevitable. However, it does capture the experience well. Here itch is defined broadly as unpleasant and a motivating desire for counterstimulation and relief.

There have been other attempts to define itch by the presumed cause and by the presumed mechanism of action. Itch can be the product of peripheral mechanisms in the skin or generated neuropathically due to presumed nerve damage or disease (Twycross et al., 2003). Much of the debate in recent years has been about the peripheral mechanisms. Earl Carstens describes how itch was once considered low frequency pain, but with the identification of specialized receptors, or *pruriceptors*, attention has shifted to a more selective mechanism. Further evidence for the selectivity of receptor pathways comes from numerous studies showing that pain can suppress or inhibit itch. According to Carstens,

> The bulk of the current evidence favors the concept of an itch-selective pathway, originating from mechanically insensitive, pruritogen-selective C-fiber afferents which project to lamina I spinothalamic tract neurons that, in turn, convey itch signals to the lateral thalamus and cortex. (Carstens, 2008, p. 118).

The evidence for central involvement in itch comes also from the novel recognition of sensitization to itch but not pain, and from the realization that cause of itch is often systemic, originating far from the skin—in particular, with the kidney or liver. Histamine as a mediator for itch perception is well documented and plays a clear role in many but not all itch experiences. Centrally, itch enters the cortex via the thalamus and then projects widely, as with other interoception, to affective, motivational, and motor control areas (Hsieh et al., 1994; Davidson and Giesler, 2010).

Function of itch

Why do we itch? The common answer is that itch operates like pain to warn of potential danger; in particular, of chemical attack from plant or animal. It is worth remembering that we share the planet with approximately 8.7 million other species (Mora et al., 2011), many of which bite, puncture, secrete, invade, or infect. Jeffrey Demain explores the causes of itchy skin weals and rashes (*papular urticaria*) in humans caused by a hypersensitive immune response to bites and stings. They come from exposure to Arachnida such as mites, ticks, and spiders; from insects such as mosquitoes, flies, midges, lice, caterpillars, and beetles; and from Reduviidae such as bedbugs. We are extremely close to many creatures who provoke severe itch. For example, "It is estimated that more than 1 million people are bitten by mosquitoes daily" (Demain, 2003, p. 297). Itch may be an important part of our overall defensive system that warns of harm inflicted.

Whereas pain promotes defensive withdrawal behavior to avoid danger, itch promotes a rubbing, wiping, or scratching to remove whatever is attacking through contact or puncturing of the skin. Although an intriguing idea, there is very little evidence that itching functions to promote scratch solely in defense of attack. There are a number of related reasons. First, the event rate of scratching is so high and occurs so often without external attack that such an explanation leaves the majority of scratch behavior unexplained by proximal causes. Second, scratching is often judged to be pleasurable and continues beyond the simple first phase of adjustment or removal of an irritant. Third, human-made barriers to external irritants such as clothing and furniture are tolerable despite constant abrasion and stimulation. Fourth, both scratching and itching are highly socially contagious in a way that almost none of our other senses are. Finally, itch can be induced by exposure to itch-relevant cues, such as images of insects.

An alternative way to think of itch is as a signal to promote broader social hygiene behavior. Itch urges scratch, but it also serves the primary purpose of promoting skin awareness in both ourselves and in observers, and it initiates a range of self-touching behaviors that function to check the integrity of the skin and elicit grooming.

Grooming

Many primates self-touch, in particular on the face. Face touching is surprisingly common. How often have you touched your face today? In one study, British students at rest with no task to perform touched their face on average 8.5 times in a ten-minute period, 51 times an hour (Hatta and Dimond, 1984). We don't know how many of these face touches are itch-relevant, or how aware people are that they are doing it, but it is clear that touching mouth, nose, and chin are common. Faces are often unclothed and accessible, and have highly innervated, cortically dominant areas such as the mouth, so may simply be the most likely target. However, faces also house structures that perhaps require defense against parasites. Self-touching of the face may be a form of abrasion to wipe away possible ectoparasitic organisms.

Whether one needs to itch in order to scratch becomes a relevant question. Scratching, rubbing, and wiping are self-grooming behaviors used by animals to reduce the parasite load. Pavol Prokop and colleagues explored human grooming. They argued that there is as yet insufficient evidence as to whether our grooming behavior needs external cuing, or whether we are more like animals whose grooming is under regular rhythmic (endogenous) control. The two may be related. It is entirely possible that we have a base rate of endogenously cued grooming, but the rate of grooming, including scratching, increases when cued externally. In an interesting study, Prokop and colleagues exposed students to cues of parasites and to cues of a biological control; in this case, images of hormones. The cues of parasites increased awareness of scratching and of formication; formication was captured with the question, "How many times during the last 45 minutes did you have a feeling that something is crawling on your body?" (Prokop et al., 2014, p. 43).

This cuing of grooming by parasites has also been reported separately. In a similar experiment, Donna Lloyd worked with a smaller group but went beyond self-report of awareness of scratch to actually observing scratching. They also captured the participants' perception of itch. In this study they had better control stimuli and used images of nonthreatening insects such as butterflies. The participants reported being more than three times as itchy when viewing the itch- compared with the non-itch pictures, and a tenfold increase in scratching behavior was observed. In a further analysis, the investigators found that the cues for itching and scratching may be highly specific. The itch pictures were of three types: itch-related stimuli in contact with the skin, such as an ant on skin; humans scratching; and objects that relate to itch but in a different context, such as an ant on the ground. Lloyd and colleagues found that images of people scratching were related to increased scratching, but images of agents of itch, such as biting insects, resulted in greater itching. (Lloyd et al., 2013). Getting closer to the exact triggers may be particularly important for people who suffer with recurrent or chronic, environmentally maintained pruritus.

Social contagion of itch and scratch

Scratching yet? These studies point to an intriguing aspect of itch; perhaps more than any of the other nine neglected senses, itch and scratch are socially contagious. Why should cues of itch and scratch increase the felt experience and lead to scratching behavior?

Although the social contagion of behavior is a very popular idea, there are still few studies, and even fewer explanations. In one modern study by Alexandru Papoiu and colleagues, 14 adult volunteers without skin complaint and 11 with mild-to-moderate atopic dermatitis (eczema) watched short films either of people scratching or a neutral comparison: same people, same place, same amount of time—but no scratching. Next, itch was induced with histamine; a placebo induction was also given. Scratching during the films was observed and self-reported itch noted. Compared to those without a skin problem, people with atopic dermatitis reported increased itching, they scratched for twice as long, and they scratched more body areas when exposed to the placebo. Similarly, when exposed to the histamine irritant, they also reported longer and more extensive itching, and scratched more than controls; these results were amplified by watching people scratch.

Two intriguing findings were hidden in this study. First, as in earlier studies, those without a skin condition scratched for more than twice as long when watching videos of people scratching, but itching was not greatly increased. But in the presence of an irritant, the itching and scratching were both amplified by social contagion. Second, the researchers found that the pattern of scratching was different after contagion in those with and without atopic dermatitis. Figure 8.1 shows the pattern of distribution.

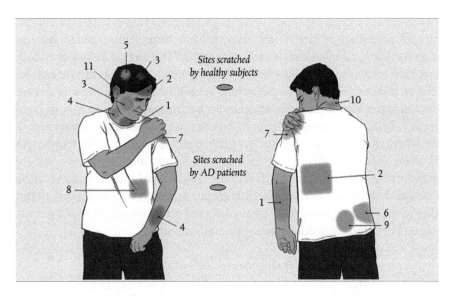

Fig. 8.1. The distribution of scratching episodes in widespread (scattered) areas, in patients with atopic dermatitis (AD) and healthy subjects. (Plate 1)

"The distribution of scratching episodes in widespread (scattered) areas, in patients with atopic dermatitis (AD) and healthy subjects, reveals that patients with AD experienced an itch that extended beyond the local itch induction site, becoming generalized, while they watched the itch video. Scratching beyond the local site in healthy participants was limited to the face [2], neck [1] and contralateral forearm [4]. The areas scratched are shown in ranking order (by mean duration) for an exposure to the itch video, when the local itch stimulus (histamine) was delivered to the right forearm (i.e., scratching on the contralateral forearm is represented). Subjects with AD scratched mostly their contralateral forearm (1), mid-back region (2), face (3), neck (4) and scalp (5)."

Reproduced from Contagious itch in humans: a study of visual 'transmission' of itch in atopic dermatitis and healthy subjects, A.D.P. Papoiu, H. Wang, R.C. Coghill, Y-H. Chan, and G. Yosipovitch, *British Journal of Dermatology*, 164 (6), pp. 1299–1303, Figure 4, doi:10.1111/j. 1365-2133.2011.10318.x Copyright (c) 2011, John Wiley and Sons.

For those with a skin disorder, the scratching was quite widespread. For those without a skin disorder, scratching was limited to face, neck, and scalp (Papoiu et al., 2011).

It is not clear whether itching, scratching, or both are contagious. There are clearly differences in the extent and pattern of scratching in response to cues between those with a propensity to itch due to a skin disorder and those without a pre-existing condition. The pattern differences shown in Figure 8.1 are particularly interesting from a functional perspective. In those without a reason to itch, observing scratching may induce self-touching of the face, perhaps as grooming—an increased hygiene response. However, in those already itching and scratching, observing others scratching may lower the threshold for attention to itch extensively across multiple sites. The same observable behavior may be functioning differently in different contexts.

The mechanism by which observing another's scratching increases our own scratching behavior, whether as increased grooming or as response to itch, is not known. Ashley Feneran and colleagues from the same Wake Forest laboratories as Alexandru Papoiu explored the idea that scratching may be due to mirror neuron involvement. However, in an observation study of pairs of monkeys, they found that the monkey behavior in response to a cage mate's behavior was not specific but general: scratching increased but was not limited to exactly the same location as observed (Feneran et al., 2013)

A hygiene paradox

Human grooming is more egocentric than that of other primates: we do not rely explicitly on others to reduce our parasite load—we do it ourselves. The extent to which we self-groom or other-groom functions in part by how fearful we are of disease: the more vulnerable we feel, the more we groom ourselves; the less vulnerable we feel, the more we touch others (Thompson, 2010). The reliance on self-grooming would, hypothetically, heighten the need for visual cuing of self-scratch. Less "You scratch my back and I'll scratch yours" and more "I see that you are scratching your back, so I should scratch mine."

The idea that itch may function as part of a larger set of behaviors that are best thought of as serving a hygiene function has some problems. Bug removal is important, and scratching may well be useful as a method of removing ectoparasites, but it also does two things that, paradoxically, increase the likelihood of infection: it transmits infection from surfaces to sites of entry of the body, and it can create new wound sites of entry.

An interesting report on home hygiene and infection behavior from the *International Scientific Forum on Home Hygiene* reminds us that when it comes to infection,

> hands are probably the single most important transmission route because, in all cases [gastrointestinal, respiratory, and skin infections] they come into direct contact with

the known portals of entry for pathogens (the mouth, nose and conjunctiva of the eyes), and are thus the key last line of defence. (Bloomfield et al., 2012, p. 8)

Putting our hands to our faces is the main method of transmission of multiple infectious diseases. Itch, and so, by extension, contagious itch, may increase the likelihood of infectious transmission. One might also expect that in an environment in which itch is common (e.g., a dermatologist's reception area), scratch would be common, and so by extension will be hand-to-mouth transmission of infectious disease. I could find no investigation of attempts to reduce scratch cues in, for example, hospital environments, and their effect of infection rates, but this could be a novel area for study.

Scratching can often, if extended, cause skin lesions and so introduce new sites of infection. It can also produce secondary complications of new injury, albeit self-inflicted. Sometimes, however, scratching goes beyond the cessation of itch and can be mediated either neurologically, behaviorally, or both, as in the interesting case of skin picking in adolescents. In these cases the immediate reward of self-attention, or distraction from other unpleasant sensations or emotions, reinforces a skin-destructive behavior (Bohne et al., 2002).

On the pleasure of itch

Much of the discussion so far has stressed the unpleasant aspects of itch, principally around the quality of urgency, that provoke scratching. However, itch may also be a pathway to pleasure. In a study of different sites of itch, itch was induced and an experimenter scratched those itches producing different but closely related judgments of pleasure in the person being scratched (bin Saif et al., 2012). Papoiu and his colleagues extended this idea, but recognized that self-scratching is motivationally different from being scratched. They investigated pleasure and itch using neuroimaging while people underwent their own itch-scratch routine. However, they did take the opportunity to compare scratching oneself with being scratched. Intriguingly, when one is in control of both the relief of itch and the pleasure of scratch, there is quite extensive involvement of reward processes in the midbrain affect systems, brain areas that are not involved when being scratched by another (Papoiu et al., 2013). Scratching yourself is much more pleasurable than being scratched.

Pleasure should perhaps be considered an inherent part of itch, rather than simply a potential consequence. The hedonic qualities of itch may arise from various sources. First, scratching an itch has a pure reward involvement and so a centrally generated hedonic quality. Second, the cessation of itch provides a quality of relief that may be experienced as pleasure in its own right. Third, just as there is evidence that pain offset enhances the pleasure of the experiences that follow, it would be interesting to examine the sensations that follow the offset of itch, to see whether they are also hedonically exaggerated; that is, are they more pleasurable because they follow itch? Finally, it is possible that itch generates not only immediate scratch, but is also a gateway into a larger class of self-stimulation, self-soothing, or patterned grooming behaviors that are experienced positively. Indeed, it is not clear when scratching turns to stroking the skin next to the site of itch, or when a rough stroke turns to a smooth and so more pleasurable stroke (Essick et al., 2010). Affective touch is a common emotional regulation behavior, but it is not well studied in psychology, with some notable exceptions (McGlone et al, 2014).

To explore the possible nonaversive, even hedonic, qualities of itch and scratch, it is helpful to explore itch in a context where it is experienced as welcome, necessary, or unavoidable. With some of the physical senses one can easily find people who engage or endure despite the aversive experience (consider pain, fatigue, imbalance, hypoxia). However, there are very few people who deliberately engage with pruritogenic environments. But there are some. Those who venture into wilderness environments—jungle, desert, mountain, or cave—encounter insect-rich places and massively increase the risk of parasite load and infection (Miller et al., 1996). Likewise, there are people who choose to work with the very itch-inducing creatures that most of us try to avoid.

To explore what it is like to be in an environment of itch, I talked to James Reynolds (Box 8.1).

Box 8.1. **James, working with itch:** *"it is the horrible looking creatures that I see a beauty in"*

James is a herpetologist. He is the keeper of the reptiles and arachnids at the Cotswold Wildlife Park, which has one of the largest collections in the UK. When I met him he was examining the delivery of amphibian food, which was a box of live jumping crickets.

Chris: What is it about working with arachnids, insects, and reptiles that attracts you?

James: It started when I was young, with an interest in bird-watching. Now, it is all the weird and wonderful stuff that I find interesting. Not the fluffy stuff. That bores me, really. It is the horrible looking creatures that I see a beauty in.

Chris: So, does being around insects and spiders all day make you itch?

James: I think you have levels. When you start your levels are low. You look at a tarantula and you might be scared. With experience and knowledge about the animals it gets better.

(Continued)

Box 8.1. *Continued*

For example, with the tarantula they have hairs they flick and they can get into your nose. They rub the back legs on the abdomen which then releases the hairs into the atmosphere and then as soon as you touch something with them on, they are there lying dormant. They go into your skin and it gets really itchy. The feeling is not like a chemical feeling; it is just really irritating. It feels like hundreds of tiny hairs digging into your skin and irritating.

Chris: Do you still get itchy when you see some insects?

James: Yes, I still get that. Not with the ones I am familiar with, but the ones that are different, like orb-weavers, which are big spiders—they are long and spindly and kind of disgusting. We are getting some in, so I hope in a couple of weeks I will get used to them and hopefully that itchiness will start to subside. Well, it should do. You get used to it. At the moment we have these lovely little tailless whip scorpions. They look disgusting. At first it is horrible. But now I can have them on my hand. No problem at all.

Chris: Why do you think people itch more with some creatures?

James: I think it is the idea of an insect getting caught on their skin that would make them itchy. When people come into contact with insects, they want to get them off their skin as quickly as possible. It is a sense of getting away from skin. Especially in the arms.

For example, we use a lot of crickets as food, and at first crickets worry people. But now the sensation is no longer itchy, you are just used to it. The only time you might itch, and you will think this funny, is if you lose one on your skin and you feel them crawling through your clothes later on.

Chris: It sounds like you no longer worry too much . . .

James: Well, don't get me wrong. I hate to be bitten. I was bitten in Costa Rica a few years ago. I was in bed and I felt like there were insects all around me. I could not sleep. So there are times when it gets too much for me.

Chris: So you are not completely immune to itch . . .

James: Yes, that is right. There are still some insects that make me itchy and there are still contexts that make me itch. I hate to be bitten and I don't like to itch. In some places I will be worried about being bitten and I will check my body. So, yes, it doesn't go away.

Chris: Do you try to educate others about which animals can itch?

James: If people ask me questions, I will help them out. But I won't go out of my way to correct people and say that what they think is itchy isn't, like spiders; because in their context it might be. So, it is hard to tell them it is not itchy because it could be.

Chris: You have said a few times that the spiders and insects are horrible, but you seem to respect them a lot.

James: I just say "horrible" because that is how they are portrayed and how people first think of them. I think that maybe if people looked at creatures as a form of beauty rather than something disgusting it would help. If you look at the structure of, for example, a stick insect, it is amazing looking. It is completely different from any other animal in the world.

Chris: Is there pleasure in being surrounded by things that itch?

James: It is about understanding their behavior. It is understanding that they are creepy and horrible looking and they make you itch and they might bite you, but that they are very basic animals. Understanding the animal and learning about its behavior. Although they are basic, they can sometimes surprise you.

Educating other people is the really positive thing. And generally being around the animals. It is a real pleasure. Sometimes you get an animal that you think, "That is smashing. I am so happy I am working with it." Or you might get a rare animal and you think, "Am I ever going to work with this again?" Yes, your knowledge and understanding is important. If you learn about them the curtain starts to lift a bit more and you see more of the beauty of an animal. Once you get past that first judgment and you look at it, I mean you really look at it, then you can get past the horror, and really see the beauty of the animal.

James lives surrounded by creatures that might itch. But the extinction of itch and scratch behavior is specific to the creature he is exposed to. It does not generalize to all. He discusses what looks like a self-delivered, graded exposure process where the more time he spends with a new creature, the less disgusted, less itchy, and more fascinated he becomes. The general, perhaps hardwired, dislike of itch is not affected. Also interesting is the role of general avoidance. A consequence of behavioral avoidance of creatures considered pruritogenic is ignorance of what actually poses a threat, and in what form. James discusses eloquently the role he plays in educating people about the beauty of insects one can marvel at if one can move beyond avoidance.

Chronic itch

For most people it is hard to find anything positive about itch; it would just be nice to be far away from things that threaten itch. Itch is a very common experience and a common symptom of many diseases. Given its function in promoting skin awareness and hygiene, we should expect itch to be highly prevalent. However, for some people itch can be frequent and chronic. The definition of chronic itch is a pragmatic one: it is itch lasting six weeks or longer, severe enough to promote complaint and request for help (Weisshaar et al., 2012). The prevalence of chronic itch has been reported as high as 10 percent in various community studies (Weisshaar and Dalgard, 2009). In a study from Heidelberg, 343 of a sample of 2,540 adults, or 13.5 percent, reported chronic itch, 72 percent of whom said they itched every day. These were people taken at random from the community. Half did not know the cause of their itch, and most found any relief from itch elusive. On closer analysis, the people with chronic itch also said that their quality of life was worse when the itch was severe (Matterne et al., 2011). Relationships, leisure, and sleep were affected on a measure of quality of life for patients with itch (Matterne et al., 2009).

Measuring quality of life is one way into thinking about experience, but it is often an unsatisfactory snapshot of that experience. Anja Bathe from the Heidelberg team led a more thorough investigation by interviewing 16 patients with chronic pruritus who were seeking treatment. The researchers asked about the labels and language used; ideas about cause, consequence, how controllable it felt; and for more detail about its consequences in wider life. Sleep disturbance often emerged as a major complaint that extended to fatigue and lack of concentration. They also reported an interesting finding not discussed elsewhere: the difficulty patients had in settling on an appropriate language for itch. Available language was considered inadequate by patients who wanted to communicate the extent of the misery of itch. Language of bites and other external agents such as cutting were used, but were very not thought satisfactory (Bathe et al., 2012).

The language of itch is peculiarly limited. For example, the itch severity scale uses only six descriptors: *stinging, stabbing, burning, annoying, unbearable,* and *worrisome* (Majeski et al., 2007, p. 672). This measure was developed from a previous clinician-administered measure, itself was taken from the famous McGill Pain Questionnaire. Of course both pain and itch share neuropathic qualities, as captured by these descriptors, but this is surely only a small part of the experience. Missing is any content relating to the interruptive and urgent qualities, and to the wider experience of emotional distress. This gap has been recognized, and plans are underway to produce more thorough methods of assessment of the broader impact of chronic itch. In a consensus paper from the International Forum for the Study of Itch, the importance of assessing not just the felt experience was clearly stated (Weisshaar et al., 2012).

The cognitive, motivational, and wider emotional aspects of itching and scratching are important when considering the person attempting to cope with itch. It is useful to think of people living within an affective-motivational cycle that starts with the interruption of attention by itch, coupled with the overwhelming desire to scratch, which is followed by concerted attempts to *not* scratch, the failure of those attempts, and then a flood of negative self-appraisals, including shame, embarrassment, and self-criticism.

Attending to itch

Itch, like pain, functions primarily to interrupt. This attention-grabbing aspect has attracted some interest. Andrea Evers from Lieden in the Netherlands leads the study of psychological influences in itch perception. In her laboratory she and her colleagues showed that attention to bodily sensations increases sensitivity to induced itch, implying a central attentional involvement (Van Laarhoven et al., 2010). But what happens when you do attend to itch? Evers reminds us of the role of anxiety, expressed with itch as worry about symptom exacerbation, stigma, and the subsequent loss of social relations; she stresses the possible role of specific beliefs, such as believing in the onset of catastrophic outcomes because of unbearable itch (L. Verhoeven et al., 2006). For Evers, the crucial cognitions are of perceived lack of control over the itch and scratch. She argues that for those who develop a pattern of helplessness, worry, and catastrophic beliefs, the impact of disease—its course and the subsequent need for treatment—increases (E.W.M. Verhoeven et al., 2008).

The importance of beliefs about itch is only beginning to be understood. Patients have long discussed the challenge of control, but how far one's beliefs are automatically invoked and what part they play in our behavior is not well investigated, even though Andrea Evers has argued the case very well. In addition, in other fields of psychology, there has been a growth of interest in cognitive biases, in how our attention, labeling, and interpretation of sensations can be altered by fear of those sensations. In many ways itch would be a much better candidate for the identification of automatic cognition. Unlike other physical sensations, itch has a direct link with a broader hygiene response, making the social cues for itch concrete and specific in a way that they have failed to be for pain, suffocation, fear of falling, and fatigue. If attention or interpretation biases can be identified for itch, it would open a novel avenue of discovery for the psychological treatment of itch and the behavioral modification of scratch.

If you have an itch, don't scratch

Once itch has interrupted, how easy is it to not scratch? Health and behavioral psychology are replete with examples of how difficult the extinction or modification of behavior can be. Habit reversal when habits are under social control is difficult enough to achieve. Consider the plethora of lifestyle advice and the fate of good intentions to change complex behaviors such as smoking, drinking alcohol, and physical activity. Success in sustained behavioral change is elusive. Behavioral extinction of conditioned behaviors such as scratch is particularly difficult to achieve. Itch is almost hardwired to deliver scratch. Is it possible to resist?

One study attempted to model this resistance in the laboratory. Elisa Filevich and Patrick Haggard developed a novel paradigm in which to study inhibition of urgent action, using itch. They were particularly interested in cases of what they call *internal inhibition*, by which they mean the decisions we make to inhibit habits (as opposed to *external* inhibition, meaning instructions from others to change): it is the difference between resolving to change and being told to change. Filevich and Haggard developed a task in which people were exposed to itch and could move to avoid it, but instead endured it. Their principal finding was that internal inhibition, or personally initiating self-control (willpower), has a stronger neural consequence than responding to instruction. Now, interpreting exactly what this stronger pattern of brain signals means will be important, but at this level of description there is evidence that when we try not to scratch an itch, it is an event of greater neural significance. They speculate that this neural involvement is about the decision making. Because we could have avoided the negative consequences, so the effect is stronger (Filevich and Haggard, 2012).

This interesting line of research into willpower and the consequences of resisting or enduring extreme urges and desires is very promising because it comes close to the experience of the battle with itch described by patients. It opens various avenues for further investigation. First, what governs the ability to resist, and under what circumstances is it difficult to resist the urge to scratch? Second, what are the consequences of planned decisions to inhibit or to resist? In a non-itch study from the same laboratory Filevich and colleagues found that immediate decisions to inhibit were less costly in terms of brain activity than planned resistance. Is this willpower in action? If so, such self-generated inhibition is costly, likely to be fatiguing, and will have consequences (Filevich et al., 2013). Finally, it would be interesting to know the consequences of repeated attempts at inhibiting scratch while experiencing an itch. We do not know, for example, whether the deliberate inhibition of scratch leads to increased intensity of the itch, as in an alarm ignored. It is also possible that inhibiting scratch will lead to an amplification of itch on its next occurrence, known as a hangover effect. What is needed is a science of resistance to scratch.

Social emotions

The fate of most attempts to inhibit scratch is that they fail. For many people with chronic itch the failure of control can be as worrying as its consequences. The itch severity scale includes *annoying* and *worrying* as part of the emotional experience. And of course chronic itch can be both of these things. However, when interviewed by Anja Bathe, patients didn't stop at *annoying* and *worrying*. They went far beyond:

> Many participants feel guilty after scratching their skin in an attempt to cope with the unbearable symptom: "One realises afterwards, oh gosh, couldn't you have kept your hands off. But then it's too late" (female aged 26: pruritus of unknown origin). Guilt also appears in the form of chronic pruritus to be constructed as punishment for committed sins: "Why am I punished again, what have I done . . ." (female aged 31: pruritus of systemic origin). Again this imposes substantial strain on the patient. The inability to withstand the urge to scratch and the resulting guilt constitute major psychological problems. Participants also said that they were highly embarrassed about scratching in

the presence of others as this constitutes a taboo. However, the urge in the person can still be felt and they need to come to terms with it. The perception that others can see secondary skin lesions (resulting from scratching) causes substantial feelings of shame and embarrassment. In one participant, who was not experiencing pruritus at the time of the interview, the thought of reappearing pruritus evoked strong emotions of fear, anxiety and helplessness as the association of pruritus and scratching and its ensuing consequences are not easily forgotten.[1]

Particular to the experience of itch is the prominent role of social emotions, in particular, guilt, shame, and embarrassment. Social emotions are the class of emotions that we feel in the context of relationships, so are sometimes called relational or self-conscious. Unfortunately, the management of itch involves the inhibition of a largely automatic behavior of scratch, which, although it can provide relief and momentary pleasure, causes damage and can further exacerbate itch. Therefore at the heart of the experience of itch are two intimately related psychological challenges: first, trying not to do something you really want to do, an immense motivational challenge of enduring and inhibiting desire; and second, when one fails to endure or inhibit and one scratches, this scratching can be accompanied by a profound sense of failure and shame. These two aspects of motivation are core to the psychology of chronic itch.

Shame and disgust

The problem with failure to control scratching is that for people with chronic itch, this failure can become psychologically toxic, leading to extensive patterns of self-destructive beliefs. There is not enough study of this aspect of self-punishment caused by the failure of attempts to control scratch. That experience tends to be lost in the broader discussion of shame of the visual manifestations of altered skin or overt scratching behavior.

For many people the context of chronic itch is the presence of skin disorders that, when aggravated by scratch, can be unsightly, and lead to social isolation and stigma. Part of the experience of skin disorders is fear and embarrassment at the thought of public display of wounds. People often report feeling unattractive and likely to attract attention that can be embarrassing (Hrehorów et al., 2012). In an interesting sociological analysis of stigma, 18 people with psoriasis, a common systemic disease that causes skin lesions, were interviewed about being socially "marked." One person exemplified the dominant theme of separation:

The worst thing with psoriasis is that it is visible and I cannot make it disappear. I feel restricted to loneliness, neither starting a new relation with a man, nor looking for a new job. (Woman, onset at age 18; Uttjek et al., 2007, p. 367)

Exploring lives lived with psoriasis reveals that everyday life is different in subtle ways; it is both more planned and routinized. Where there is skin there is grooming, and the practices of grooming for the person with marked skin involve elaborate hygiene and clothing routines that become an important part of life. Participants described the lengthy deliberations about clothing, about its use in hiding markings, and about the many embarrassments of leaving flaked skin behind. The researchers say of everyone interviewed:

> All participants said that psoriasis had some impact on their quality of life. They never felt fresh; instead they felt messy, unclean, and/or restricted in their life and that the rash's scales made their clothes and spaces around them look untidy. (Uttjek et al., 2007, p. 369)

In this study, however, shame was never openly discussed, and when raised the topic was quickly changed. However, if asked directly, patients with psoriasis do report shame. In a large study from Rome, 936 patients with psoriasis were asked to report on the emotions they felt. Forty-eight percent said they sometimes, often, or always felt humiliated. Embarrassment, anger, and shame were similarly frequent features for more than 60 percent (Sampogna et al., 2012). Parker Magin, a primary care physician from Australia, has led extensive research into the experience of social emotions. In a variety of studies, he asked patients with psoriasis to describe in more depth their experience. For many, the experience of shame and humiliation comes back to a social understanding of hygiene and disease transmission that is part of the social meaning of skin. Patients report feeling not only dirty, but of others' perceptions of them as carriers of infectious disease. This is captured well in one study in which a 42-year-old woman said, "People tend to back away from it or think that it might be contagious. That seems to be a big factor, 'Can I catch it?'" (Magin et al., 2009, p. 157).

The social emotions of shame, embarrassment, and anger operate freely in the context of itch. Scratching is a visible sign of potential skin attack and functions to make others skin-vigilant. Visible skin disorders and recognizable scratch behavior also trigger skin hygiene beliefs. The stigma that is central to the experience of those with chronic skin disease and pruritus is part of a broad set of protective behaviors that rely on *disgust* as a primary driver of avoidance. In their massive global study of disgust, Val Curtis, Robert Aunger, and Tamer Rabie had over 30,000 people worldwide make judgments about how disgusting certain pairs of images were. In one image, a man "was sprayed with a water mist and photo-morphed to look feverish and spotty-faced." As a consequence, "the respondent average disgust score more than doubled, from 1.5 to 3.1." (Curtis et al., 2004, pp. 131–132).

Another pair of images included skin lesions. Both were judged to be disgusting, but the less disgusting one was of a healing wound. A further set of images was of ectoparasites. Of the seven images judged to be disgusting, three were directly

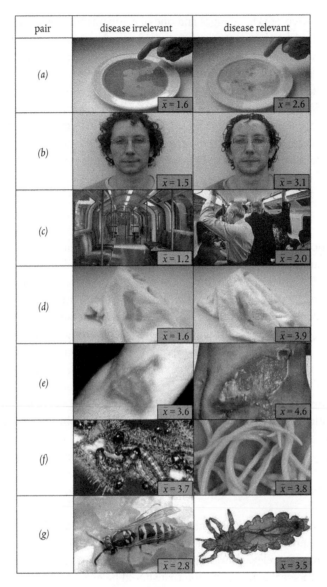

pair	disease irrelevant	disease relevant
(a)	$\bar{x} = 1.6$	$\bar{x} = 2.6$
(b)	$\bar{x} = 1.5$	$\bar{x} = 3.1$
(c)	$\bar{x} = 1.2$	$\bar{x} = 2.0$
(d)	$\bar{x} = 1.6$	$\bar{x} = 3.9$
(e)	$\bar{x} = 3.6$	$\bar{x} = 4.6$
(f)	$\bar{x} = 3.7$	$\bar{x} = 3.8$
(g)	$\bar{x} = 2.8$	$\bar{x} = 3.5$

Fig. 8.2. Stimuli used in the paired disgust sensitivity task ($\bar{x}$ is the average disgust score out of 5 as the most disgusting). (Plate 2)

Reproduced from Val Curtis, Robert Aunger, and Tamer Rabie, Evidence that disgust evolved to protect from risk of disease, Proceedings of the Royal Society of London (1800–1905), 282 (1804), S131–S133, Figure 1 © 2004, The Royal Society.

scratch-related—two of skin changes and one of ectoparasites—and one other was indirectly scratch-related: an image of a crowded subway train. Disgust, Curtis and her colleagues argue, "is an adaptation designed to prevent the acquisition of infectious diseases" (p. 132). Figure 8.2 reproduces the pairs of images used in the study together with their mean disgust scores.

It would be interesting to discover whether just knowing that another person is itching, or the observation of another scratching, is sufficient to communicate disgust and fear of infection, or whether it is only the direct observation of possible causes of infection (like parasites and broken skin) that function to promote hygiene by stimulating disgust.

Formication

The close relationship of itch and scratch to hygiene behavior and parasite load is at its most pronounced when people actually experience the feeling of insects on or under the skin. *Formication* can usefully be thought of as an extreme form of the itch-scratch phenomenon. It is not extreme in the sense of high intensity, but extreme in its function of signaling potential infection, first by mimicking the experience of insects crawling on and under skin, and then generating a strong belief of infestation. Formication, as the actual paresthesia sensation, can be distinguished from the rare delusional state of parasitic infection. In delusional parasitosis, patients believe that they are infested with parasites, which drives behaviors such as attempting to remove the offending insects (Levin and Gieler, 2013). Nancy Hinkle gives a good summary of Ekbom's variation of delusional parasitosis. She makes the point that "although ES [Ekbom's syndrome] is a delusion that the body is infested by bugs, it is almost always accompanied by tactile hallucination of a crawling sensation, or a feeling of biting or stinging" (Hinkle, 2011, p. 178). She also briefly discusses the folie à deux phenomenon that occurs in many delusions in which a close person can come to share the delusional belief.

In order to provoke scratch, all that is normally needed is itch. Beliefs about the cause and consequence of itch do play a role in predicting defensive and hygiene behavior, but are more relevant in chronic pruritus caused by skin disease. Formication, however, is a specific phenomenon that should be explored further because it may hold the key to understanding how bodily senses are interpreted. It is not clear why such a specific paresthesia has evolved. One can speculate that it may be a last line of defense when itch-scratch fails, in digging out a burrowing parasite from the skin, but it is clear that when formication appears what becomes important is not the sensation but the belief. What distinguishes simple formication paresthesia from delusional parasitosis is the role of belief. In the former, one knows that it only *feels like* insects crawling under the skin; in the latter, one believes, and can convince others to believe, that there *are* insects crawling under the skin. Beliefs about itch, its causes and consequences—even rare beliefs like this—are at the heart of the experience of itch and are also the main targets of psychological treatments of chronic itch and chronic scratch.

Psychodermatology

The causes of itch are not always skin-relevant. But for patients the skin is the principal observable organ involved. Whether or not skin is implicated in the cause, it is nearly always involved in the consequences when itch-scratch behaviors take hold. The recognition that skin is psychological has led to the development of the field of *psychodermatology* that covers the treatment of skin disorders in psychiatric populations, the co-presentation of skin and psychological problems, and the role of psychological factors in the experience and adjustment to primary dermatological problems, such as psoriasis, atopic dermatitis, and acne (Bewley et al., 2014). Primary psychological treatments have been developed that focus specifically on itching and scratching, and broader treatments have been developed with the goal of changing beliefs and behaviors to promote the self-management of symptoms and improve quality of life.

In a meta-analysis of psychological treatments, 23 studies of psychological interventions were identified. The studies are varied and cover outcomes that range from itch frequency to shame. In general, the outcomes are promising (Lavda et al., 2012). A few studies focused specifically on the management of itch. Andrea Evers's team have published the most comprehensive study. They undertook a group treatment for adults with atopic dermatitis, which included content on itch management (in particular, techniques of habit reversal) and a focus on beliefs. They used a three-pronged approach: teaching skills to reduce the urge to scratch, building belief in the ability to control and change (self-efficacy), and reducing catastrophic beliefs and worry. Compared to patients who were waiting for treatment, treated patients experienced less itch and scratched less. Treatment was also effective in increasing self-efficacy and reducing worry on an itch-catastrophizing scale (Evers et al., 2009). This is a promising study; it shows that altering scratch behavior is possible.

The psychological treatment of itch is still in its infancy. We lack tools and techniques. Assessment tools are borrowed from other areas and methods are attempted but not yet well specified. Advances in behavior therapy have been slow to transfer to psychodermatology, probably because of the small number of researchers focused on this area. However, the specificity of the itch-scratch behavioral loop makes it an extremely promising target for psychotherapeutic intervention. Given that 10 percent of the population report that itching and scratching are unpleasant and unwelcome in their lives, the development of successful self-management treatments could have far-reaching benefits. First, Evers pioneering work should be built upon. In addition, research into four novel areas could be promising. First, it is important to demonstrate the extent to which scratch can be reduced by graded exposure to itch-inducing stimuli. Second, research into goal planning and motivation to stop scratching is needed. Critical in this will be the study of dealing with setbacks, which many patients report as catastrophic and can generate a wave of self-defeating cognition. Third, negative social emotions are a core part of the experience of chronic itch. Unexplored is the effect of promoting positive social emotions in treatment, in particular of self-compassion, empathy, and pride. Finally, we need to know more about the beliefs that occur in different contexts associated with itch. Many of the studies of cognition in chronic itch have relied on advances in other fields, such as pain, or from general theory. Specific itch theory should guide research. To help, there are qualitative studies of the experience of chronic itch, although more of these studies are needed, especially if they can sample the content, valence, and strength of cognition.

To explore the experience of living with chronic itch, I talked with Neil Carrier (Box 8.2).

Box 8.2. Neil, living with itch: *"it is hard for me to imagine what it is like not to itch"*

Neil is an anthropologist and an expert on East Africa; in particular, the ethnography of drug use. For as long as he can remember, he has had a constant itch in all of his face, which is temporarily relieved by contact—in particular, moving, touching, or rubbing.

Chris: Can you describe for me the sensation of itch?

Neil: That is a difficult question. It seems an obvious sensation. It is just an intensity of feeling. Gosh, it is tricky to describe. It is the intensity of a feeling that is urging me to put pressure on my face to take that feeling away. It is uncomfortable. A tickling, but with moments of real intensity—almost like a rush of it, almost like a piercing itch that demands attention straight away. But other times it is more dull. Sometimes, when it is at its worst, there is an intensity of it. Yes, I wish we had a better language to describe it, really.

Chris: Why don't we have a better language to describe itch?

Neil: It would be easier if we did. To most people an itch is an itch is an itch. But it isn't; it is so much more than that.

Chris: What would happen if you could not move and you could not touch yourself? Would the sensation change?

Neil: It would get much worse—the feeling that I have to do something. I am not sure how I would cope with it if I could not have my hands near my face. I would probably contort myself trying to do something. I would probably tense up to try and take some pressure away. If I could not move I would probably try and do it within me. So probably

Box 8.2. *Continued*

internalize it. I have never got to the point of testing it. Probably I should try that. I have never got to that stage. I always feel it so intensely that I have to respond.

Chris: How do you respond to the itch? Do you scratch?

Neil: I don't really scratch my face. I manage it by putting pressure on different points. If I scratched, then it would just irritate it more in the long run. My strategies have always been to touch my face in a way that puts pressure on it to take away the itch, or causing pain elsewhere for distraction. It is not really scratching. I wonder if I ever really scratched. I used to be more aggressive with pushing my face, and I think I have misshapen my nose through that. But now it is more just putting pressure.

Chris: So is it fair to say that it is experienced through your whole body?

Neil: It is only recently that I begin to realize more and more how much it has affected my life, and how it is lived more and more in my body. I have even damaged my left eye now because I have been rubbing it too much. Because it relieves me a bit. I suspect I might have damaged it. I have pushed that side of my face in a bit with rubbing so much.

Chris: How else does it change your body?

Neil: I am always trying to find ways to keep my hands close to my face. I will always be sitting in a way that keeps my hands in reach of my face. It looks casual but it is deliberate. There are a lot of small things. I will be in seminars and there is a moment when you are not quite ready to ask a question, but the way I sit communicates that I have my hand up. It has happened a couple of times recently when I am not ready to ask a question and I am called upon. I should never go to an auction!

Chris: Does needing to keep your hands near to your face change what you can do socially?

Neil: Yes, I become a lot more aware of it around other people. If I am alone doing my writing then I can sit in whatever position I need to. I always write one-handed, so I have my other hand up to my face. But, yes, when I am around other people in a social environment, then I become more aware of what I am doing that is different from others. It does make me more antisocial than it would otherwise. Depends on the situation. If it is somewhere where you have to stand around, like a drinks reception, I don't like those, because my hands will be full and I won't be able to free them easily.

Chris: Is it itch or embarrassment?

Neil: It is the itch. Some of these receptions can be laborious, but it is definitely something about knowing that I am going to be uncomfortable and itchy. And even when you talk to someone and you realize that you are not giving your best because you are so focused on how to cope. I think, "I am not comfortable, I am feeling really itchy," but I have to keep on talking. My mind starts to focus on the itch rather than engaging with the person. Yes, it definitely makes me uncomfortable in these situations.

(Continued)

Box 8.2. *Continued*

Chris: Are there times of embarrassment?

Neil: Going back quite a long way, when I was younger. If you are constantly touching your face it is noticeable. I just went into my shell about it and didn't want to talk, it was too embarrassing a thing to speak of, really. I just felt so different, and obviously you would get teased about it at school. So over the years I really didn't want to talk about it. Whereas nowadays, I understand partly that I will never improve these things if I don't discuss them. Now I find it quite interesting myself. Intellectually interesting: about how these sensations are embodied. Or perhaps I am just getting older and realize that it is something I have got and there is no reason to be embarrassed about it, as I was when a teenager.

Chris: Has it changed who you are and what you can do?

Neil: Who knows? If I had not had the itch I might be doing something completely different. But I suspect that is putting too much determinism onto the itch. I don't know. I love what I do and the contribution I can make.

I have no idea what life would be like without itch. I wonder what life must be like for people who don't itch. It is a factor every day of my life: how to cope with it, how to adjust, what social things I don't want to go to because I will be uncomfortable. So, yes, it is hard for me to imagine what it is like not to itch.

We think of itch as related to scratching of the skin. Neil's account is fascinating because three ideas dominate. Some we have discussed and others are new. The qualities of itch as urgent and interruptive are reported, and the strange ability of itch to escape description is pondered. But also, we are reminded that *scratch* as a category should include various forms of counterstimulation in response to itch. Novel was Neil's recognition that itch has a whole-body effect. Itch has an effect on Neil's posture, physical poses, habits, and lifestyle choices. And lastly, the extreme of itch, unlike the extreme of dyspnea, pain, or fatigue, was avoided. Any derealization was avoided. Itch is never allowed to go unscratched.

Summary

Itch it is intimately related to the specific behavior of scratch. It operates in the symbolic context of possible external attack to the skin, and it functions to promote a range of hygiene and grooming self-protective behaviors. In a chronic state, much of the suffering of people with itch is about living with constant distraction, personal loss, fear of social rejection, and being different, all of which are expressed as negative social emotions in embarrassment and shame. Itch has a preoccupying attentional quality that makes an external motivational focus difficult. The psychology of itch could provide novel understandings of embodied protective behavior, and there is a very strong case for a growth in psychodermatology, focusing on how to change the lived experience of itch.

Note

1. Reproduced from Chronic pruritus—more than a symptom: a qualitative investigation into patients' subjective illness perceptions, Anja Bathe, Elke Weisshaar, and Uwe Matterne, *Journal of Advanced Nursing*, 69 (2), p. 321, doi:10.1111/j.1365-2648.2012.06009.x Copyright © 2012 Blackwell Publishing Ltd.

References

Bathe, A., Weisshaar, E. and Matterne, E. (2013). Chronic pruritus—more than a symptom: a qualitative investigation into patients' subjective illness perceptions. *Journal of Advanced Nursing*, 69, 316–326.

Bewley, A., Taylor, R.E., Reichenberg, J.S. and Magid, M. (2014). Practical psychodermatology. Chichester: Wiley Blackwell.

bin Saif, G.A., Papoiu, A.D.P., Banari, L., McGlone, F., Kwatra, S.G., Chan, Y.-H. and Yosipovitch, G. (2012). The pleasurability of scratching an itch: a psychophysical and topographical assessment. *British Journal of Dermatology*, 166, 981–985.

Bloomfield, S.F., Exner, M., Carlo Signorelli, C., Nath, K.J. and Scott, E.A. (2012). The chain of infection transmission in the home and everyday life settings, and the role of hygiene in reducing the risk of infection. http://www.ifh-homehygiene.org/IntegratedCRD.nsf/111e6 8ea0824afe1802575070003f039/9df1597d905889868025729700617093?OpenDocument 2012. Accessed January 2015.

Bohne, A., Wilhelm, S., Keuthen, N.J., Baer, L. and Jenike, M.A. (2002). Skin picking in German students: prevalence, phenomenology, and associated characteristics. *Behavior Modification*, 26, 320–339.

Carstens, E. (2008). Itch. In C. Bushnell and A.I. Basbaum (Eds.), The senses: a comprehensive reference, vol. 5: pain (pp. 115–126). Amsterdam: Elsevier.

Curtis, V., Aunger, R. and Rabie, T. (2004). Evidence that disgust evolved to protect from risk of disease. *Proceedings of the Royal Society, London, Biological Sciences (Suppl)*, 271, S131–S133.

Davidson, S. and Giesler, G.J. (2010). The multiple pathways for itch and their interactions with pain. *Trends in Neuroscience*, 33, 550–558.

Demain, J.G. (2003). Papular urticarial and things that bite in the night. *Current Allergy and Asthma Reports*, 3, 291–303.

Essick, G.K., McGlone, F., Dancer, C., Fabricant, D., Ragin, Y., Phillips, N., Jones, T. and Guest, S. (2010). Quantitative assessment of pleasant touch. *Neuroscience and Biobehavioral Reviews*, 34, 192–203.

Evers, A.W.M., Duller, P., de Jong, E.M.G.J., Otero, M.E., Verhaak, C.M., Van der Valk, P.G.M., van de Kerkhof, P. and Kraaimaat, F. (2009). Effectiveness of a multidisciplinary itch-coping training programme in adults with atopic dermatitis. *Acta Dermato-Venereologica*, 89, 57–63.

Feneran, A., O'Donnell, R., Press, A., Yosipovitch, G., Cline, M., Dugan, G., Papoiu, A.D.P., Nattkemper, L.A., Chan, Y.H. and Shively, C.A. (2013). Monkey see, monkey do: contagious itch in non-human primates. *Acta Dermato-Venereologica*, 93, 27–29.

Filevich, E. and Haggard, P. (2012). Grin and bear it! Neural consequences of a voluntary decision to act or inhibit action. *Experimental Brain Research*, 223, 341–351.

Filevich, E., Kühn, S. and Haggard, P. (2013). There is no free won't: antecedent brain activity predicts decisions to inhibit. *PLoS One*, 8, e53053.

Hanfield-Jones, S. (2009). Itching. *Medicine*, 37, 273–276.

Hatta, T. and Dimond, S.J. (1984). Differences in face touching by Japanese and British people. *Neuropsychologia*, 22, 531–534.

Hinkle, N.C. (2011). Ekbom syndrome: a delusional condition of "bugs in the skin." *Current Psychiatry Reports*, 13, 178–186.

Hrehorów, E., Salomon, J., Matusiak, L., Reich, A. and Szepietowski, J.C. (2012). Patients with psoriasis feel stigmatized. *Acta Dermato-Venereologica*, 92, 67–72.

Hsieh, J.-C., Hägermark, Ö., Ståhle-Bäckdahl, M., Ericson, K., Eriksson, L, Stone-Elander, S. and Ingvar, M. (1994). The urge to scratch represented in the human cerebral cortex during itch. *Journal of Neurophysiology*, 72, 3004–3008.

Lavda, A.C., Webb, T.L. and Thompson, A.R. (2012). A meta-analysis of the effectiveness of psychological interventions for adults with skin conditions. *British Journal of Dermatology*, 167, 970–979.

Levin, E.C. and Gieler, U. (2013). Delusions of parasitosis. *Seminars in Cutaneous Medicine and Surgery*, 32, 73–77.

Lloyd, D.M., Hall, E., Hall, S. and McGlone, F.P. (2013). Can itch-related visual stimuli alone provoke a scratch response in healthy individuals? *British Journal of Dermatology*, 168, 106–111.

Magin, P., Adams, J., Heading, G., Pond, D. and Smith, W. (2009). The psychological sequelae of psoriasis: results of a qualitative study. *Psychology, Health and Medicine*, 14, 150–161.

Majeski, C.J., Johnson, J.A., Davison, S.N. and Lauzon, G.J. (2007). Itch Severity Scale: a self-report instrument for the measurement of pruritus severity. *British Journal of Dermatology*, 156, 667–673.

Matterne, U., Apfelbacher, C.J., Loerbroks, A., Schwarzer, T., Büttner, M., Ofenloch, R., Diepgen, T.L. and Weisshaar, E. (2011). Prevalence, correlates and characteristics of chronic pruritus: a population-based cross-sectional study. *Acta Dermato-Venereologica*, 91, 674–679.

Matterne, U., Strassner, T., Apfelbacher, C.J., Diepgen, T.L. and Weisshaar, E. (2009). Measuring the prevalence of chronic itch in the general population: development and validation of a questionnaire for use in large-scale studies. *Acta Dermato-Venereologica*, 89, 250–256.

McGlone, F., Wessberg J., Olausson H. (2014). Discriminative and affective touch: sensing and feeling. *Neuron*, 82, 737–755.

Miller, D.M., Brodell, R.T. and Herr, R. (1996). Wilderness dermatology: prevention, diagnosis, and treatment of skin disease related to the great outdoors. *Wilderness and Environmental Medicine*, 2, 146–169.

Mora, C., Tittensor, D.P., Adl, S., Simpson, A.G.B. and Worm, B. (2011). How many species are there on earth and in the ocean? *PLoS Biology*, 9, e1001127.

Papoiu, A.D.P., Nattkember, L.A., Sanders, K.M., Kraft, R.A., Chan, Y.-H, Coghill, R.C. and Yosipovitch, G. (2013). Brain reward circuits mediate itch relief: a functional MRI study of active scratching. *PLoS One*, 8, e82389.

Papoiu, A.D.P., Wang, H., Coghill, R.C., Chan, Y.-H. and Yosipovitch, G. (2011). Contagious itch in humans: a study of visual "transmission" of itch in atopic dermatitis and healthy subjects. *British Journal of Dermatology*, 164, 1299–1303.

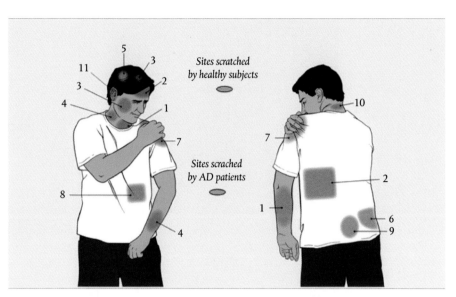

Plate 1: The distribution of scratching episodes in widespread (scattered) areas, in patients with atopic dermatitis (AD) and healthy subjects.

"The distribution of scratching episodes in widespread (scattered) areas, in patients with atopic dermatitis (AD) and healthy subjects, reveals that patients with AD experienced an itch that extended beyond the local itch induction site, becoming generalized, while they watched the itch video (in red). Scratching beyond the local site in healthy participants was limited to the face, neck and contralateral forearm (in blue). The areas scratched are shown in ranking order (by mean duration) for an exposure to the itch video, when the local itch stimulus (histamine) was delivered to the right forearm (i.e., scratching on the contralateral forearm is represented). Subjects with AD scratched mostly their contralateral forearm (1), mid-back region (2), face (3), neck (4) and scalp (5). Note that colored areas indicate in a figurative manner the location of scratching sites and are not intended to depict to scale the extent of the skin surface scratched."

Reproduced from Contagious itch in humans: a study of visual 'transmission' of itch in atopic dermatitis and healthy subjects, A.D.P. Papoiu, H. Wang, R.C. Coghill, Y-H. Chan, and G. Yosipovitch, *British Journal of Dermatology*, 164 (6), pp. 1299–1303, Figure 4, doi: 10.1111/j.1365–2133.2011.10318.x Copyright (c) 2011, John Wiley and Sons.

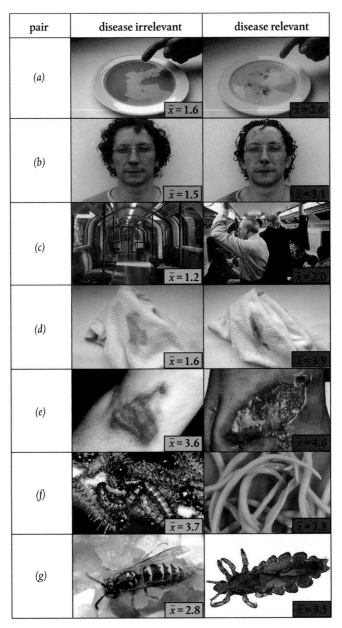

pair	disease irrelevant	disease relevant
(a)	$\bar{x} = 1.6$	$\bar{x} = 2.6$
(b)	$\bar{x} = 1.5$	$\bar{x} = 3.1$
(c)	$\bar{x} = 1.2$	$\bar{x} = 2.0$
(d)	$\bar{x} = 1.6$	$\bar{x} = 3.9$
(e)	$\bar{x} = 3.6$	$\bar{x} = 4.6$
(f)	$\bar{x} = 3.7$	$\bar{x} = 3.8$
(g)	$\bar{x} = 2.8$	$\bar{x} = 3.5$

Plate 2: Stimuli used in the paired disgust sensitivity task ($\bar{x}$-is the average disgust score out of 5 as the most disgusting).

Reproduced from Val Curtis, Robert Aunger, and Tamer Rabie, Evidence that disgust evolved to protect from risk of disease, Proceedings of the Royal Society of London (1800–1905), 282 (1804), S131–S133, Figure 1 © 2004, The Royal Society.

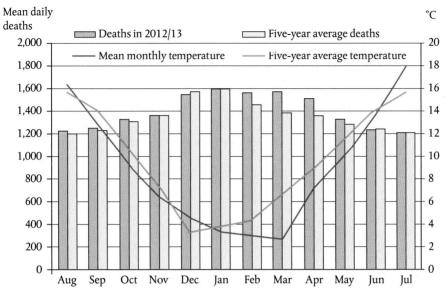

Plate 3: Average daily deaths and monthly temperatures in England and Wales in 2012/13 and a five-year average.

Plate 4: Coughs and Sneezes Spread Diseases. Circa 1960.

©The British Library Board, B.S.81/19.

Prokop, P., Fančovičová, J. and Fodor P. (2014). Parasites enhance self-grooming behaviour and information retention in humans. *Behavioural Processes*, 107, 42–46.

Sampogna, F., Tabolli, S., Abeni, D. and the IDI Multipurpose Psoriasis Research on Vital Experiences (IMPROVE) investigators. (2012). Living with psoriasis: prevalence of shame, anger, worry, and problems in daily activities and social life. *Acta Dermato-Venereologica*, 92, 299–303.

Savin, J.A. (1998). How should we define itching? *Journal of the American Academy of Dermatology*, 39, 268–269.

Thompson, K.P.J. (2010). Grooming the naked ape: do perceptions of disease and aggression vulnerability influence grooming behavior in humans? A comparative ethological perspective. *Current Psychology*, 29, 288–296.

Twycross, R., Greaves, M.W., Handwerker, H., Jones, E.A., Libretto, S.E., Szepietowski, J.C. and Zylicz, Z. (2003). Itch: scratching more than the surface. *Quarterly Journal of Medicine*, 96, 7–26.

Uttjek, M., Nygren, L., Stenberg, B. and Dufåker, M. (2007). Marked by visibility of psoriasis in everyday life. *Qualitative Health Research*, 17, 364–372.

Van Laarhoven, I.M., Kraaimaat, F., Wilder-Smith, O. and Evers, A.W.M. (2010). Role of attentional focus on bodily sensations in sensitivity to itch and pain. *Acta Dermato-Venereologica*, 90, 46–51.

Verhoeven, E.W.M., de Klerk, S., Kraaimaat, F., van de Kerkhof, P.C.M., de Jong, E.M.G.J. and Evers, A.W.M. (2008). Biopsychosocial mechanisms of chronic itch in patients with skin diseases: a review. *Acta Dermato-Venereologica*, 88, 211–218.

Verhoeven, L., Kraaimaat, F., Duller, P., van de Kerkhof, P. and Evers, A. (2006). Cognitive, behavioral, and physiological reactivity to chronic itching: analogies to chronic pain. *International Journal of Behavioral Medicine*, 13, 237–243.

Weisshaar, E. and Dalgard, F. (2009). Epidemiology of itch: adding to the burden of skin morbidity. *Acta Dermato-Venereologica*, 89, 339–350.

Weisshaar, E., Gieler, U., Kupfer, J., Furue, M., Saeki, H. and Yosipovitch, G. (2012). Questionnaires to assess chronic itch: a consensus paper of the Special Interest Group of the International Forum on the Study of Itch. *Acta Dermato-Venereologica*, 92, 493–496.

Weisshaar, E., Szepietowski, J.C., Darsow, U., Misery, L., Wallengren, J., Mettang, T., . . . and Ständer, S. (2012). European guideline on chronic pruritus. In cooperation with the European Dermatology Forum (EDF) and the European Academy of Dermatology and Venereology (EADV). *Acta Dermato-Venereologica*, 92, 563–581.

CHAPTER 9

TEMPERATURE

We need help when it comes to managing body temperature. Although we have good physiological mechanisms of thermoregulation, they are not perfect. There are limits to our unconscious ability to automatically adjust body temperature in response to a changing environment. Human core temperature is approximately 37°C but we can only operate safely within a narrow range: with hypothermia starting at 35° and hyperthermia at 39°, if not earlier. Before we get to these temperatures, or stay at them for too long, we need to intervene and engage in a variety of exogenous thermoregulatory behaviors. Or to put it more simply: we need to know when to put on or take off a hat. Effective thermoregulation needs thermoperception.

This chapter is about our experience of perceiving temperature, of being hot and warm, cold and cool, and everything in-between. The physiological mechanisms of thermoperception occur at the periphery of skin and centrally in the brain. How we perceive and make sense of the temperature of the outside world and at the same time maintain our own temperature is a remarkable achievement. It is so important that the language of heat and its loss extends far beyond the simple judgment of body temperature, with *hot* and *cold* being used to refer to emotions, characters, situations, and actions. Is the tendency to describe anything and everything with reference to temperature more than just linguistic laziness? Perhaps this is how cognition works, grounded in everyday base realities like temperature.

Equally intriguing is what I think is one of life's great puzzles: why don't people put on a hat when it gets cold? I admit it might not seem the most pressing challenge of the human condition. But the decisions we make to protect ourselves, and how they go wrong, are what hide behind the statistics on winter deaths; life and death decisions in response to environmental pressure. One answer of why people behave in particular ways is a social one: we make thermoregulatory decisions, like hat wearing, in a social context. Shivering or sweating in public, for example, communicate more than body temperature, and sweating in particular can be very challenging. Body temperature is one of the primary vitals sign of health, measured repeatedly and often, everyday, all across the world. Exactly what meanings temperature acquires and how it is experienced in specific health contexts teaches us a lot about the psychology of bodily perception. I close with an examination of a primary disorder of thermoregulation known as Raynaud's phenomenon. It is a good test of whether psychology can be useful, and go beyond observation and explanation.

Two people helped me explore the experiences of temperature. First I spoke with Alex who is a blacksmith. He spends his working life in high ambient temperatures and close to white hot metal. He has thought carefully about the effects of heat on his body. Euphemia was also kind in talking to me about what it is like to live with Raynaud's phenomenon. An awareness of temperature, temperature change, and the importance of clothing are never far from her thoughts.

Thermoregulation

The skin is the main sense organ for temperature:

> Thermosensation . . . is one of the sensory modalities of the skin. It provides (1) a thermoregulatory afferent signal for homeostatic mechanisms which keep the body at an optimal working temperature, (2) the capability to detect potentially noxious thermal stimuli that pose an immediate threat to the integrity of the integument (i.e., noxious cold and heat stimuli) (3) afferent signals which contribute to the identification of objects and materials through touch, e.g., metals are easily discriminated from wood because metals feel colder than wood.[1]

This rather neat summary shows the various functions of temperature perception in the skin. It functions to do three things simultaneously: to promote biological homeostasis, to protect the organism, and to support haptic exploration.

Neurophysiological studies have now shown a relative specification in cold and warm fibers that function only in response to their temperature ranges, and do not operate as mechanoreceptors or as nociceptors. These dedicated afferents also project spinally, in the thalamus and to the cortex, relatively intact. Joris Vriens and his colleagues give a clear summary of the current state of research in the peripheral and central mechanisms, discussing the progress in our understanding of ion channels, which they describe engagingly as "molecular thermometers that translate environmental and internal thermal cues into electrical activity in the somatosensory system" (Vriens et al., 2014, p. 586). Thermoreceptors are also found outside of the skin: in muscle, viscera, and particular organs including the eye, the mouth, and the trachea.

Sensory neurons have their cell bodies clustering in either the dorsal root ganglia for the body, or in the trigeminal ganglia for innervated structures of the head, including the face. Neuroimaging studies of temperature challenges show the involvement of both the thalamus and hypothalamus, as well as cortical structures such as the somatosensory cortex. As with other interoceptive states such as fatigue, pain, itch, hunger, and thirst—which all require behavior to alter homeostasis— older regulatory structures such as the hypothalamus that drive urgent behavior are implicated (Egan et al., 2005). Physiologically, what is remarkable about temperature is the maintenance of core body temperature within an extremely tight temperature range, despite major fluctuations in environmental temperature. The system is best thought of as an integrated pattern of multiple looping feedforward and feedback sensory and effector systems, with conscious experience emerging as a by-product that provokes behavioral regulation only when autonomic regulation fails (Romanovsky, 2006).

Primary regulation is achieved physiologically by changes in heat output and changes in the movement and flow of blood. Increases in core heat will lead to blood moving heat away from the core, flushing near to the skin (hence the change in skin color) where heat is lost from the skin in sweat. We tend to think of the movement of blood in terms of oxygen carriage; however, blood circulation also functions successfully as part of the temperature regulation system, transporting heat. Similarly, in preserving core temperature blood is transported centrally, and muscle activity is increased in an attempt to increase heat production. The most observable examples are shivering and teeth chattering.

Secondary regulation, by which I mean behavior aimed at changing body temperature (seeking shade or sun, or adjusting clothing), is often invoked only after primary regulation reaches its limits. However, it operates to support the same functions of temperature regulation by attempts to either insulate from or promote heat loss, and/or by attempts to produce or conserve heat. We don't think of the choices we make in dressing as a form of secondary behavioral thermoregulation, but that is exactly what they are. When we decide to put on a coat we are assisting the three functions of temperature: maintaining biological homeostasis, protecting the self, and allowing touch to be more discriminating when we explore the world.

However, as we have come to understand, our psychology of the body does not always follow simple physiological rules. It misbehaves. The decisions we make about temperature are not very straightforward and are open to a variety of influences. The distinction I made between primary and secondary is maybe too simple, too dualistic. Secondary regulation does not operate slavishly in response to a failure of primary regulation. Consciousness gets in the way. Consider that we can be planful, putting on clothes in preparation for cold temperatures; willful, taking off a shirt in −5°C at a soccer game in celebration; or just fashionable, wearing branded wellingtons in a 35°C New York thoroughfare.

Let's explore this interplay of primary and secondary regulation. There are two specific cases that demonstrate how the perception of temperature has a strong influence on our behavior and how behavior has a strong influence on our perception of temperature. The first is in how body temperature affects our judgment of others' character. The second is in how far our emotions can actually change our judgment of temperature, and influence our thermoregulatory behavior.

Blowing hot and cold: judging others' character

The language of temperature has been very useful for describing a broad range of human behaviors. Consider, for example, that we often describe people who show anger as *hot-headed* or *fiery*, and those whom we consider to be calculating and less influenced by emotion as *cool* under pressure or *cold-hearted*. Perhaps this may be because emotional arousal can often look like thermoregulation (e.g., turning red). But this goes beyond arousal. When I reject you I can be said to give you the *cold* shoulder, but if you accept me, you might give me a *warm* welcome. Away from the extremes of hot and cold, we can unfavorably describe those who appear inconsistent as *intemperate*, implying that we cannot tolerate their extremes. These are people who blow *hot and cold*, implying they are unpredictable. Linguistically, at least, it seems that we value certainty, control, and order, and that metaphors that refer to basic features of life such as hot and cold work well for us. But language is fundamentally metaphorical. We consistently talk about things in reference to other things. It is not that surprising that temperature is used metaphorically. Lawrence Williams and John Bargh, however, suggested that the association between temperature and the judgments of others' character goes beyond metaphor, is more than linguistic coincidence. In two intriguing experiments, they adapted a well-established test of this idea and exposed people to warming or cooling prior to making judgments.

Please hold my coffee

In a classic social psychology deception study, an experimenter met the student subjects at the entrance to a university building and they took an elevator together to the laboratory four floors up. While in the elevator the experimenter asked the subject to hold either a warm coffee or an iced coffee for them while they wrote notes. After this warm-cold exposure, the students underwent what they thought was the experiment, which involved making judgments about many things, including people's character. Those exposed to the warmth judged the characters of strangers to be warmer (more trustworthy and likable) and those exposed to the cold judged the opposite. In a second, improved experiment, they replaced the outcome of a judgment of character with a behavior of whether they would act more prosocially (less selfishly) toward another person after feeling warm. Again, they found that people are more egocentric following a cold experience. The researchers concluded that "experiences of physical temperature per se affect one's impressions of and pro-social behavior toward other people, without one's awareness of such influences" (Williams and Bargh, 2008 p. 607). This finding has been replicated and also extended to judgments of how close one feels to other people, as an attempt to explore social warmth (Ijzerman and Semin, 2009).

Cold and lonely: a Bridget Jones effect

Is it really possible that one's perception of physical temperature directly affects a judgment of another's social warmth? If so, then the opposite might also be true: that emotions directly affect a judgment of temperature and liking. Chen-Bo Zhong and Geoffrey Leonardelli asked just this question in two experiments. Specifically, they were interested in whether rejecting somebody led to them judging the temperature of a room as colder. In one experiment they simply asked students to recall a time when they had been socially excluded, with another group recalling a time of social acceptance. After this remembering, the participants were asked to judge various aspects of their environment, including room temperature. Real room temperature was held constant. Those who thought about being rejected gave an average room temperature of 21.44°C compared to those who thought about feeling accepted, who judged the room to be an average of 24.02°C. A small difference, perhaps, but not a chance difference. And when it comes to temperature, a difference of 2.5°C can be a life-or-death matter (Zhong and Leonardelli, 2008).

Taking these ideas further, John Bargh and Idit Shalev were interested in those who feel chronically rejected, not just by an experimenter. In their own words, they hypothesized

> that people (implicitly) compensate for the lack of social warmth in their lives with increased physical warmth experiences. Specifically, we hypothesized that chronic or "trait" loneliness . . . of our participants would be positively associated with the frequency, duration, and preferred water temperature of the showers and baths that they take. (Bargh and Shalev, 2012, p. 156)

The first study was with students and the second with people from the community. The researchers' methods were simple. They masqueraded as undertaking a survey about everyday habits, and included questions about frequency, length of exposure, and water temperature in bathing habits, which they combined into a measure of how much heat is taken. They then measured loneliness. In both samples, significant correlations were found between loneliness and heat extraction. Bargh and Shalev concluded that social exclusion leads to physical comfort behaviors: if you feel rejected you will seek out physical warmth.

That we seek comfort when we are lonely is perhaps a simpler explanation for such effects. We could usefully call it a Bridget Jones effect, after Helen Fielding's popular character who is unlucky in love and becomes expert at self-comforting (Fielding, 1996). However, investigators propose more specific effects. For example, in one study using similar experimental methods, social rejection was not only associated with the judgment of body temperature, but with skin temperature measured objectively. In a perhaps unforgivable pun the authors call this effect *cold-blooded loneliness* (Ijzerman et al., 2012).

The extent to which such effects are robust and specific to temperature need to be properly established, because attempts at replication are proving elusive (Lynott et al., 2008; Wortman et al., 2014). This research is only at its beginning, but the trail may already be going cold.

The idea that the linguistic coding of social and personal judgments using a language of temperature is more than metaphorical is a form of embodied cognition, in which experience can directly affect and be affected by sensorimotor processes. In a weak form, there is the idea that moral, social, and relational thoughts and emotions are played out on and in the body. If we are disgusted by a thought, do we want to wash? Similarly, if we are given the *cold shoulder* of rejection, do we seek out comforting warmth? In this weak form, the shared language is just a metaphorical clue. But in a stronger form, embodied cognition holds that physiology and psychology are inextricably linked: that perception—in this case, the perception of temperature—can make sense only within its social and personal environment, and as such, "the environment is part of the cognitive system" (Wilson, 2002, p. 626).

The possibility that being cold can lead to less generosity or social sharing, or that being rejected makes one feel cold and seek warmth, can be interpreted within the context of the broader function of self-protection. For a social animal such as a human, rejection can indeed lead to isolation and possible exposure. If you are going to be cast out from a group, you are going to be exposed to the elements, and so better find protection.

Protecting ourselves from the elements: secondary regulation

How successful are we at avoiding the extremes of temperature and taking action to protect ourselves from exposure to the elements? In part the answer depends on what experience we have of living exposed to those elements. Many people live in extreme climates. I am writing this chapter in a country with a famously temperate and wet climate, but even here in the UK, we have recorded a highest temperature of 38.5°C in August 2003, and a lowest temperature of −26.1°C in January 1982 (http://www.metoffice.gov.uk/). We need to behave to protect ourselves from the elements.

Secondary regulation operates in exactly the same two modes as primary regulation. When cold, we act to preserve the heat we have and generate new heat, and when hot, we act to lose the heat we have and prevent new heat from building: a simple, well-mapped functional system. Except this means we need to have a good understanding of how to behave to support these two mechanisms. And, of course, we need to behave in accordance with good thermodynamic and physiological principles.

Mad dogs and Englishmen

Psychology teaches us repeatedly and often that humans are just not rational. We do not behave in line with thermodynamic principles, however much it would be in our interest. Frances Ashcroft, in her engaging and entertaining study *Life at the Extremes*, discusses how different approaches to secondary thermoregulation have been attempted. The Noel Coward observation that only mad dogs and Englishmen go out in the Indian midday sun, says Aschroft, was due to a mistaken belief that vigorous exercise in the sun protected against tropical disease. A more simple error can be seen in the removal of clothing in the sun believing it cooling, when people who live in hot climates often do the opposite, wearing loose-fitting ventilated clothes. It is the difference between sun-basking tourists and shade-seeking locals (Ashcroft, 2001).

Climate-driven behavior is particularly interesting and only rarely studied at a psychological level. For example, we know that deaths from both hot and cold weather are common. A recent study of cold-related mortality, or excess winter deaths, gave an estimate of over two million deaths in Europe in 2002–2010 (Fowler, 2015). Older people are significantly more at risk, a finding also reported for heat-related mortality (Baccini et al., 2011). At a population level, it seems we are unprepared for these extreme temperatures. Perhaps our secondary regulation is failing; we are not making good decisions.

A hint of what may be happening was found in a landmark study by the large Eurowinter research team. They explored differences in the decisions that individuals make about temperature. People respond very differently to the same temperatures:

> Outdoors at 7°C, people living in regions with warm winters were less likely to wear a hat (13% Athens, 72% south Finland), an anorak, gloves, or trousers (among women), though total clothing area was similar; they were more likely to wear a skirt (women), an overcoat, or a sweater, and more likely also to stand still and to shiver, and less likely to sweat.[2]

What seems to matter in the decision to put on a hat is not whether it is cold but whether the cold temperatures are out of the ordinary for your normal climate. They conclude, "Although we know that the middle-aged and elderly should wear protective clothing and keep active in cold weather outdoors, our surveys show that in relatively warm countries they often fail to do so."[3] We don't seem to be heeding the advice of our grandmothers (Sperber and Weitzman, 1997), perhaps worried about the impression that "old-fashioned" behaviors might have on our social standing (Day and Hitchings, 2011).

"The apparel oft proclaims the man"

Shakespeare was aware that clothes matter. But perhaps he should have written, "Ignorance of apparel oft undoes the man." Clothing can be a matter of life and death. Psychology has not been very interested in clothes as protection. There is a rich psychology of clothing; however, virtually none of it concerns human decision making about the thermal properties of different garments. Perhaps that is unsurprising. If we take heat for granted, then clothes serve a variety of functions more interesting to the social scientist: for body adornment, for bodily satisfaction, in communication, and in establishing social status, role, and desire. For example, in a study of 223 young women in the United States on how fitted they liked their clothes to be, the various benefits of the clothes they liked were examined, with "fashion innovativeness" coming out top (Alexander et al., 2005). Perhaps we should expect this from young women in a warm California. So what about older women in Helskinki? The same. In an in-depth qualitative study of ten women in Finland, comfort was mentioned but fashion and cut were the highest concerns (Holmlund et al., 2011). Perhaps when it comes to clothing, in affluent societies at least, we take the thermal properties of clothing for granted. The challenge in temperate climates is in knowing when to pay attention to changes in temperature that require changes in clothing behavior.

Entering the extremes

There are places where extreme conditions demand more careful consideration of temperature—where survival would be measured in minutes and seconds if you *didn't* think about temperature. Some people, and all of us some of the time, are motivated by more than keeping warm. We have goals that threaten thermoregulation, whether in pursuit of work, sport, play, or adventure. But overriding thermoregulation with another goal puts us at risk: homeostasis may be compromised, the ability to protect ourselves sacrificed, and our ability to explore the world challenged.

Humans make mistakes when temperature-stressed. For example, in one study of helicopter pilot accidents, the number of accidents increased proportionally with the heat of the helicopter cab (Froom et al., 1993). Vigilance and attention to change are at particular risk in higher temperatures. In one well-controlled study in which cognitive performance was measured at 0°C, 23°C, and 40°C, it was only at 40°C that vigilance failed and errors increased. What seems to matter, however, is not ambient external or even skin temperature, but changes in core temperature. Only when primary regulation is insufficient and homeostasis fails does attention fail (Faerevik and Eidsmo Reinertsen, 2003).

Firefighters are particularly at risk of challenges to decision making. In the specific environment of fire, rescue motivation may be high, but critical decisions need to be made: decisions about harm, in environments defined by danger; decisions about time, when duration of exposure to high temperatures and thermal radiation matters; indeed, decisions about survival itself. Unfortunately, the psychological study of real-world heat stress has been limited. There are general effects of exposure to extreme heat, nearly all showing decrement. Most studies are undertaken in controlled environments with specific cognitive tasks (Pilcher et al., 2002). It has not been possible to recreate the emotional and motivational contexts that would teach us how temperature affects life or death decisions. In the case of firefighting, for example, we don't know whether a motivationally rich and extreme environment of rescue will impair or improve mental performance, or have no effect at all. (Barr et al, 2010)

Similar findings of exposure to cold have been reported. Mathew Muller and colleagues explored the effects of cold on cognitive performance. They measured attention, memory, and aspects of decision making when acutely exposed to 10°C for two hours, and on re-warming. Working memory—the attention and updating aspect of cognition—was particularly impaired in cold temperatures (Muller et al., 2012). Although this study was very well controlled, the findings need replication, in particular to determine how important the losses are in complex, real-world decisions. Field studies of people living and working in extreme cold environments suggest that such cognitive changes are at worst just temporary (Paul et al., 2010).

There is a gap to cross between controlled experiments showing that extreme temperatures can affect psychological function and the fact that many people appear to function in those environments (Burke and Orlick, 2003). Not only do they function, but they are motivated to put themselves into those extreme temperatures. The data from the winter mortality studies suggest that we are not good at making the necessary adjustments when the temperature changes, that we have low "situational awareness." Perhaps those who choose to live or work in extremes of temperature are better prepared, more reactive, or have learned the warning signals. Those who expect and prepare for extreme temperatures may do better than those who do not expect and fail to prepare for minor changes. How do we notice when the danger creeps up on us, or when secondary regulation of temperature is sorely needed?

To explore the ideas of how one can live or work in extremes of temperature, making decisions in the moment, and whether heat changes one's world-view I talked with Alex Coode (Box 9.1).

Box 9.1. Alex, the heritage blacksmith: *"you have a holiday from your body"*

Alex is a blacksmith who works now on heritage projects. He has a passion for iron and its use in restoration work, and just how far nature can be represented in forging. He has three forges situated in a historic foundry in the UK. Alex describes himself as single-minded and stubborn. He knew he wanted to work with iron and said of forging, "It is so physically and mentally demanding. I love it. In several lifetimes I would never master it. There would always be more to learn." In this interview it will help to know that the word *forge* has multiple referents. It is confusingly used as a verb to mean working the metal, as a noun to describe the fire, and as the building that houses the forges and where the forging is done. So Alex forges at a forge in a forge.

Box 9.1. *Continued*

Chris: How hot does it get in a forge?

Alex: The ambient temperature in the workshop can get up into the late 40s, which is hot. You can tell it is hot because you have to drink a lot.

Chris: In working the metal how close to the heat do you need to get?

Alex: There are a lot of processes where you need to be seeing what is happening in the fire and so being quite close to it. The nature of forging is that it has to be accurate with the right amount of force and done quickly. Because what you have taken out of the forge is at the right temperature, then it is immediately trying to cool down. The second law of thermodynamics is doing its very best to make everything the same temperature.

Chris: So speed matters?

Alex: Not just speed but accuracy. Forging is technical and physical. You want to be working the metal when it is white hot, or orange, preferably light orange; otherwise it is too late. They say that there are two ways for a blacksmith to go to hell: one is undercharging and the other is working the metal when it is too cold. While a piece is in the fire, resource is going into making it ready to work. If you don't work fast and accurately, and you don't have the right equipment to hand, then you will waste that resource.

Chris: Do you get used to the heat?

Alex: Sometimes the heat can be quite shocking, but it does not last long. Once you have established that it is not going to hurt you. You don't worry about it. You just ignore it.

Chris: How do you know it is not going to hurt you?

Alex: Because after the first few times you have not been hurt. It is a bit like hot sauce on food. If you were not expecting it and you didn't know it was safe, your mouth would be telling you that you are injured. But you learn from experience that it is not harming you.

One of the most important reflexes you build up as a blacksmith is the one that makes you let go if you feel any residual heat in what you have just picked up. If something is white or orange or even red heat. If you pick it up you will very rarely get burned because you sort of know. There will be a hissing noise and a slight smell of bacon. I have a theory that the hiss does not have far to go to get to your brain. Burns happen when you get hold of something that is black and does not make a hissing noise when you grab it. By the time the message has reached your brain that there is danger, that you are being burned, it is too late and you have a nasty burn.

Chris: Is discomfort a necessary part of being exposed to heat in forging?

Alex: No. The opposite is true. Because the work itself is so absorbing, you don't notice the discomfort and the small injuries like burns. You can finish a session at a forge and realize that you have strained something or burned something. That twisted ankle that bothered you in the morning you have forgotten about. Because you have to work so fast

(Continued)

Box 9.1. *Continued*

and hard it takes your full attention. So you don't feel the heat. You tend not to notice it. The activity of forging itself is so absorbing, it requires your complete focus so you switch off anything that is unrelated to what you are doing.

Chris: I can't work out whether being so absorbed is good or bad. Do you see it as a benefit or a danger?

Alex: I would say it is a benefit. You have a holiday from your body. When you repeat it again and again it liberates you to a large extent from your perceived limitations. You realize that you can do more. And so I think it does alter the way you think about yourself, the way you interact with the world and with your own body. If you can so easily forget, completely forget, about whatever you thought was so important that morning, then it is obviously a choice.

Chris: Have we become too aware of discomfort, too ready to avoid too much or too little heat?

Alex: The heat of forging is not comfortable—I wouldn't say that. I am aware of it but just choosing not to address it. I do think in general that people's comfort zones have shrunk. On a hot day we go from air-conditioned house to car to office. People can isolate themselves from discomfort. For many people a lot of things that are uncomfortable are not worth considering. Anything that involves extremes of physical labor or temperature have all been cushioned. I think that is the challenge of modern life. What is the point of complaining about the heat? It is what it is.

For Alex, living with the extremes of heat appeared to be unusually edifying, not something much discussed in the psychology of temperature studies. It will be interesting to know the extent to which those who routinely live or work outside of normal ranges of temperature believe that this confers benefits in general self-preservation, self-determination, or grit. Being absorbed was also seen here as positive, allowing freedom from restriction or challenge from one's body.

The paradox of sweating

Not everyone wants or is able to escape their physical experience. For many people, the experience of being hot can be overwhelming and come to dominate their lives, especially when it results in the observable forms of primary regulation such as sweating.

Sweating is normal, and a useful mechanism of heat loss. However, despite this normal, functional, and highly useful mechanism, it is not often personally enjoyed or socially celebrated. In fact, for many people it is experienced as unpleasant, unwelcome, and even disgusting. In part this may be due to the ability of thermo-regulation to be shaped by influences other than its primary functions. Autonomic arousal in anxiety can be thought of as highjacked thermoregulation: in sweating, in blushing, and in trembling (Harker, 2013). For some people, sweating that serves no obvious thermoregulatory function is a clinical problem seen in dermatology as a major limiting factor on people's lives. Paradoxically, anxiety about sweating can create further sweating, leading some to explore whether a primary treatment might be psychological: to alter the unhelpful and anxiety-exacerbating beliefs people hold about sweating.

One measure of common cognitions in *hyperhidrosis* (excessive sweating) captured the range of negative beliefs commonly expressed. In the main they relate to fear of embarrassment, negative evaluation of self-competence, and social rejection (e.g., "people will think I'm incompetent if I sweat"); but also a belief that sweating is asso-ciated with poor personal hygiene (e.g., "people will think I didn't shower because I'm sweaty"); and its social consequences (e.g., "people are disgusted by my sweat") (Wheaton et al., 2011). These items show how sweating, perhaps because it often hap-pens with fever, is so often associated with illness and disease, and therefore with the protective reactions of fear and disgust (Curtis, 2001).

The treatment of fear and loathing of sweating is lost within the wider constructs of social phobia and fear of social rejection. For many people with such a fear, *blushing* is often the primary focus because of its autonomic immediacy and its visibility. Sweat-ing takes a secondary position. However, for those who develop an emotionally main-tained hyperhidrosis, specific beliefs may well be important. For a well-cited example, Agnes Scholing and Paul Emmelkamp explored a typical cognitive therapy approach of addressing the reality of dominant self-statements such as "blushing means that you hide something." (Scholing and Emmelkamp, 1993, p. 159). They step-by-step helped people to test these beliefs and found them to be largely without evidence. The problem that is often unexplored in standard cognitive therapy for social phobia is that sweating does actually elicit disgust and avoidance. It is not an irrational belief. People don't like it. It is not clear how far the challenging of the veracity of beliefs that have a strong basis in reality is helpful. Exploring the specific fear associated with sweating—be it unwelcome scrutiny, public disapprobation, loss of personal control, or even a fear of the consequences of heat loss—will be important (Moscovitch, 2009).

In some situations, however, sweating is considered normal. In exercise, for example, sweating connotes hard work and application. In one qualitative study using a group-memory technique, women discussed positive experiences of sweat-ing within a context of mastery, control, and physical effort, an example of which is worth repeating in full because it is a rare and rich evocation:

> I start to pedal my exercise cycle and I feel comfortable and under-stretched. Push-ing the pedals feels boringly easy and I'm convinced that I could continue at this pace

indefinitely. After about ten minutes or so, I start to feel hot and a bit out of breath and I can feel the sweat collecting on my forehead and my upper lip. The action of pushing the pedals feels more difficult and I want to stop but I force myself to think of the good it must be doing me. As I grip the handlebars I start to feel the sweat seeping between my fingers and although this feels uncomfortable I take it as a sign that I am exercising properly. I wipe my hand on my jogging pants, lift my tee-shirt and check my back for sweat. I feel quite disappointed because it only feels damp and so I carry on at a faster rate. Eventually I feel trickles of sweat running down my face and my back and I remind myself again that this discomfort is worthwhile. When I check my back for the second time it feels slippery wet and I experience a mixture of satisfaction and disgust. When I stop cycling I head straight for the shower and enjoy the feeling of my heart beating fast as I wash away the sweat.[4]

Unfortunately, for some, the disgust of sweating wins over the potential satisfaction and benefits of exercise. For many people, in many communities, sweating on exercise is seen as highly undesirable and something to be avoided (Lucas et al., 2013). For example, in their review of barriers to exercise among older people, Karen Schutzer and Sue Graves suggested that "sweating, labored breathing, and muscle soreness typical during exercise is believed by some to do more harm than good. Older women, in particular, were often raised to believe exercise is not 'ladylike'" (Schutzer and Graves, 2004, p. 1057).

The researchers do not provide evidence for this assertion, although I think it is a commonly held view, often anecdotally reported. In a recent qualitative study one woman remarked, "Some of us ladies were born at a time where girls didn't sweat" (Bethancourt et al., 2014, p. 15). A better understanding is needed of exactly why sweating is experienced as undesirable for so many people, why it was constructed as "unladylike," how these narratives persist, and how stable they are.

As Val Gillies and her colleagues showed, it is possible for sweating to be constructed positively as socially and personally rewarding, but for many people "getting hot and sweaty" may be a primary source of avoidance, not only of exercise but even of the contemplation of exercise. Gordon Waitt argues that to understand what is acceptable for bodily experience is dependent upon the place it happens. He calls this, rather engagingly, "a geography of sweating." The social meaning of sweating matters, and the meaning is in part determined by its location. Sweating during garden work, after sex, and in the gym, were all acceptable to his participants, whereas socially and at work it was the subject of disgust and horror (Waitt, 2014). The physiology of human sweating does not change very much. However, the psychology of sweating is in constant flux. Sweating can be experienced as intensely positive, coming at the apogee of human endeavor and success; it can also be experienced as dirty, filthy, bestial, and disgusting, at the nadir of human misery.

Hot flushes

The idea that sweating is not "ladylike" is odd when one considers the common experience of menopause, in which sudden, unbidden changes in temperature and sweating are signature features. Alterations in primary thermoregulation lead to unwanted heat retention. Symptoms can last for many years and, although a normal part of life, can have far-reaching detrimental effects (Politi et al., 2008). Symptoms of menopause go beyond the classical hot flush, often extending to include pain, anxiety, emotional lability, cognitive loss, and unwelcome bodily changes. But overheating and sweating, especially at night, are common complaints (Pimenta et al., 2012).

Myra Hunter has championed the view that the attitudes and beliefs that people hold about menopause—its meanings, cause, consequence, controllability, and social acceptance—are all at the heart of women's experience. For example, with colleagues she developed the Hot Flush Beliefs Scale as a tool to capture experience. The final instrument has three subscales that concern negative emotion and social acceptance (e.g., "When I have a hot flush I look stupid in front of others"), beliefs about coping with hot flushes ("Other people seem to manage their hot flushes better than I do"), and beliefs about how to cope with sweating at night ("When I have night sweats, it is harder to cope the next day") (Rendall et al., 2008, p. 164).

Like much health psychology, the focus can be on the negative. There is some evidence that those who have a dominant belief of menopausal symptoms as negative do experience worse symptoms. In a thorough review of the role attitudes toward menopause play on symptoms, Beverley Ayers and colleagues found that holding negative attitudes about menopause seemed to contribute to worse experience, and vice versa (Ayers et al., 2010). Mind you, when you look at the list of symptoms reported by Pimenta and colleagues, it is hard to find a positive story to tell. Lotte Hvas did find some, although none were related to symptoms. When asked for the positive, women in her studies reported the lack of anxiety over sex and pregnancy, the absence of menstruation, and general aspects of confidence gained in older age (Hvas, 2001, 2006). Being hot and finding it difficult to regulate body temperature were uncomplicatedly negative.

The psychological ambiguity of heat

The psychology of temperature, at least as it relates to heat, is intricately linked with the psychology of arousal. Many of the physiological systems of thermoregulation serve multiple alternate functions in arousal, flight, and the social communication of danger. Growing red in the face could signal anger, embarrassment, or re-warming on a cold day. Sweating profusely could signal fear, menopause, or cooling. People's experience of being hot emerges directly from the social context of the heat. Because of the ambiguity of the communication of heat, it will demand scrutiny from others. If I see you red-faced and sweating, I will automatically attend more closely to gather further information on your needs, and determine whether I need to protect myself from disease or aggression, or come to your aid. At times, the functions of thermo-regulation can compete: in altering the movement of heat to and from the periphery to maintain physiological homeostasis, one may expose oneself to undue attention and negative social judgment, challenging self-protection.

The public display of thermoregulation will always, therefore, be a site of social scrutiny and negotiation. The challenge for those who want to encourage people to get hot and sweaty—for example, in public health campaigns of promoting exercise—will be to communicate positive contexts for physical sensations. For many people, being encouraged to exercise means being encouraged to confront physical self-disgust. Much of the health promotion and exercise encouragement literature focuses on the science of motivation; it is interested in how to instill and maintain goals of self-improvement and make concrete the abstract reward of future benefits; it is dominated by theories of self-regulation and self-determination (Teixeira et al., 2012). Missing is a concern for the psychology of the body; in par-ticular, for the thermoregulating body. We will need to understand how to con-struct a positive framing of heat and sweat as nondisgusting, natural, and part of a healthy response to movement and activity. Of course, this will mean countering the significant marketing investment spent encouraging us to think the opposite. The size of the global market in antiperspirants is in the order of US$13 billion (Statista, 2014).

Being cold

For many people, however, sweating is not a daily concern. Staying warm and avoid-ing the cold are basic human motivations. The cold kills. In England and Wales, for example, there were 31,100 preventable winter deaths in 2012–13. Many of these were due to cold stress, and, as shown in Figure 9.1, there is a clear relationship with tem-perature drop (ONS, 2013). The main culprits, unsurprisingly, are cardiovascular and respiratory compromise. Average winter temperatures in the United Kingdom rarely go below 0°C for long, although in other countries this would be a mild winter. Inter-view and lifestyle data from eastern Russia, where average winter temperatures are around −7°C, show how important cold stress can be. Mortality below 0°C increased by 1 percent for every −1°C (Donaldson et al., 1998).

For some people, however, cold can strike when the temperature falls well within a normally comfortable range. There are many people who live feeling constantly challenged by disorders of thermoregulation that throw them into sudden, often unpredictable, episodes of being cold.

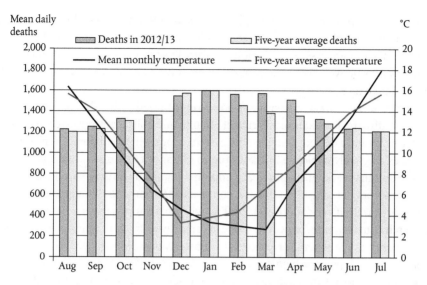

Fig. 9.1. Average daily deaths and monthly temperatures in England and Wales in 2012/13 and a five-year average. (Plate 3)

Reproduced from Office of National Statistics, Excess Winter Mortality in England and Wales, 2012/13 (Provisional) and 2011/12 (Final), 2013, p. 5, Figure 2, http://www.ons.gov.uk/ons/dcp171778_337459.pdf © Crown Copyright 2013. This figure is published under the terms of the Open Government Licence (http://www.nationalarchives.gov.uk/doc/open-government-licence/version/3/).

Raynaud's phenomenon

One of the most common vascular disorders related to the perception of cold temperature is known as Raynaud's phenomena, named after Maurice Raynaud, a French physician who first described cold extremity damage and its relationship with gangrene. Today, it is often referred to as a disease, but is more accurately a phenomenon associated with many diseases. Janet Pope, summarizing for the *British Medical Journal*, defines Raynaud's phenomenon as

> an episodic, reversible vasospasm of the peripheral arteries (usually digital). It causes pallor, followed by cyanosis and/or erythema, which can cause pain and, at times, paraesthesia. On rare occasions, it can lead to ulceration of the fingers and toes (and, in some cases, of the ears or nose). Primary or idiopathic Raynaud's phenomenon (Raynaud's disease) occurs without an underlying disease. Secondary Raynaud's phenomenon (Raynaud's syndrome) occurs in association with an underlying disease—usually connective tissue disorders, such as systemic sclerosis (SSc; scleroderma), systemic lupus erythematosus, rheumatoid arthritis, Sjogren's syndrome, or polymyositis.[5]

The causes of primary Raynaud's phenomena are often unknown but are thought to be either genetic or environmental, with prolonged exposure to cold stress or vibration. It is a surprisingly common problem. Pope (2013) reviewed the prevalence, which varies between countries but could be as high as 6 percent, and is higher in women than men.

The experience of secondary Raynaud's is often buried within the challenges of the primary disease. For example, Bernadet Sutanto and colleagues reviewed 46 studies of the experience of people living with systemic lupus erythematosus. Temperature changes are rarely explored in these studies (Sutanto et al., 2013). Perhaps because of the dominance of other physical symptoms in the adjustment to a life-changing polysymptomatic long-term disease, concerns about how to manage thermoregulation are rarely, if ever, addressed. Dealing with cold temperatures is banished from research consideration. However, if one specifically asks about temperature, people do discuss it as a problem. For example, in one study of the unmet needs of 112 patients with systemic lupus erythematosus, after pain and tiredness came the problems of managing temperature changes. Sixty-seven percent of patients reported having some or a moderate-to-high level of need when it came to coping with the cold, and as many as 80 percent reported a similar level of fear that all symptoms would worsen (Danoff-Burg and Friedburg, 2009).

Primary Raynaud's is a classic case of an idiopathic disorder. It is common, unpleasant, not generally very disabling, diagnostically relevant in only a small number of cases, but a significant nuisance for many people who find the attacks of vasospasm painful, worrying, and disabling. These types of high-prevalence, subclinical, idiopathic problems can be the cause of major if rarely calculated burden.

Cold comfort

What little psychological study there is of possible interventions for people with Raynaud's has focused on either specific aspects of symptom management or on the broader issues of adjustment to, and support of life with, a chronic condition. In these studies, Raynaud's is only one part of another disorder.

In the early 1980s both cold and stress were identified as playing a role in triggering an attack (Freedman and Ianni, 1983). It became clear that emotional experience seemed to matter, but it was not clear whether it precipitated an attack, or whether emotional control could mitigate an attack. Kathleen Brown and her colleagues explored this idea of stress further in their study of 313 people with primary Raynaud's and found that anxious thoughts were more relevant to triggering events in warmer temperatures. Worry and anxiety were risk factors, but they may be hidden in studies that focus on multiple risk factors in cold environments (Brown et al., 2001). There was then both a physiological and a psychological case emerging for the role of treatments that teach mastery of a possibly learned vasomotor response to arousal. In short, biofeedback looked like it should be successful.

This population of 313 patients remains the largest study of patients with Raynaud's. These patients were entered into a randomized, controlled, multicenter trial of temperature and EMG biofeedback. They followed a tradition of biofeedback studies in which patients were taught methods of identifying when temperature changes were happening in advance of an attack through observable changes in the skin. The idea is to condition peripheral vasomotor function by either reducing the onset of vasoconstriction or increasing vasodilation, often with the use of hand-warming.

Unfortunately, no treatment effects were found. It didn't work. Or, to be fair, the treatment was not able to work because people with Raynaud's disease could not master it. The authors reported that "the Temperature Biofeedback group . . . not only had problems with learning basic hand-warming skills, but also had problems applying hand-warming skills to reduce RP [Raynaud's Phenomenon] attacks" (Middaugh et al., 2001, p. 274). The authors speculate on the possible reasons for biofeedback failure.

Indeed, the literature on psychological interventions for people with Raynaud's phenomena has continued in this speculative vein. In a narrative review of the ten available studies, all of which are small, except for the Middaugh study, the effects of biofeedback are at best inconclusive, and more likely missing (Karavidas et al., 2006). Research in this important area has stopped. A large negative trial may well have the effect of closing a field of research, but unfortunately no further avenues of research have been developed to replace it.

Although it needs to be further explored, the apparent inability of patients to master biofeedback is intriguing. Middaugh and colleagues suggest that part of the problem with the failure of the treatment lies with the patients who approach it negatively:

> A negative strategy, Denial, predicted less successful learning and early drop out with temperature biofeedback (e.g., I act as though it hasn't even happened). This suggests that learning may be enhanced by instruction on coping skills to foster positive engagement and counteract denial-associated withdrawal. (Middaugh et al., 2001, p. 272)

I suspect this interpretation misses the point. Given what we know about the modern psychology and physiology of thermoregulation, it may just not be possible or even feasible to learn how to control bloodflow in the periphery.

Nevertheless, there are at least three avenues of investigation needed before abandoning hope—or trying to change the patient to fit the treatment. First, what matters in the movement of blood (and hence heat) to and from the periphery is not skin temperature so much as core temperature. Temperature biofeedback that makes use of changes in core temperature is potentially more relevant. Second, the overlapping and interwoven relationship between thermoperception, emotion, and embodiment is only just being explored (Moseley et al., 2008). Central mechanisms that drive vaso-motor function associated with bodily threat are a promising target for investigation. Third, we have not really covered first base, in that we do not understand the experience of sudden loss of heat from hands and feet and when it is noticed. What is really meant by *denial*? Perhaps what is meant is closer to what we saw with Alex Coode—a state of being absorbed and an uncomplaining attitude. Qualitative investigation is needed into the experience of people with Raynaud's phenomenon and how bodily sensation is interpreted.

To explore the idea of how the sudden onset of an attack of cold temperature feels, I talked with Euphemia Graham (Box 9.2).

Box 9.2. Euphemia, living with Raynaud's: "*I guess I am learning all of the time*"

Euphemia works in a large telecommunications company in a corporate leadership role, but she worked originally in physiotherapy. She has had Raynaud's disease, as she thinks of it, for the last 12 years. I was particularly interested to learn more about her experience of the onset and offset of an episode, and about how it has changed her attitude to life.

Chris: How long have you had Raynaud's?

Euphemia: I first noticed it about ten years ago. I was working in an air-conditioned gym. When I left and got into my car I started to have bad attacks. I knew about Raynaud's because I had worked with patients with it, but I didn't really think about it for myself until those first attacks when I was driving home. Now my Raynaud's is quite bad.

Chris: What does "quite bad" mean? Talk me through an attack.

Euphemia: It means that my fingers lose all their sensation and go white and I can't feel them. I just have total loss of sensation. I don't really know where they are in space. What "bad" to me means is that I can't feel them. If I go for a shower, it is as if they are not mine. I can't wash or scrub my hair or do anything. I can move them around my body but I can't feel them in the same way. And then after an attack it takes quite a long time, about 20 to 30 minutes, before it starts to get better. If I want to go onto my computer and start working, there is no chance of that happening because I can't type. It feels like I have very fat fingers so it just feels like I am slapping the keyboard.

Chris: How disabling can it be?

Euphemia: It is disabling in the instant because you can't do the things you want to do. It feels like you've got somebody else's hands. It is odd. There is no way I can do anything intricate. I also don't trust myself because I don't know the temperature of things, so

---

Box 9.2. *Continued*

there is a risk involved. One of the things I want to do when I am cold is run a nice warm bath, but I couldn't tell with my hand whether the bath is hot or not.

It can be very annoying, but at least I know it is going to go away. Other people have much worse things to deal with. And I tend to think it was my own fault because I did not look after my hands when I was younger. I know I didn't. When I was younger I used to ride horses a lot, but that would be more difficult now. Not just the riding, but looking after the horses. Simple tasks like undoing the buckles on the bridle or loosening the girth, would be really hard and sometimes impossible if I could not feel my hands.

Chris: Are there times or occasions that make it worse?

Euphemia: Almost you can say that it is the twilight of each season—that is the danger because you don't notice the change in temperature. When you are in the season it is fine. I probably get more bad attacks in autumn on a sunny bright day when it is cold but I still think it is summer and I am not wearing my gloves, whereas once I have got into the middle of winter I wouldn't dream of going out without gloves. I like the seasons to change; I just have to try and get better at it.

Chris: Has it changed the way you think about clothes?

Euphemia: Yes, I am very aware. I really like to look nice, but the overriding decision is that I have to either be warm or not get too hot. So if I am going to a summer wedding, I would hate to be sweaty and hot, and I don't like to get too cold. So I do now pay much more attention. So now for example at work I only have to get from the car to my office five minutes away, but I would always get a coat to make that small journey because otherwise I know I am risking having an attack when I get into the building. So I try to be sensible.

And I have gloves everywhere, everywhere I go, in the car, in my bags, everywhere. I have got so many pairs. And I now think about what clothes are made of. I buy cashmere if I can because I know it is going to keep me warm; man-made fibers don't keep you as warm.

Chris: Some people think of being spontaneous as romantic. Is that spontaneity denied to you?

Euphemia: It is just planning. Once you start having the attacks regularly, and you lose 20 or 30 minutes of your life at a time, it is quite annoying because you can't do what you want to do for quite a while so you start to think, "What can I do to prevent it?" So this romantic spontaneity you speak of is not worth the disability.

Chris: Is there anything positive that has come from your experience?

Euphemia: I don't think of it as negative. We are all going to get something and if this is it, then that is fine. I do try and tell people to look after their bodies when they are young. Not just around hand care. We joke about young people thinking they are indestructible.

(Continued)

Box 9.2. *Continued*

I am sure I was like that. I try to tell my daughter that you should look after your hands because you are going to need them for the next 70 to 80 years. Nobody ever said that to me. They were just there to be used. I just took them for granted that they would always be there. It is also positive, I think, when it comes to clothes. I definitely have more hats than I ever thought possible. And it has given me the confidence to wear them. It is not a fashion statement because I am wearing them to get warm, but I get to wear some great hats.

Living with the possibility of sudden severe cold stress for Euphemia at least is partly controlled by a new regime of secondary regulation that is based on detailed planning, situational awareness, and clothing choice. Not spontaneous but effective. Not mentioned, however, is any strategy of thinking about bodily sensation and how warm one is. Denial? No. I would call it a determination to plan and to not let the cold matter. We need a new psychology of chronic thermoregulatory disorders that accounts for beliefs about temperature, how we naturally adapt to challenges of heat and cold—one that is sensitive to the social meaning of heat and cold in context.

Summary

Secondary thermoregulation has been largely ignored in psychology. A psychology of temperature is needed that seeks to explain how protection from cold and heat stress is achieved. This psychology will range from the psychology of clothing to embodied cognition. Deciding to adjust clothing can be a life-or-death decision, but we know very little about this common behavior. Equally, we know very little about the uncommon behaviors, such as how firefighters make decisions. We can learn a lot from people who inhabit extreme temperature environments, and from those who struggle every day to regulate their temperature. Psychology has neglected thermoregulation. We are constantly making decisions that change our body temperature. Needed is a practical psychology that can improve health interventions both to prevent excess winter and summer deaths, and to treat those struggling with seemingly out of control extremes of body temperature.

Notes

1. Reprinted from *Neuroscience & Biobehavioral Reviews*, 34 (2), Raf J. Schepers and Matthias Ringkamp, Thermoreceptors and thermosensitive afferents, p. 177, doi:10.1016/j. neubiorev.2009.10.003 Copyright (2010), with permission from Elsevier.

2. Reprinted from *The Lancet*, 349 (9062), The Eurowinter Group, Cold exposure and winter mortality from ischaemic heart disease, cerebrovascular disease, respiratory disease, and all causes in warm and cold regions of Europe, p. 1344, doi:10.1016/S0140–6736(96)12338–12,332 Copyright (1997), with permission from Elsevier.
3. Reprinted from *The Lancet*, 349 (9062), The Eurowinter Group, Cold exposure and winter mortality from ischaemic heart disease, cerebrovascular disease, respiratory disease, and all causes in warm and cold regions of Europe, p. 1345, doi:10.1016/S0140–6736(96)12338–12,332 Copyright (1997), with permission from Elsevier.
4. Reproduced from Women's collective constructions of embodied practices through memory work: Cartesian dualism in memories of sweating and pain, Val Gillies, Angela Harden, Katherine Johnson, Paula Reavey, Vicki Strange, and Carla Willig, *British Journal of Social Psychology*, 43 (1), p. 109, doi:10.1348/014466604322916006 Copyright (c) 2004, John Wiley & Sons, Inc.
5. Reproduced from Janet Elizabeth Pope, Raynaud's phenomenon (primary), *BMJ Clinical Evidence*, 10, p. 1119 © 2013, BMJ Publishing Group Limited.

References

Alexander, M., Connell, L.J. and Presley, A.B. (2005). Clothing fit preferences of young female adult consumers. *International Journal of Clothing Science and Technology*, 17, 52–64.

Ashcroft, F. (2001). Life at the extremes: the science of survival. London: HarperCollins.

Ayers, B., Forshaw, M. and Hunter, M.S. (2010). The impact of attitudes towards the menopause on women's symptom experience: a systematic review. *Maturitas*, 65, 28–36.

Baccini, M., Kosatsky, T., Analitis, A., Anderson, H.R., D'Ovidio, M., Menne, B., Michelozzi, P., Biggeri, A. and the PHEWE Collaborative Group. (2011). Impact of heat on mortality in 15 European cities: attributable deaths under different weather scenarios. *Journal of Epidemiology and Community Health*, 65, 64–70.

Bargh, J.A. and Shalev, I. (2012). The substitutability of physical and social warmth in daily life. *Emotion*, 12, 154–162.

Barr, D., Gregson, W. and Reilly, T. (2010). The thermal ergonomics of firefighting reviewed. *Applied Ergonomics*, 41, 161–172.

Bethancourt, H.J., Rosenberg, D.E., Beatty, T. and Arterburn, D.E. (2014). Barriers to and facilitators of physical activity program use among older adults. *Clinical Medicine and Research*, 12, 10–20.

Brown, K.M., Middaugh, S.J., Haythornthwaite, J.A. and Bielory, L. (2001). The effects of stress, anxiety, and outdoor temperature on the frequency and severity of Raynaud's attacks: the Raynaud's Treatment Study. *Journal of Behavioral Medicine*, 24, 137–153.

Burke, S.M. and Orlick, T. (2003). Mental strategies of elite high altitude climbers: overcoming adversity on Mount Everest. *Journal of Human Performance in Extreme Environments*, 7, 15–22.

Curtis, V. (2001). Hygiene: how myths, monsters, and mothers-in-law can promote behavior change. *Journal of Infection*, 43, 75–79.

Danoff-Burg, S. and Friedberg, F. (2009). Unmet needs of patients with systemic lupus erythematosus. *Behavioral Medicine*, 35, 5–13.

Day, R. and Hitchings, R. (2011). "Only old ladies would do that": age stigma and older people's strategies for dealing with winter cold. *Health and Place*, 17, 885–894.

Donaldson, G.C., Tchernjavskii, V.E., Ermakov, S.P., Bucher, K. and Keatinge, W.R. (1998). Winter mortality and cold stress in Yekaterinburg, Russia: interview survey. *British Medical Journal*, 316, 514–518.

Egan, G.F., Johnson, J., Farrell, M., McAllen, R., Zamarripa, F., McKinley, M.J., Lancaster, J., Denton, D. and Fox, P.T. (2005). Cortical, thalamic, and hypothalamic responses to cooling and warming the skin in 109 awake humans: a positron-emission tomography study. *PNAS*, 102, 5262–5267.

Eurowinter Group. (1997). Cold exposure and winter mortality from ischaemic heart disease, cerebrovascular disease, respiratory disease, and all causes in warm and cold regions of Europe. *The Lancet*, 349, 1341–1346.

Faerevik, H. and Reinertsen, R.E. (2003). Effects of wearing aircrew protective clothing on physiological and cognitive responses under various ambient conditions. *Ergonomics*, 46, 780–799.

Fielding, H. (1996). Bridget Jones's diary: a novel. London: Picador Press.

Fowler, T., Southgate, R.J., Waite, T., Harrell, R., Kovats, S., Bone, A., Doyle, Y. and Murray, V. (2015). Excess winter deaths in Europe: a multi-country descriptive analysis. *European Journal of Public Health*, 25 339–345.

Freedman, R.R. and Ianni, P. (1983). Role of cold and emotional stress in Raynaud's disease and scleroderma. *British Medical Journal*, 287, 1499–1502.

Froom, P., Caine, Y.G., Shochat, I. and Ribak, J. (1993). Heat-stress and helicopter pilot errors. *Journal of Occupational and Environmental Medicine*, 35, 720–724.

Gillies, V., Harden, A., Johnson, K., Reavey, P., Strange, V. and Willig, C. (2004). Women's collective constructions of embodied practices through memory work: Cartesian dualism in memories of sweating and pain. *British Journal of Social Psychology*, 43, 99–112.

Harker, M. (2013). Psychological sweating: a systematic review focused on aetiology and cutaneous response. *Skin Pharmacology and Physiology*, 26, 92–100.

Holmlund, M., Hagman, A. and Polsa, P. (2011). An exploration of how mature women buy clothing: empirical insights and a model. *Journal of Fashion Marketing and Management*, 15, 108–122.

Hvas, L. (2001). Positive aspects of menopause: a qualitative study. *Maturitas*, 39, 11–17.

Hvas, L. (2006). Menopausal women's positive experience of growing older. *Maturitas*, 54, 245–251.

Ijzerman, H. and Semin, G.R. (2009). The thermometer of social relations: mapping social proximity on temperature. *Psychological Science*, 20, 1214–1220.

Ijzerman, H., Gallucci, M., Pouw, W.T.J.L., Weißgerber, S.C., Van Doesum, N.J. and Williams, K.D. (2012). Cold-blooded loneliness: social exclusion leads to lower skin temperatures. *Acta Psychologica*, 140, 283–288.

Karavidas, M.K., Tsai, P.-S., Yucha, C., McGrady, A. and Lehrer, P.M. (2006). Thermal biofeedback for primary Raynaud's phenomenon: a review of the literature. *Applied Psychophysiology and Biofeedback*, 31, 203–216.

Lucas, A., Murray, E. and Kinra, S. (2013). Heath beliefs of UK South Asians related to lifestyle diseases: a review of qualitative literature. *Journal of Obesity*, Article ID 827674, 1–3.

Lynott, D., Corker, K.S., Wortman, J., Connell, L., Donnellan, M.B., Lucas, R.E. and O'Brien, K. (2008). Replication of "Experiencing physical warmth promotes interpersonal warmth" by Williams and Bargh (2008). *Social Psychology*, 45, 216–222.

Middaugh, S.J., Haythornthwaite, J.A., Thompson, B., Hill, R., Brown, K.M., Freedman, R.F., Attanasio, V., Jacob, R.G., Scheier, M. and Smith, E.A. (2001). The Raynaud's Treatment Study: biofeedback protocols and acquisition of temperature biofeedback skills. *Applied Psychophysiology and Biofeedback*, 26, 251–278.

Moscovitch, D.A. (2009). What is the core fear in social phobia? A new model to facilitate individualized case conceptualization and treatment. *Cognitive and Behavioral Practice*, 16, 123–134.

Moseley, G.L., Olthoff, N., Venema, A., Don, S., Wijers, M., Gallace, A. and Spence, C. (2008). Psychologically induced cooling of a specific body part caused by the illusory ownership of an artificial counterpart. *PNAS*, 105, 13169–13173.

Muller, M.D., Gunstad, J., Alosco, M.L., Miller, L.A., Updegraff, J., Spitznagel, M.B. and Glickman, E.L. (2012). Acute cold exposure and cognitive function: evidence for sustained impairment. *Ergonomics*, 55, 792–798.

ONS. (2013). Excess winter mortality in England and Wales, 2012/13 (Provisional) and 2011/12 (Final). http://www.ons.gov.uk/ons/dcp171778_337459.pdf. Accessed 5 September 2014.

Paul, F.U.J., Mandal, M.K., Ramachandran, K. and Panwar, M.R. (2010). Cognitive performance during long-term residence in a polar environment. *Journal of Environmental Psychology*, 30, 129–132.

Pilcher, J.J., Nadler, E. and Busch, C. (2002). Effects of hot and cold temperature exposure on performance: a meta-analytic review. *Ergonomics*, 45, 682–698.

Pimenta, F., Leal, I., Maroco, J. and Ramos, C. (2012). Menopause Symptoms' Severity Inventory (MSSI-38): assessing the frequency and intensity of symptoms. *Climacteric*, 15, 143–152.

Politi, M.C., Schleinitz, M.D. and Col, N.F. (2008). Revisiting the duration of vasomotor symptoms of menopause: a meta-analysis. *Journal of General Internal Medicine*, 23, 1507–1513.

Pope, J. (2013) Raynaud's phenomenon (primary). *BMJ Clinical Evidence*, 10, 1119, 1–10.

Rendall, M.J., Simonds, L.M. and Hunter, M.S. (2008). The Hot Flush Beliefs Scale: a tool for assessing thoughts and beliefs associated with the experience of menopausal hot flushes and night sweats. *Maturitas*, 60, 158–169.

Romanovsky, A. (2006). Thermoregulation: some concepts have changed. Functional architecture of the thermoregulatory system. *American Journal of Physiology: Regulatory, Integrative and Comparative Physiology*, 292, R37–R46.

Schepers, R.J. and Ringkamp, M. (2010). Thermoreceptors and thermosensitive afferents. *Neuroscience and Biobehavioral Reviews*, 34, 177–184.

Scholing, A. and Emmelkamp, P.M.G. (1993). Cognitive and behavioral treatments of fear of blushing, sweating or trembling. *Behavior, Research and Therapy*, 31, 155–170.

Schutzer, K.A. and Graves, B.S. (2004). Barriers and motivation to exercise in older adults. *Preventive Medicine*, 39, 1056–1061.

Sperber, A.D. and Weitzman, S. (1997). Commentary: mind over matter about keeping warm. *The Lancet*, 349, 1337–1338.

Statista: The Statistics Portal. (2014). Size of the global antiperspirant and deodorant market from 2012 to 2021 (in billion U.S. dollars). http://www.statista.com/statistics/254668/size-of-the-global-antiperspirant-and-deodorant-market/. Accessed 5 September 2014.

Sutanto, B., Singh-Grewal, D., McNeil, H.P., O'Neill, S., Craig, J.C., Jones, J. and Tong, A. (2013). Experiences and perspectives of adults living with systemic lupus erythematosus: thematic synthesis of qualitative studies. *Arthritis Care and Research*, 65, 1752–1765.

Teixeira, P.J., Carraça, E.V., Markland, D., Silva, M.N. and Ryan, R.M. (2012). Exercise, physical activity, and self-determination theory: a systematic review. *International Journal of Behavioral Nutrition and Physical Activity*, 9, 78, 1–30.

Vriens, J., Nilius, B. and Voets, T. (2014). Peripheral thermosensation in mammals. *Nature Reviews Neuroscience*, 15, 573–589.

Waitt, G. (2014). Bodies that sweat: the affective responses of young women in Wollongong, New South Wales, Australia. *Gender, Place and Culture*, 21, 666–682.

Wheaton, M.G., Braddock, A.E. and Abramowitz, J.S. (2011). The Sweating Cognitions Inventory: a measure of cognitions in hyperhidrosis. *Journal of Psychopathological Behavioral Assessment*, 33, 393–402.

Williams, L.E. and Bargh, J.A. (2008). Experiencing physical warmth promotes interpersonal warmth. *Science*, 322, 606–607.

Wilson, M. (2012). Six views of embodied cognition. *Psychonomic Bulletin and Review*, 9, 625–636.

Wortman, J.M., Donnellan, M.B. and Lucas, R.E. (2014). Can physical warmth (or coldness) predict trait loneliness? A replication of Bargh and Shalev (2012). *Archives of Scientific Psychology*, 2, 13–19.

Zhong, C.-B. and Leonardelli, G.L. (2008). Cold and lonely: does social exclusion literally feel cold? *Psychological Science*, 19, 838–842.

CHAPTER 10

APPETITE

We need fuel to live. As a general guide, each adult needs to source more than 2,100 kilocalories each day to sustain function. For many people, 2,100 kilocalories of energy are extremely difficult to achieve and daily life is spent in hunger. To be more precise, according to the United Nations World Food Programme the number of people in food poverty is 805 million or 1 in 9 people (World Food Programme, 2014). Hunger is typically defined as both a physical discomfort caused by lack of food and the drive to find food. Appetite is best thought of as the embodied urge, want, need, drive, or desire to consume food and drink.

Appetite is perhaps an unusual choice for a focus on neglected physical sensations. After all, there is no shortage of academic and popular discussion about wanting for food and drink. In fact, today our relationship with food and drink is a major source of debate. What has been neglected, however, is a focus on the experiences of needing and wanting. What does it feel like to be distracted by the physical pull toward food? I review briefly the physiological and anatomical mechanisms of appetite, and then discuss the broader social and political expression of appetite in a world in which food and water are scarce resources. Next, I consider the psychology of appetite with a focus on how appetite functions in the normal case, and in a variety of abnormal cases. Throughout, I deliberately avoid any consideration of taste and smell. Of course taste and smell are important, but I judged them less neglected in terms of psychological research. They are already well studied. My focus is on this felt experience of the *desire to consume*.

I sought the help of two people who are experts in appetite. First, I spoke with Jean Christophe. He is a chef and restaurateur who lives surrounded by the objects of his desire. Second, I spoke with Tom. Tom is a professional jockey. In order to ride he needs to make a weight of under 150 pounds, which means that he must regularly stay undernourished and reach a body mass index of 18.5. For him appetite is a complex subject, a balance between the desire to eat and drink and the desire to win.

Appetite regulation

Appetite is only one part of a complex set of conditions that structure how we eat and drink, including habit, emotion, availability of food, and other people. All of these influences determine what and when we consume. In particular, appetite functions sometimes as a signal to seek food and drink. At other times it operates as a check during eating or as a signal to pause or stop altogether: these stop signals can then provoke food avoidance even when there is more that could be consumed.

There are peripheral sensory mechanisms that operate in specific phases of eating, from olfactory preparation triggering local changes in mouth and stomach, to the experience of stomach pressure discussed in Chapter 4. However, unusually for the physical senses, more research attention has been paid to the involvement of endocrine and central nervous systems. Appetite is best considered as a function of two related systems that involve the peripheral, central, and psychological influences. These two appetite systems can be described as *homeostatic* and *hedonic*.

Homeostatic appetite manages biological energy reserves. This system operates outside of awareness to manage the storage and release of energy. Critical to this system is the signaling from adipose tissue. Emerging as particularly important in the homeostatic drive to consume are the hormones leptin and ghrelin, which are in constant circulation (Lutter and Nestler, 2009). As with other aspects of urge, the hypothalamus is centrally implicated in the regulation of appetite. Neuropeptides released by neurons in the hypothalamus underpin homeostasis in promoting or reducing feeding behavior (Parker and Bloom, 2012).

Hedonic appetite, as its name suggests, is also under the control of neural mechanisms; not those that drive need, but those that drive reward and pleasure. This hedonic system is attracting more research interest because of its prominent role in theories of food consumption and obesity in societies where dense and energy-rich foods are plentiful. Eating beyond any homeostatic benefit is thought now to be reward-based, operating partly under the influence of both the opioid and dopamine systems. Hans-Rudolf Berthoud summarizes the two dominant theories of overeating. The first he pejoratively calls the *gluttony* hypothesis and refers simply to overeating, producing more dopamine-mediated pleasure. The second he called the *deficiency* hypothesis: that one's appetite drives overconsumption due to a pleasure regulation strategy of increasing dopamine through repeated stimulation (Berthoud, 2011). There is evidence that fits both hypotheses but none currently that discriminates between them.

Homeostatic and hedonic influences on appetite do not operate in isolation; a rich area of research investigates how they interrelate. Maximizing signals used in homeostasis may be essential in counteracting hedonic drive, and likewise a better understanding of what governs hedonic drive could be enough to "override homeostatic control" (Harrold et al., 2012). The extent to which these two systems interact at a psychological level has not been well investigated. Berthoud argues, perhaps simplistically, that by physiological definition, eating past the replacement of energy supplies has to be hedonic as it no longer functions to maintain homeostasis, and may actually put an organism at risk. However, these dual evolved systems of appetite mean that we are living with many paradoxical effects of appetite.

The world is replete with examples of how appetite can operate in a nonrational or illogical way. The case exemplars are of the reports of loss of appetite in starvation, and the report of great hunger in the obese. To understand appetite we need to understand the core experience of hunger and thirst—the experience of being driven to consume.

Power

Unique to appetite as a neglected sense is its relationship with power. Appetite functions to promote a search for food and drink. But food and drink are scarce resources that are not universally available. In general, our access to gravity, space, and breathable air are not under central economic control; similarly, avoidance of itch, pain, and fatigue are not rationed among us. None of the targets of these urges are as scarce, potentially unobtainable, or socially mediated as nourishing food and clean drinkable water. Imagine a world in which gravity was a scarce resource to be shared, or in which breathable air was available only to eight out of nine of us. Imagine the political significance they would take on, and the economy that would develop around them. A useful definition of power is the control over a shared resource. In this sense, appetite is always an expression, however unwittingly, of power in action. The provision and consumption of food is always under political influence, often the macro political, but also the micro political of everyday negotiation.

From the day we are born appetite ties us to others, to those who can choose to feed and water us, or choose not to. The relational aspect of appetite is core to its experience. And the idea that one can choose to satisfy appetite is part of that experience of power. The choice to feed oneself or to feed another is a political and social act. We can see this in evidence in extreme and abnormal cases. For example, starvation is a common form of torture; it is used to debase, as a means to dehumanize. Ray Tallis, for example, argues in his philosophical discussion of hunger, that although we appear more bestial in starvation, it is the knowledge of our behavior, even in self-observation, that grounds us. Reflecting on accounts of survival of Nazi death camps in Auschwitz, he says:

> What happens to us when we are savagely hungry seems to be a kind of critique of all those aspects of ourselves we take pride in as human beings. The knowledge that one would fight to protect one's full plate while others have empty ones, that one would hoard food while others around one are dying—glossed as prudence—remains as a guilty shadow at the heart of one's self-esteem.[1]

Withholding food and drink with the aim to starve is torture. However, resisting or refusing food for oneself is also a political act, one that is highly challenging to others. Often it arises within a context of reduced options for control, as in the case of a hunger strike. The political power of the hunger strike comes from its transgression, from its social defiance, from its visibility. In the language of social science, it is performative, acted, and communicated. It must be visible and known.

In rare cases, self-starvation is not constructed as a political act but instead as an abnormal psychiatric act. For an interesting example, Fiona McNicholas and her colleagues in Ireland described an unusual and extreme case of "pervasive refusal" in which an eleven-year-old girl, "J," ultimately became hospitalized as her homeostasis was put at risk:

> After a total of 18 months in hospital J had shown no response to any intervention provided. During the latter nine months of this admission she had refused to eat, drink, engage in self-care or communicate in any way with staff, other patients or family. (McNicholas et al., 2013, p. 140)

J eventually had a "flight into health" when presented with a referral to a foreign specialist unit. The case is interesting in itself, but here the very fact that food refusal can be used in such a way emphasizes its political role in social control when there are few avenues of independent control. These are extreme examples of a common feature of appetite—the suppression of appetite for a higher goal. But for a psychology of appetite, it is important to remember that embodied desire is always a social expression of human interdependence; it is always relational.

Setting priorities

Like being tired, cold, or in pain, appetite imposes a motivational priority. When we are hungry or thirsty, or are presented with the option of feeding, appetite can win out over all other drives. What governs that priority and what predicts eating behavior are major preoccupations in psychology. The literature is mostly concerned with modern dilemmas of hedonic or controlled eating. Chief among them is the current concern for eating disorders, the most common of which is obesity. The prevalence of obesity in adults in the United States, defined as a BMI over 30, is now 35.5 percent in men and 35.8 percent in women (Flegal et al., 2012). Similar prevalence data have been reported in Europe (Gallus et al., 2015). The psychology of appetite has become important as never before. When food is scarce, overconsumption is only a fantasy. However, when energy-rich foods are easily within reach, mass obesity may become a reality. Jo Harrold and colleagues state the nature of the problem very well:

> We occupy a world of abundant and heavily promoted highly palatable and energy dense food. In this situation obese individuals possess an over responsiveness to the

pleasures of eating which appears not to be quenched by the physiological consequences of ingestion. In effect their appetite system appears overwhelmed. (Harrold
et al., 2012, p. 3)

For psychology to be relevant to the study of obesity, we need to offer explanation for
the role of wanting, desiring, and craving in the promotion of food search.

Less common, but also often seen in food-plentiful societies, is the problem
of food avoidance or refusal, clinically presenting as versions of anorexia disorders. Appetite or craving may actually be diminished in those with anorexia
who restrict all food intake (Veensta and de Jong, 2011). But, anorexia is not really
about appetite. Appetite is merely a casualty of attempts at control and perfection. For example, Sarah Williams and Marie Reid analyzed how people with
self-defined anorexia nervosa relate to food and their sense of self. They found
that people were mainly concerned with personal control and with perfection.
In general, people with anorexia framed hunger positively as a form of experiential avoidance: they talked about hunger being useful because it stops one from
thinking about the pain of rejection and loss (Williams and Reid, 2012). It may
simply be that the meanings of craving, desire, want, and need are altered to sig-
nify broader personal challenges. Hunger becomes less about food and is instead
captured—kidnapped, if you like—and used to function as a vehicle of denial and
control. In this sense resistance to appetite serves an overall emotional purpose
of self-protection.

These are abnormal cases. Extreme, deliberate undernourishment or overnour-
ishment fall at the limits of the distribution of food and drink behavior. Perhaps
more common, but less investigated, are the interesting everyday expressions of
appetite in those who don't have an eating disorder. What role does appetite play,
for example, in those who manage hunger and thirst as a pleasurable desire, and
those who resist the urge to ingest as part of a regular strategy of diet or weight
control?

The pleasures of desire

Hedonic appetite—the desire for food for pleasure, beyond homeostasis, beyond
the provision of fuel and hydration—is a core part of modern eating and drinking in
wealthy societies. Hedonic it may well be, but it is not at all clear that we understand
what the pleasure of appetite is. David Mela has tried to explore exactly this question by proposing a stronger distinction between food "liking" and food "wanting."
He reflects that most animal studies, and many human studies, don't study pleasure
but actually study *preference*. Typical paradigms involve a choice between competing
rewards, from which one assumes liking from the choice that is labeled a preference.

For humans, the hedonic question is whether one is motivated by the pleasure of liking or by the wanting of food. This distinction may be crucially important, because the wanting of food is under the control of a range of learned cognitive and emotional associations, which are different to those for the liking of food. These associations are those most used in marketing and advertising. Rather engagingly, in this argument Mela allows himself a moment of criticism of the moralistic tone that he believes pervades the science of eating behavior, and in particular the science of obesity:

> There is a subjective element of Calvinism colouring even professional discussions of food pleasure, an unstated expression of the view that "If it tastes nice, it must be bad for you." Valid or not, from the perspective of evolutionary biology this is certainly a modern and unnatural view of the mechanistic links between food selection and nutritional requirements. More worrying is that this also positions pleasure as a foe, rather than a potential ally of healthy eating behaviours. The corollary, "In order to be good for you, it cannot taste nice" will assuredly get us nowhere in making progress toward attracting consumers to a healthy, balanced food choice and intake.[2]

How we come to decide whether we want or like certain substances is a source of much psychological interest. There is clearly huge variability in our appetites and we are used to expressing our like or dislike of certain foods. Consider the broad differences in diets across the world. In China, for example, the staples are rice and noodles, while in northern Europe it is the potato, although for most of the world it remains maize. But there are some foods that people actively avoid, even when others seek them as a delicacy. For example, how fond are you of fried cricket or the protein-rich pupae of the silkworm? The Western rejection of insects, many of which are commonly eaten across the world, has been a stubborn population avoidance that has so far resisted any public policy attempts at change. Alan Yen, for example, reminds us that "apart from Europe and North America, approximately 1500–2000 species of insects and other invertebrates are consumed by 3000 ethnic groups across 113 countries in Asia, Australia, and Central and South America" (Yen, 2009, p. 290). Attitudinal barriers to the selective consumption of insects in the West are well established, and Alan Yen does a good job of explaining the many benefits of voluntarily introducing insects into our diet. He accepts that it is going to be a hard sell. As Mary Roach puts it in her excellent book *Gulp*, "Culture writes the menu" (Roach, 2014, p. 53).

Eat your greens

How do you encourage people to eat and drink things they judge unappetizing or even disgusting? Many of us have had the experience of attempting to persuade a reluctant child to eat something they don't want to eat. Indeed, many of us were those reluctant children—and some of us remain reluctant adults. For a dominant example, eating adequate amounts of fruit and vegetables is considered protective against vascular diseases (Steffen, 2006). Despite many public health campaigns on the value of eating fruit and vegetables, the average consumption remains low. In an American survey undertaken in 2000, the percentage of people meeting the WHO-recommended level of consumption of five 80-gram portions of fruit or vegetables a day was 40 percent. Adolescent boys achieved the lowest consumption—at a remarkable 0.7 percent. This figure means many consumed none (Guenther et al., 2006). This is a stubbornly stable finding, not changing very much over time, geography, or generation, and has been repeated in a variety of U.S. studies. The State of the Plate review in 2010, for example, showed no change: "Fruit and vegetable consumption has remained quite stable at just under 2 cups per person per day across the total population since 1999" (State of the Plate, 2010, p. 11). An interesting observation of those interested in obesity prevention is that figures such as these often include fruit juice and fried potatoes. These data are not peculiar to the United States. Global data show similar patterns, with countries such as Pakistan having diets that are almost vegetable-free (Hall et al., 2009).

There are many studies of the potential reasons for fruit and vegetable avoidance. The factors implicated range from social and economic barriers to ethnic and cultural history, social modeling, and habit. In a systematic review of all of the psychological attempts to change eating behavior and increase the consumption of fruit and vegetables, it was judged that it is possible to increase self-reported consumption of fruit and vegetables. However, the changes achievable are quite small: across all of these, fruit and vegetable consumption increased by an average of one serving a day. This modest increase shrinks to below half a serving a day for adolescents (Thomson and Ravia, 2011).

So children don't eat their greens, and it is hard to make them. Perhaps that is hardly news. Parents have a significant role in shaping the context in which food attitudes and beliefs are developed. The purchasing, carrying, storing, preparing, and consuming of food are all modeled repeatedly and often in the home (Birch and Fisher, 1998). What doesn't positively influence behavior is direct assertive parental instruction—saying "Eat it!" in a shrill or loud voice. Julie Lumeng and her colleagues at the University of Michigan, as part of a larger study in child development across ten sites in the United States, videotaped children and mothers discussing a snack that was introduced. They observed 1,218 young children (15, 24, and 36 months old) and their mothers for ten minutes, and coded all of the mothers' interventions, from encouragements to instructions. The researchers found that the use of "assertive" and "intrusive" eating instructions were associated with greater adiposity in the child (Lumeng et al., 2012). Although there was nothing green in the snack offered in this study, the general findings are rather startling when it comes to nutritional awareness. It seems that knowledge and skills in motivating, directing, encouraging, or negotiating positive eating are not common. In fact, the State of the Plate study even argued that these are in decline, with generation-Y mothers in the United States less knowledgeable than ever about the appropriate portions of fruit and vegetables recommended for their children.

Conspicuously missing from the forest of papers on public health and psychological interventions aimed at altering eating behavior is any consideration of what David Mela (2006) called liking and wanting. It is almost as if the psychology of eating has lost sight of the importance of the experience of consuming, not only taste, but its effects on appetite, on desire. Psychological theories tend to focus on social and personality determinants of behavioral choice within a specific context. The few studies there are on pleasure show that when it comes to answering the dominant social question—"Do you like this?"—the answers do indeed revolve around beliefs about texture and appearance, as well as taste (Zeinstra et al., 2007). Hedonic experience and how it can be altered with information hold the greatest interest for those who are trying to influence our consumption, those who are trying to get us to switch to their products and consume more.

Lipsmackinthirstquenchinacetastinmotivatingoodbuzzincooltalki nhighwalkinfastlivinevergivincoolfizzin Pepsi

Significant investment goes into influencing our hedonic judgments about food and drink, with advertising drawing on qualities that go well beyond the taste. This commercial from the 1970s is an iconic example of the trade. One could describe a carbonated flavored sugar drink in simpler terms, but this innovative and humorous approach packs in multiple associations that accentuate both the characteristics of the drinking experience (*fizzin*) and prime desirable social attributes (*fastlivin*). Aradhna Krishna has led this field in studying the use of sensory characteristics outside of taste to promote consumer experience. She calls it "sensory marketing." The experience of purchasing and consuming is a multisensory one. From the unwrapping of a chocolate to the crackle provided by carbonation of water in a soda drink, all, she argues, are crucial to the experience of consumption inasmuch as they give structure, purpose, and focus to appetite, and guide purchase or consumption behavior (Krishna, 2012). She is beginning to unravel how the foundational metaphors, such as height, weight, and temperature, discussed in studies of embodied or grounded cognition, can be used in consumer psychology (Krishna and Schwarz, 2014).

The efficacy of such marketing strategies in influencing consumption is not in doubt. Less clear is whether the experience of food information can actually change the experience of the food, including one's hedonic appetite. In other words, marketing can clearly change our wanting behavior, but can it change our liking behavior? Important here is not just the influence on taste but also the influence on the desire for more, and on judgments of satiety.

Jeffrey Larson and his colleagues took a novel approach to studying the influence of marketing on appetite. They recognized that there had been very little interest in the potentially saturating effects of the high volume of food and drink advertising we are exposed to on a daily basis. In two experiments, they asked students to actively consider and evaluate images of food. One group viewed 60 images and another only 20. All of the students evaluated how much they liked the food, and how appetizing they found it. The idea was that those exposed to three times as much "considering and evaluating" of food images would behave differently when faced with that food. Immediately following the image evaluation, the participants were given three peanuts and asked how much they enjoyed them. Intriguingly,

> as participants evaluated more salty foods in pictures, their enjoyment decreased when subsequently eating a different salty snack of peanuts. This happened even though participants never saw a picture of peanuts, and they were never instructed to think about consuming peanuts (or any other food). (Larson et al., 2014, p. 190)

Perhaps an unintended consequence of overexposure to food images is the stimulation of satiety. If food is thought plentiful, wanting is reduced. Equally speculative is the idea that this is simply a function of scarcity. The value of the peanut is reduced because it is presented in a salted food–rich context. Larson and colleagues argue, with a supporting second experiment, that what matters is that participants had to actively imagine food, and that this operates through provoking judgments of satiety and so reduced pleasure.

How you describe food, and how often you are exposed to and consider those descriptions can matter. As well as making recommendations to marketers about possible counterintuitive effects of communication, Larson and colleagues offer advice to all of us. Perhaps, they suggest, people "might benefit from limiting their sensory simulations before eating with the potential result that food may become more enjoyable" (Larson et al., 2014, p. 193). Too much research on a food blog or restaurant review website might reduce your pleasure. An optimal "hedonic strategy" for food is to spend as little time considering it as possible until the moment of food choice.

What's on the menu?

That moment of food choice is critical to those who want to provide the best possible experience of eating and drinking, to chefs, restaurateurs, and food writers.

Brian Wansink and colleagues focused exactly on the moment of food choice in a restaurant. They were interested in whether the description of food on the menu could affect not only the wanting but also the liking—in other words, whether seeing something more extensively described makes any difference to the pleasure of its consumption. In an interesting field experiment, Wansink and colleagues manipulated menus in a canteen. Some people had menus that were merely descriptive, whereas others, on different days, had menus that were more expressive. The choices were:

> Traditional Cajun Red Beans with Rice (vs. Red Beans with Rice), Succulent Italian Seafood Filet (vs. Seafood Filet), Tender Grilled Chicken (vs. Grilled Chicken), Homestyle Chicken Parmesan (vs. Chicken Parmesan), Satin Chocolate Pudding (vs. Chocolate Pudding), and Grandma's Zucchini Cookies (vs. Zucchini Cookies). (Wansink et al., 2005, p. 395)

The diners were asked three questions about their experience: how good the food tasted, how sated they felt, and how appealing the food looked. The first finding was that more words produced more words. Twice as many positive comments were received about the meals that were described expressively. Diners also reported that the expressively described food was more appealing and tasted better, but did not report it as more filling (Wansink et al., 2005).

Once we are in the realm of hedonic appetite, it seems that the exact experience is highly sensitive to external cues, and can be manipulated by information and expectation. Perhaps the best scientific expression of this was given by Martin Yeomans, working with the chef Heston Blumenthal. Together with Lucy Chambers and Anthony Blake, they created what they hoped would be everybody's favorite new dessert: smoked salmon ice-cream. They were interested not so much in whether one can enhance experience by describing it in a more evocative way, but what exactly the role of food expectation was. They used a method of priming for a sweet experience by describing something as "ice-cream" and providing a conflicting and countercultural (at least in England) experience with a "salted fish" ingredient. The results are shown in Figure 10.1. When the same food was described as "smoked salmon ice-cream," it was rated as less pleasant and more salty than when it was described as "frozen savory mousse." In repeated experiments this finding held strong. We expect ice-cream to be sweet, and we don't like it when it is not (Yeomans et al., 2008).

The food and drink industries are getting more interested in the idea that perception can be influenced by the cognitive and emotional context in which the food is presented. We are only just beginning to explore how the description, labeling,

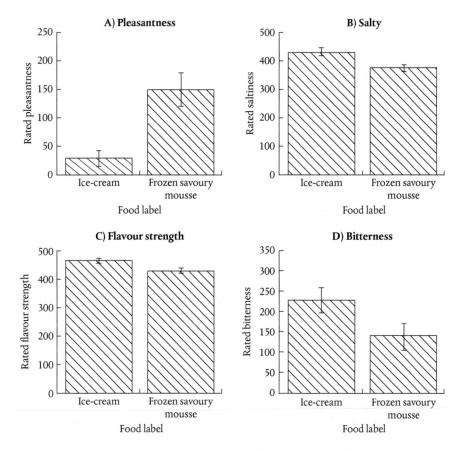

Fig. 10.1. Rated characteristics of salmon-flavored food presented as either "ice-cream" or "frozen savory mousse."

"Rated pleasantness (A), saltiness (B), strength of flavor (C) and bitterness (D) of smoked salmon ice-cream depending on whether this was labelled as frozen savory mousse or ice-cream. Data are mean ± SEM."

Reprinted from *Food Quality and Preference*, 19 (6), Martin R. Yeomans, Lucy Chambers, Heston Blumenthal, and Anthony Blake, The role of expectancy in sensory and hedonic evaluation: The case of smoked salmon ice-cream, pp. 565–73, Figure 1, Copyright (2008), with permission from Elsevier.

presentation, and other nontaste characteristics of consumption can be used to alter appetite and consumption. Can we stimulate desire or increase avoidance with the simple use of an adjective such as *succulent* or the presentation of a dessert menu at just the right time?

To explore the idea of how we manage expectations around food and drink, I talked to Jean Christophe Slowik (Box 10.1).

Box 10.1. Jean Christophe, the restaurateur: "*I love what we serve and we serve what I love*"

Jean Christophe is a celebrated chef who lives surrounded by the objects of his desires. He is passionate about food and about the social experience of eating and drinking. We talked at his restaurant L'Absinthe, in Primrose Hill, North London

---

Chris: Is there a difference between eating because you need to and eating because you want to?

JC: I think so. We see it often in the restaurant. Because of the size of portions we serve, when people have two courses they have more than their share of what they need. Then the pudding [dessert] becomes interesting. One out of three times we give the pudding menu and people say, "No. But maybe I will just look." They are not hungry anymore. Then they look at the menu and see something they are interested in. Then they will find the space. They do not *need* it. But most of the time it is, how can I say, they are interested and want to experiment a bit more. They want to try something they have wanted for a long time, or something they have an urge for. So pudding is always more to do with desire than need. I don't think anybody ever really needs pudding when it is part of a three-course meal, not in the way you mean "need."

Chris: How do you influence that desire? Does description matter?

JC: I don't like to overdescribe. You go to some restaurants and there are four lines explaining where the potatoes come from, where the garlic they use in the sauce comes from, and they are all fancy names from fancy farms. Because of the school of thought from my upbringing, my training, I believe that you cannot have a restaurant if you do not deal with good produce to start with. So there is no need to go into the detail of source, because the bottom line is: if you are passionate about your job, you are only going to get the best.

I understand that the label matters, but I have decided that we do not need to do this. The restaurant will do the talking. There is no point of fancying it all up. It is about the substance. If you do all that and there is no substance, then you fail anyway.

Chris: But doesn't expectation matter?

JC: I have thought about expectation a lot. The lower the expectation then the greater the pleasure. The higher the expectation the lower the pleasure. Most of the time people come in and discover us and then come back. We have a higher rate of return on walk-ins than on bookings. Because the bookings have read about us or researched us, or a journalist has sold a specific experience, and they expect exactly the same. People who walk in from the street are more interested in what they find.

Chris: Do you experiment with the menu?

JC: I try to experiment, but once you are on a path it can be very difficult because it is hard to twist. You want to twist, but every time you twist you have to twist back. So we

---

Box 10.1. *Continued*

very rarely change the menu, because for us quality comes in repetition. The more you do the dish the better the dish becomes. If you change the dish every day, it is very hard for the chef to do that well. But we change three or four times in the year. We can't have a long menu. The only way you get quality out of a small kitchen is to have a small menu. Sometimes people ask for what is not on the menu. I can't do that, because I cannot guarantee the quality. We will get lost. I always find a long menu very suspicious in a restaurant because you have to ask: how is that possible?

Chris: Have you tried to offer a wider French cuisine, for example, with the use of offal?

JC: We tried. We wanted to do French cuisine with British produce. So we tried to bring some offal on the table. And it was a disaster. We made andouillette—tripe sausage. Try to get a British person to eat tripe sausage! Or tripe, full stop! It is not produce that British people eat.

Chris: We used to eat offal. Who sets these cultural expectations on what is possible?

JC: It must be a slow process of revolution of the generations. We are the middle generation where some of us eat offal and some do not anymore. Maybe in 20 years time it won't be seen. People will think us strange. Perhaps people think they have bettered themselves. We all want to better ourselves. So they do not need to eat that sort of food. You have gone up one notch in society and now you can afford to have the pork chop. This probably is a class issue, more so in this country.

Chris: So it is not about the taste or about appetite.

JC: No, completely not. No: it is the idea. If I said to someone, You can have a plate of tripe, it is irrelevant to how it is going to be prepared. He will not like it.

Chris: You are surrounded every day by the food and wine of the highest quality that you have chosen. Is that a temptation?

JC: Oh, no, it is very easy. It is like when you start in a chocolate shop. They make sure you eat as much chocolate as you can. Once you are sick of it you don't touch it any more. In the restaurant, professionalism takes over very quickly. We have to eat before the service. So we eat at 11:30 in the morning. And 5:30. So when you are providing the food, you are either not hungry or you are too busy to eat.

Chris: Does working with food and wine change your desire and pleasure?

JC: No, it doesn't. What it does change is your standard. It goes up and up and up. Take wine. So if I started at the bottom of the range: I used to drink house wine and I thought that was quite good. Then maybe I shifted to the Côtes du Rhône. Now that has become my norm. Now the Gevrey-Chambertin has become the norm. So my taste has gone up. Now my everyday wine has become a higher standard. I can afford it. I don't mean financially—I mean I can now appreciate it, appreciate the difference. Obviously I still try different things. But once you get used to something you have to go to the next level. I love what we serve and we serve what I love. Same with the wine. Everything we serve has to be excellent.

(Continued)

Box 10.1. *Continued*

Chris: Can you go back down a level?

JC: No, I cannot drink bad wine any more. I am too old for that!

JC has an expert understanding of the relationship between wanting and needing and the role that description and expectation can play on the choice and enjoyment of food and drink. In support of Jeffrey Larson's ideas, it is interesting that JC believes that less information increases the possibility of pleasure. In reducing any prior influence by not reading reviews, not thinking about the farm that produced the produce, and simply trusting chefs to know their business, one can allow an appetite to be expanded through discovery. Also interesting and not explored in the scientific literature, is an adaptive response to food plenty: a change in preferences. When surrounded by objects of desire, one's preference becomes more particular, nuanced, and discriminating.

Personal responsibility

The expert appetite of an expert chef is an extreme example of how appetite can be shaped and tamed. This is something JC takes for granted. He is in control of his desires. The issue of control, however, is at the center of arguments over how individuals and societies should respond to the obesity pandemic. For many people it is simple: if you are overweight, then exercise personal responsibility and consume less. Kelly Brownell and colleagues discuss the fraught issue of personal responsibility in the context of the American discourse on obesity. They argue as follows:

> The notion that obesity is caused by the irresponsibility of individuals, and hence not corporate behavior or weak or counterproductive government policies, is the centerpiece of food industry arguments against government action. Its conceptual cousin is that government intervention unfairly demonizes industry, promotes a "nanny" state, and intrudes on personal freedoms. This libertarian call for freedom was the tobacco industry's first line of defense against regulation. It is frequently sounded today by the food industry and its allies, often in terms of vice and virtue that are deeply rooted in American history and that cast problems like obesity, smoking, heavy drinking, and poverty as personal failures.[3]

This combative discourse gives a good flavor of the current battle over our appetites. The regulation and control of the social drivers of appetite are being fought over, in particular when it comes to sugar (Lustig et al., 2012). However, it is worth remembering that the personal is always social. When I decide to eat a snack, I can bring to mind its surface characteristics, and my perception of want and need. What I cannot access are the influences over time in shaping my perceptions, or the ingredients and their effect on my subsequent appetite and behavior. Other people, people I don't know, are involved in my choices. The involvement of others in our personal responsibility for food is becoming better understood, at least by academics and policy makers (Swinburn et al., 2011; Roberto et al., 2015).

This knowledge has, however, barely transferred to any clear public understanding of appetite. When I choose to eat a snack it feels like solely personal choice, and other people treat me like I am making only a personal choice. If I "lose control" and eat ten snacks the consequences will be physical and social. Where there are judgments of responsibility, there will be judgments of irresponsibility. Stigma and discrimination are core to the experience of obesity (Puel and Heuer, 2009). Overweight and obese people are often considered to be unattractive, lazy, and lacking in willpower and self-control. In obesogenic environments characterized by the oversupply of energy-dense, nutrient-free food and drink, people are described as simply having lost control of their appetites.

Not everyone believes that we have lost control. Biology is perhaps not so easily beaten. Ruud van den Bos and Denise de Ridder offer an interesting challenge to the dominant idea that our appetite system is no longer fit for purpose. Instead, they argue that the defining feature of evolved human adaptivity is the existence of conscious control, of our ability to override otherwise automatic systems. With consciousness and language comes self-regard. We are able to question our physiology rather than slavishly respond to it. Self-control, in their view, allows for temporal planning and the prioritizing of longer-term outcomes against immediate rewards (van den Bos and de Ridder, 2006). This is exactly what we are doing when we deliberately attempt to change our diet. But just how easy is it to individually change a behavior so fundamentally social, relational, and shaped by external forces?

"I'm on a diet"

Most of us have tried at some point to change our dietary habits, typically to lose weight, but often for other health or social goals. It is hard. Denise de Ridder and her colleagues were interested in why we decide to calorie-control diet, what happens when we do, and in particular what it means when someone declares themselves to be on a diet (de Ridder et al., 2014). The answer might seem obvious. Surely people who say they are on a diet are those who are overweight or want to lose weight. However, the answers to the questions posed by de Ridder and colleagues are not so straightforward. They observed that the declaration of being on a diet, or the social label of being a dieter, is unrelated to weight loss. In fact, the chances are that if you declare yourself on a diet, you will not lose weight. In a relatively large sample, they identified that dietary restraint was common (van Strien et al., 1986). However, dietary restraint is highly related to negative perceptions and concerns about food. The researchers discovered that "dieting and concerns go hand in hand while both leave actual consumption largely unaffected" (de Ridder et al., 2014, p. 106). In plainer words, worrying about food and attempting to control diet have nothing to do with subsequent weight loss.

Perhaps we need help. Dieting alone appears to be just too difficult. There is no shortage of commercially available help in the form of weight loss programs, many of which are either prescribed or provided within formal health care systems. Studies of such dieting programs show that modest short-term gains are possible, although even the studies showing modest gains may be flawed by biases toward positive evaluation (Mann et al., 2007). A recent systematic review of therapist-delivered weight loss programs also showed a mixed picture. They were not effective when delivered in primary care, although they may be effective when delivered commercially by people who are specialist trainers (Hartmann-Boyce et al., 2014). Weight loss is possible, then, with behavioral intervention; in particular, when delivered by behavior change specialists, but self-dieting may be closer to an anxiety- or impression-management strategy, operating in the context of food-plentiful societies.

"Diet talk" is more of a ritualistic performance of mild self-punishment that may serve only to manage the negative impact of shame and worry. Self-initiated dietary restriction has now lost its power to function as part of a weight-management strategy, but instead has taken on a new role as defense of self-respect. The behavior of expressing an intention for change has become totally decoupled from the behavior of food search or of eating: it operates free of any planning or implementation (de Ridder et al., 2014). Intriguing though these ideas are, what's missing from this developing view of the psychology of appetite is a discussion of changes in food wanting when people attempt to restrict food intake and declare themselves "on a diet." What role does appetite play in food restraint or its failure?

Hungry behavior

There are surprisingly few qualitative studies of the actual experience of dieting, of what it feels like when one is hungry. Perhaps food and drink restraint is so common a behavior that it escapes serious investigation. There are studies of specific populations—in particular, those with an eating disorder—but there is less interest in the ordinary. Social scientists appear to be more interested in core subjects of identity, body image, and choice. However, hunger—an increase in the salience of physical discomfort and attentional bias to cues for possible food—has a number of effects on behavior. Principally, hunger acts to raise awareness to possible food, motivates one to forage, broadens the category of what might satisfy, and increases exposure to our own core behavioral tendencies. In other words, hunger disinhibits.

Anne Hammarström and colleagues undertook a trial of a weight loss intervention. They chose 12 women from the trial and interviewed them in more detail about their experience of dieting. The results are quite revealing. The women were not interested in any technical aspects of energy consumption, nor with the overall purpose of dieting. And they did not talk much about food *liking*. No. What they talked about were the demands of food *wanting* and its assault upon the self, and about their battle for self-respect, self-determination, and change. They talked about their inner battles with food and drink, with desire and craving; with the challenge of self-loathing and self-respect. One woman described her hunger in terms of a "craving" for sugary foods that was similar to the trials of being an alcoholic:

> I cannot buy sweets, which is why I call myself an alcoholic because I'm like them in that they can't buy themselves a bottle of alcohol. And I have to eat all sweets at once. Nothing else is possible. I wish the sweets were as far away in the shop as possible.

Another spoke of how she felt when failing to resist eating sweets: "Afterwards when I have eaten it I feel sick and I think—hell, why did I eat it … when I know that I should not and that I feel bad afterwards."[4]

Craving

At its extreme hunger becomes craving, which is a highly intense desire accompanied by thoughts that are intrusive, hard to ignore, and hard to control. The same word is used for a range of motivational disorders for all substances of abuse, including food, drugs, and alcohol (Pelchat, 2002). Food craving, as was seen in the example from Anne Hammarström's study, is often experienced negatively as abandonment to an external force or as a character weakness. But the psychology of craving in appetite is not very well understood. It is dominated by models borrowed from addiction, which are more relevant to a craving for a specific, often illegal or illicit substance, such as drugs of abuse. Craving for normal, everyday food and drink is different. Craving is likely to be highly context dependent. Three different contexts of food denial and craving exemplify how important context can be. The first is a study of dieters; the second is a study of craving in pregnancy; and the last is a different context of food denial: those deliberately avoiding food in order to achieve a positive, often occupational goal.

Andrew Hill in the UK has done much to develop a psychology of craving and appetite. For example, in a study with Anna Massey, he introduced two important methodological developments to the study of diet and craving. First, the investigators made a distinction between those who are restricting their diet to *lose* weight and those who are restricting their diet to *maintain* their weight. They call the first group "dieters" and the second "watchers." Second, they went back to basics and captured detailed observations in diaries of each craving target, intensity, and emotion over a seven-day period by 129 women. In all, they captured 393 records of craving in the week. They found:

> Chocolate was the most frequent target of cravings (37% of episodes), followed by savoury (31.6%), and sweet foods (22.4%). Savoury food cravings included crisps (potato

fries), bread, cheese, and meal foods, while sweet food cravings were most commonly for biscuits, cake, desserts, and confectionery.[5]

And without any hint of irony, they report that "the majority of cravings were fulfilled by eating the craved food (70%), a proportion that did not differ by dieting group."[6] The context of food restraint was important. Self-defined dieters had more frequent and stronger cravings than both watchers and those not on a diet. Furthermore, "Dieters rated their cravings as slower to disappear and their mood to be lower in hedonic tone" (Massey and Hill, 2012, p. 783). In this context, defining oneself as a dieter was associated with increases in craving, decreases in positive mood—and no sign of changed behavior.

A different context of craving was explored by Natalia Orloff and Julia Hormes from New York. They were interested in the experience some women have of craving during pregnancy. Appetite often changes during pregnancy. For example, the incidence of pica, the ingestion of non-foods, is thought to increase. And craving, often for sweet substances such as chocolate, increases (Orloff and Hormes, 2014). The researchers argue that craving is largely due to a pattern of approach and avoidance around socially sanctioned denial of desired food. The more one self-denies, the more likely it is one will crave. In pregnancy the social meaning of eating is changed and the social sanctions on satisfying one's craving by consuming are relaxed. This is an intriguing idea, although it certainly needs further study. However, the positioning of a highly motivated and specific behavior so squarely in the realm of the social context is welcome. A psychology of appetite needs to be relational in understanding the meaning of self-denial and the social costs of the failure of attempts at self-denial.

Approaching the question of context and appetite from a different angle is the third interesting case of occupational dieting. For some people diet is constructed as an occupational requirement, either in what is becoming known as "aesthetic labor," as in aspects of the hospitality industry (e.g., flight attendants, reception workers), or in modeling, acting, or sport. Take acting, for example. In one study, both student and professionals were asked what lengths they would go to in order to secure a "dream job." Figure 10.2 gives the results of twelve body alterations. Most agreed that losing and gaining weight is a body modification they are willing to undertake to achieve an acting job. One young male actor captured this well when he said:

> I am the kind of actor who diets ridiculously, goes through binge diets of "I'm going to not," you know, "I'm going to cut major food groups out of my diet." In order to achieve something . . . Equally, I'm also the kind of actor who [will] go to the place of transforming my body to the extreme by putting on weight to play a part.[7]

Another common example is professional jockeys. Using diary methods, Eimer Dolan and colleagues studied jockeys' nutritional habits prior to racing. All jockeys reported a range of weight-loss practices, not least dieting, dehydration, use of saunas, and excessive exercise. According to the researchers, "It appears likely that

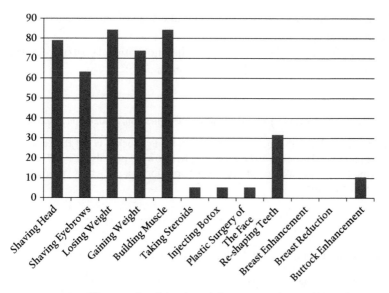

■ % willing to undertake each modification, out of 19 student actors

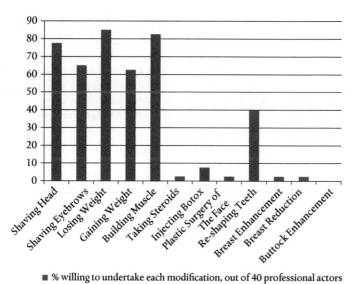

■ % willing to undertake each modification, out of 40 professional actors

Fig. 10.2. Body modifications student and professional actors would undertake to achieve their "dream job."

a substantial proportion of jockeys remain in a state of chronic energy deficiency" (Dolan et al., 2011, p. 796).

To explore appetite in the context of a higher motivational goal of sport, I talked to Tom Strawson. Tom is 26 and a jockey (Box 10.2).

Box 10.2. Tom, the jockey: *"the discipline comes from an ambition to succeed"*

At 6 feet, 2 inches (188 cm), with size-11 feet, being a jockey is not the easiest of life choices for Tom. He has to make a race weight below 147 pounds (66 kg). This involves reducing his food intake to between 600–700 calories a day, effectively making him hungry all the time.

_____

Chris: How would you describe this lifestyle you lead?

Tom: It is a challenge. You have to constantly manage your weight. I think I am now getting better at it.

Chris: How do you achieve it?

Tom: You have to have a really good regime and a well-planned diet. Generally you are meant to eat in the region of 2,000 to 3,000 calories a day, but I get down to 1,000 calories, and when I am dieting hard, 600 to 700. Your body has to get used to it, and adapt to it. You have to learn to eat the right things. This year is the first time I have consulted a professional dietician who has helped me eat the right things. I have probably been starving myself a little bit too much. And now I have a bit more of a protein diet. More meat. I don't eat bread any more. I eat protein. It is one constant battle, but you have to try and make it easier.

Chris: Do you keep a constant weight or does it fluctuate?

Tom: Yes, you do fluctuate. The more rides you get the easier it is. I think getting your weight down is the hardest thing. Keeping it down is easier. In the summer I can put weight on, this summer I got up to 12.4, even 12.8 stones [172, 176 pounds]. I fluctuate a bit at this time of year.

Chris: What else do you do to achieve weight loss?

Tom: I have to do a lot of exercise. I have to be physically very fit, and that involves riding five or six days a week. Then I live a life on an exercise bike in front of the TV at home or working harder at the office, then going to the gym at lunchtime, swim a kilometer, bike 15 kilometers, then go back to work feeling refreshed. Your body gets used to it.

Chris: Your body gets used to it, but does your mind? Are you still hungry?

Tom: Oh, yes, you are hungry the whole time. That does not change.

Chris: Does the desire for food change?

Box 10.2. *Continued*

Tom: Desire? Yes, it does. Yes. For example, there are some things I will never touch. In the last five years I have not eaten a McDonalds burger. Before I would happily have had a burger or a pizza or a fry-up. I look at that now and think of the calories. For the whole time I am thinking of calories.

Chris: Is it the calories that stop you or has the wanting changed?

Tom: I don't desire it anymore. It is not something I want. My diet has changed a lot. I now eat a lot of fish and fresh vegetables.

Chris: Marathon runners say they have thoughts about stopping all the time. Do you have thoughts about eating?

Tom: Oh, gee! Yes, you do get that. It happens all the time. I don't say it out loud but I do think about it all the time. But you get better with it. I just keep reminding myself of the achievements. I achieved more than I wanted to achieve last year and I just keep reminding myself of that. That is exactly why I do it: to achieve. I just have to man-up and get on with it. I don't find it particularly easy to fast in the week, but to me it is all about succeeding. And whenever I question myself, which I do the whole time, I think, "Well, what else would I be doing?" I put everything into what I do and I want to be the best at what I do.

Chris: What is the biggest challenge?

Tom: It can get you down. At one point nothing was going well, but in the last eighteen months it is all getting better and I feel like it is now moving forward. The success helps you cope with feeling hungry all the time, and starts to justify why you are doing it.

Chris: It sounds like a life that is defined by discipline. Are there positives from being so disciplined that transfer to the rest of life?

Tom: Of course. Massively. Discipline is organization. You have to be organized and determined. I am all about trying to achieve something. I will work until I get there. I might fail at first, but I will get there. You get out of life what you put into it. That is my motivation. The discipline comes from an ambition to succeed, and finding a way to make it all happen.

For Tom as a jockey, dieting is still difficult, still challenging, and something that requires tremendous personal discipline. Interestingly, his motivation is indirect. He is not dieting to lose weight; he is dieting to lose weight so he can compete and win. Perhaps in this way jockeys escape the failure discussed by Denise de Ridder. Appetite does not seem to alter: the being hungry and wanting of food remains intact, regardless of the motivation. However, there are changes in the targets. Just as Jean Christophe's appetite changes with experience, in demanding higher-quality foods, so Tom's appetite changes with the loss of desire for high-fat, high-sugar foods from fast-food restaurants.

Summary

The experience of desiring, wanting, and craving to eat and drink is oddly neglected in psychology. Appetite is always relational: consuming too much or too little can always be explained by power relations. The role of power can be observed in food refusal and avoidance, but is also at play in "diet talk" and in the lengths the food industry will go to shape and influence our choices. A psychology of appetite will need to understand the limits of personal choice when it comes to availability of food and drink. Egocentric explanations of self-determination focused on "personal responsibility" will fail, as will wholly sociological explanations of social determination. Individuals repeatedly exercise choice in the very specific contexts of their own goals and values. Needed is a psychology of desire that takes account of the physical experience of appetite, of wanting and needing, of the desire to consume.

Notes

1. Reproduced from Raymond Tallis, *Hunger*, 1e, p. 32 © 2009, Routledge.
2. Reprinted from *Appetite*, 1 (8), David J. Mela, Eating for pleasure or just wanting to eat? Reconsidering sensory hedonic responses as a driver of obesity, p. 16, Copyright (2006), with permission from Elsevier.
3. Reproduced from Kelly D. Brownell, Rogan Kersh, David S. Ludwig, Robert C. Post, Rebecca M. Puhl, Marlene B. Schwartz, and Walter C. Willett, Personal Responsibility And Obesity: A Constructive Approach To A Controversial Issue, *Health Affairs*, 29 (3), p. 379, doi:10.1377/hlthaff.2009.0739 (c) 2010, Project HOPE. The published article is archived and available online at http://www.healthaffairs.org.
4. Reproduced from Anne Hammarström, Anncristine Fjellman Wiklund, Bernt Lindahl, Christel Larsson, and Christina Ahlgren, Experiences of barriers and facilitators to weight-loss in a diet intervention—a qualitative study of women in Northern Sweden, *BMC Women's Health*, 14 (59), p. 5, doi:10.1186/1472–6874–14–59 © 2014 Hammarström et al.; licensee BioMed Central Ltd. Quotation used under the terms of the Creative Commons Attribution License (http://creativecommons.org/licenses/by/2.0).
5. Reprinted from *Appetite*, 58 (3), Anna Massey and Andrew J. Hill, Dieting and food craving. A descriptive, quasi-prospective study, p. 783, Copyright (2012), with permission from Elsevier.
6. Reprinted from *Appetite*, 58 (3), Anna Massey and Andrew J. Hill, Dieting and food craving. A descriptive, quasi-prospective study, p. 783, Copyright (2012), with permission from Elsevier.
7. Reproduced from Seen but not heard: an embodied account of the (student) actor's aesthetic labour, Roanna Mitchell, *Journal of Theatre Dance and Performance Training*, 5 (1), p. 65, doi:10.1080/19443927.2013.868367 (c) 2014, Taylor & Francis. Reprinted by permission of the publisher (Taylor & Francis Ltd, http://www.tandfonline.com).

References

Berthoud, H.-R. (2011). Metabolic and hedonic drives in the neural control of appetite: who is the boss? *Current Opinion in Neurobiology*, 21, 888–896.

Birch, L.L. and Fisher, J.O. (1998). Development of eating behaviors among children and adolescents. *Pediatrics*, 101, 539–549.

Brownell, K.D., Kersh, R., Ludwig, D.S., Post, R.C., Puhl, R.M., Schwartz, M.B. and Willett, W.C. (2010). Personal responsibility and obesity: a constructive approach to a controversial issue. *Health Affairs*, 29, 379–387.

de Ridder, D., Adriaanse, M., Evers, C. and Verhoeven, A. (2014). Who diets? Most people and especially when they worry about food. *Appetite*, 80, 103–108.

Dolan, E., O'Conner, H., McGoldrick, A., O'Loughlin, G., Lyons, D. and Warrington, G. (2011). Nutritional, lifestyle, and weight control practices of professional jockeys. *Journal of Sports Sciences*, 29, 791–799.

Flegal, K.M., Carroll, M.D., Ogden, C.L. and Curtin, L.R. (2012). Prevalence of obesity and trends in the distribution of body mass index among US adults, 1999–2010. *JAMA*, 307, 491–497.

Gallus, S., Lugo, A., Murisic, B., Bosetti, C., Boffetta, P. and La Vecchia, C.L. (2015). Overweight and obesity in 16 European countries. *European Journal of Nutrition*, 54, 679–689.

Guenther, P.M., Dodd, K.W., Reedy, J. and Krebs-Smith, S.M. (2006). Most Americans eat much less than recommended amounts of fruits and vegetables. *Journal of the American Dietetic Association*, 106, 1371–1379.

Hall, J.N., Moore, S., Harper, S.B. and Lynch, J.W. (2009). Global variability in fruit and vegetable consumption. *American Journal of Preventative Medicine*, 36, 402–409.

Hammarström, A., Fjellman Wiklund, A., Lindahl, B., Larsson, C. and Ahlgren, C. (2014). Experiences of barriers and facilitators to weight-loss in a diet intervention—a qualitative study of women in Northern Sweden. *BMC Women's Health*, 14, 59 (1–10).

Harrold, J.A., Dovey, T.M., Blundell, J.E. and Halford, J.C.G. (2012). CNS regulation of appetite. *Neuropharmacology*, 63, 3–17.

Hartmann-Boyce, J., Johns, D.J., Jebb, S.A., Summerbell, C. and Aveyard, P. (2014). Behavioural weight management programmes for adults assessed by trials conducted in everyday contexts: systematic review and meta-analysis. *Obesity Reviews*, 15, 920–932.

Krishna, A. (2012). An integrative review of sensory marketing: engaging the senses to affect perception, judgment and behavior. *Journal of Consumer Psychology*, 22, 332–351.

Krishna, A. and Schwarz, N. (2014). Sensory marketing, embodiment, and grounded cognition: a review and introduction. *Journal of Consumer Psychology*, 24, 159–168.

Larson, J.S., Redden, J.P. and Elder, R.S. (2014). Satiation from sensory simulation: evaluating foods decreases enjoyment of similar foods. *Journal of Consumer Psychology*, 24, 188–194.

Lumeng, J.C., Ozbeki, T.N., Appugliese, D.P., Kaciroti, N., Corwyn, R.F. and Bradley, R.H. (2012). Observed assertive and intrusive maternal feeding behaviors increase child adiposity. *The American Journal of Clinical Nutrition*, 95, 640–647.

Lustig, R.H., Schmidt, L.A. and Brindis, C.D. (2012). The toxic truth about sugar. *Nature*, 482, 27–29.

Lutter, M. and Nestler, E.J. (2009). Homeostatic and hedonic signals interact in the regulation of food intake. *The Journal of Nutrition*, 139, 629–632.

Mann, T.A., Tomiyama, J., Westling, E., Lew, A.-M., Samuels, B. and Chatman, J. (2007). Medicare's search for effective obesity treatment: diets are not the answer. *American Psychologist*, 62, 220–233.

Massey, A. and Hill, A.J. (2012). Dieting and food craving: a descriptive, quasi-prospective study. *Appetite*, 58, 781–785.

McNicholas, F., Prior, C. and Bates, G. (2013). A case of pervasive refusal syndrome: a diagnostic conundrum. *Clinical Child Psychology and Psychiatry*, 18, 137.

Mela, D.J. (2006). Eating for pleasure or just wanting to eat? Reconsidering sensory hedonic responses as a driver of obesity. *Appetite, 47,* 10–17.

Mitchell, R. (2014). Seen but not heard: an embodied account of the (student) actor's aesthetic labour. *Theatre, Dance and Performance Training, 5,* 59–73.

Orloff, N.C. and Hormes, JM. (2014). Pickles and ice cream! Food cravings in pregnancy: hypotheses, preliminary evidence, and directions for future research. *Frontiers in Psychology, 5,* 1076 (1–14).

Parker, J.A. and Bloom, S.R. (2012). Hypothalamic neuropeptides and the regulation of appetite. *Neuropharmacology, 63,* 18–30.

Pelchat, M.L. (2002). Of human bondage: food craving, obsession, compulsion, and addiction. *Physiology and Behavior, 76,* 347–352.

Puel, R.M. and Heuer CA. (2009). The stigma of obesity: a review and update. *Obesity, 17,* 941–964.

Roach, M. (2014). Gulp: adventures on the alimentary canal. London: Oneworld.

Roberto, C.A., Swinburn, B., Hawkes, C., Huang, T.T.-K., Costa, S.A., Ashe, M., Zwicker, L., Cawley, J.H. and Brownell, K.D. (2015). Patchy progress on obesity prevention: emerging examples, entrenched barriers, and new thinking. *The Lancet, 385,* 2400–2409.

State of the Plate. (2010). 2010 study on America's consumption of fruits and vegetables. Produce for Better Health Foundation. http://www.pbhfoundation.org. Accessed November 2014.

Steffen, L.M. (2006). Eat your fruit and vegetables. *The Lancet, 367,* 278–279.

Swinburn, B.A., Sacks, G., Hall, K.D., McPherson, K., Finegood, D.T., Moodie, M.L. and Gortmaker, S.L. (2011). The global obesity pandemic: shaped by global drivers and local environments, *The Lancet, 378,* 804–814.

Tallis, R. (2008). Hunger. Stocksfield: Acumen Press.

Thomson, C.A. and Ravia, J. (2011). A systematic review of behavioral interventions to promote intake of fruit and vegetables. *Journal of the American Dietetic Association, 111,* 1523–1535.

van den Bos, R. and de Ridder, D. (2006). Evolved to satisfy our immediate needs: self-control and the rewarding properties of food. *Appetite, 47,* 24–29.

van Strien, T., Fritjers, J.E.R., Bergers, G.P.A. and Defares, P.B. (1986). The Dutch Eating Behavior Questionnaire (DEBQ) for assessment of restrained, emotional, and external eating behavior. *International Journal of Eating Disorders, 5,* 295–315.

Veensta, E.M. and de Jong, P.J. (2011). Reduced automatic motivational orientation towards food in restricting anorexia nervosa. *Journal of Abnormal Psychology, 120,* 708–718.

Wansink, B., van Ittersum, K. and Painter, J.E. (2005). How descriptive food names bias sensory perceptions in restaurants. *Food Quality and Preference, 16,* 393–400.

Williams, S. and Reid, M. (2012). "It's like there are two people in my head": a phenomenological exploration of anorexia nervosa and its relationship to the self. *Psychology and Health, 27,* 798–815.

World Food Programme. (2014). http://www.wfp.org/hunger/stats. Accessed October 2014.

Yen, A.L. (2009). Edible insects: traditional knowledge or western phobia? *Entomological Research, 39,* 289–298.

Yeomans, M.R., Chambers, L., Blumenthal, H. and Blake, A. (2008). The role of expectancy in sensory and hedonic evaluation: the case of smoked salmon ice-cream. *Food Quality and Preference, 19,* 565–573.

Zeinstra, G.G., Koelen, M.A., Kok, F.J. and de Graaf, G. (2007). Cognitive development and children's perceptions of fruit and vegetables; a qualitative study. *International Journal of Behavioral Nutrition and Physical Activity, 4*(30), 1–11.

CHAPTER 11

EXPULSION

The final consideration is of the sensation of expulsion, the removal of gas, liquid, and solids from one's body. I explore a group of ten physical experiences, most of which are associated with proprioceptive actions whose principal operation is to separate matter from the body, to move it from inside to outside. These are the senses that function to expel, expunge, make matter other to oneself; these are the sensations we experience as we literally dis-embody.

The *removal senses* of interest in this penultimate chapter all share a common phenomenological feature: once they start they are difficult to stop. Most involve a limited and defined set of physical parameters (effector systems or triggering events) and have very different hedonic qualities. But they all share this principal feature of needing to run their course; a quality of being almost semi-automatic. One is often relegated to the role of observer, travelling with the sensation, but held responsible for it and for what happens next.

Removal and separation are achieved either through the action of air or the action of fluids and semi-solids. The air removal senses include sneeze (*sternutation*) cough (*tussis*), hiccup (*singultus*), burping (*eructation*), and farting (*flatulence*). The fluid and semi-solid removal senses include defecation, urination (*micturition*), vomiting (*emesis*), menstruation, and ejaculation. Physiologically, most involve a set of muscles that operate for the specific purpose. Some are arced reflexively through the spinal cord—the best examples being perhaps hiccupping and vomiting—whereas others have more central control, if only over sphincters, such as in urination.

There are very different sets of social understandings and practices that each of these senses operates within, which are at least partially determined by their physiological character. In what follows I explore first the air removal senses in two parts. The two senses of sneeze and cough are dominated by discourses of disease, contagion, and protection. The other three air senses of hiccup, burp, and fart escape this disease association, but are instead constructed within a discourse of manners, of social propriety. Next, I explore the fluid removal senses in three parts. First, defecation and urination are discussed as the routine removal of bodily waste—as the final stage of digestion. Vomit is an interesting case because it involves the specific expulsion of ingested but potentially toxic material before digestion. Finally, the last two fluid removal senses are reproduction-related with the vaginal discharging of blood and tissue, and both male and female ejaculation.

Each of these ten removal senses has a clear and well-defined physical function. However, how they are experienced depends on their social context and personal meanings. Across all of them, there is a public-private dynamic at play. Always at stake with these senses is how far one is physically or socially able to publically remove air or fluid from the body, made more complicated by their aural, olfactory, or visible qualities. And always with this public-private dynamic is the need to control, plan, manage, or mitigate the consequences of the public display of physical removal.

Two people helped me explore expulsion. In failing to understand from the academic literature why some air removal senses are funny and others are not, I sought the advice of a professional comedian, Arthur, who talked to me about why farting is funny. Later, intrigued by how the fluid removal sense of vomiting can change dependent upon its place and time, I talked to Connie about voluntary vomiting. Vomiting for her is a method of controlling the consequences of alcohol consumption.

Human jets

Both coughing and sneezing function to defend the airway from irritation or blockage. We inspire air and explosively propel it through the airway with force. For cough, there is much debate as to its separation from breathing and its unique characteristics, not least its repetitive and rhythmic character (Bolser et al., 2006). Adult human coughing and sneezing can be seen as a form of human jet propulsion. Both coughing and sneezing velocity can be as fast as 4.5 meters per second, and sneeze has recently been measured as reaching at least half a meter (Tang et al., 2013). It is an effective system for projecting a foreign body or internal blockage away from the body, and may also function to promote mucus secretion triggered by pharynx and buccal pressures (Burke, 2012). Increased buccal mucus secretion itself also functions to remove debris from the airway by swallowing.

It is exactly our success in jet propelling mucus away from the body that causes social concern because it is a highly effective way of transmitting disease. Much of the mucus sharing is done indoors and in confined spaces. In simulation studies, both position in a room and the quality of the ventilation influence personal exposure to mucus droplets from another's sneeze (Seepana and Lai, 2012). Sneezing indoors is by far a more effective way of transmitting disease than sneezing outdoors.

The explosive and projectile qualities of these human jet propulsions also communicate to others that one may have a blocked airway and need assistance, or that the air may itself be dangerous (e.g., smoke). It may also communicate potential illness and possible infection. Sneezing, however, is also known to occur with other triggers. For example, there are reports of sneeze on exposure to direct sunlight, on overeating, after orgasm, or simply brought about by thoughts of a sexual nature. The causes of orgasmic sneezing are unknown but are likely to be centrally mediated. Early theories of cause were often psychogenic, especially psychosexual. But it is more likely that a better understanding of the evolution of sneeze and the relationship of vestigial cortical sharing of nasal and genital projections will provide an explanation of these seemingly unrelated phenomena. Because it causes embarrassment, sexual sneeze is thought to be underreported. When it is reported, the descriptions are often of distress rather than pleasure (Bhutta and Maxwell, 2008, 2009).

"Coughs and sneezes spread diseases"

Murat Songu and Cemal Cingi discuss an interesting hypothesis about our preoccupation with sneeze and disease. They suggest that sneezing has always attracted beliefs around health, morality, and even prescience. It is still common for people to think that when someone sneezes it is a sign that others are thinking of them, or that the number of sneezes can bring good or bad luck. The meaning of sneeze has changed since the occurrence of great European pandemics such as plague and the more recent major flu epidemics: sneezing is now always symbolically related to infectious disease and illness (Songu and Cingi, 2009). Whatever the cultural history of the place of coughing and sneezing as methods of transmitting infection, this idea is now well embedded, perhaps best captured by the 1940s UK Ministry of Health campaign declaring that "coughs and sneezes spread diseases" (see Figure 11.1). These health promotion campaigns were unflinching in their positioning of the person who does not use a handkerchief as stupid, a public menace, and deserving of prosecution (Welch, 2013). This campaign is still used in the United Kingdom, although the use of the handkerchief has become confused and lost from this message, being a less popular practice. Other barrier methods are emerging, such as the wearing of face masks (Suess et al., 2012). Wearing a face mask is a public display of infection concern and may mark a shift away from the 1940s public health attempts to control transmission by changing the behavior of the carrier. The focus now is on individual attempts to protect oneself from others.

Common and public

Upper respiratory tract infections (the common cold) are the most common diseases we know, with most adults experiencing more than two a year, and children having more (Eccles, 2005). Chronic cough, typically one lasting for longer than eight weeks, is thought to affect one in five of us (Morice et al., 2004). Although possible causes and treatments are well documented, the experience of chronic cough is not. Exactly how people experience persistent cough and make sense of it as part of their lives is not well described.

Measuring cough severity is challenging but not impossible. In one study of 22 people with chronic cough, frequency and intensity were reported as being very

Fig. 11.1. Coughs and sneezes spread diseases. Circa 1960. (Plate 4)
©The British Library Board, B.S.81/19.

important to the experience. But as important was the discussion of the consequences of the public display. Coughing is not easy to hide. It is often a public activity because it is interruptive. It signals distress, raises the question of proximity to disease, and it might quickly transfer into a call for help. However, it does not always produce help. In a study of the experience of cough, one participant talks about coughing and the experience of mucus being stuck in the throat:

And that then trickles down here, and then I cough like the devil. . . . I get—it sticks here, great big chunks of it will stick here—can't get it out. And I cough, and cough, and cough, and then if you go to a restaurant and start coughing, they throw you out.[1]

Both coughing and sneezing publically display personal distress and social threat. Despite their ubiquity, there are few considerations of the public experience of coughing and sneezing, and fewer still on the stability and influence of beliefs about coughing and sneezing and their relationship with hygiene behavior. For example, how do people change their behavior when others cough and sneeze near to them?

Also unclear is how easy it is to change behaviors that are so common, and whether public health campaigns, like that shown in Figure 11.1, have any effect on mass hygiene behavior. A psychology of sneeze and cough will need to understand lay perceptions of disease transmission, beliefs about sneeze, the social control of sneeze within specific knowledge communities, and why health practices such as wearing a mask, using a handkerchief, being temporarily isolated, and using vitamin supplements move in and out of popularity, dominating in some but not other societies.

Hiccup

Hiccups are the "repeated spasms of the diaphragm followed by sudden closure of the glottis" (Krakauer, 2005, p. 822). Functionally they appear to have no physical or protective role and play no part in disease expression or management. They are thought to be only a vestigial reflex, one that has no adaptive value (Kahrilas and Shi, 1997). Typically we experience hiccup as sudden and hard to control. They are often judged to be loud and socially disturbing. In fact, they are named after their sound: consider the English *hiccup*, the French *hoquet*, and the Spanish *hipo*. Hiccups are, then, aural and public. They are normally short-lived and the source of humor and mild frustration or consternation. Consider that the word *hiccup* is often used metaphorically to mean a minor problem, or a pause for correction in a process. When we say, "There has been a hiccup," we generally mean to downplay a problem as minor, temporary, and manageable.

Chronic hiccup, however, is a serious problem and can cause severe distress, disability, and anxiety. It is anything but minor and is often not manageable. Thankfully it is not common, but it does occur more with advanced cancers and can be a major challenge in end-of-life care. There is a surprisingly large literature on potential pharmacological treatments for persistent hiccup in palliative care, although little guidance on their effectiveness (Moretto et al., 2013).

Patients with persistent hiccup often experience it as challenging in the extreme. For example, I know of only one study that looks in detail at the experience of people with chronic hiccup. Alvisa Palese and her colleagues took five years to undertake a study of adults with cancer-related persistent hiccup. It is a very challenging environment in which to do research, research that has to be done sensitively and with clinical expertise. In this study, five adults talked in detail about their experience of symptoms from neurological cancer and in particular of hiccup. Their narratives were dominated by a sense of despair at being powerless, at being unable to control unpredictable and automatic experiences, without any known trigger or mechanism for stopping them. The longer-term prospect was equally challenging as the patients reported fighting each hiccup, but eventually shifting to managing the frequency:

> Patients' attitude started to modify radically. With the growing understanding of the malign nature of the symptom, and its invincibility even against pharmacological treatments, over time, patients learned to lengthen pauses between one hiccup and the next and to reduce the number of spasms. (Palese et al., 2014, p. 399)

The study of psychological treatments for hiccup is sparse. There are case studies of highly unusual problems such as in hiccup associated with compulsive fluid consumption (Thomas et al., 2001), and there have been attempts at using biofeedback. For example, there is one clinical case with the successful use of respiratory control and heart rate biofeedback in a young woman with persistent hiccup (Hurst et al., 2013). The lack of consideration and treatment development for hiccup reflects badly on psychology as an applied and clinical discipline. We are only at the very beginning of considering treatments for these distressing conditions.

Releasing gases

Coughing, sneezing, and hiccup all require a respiratory inspiration phase in which air is taken and used to create a force. The final two air removal sensations relate to the release of gases from physical cavities, sometimes actively, often passively. There is a specific case of the release of air trapped in the vagina, typically during or after penetrative sex. It may be common, although its incidence is unknown, but in the normal case is virtually always medically benign. For some women, however, it can be embarrassing and in rare cases worrying and socially disabling (Allahdin, 2011). By far the more common cases of the buildup of bodily gases to be released are at either end of the digestive tract, in the burp and fart.

Burping

Burping is thought to occur approximately twenty times a day. It is a normal mechanism for returning swallowed air, but can become a concern when its frequency increases, it becomes associated with food regurgitation (rumination), or its social

display creates embarrassment or fear of embarrassment. Gastrointestinal disturbance is an everyday occurrence and perhaps to be expected when we consider the
complexity of normal human digestion. But for many people, dysfunctional digestion, or dyspepsia, is also common and sometimes troubling (Wallander et al., 2007).
One interesting household survey showed burping to be a common gastrointestinal
event across the world (Enk et al., 1999).

For most people, burping is not a worry but a form of gastric self-management.
Uncontrolled and sudden burping in an inappropriate social setting is often considered rude because it is associated with slovenly, uncouth, and poorly disciplined eating behavior. Modern eating involves various practices of distancing oneself from the
immediacy of food and the urgency of appetite, such as the regular timing of meals,
the use of cutlery and dishware, and the habit of eating in a slow and considered manner. These are forms of restraint that operate as marks of civilization, and signal our
separation from the bestial. Because burping is often caused or exacerbated with
swallowing air on eating rapidly, it can be an unwelcome reminder of physicality. The
public burp operates often as a social challenge to finely crafted and fragilely maintained social mores. Shakespeare understood this well in his invention of Sir Toby
Belch, who appears in *Twelfth Night* to crudely deliver basic truths, offering a chaotic
alternative to order. To deliberately burp is to challenge. A burp rarely goes unjudged.
It says: Reject me as uncouth, or accept us all as animal.

The humor in burping arises exactly from the social transgression of manners and
the positioning of the dominant concern as suddenly ridiculous. The burp operates
in humor bathetically. In other words, it challenges the pompous and over-serious.
One of the most successful ever clip-television shows in the United Kingdom is called
TV Burp. It operates exactly as its name suggests. Short clips of life (at least TV life) are
presented out of context and their seriousness undermined as a reminder ultimately
of our shared human ridiculousness (Leggott, 2010).

For some people, however, burping is neither funny nor socially useful. It is a
menace. For those with advanced cancer, for example, gastrointestinal symptoms,
including burping, can be challenging (Komurcu et al., 2002). Others suffer from a
primary belching disorder that can occur either with or without excessive air swallowing (*aerophagia*) (Tack et al., 2006). Also problematic, although not as commonly
mentioned, is the inability to burp.

There are no developed psychological interventions for chronic and severe burping. One can find case studies that give some insights. Although there are historical
studies showing how gastrointestinal and muscular changes can be altered psychologically, this area of research never flourished (Kamolz and Velanovich, 2002). There
were flirtations with hypnosis and relaxation training, but burping has escaped any
concerted psychological attention. There is a sign that interest has not completely
collapsed. Case studies are beginning to emerge that discuss burping as a serious area
of clinical interest. One proposes a role for simple education and reassurance (Disney

and Trudgill, 2014); another discusses a first case of burping as relief of distress (*eructophilia*) in the context of an eating disorder (Jones and Morgan, 2012). Nobody has yet described a case of the fear of burping either privately or publically, which logically must exist, and could perhaps be called *eructophobia*.

Farting

Farting is the removal or release of intestinal gas, most of which is produced in the intestine itself, although it can be caused by the excessive swallowing of air. It helps in the study of flatulence to recognize three principal features that are worth exploring separately: the volume of gas produced and hence released (including a concern for the frequency and duration of flatus); the noise associated with the release; and the smell.

Fabrizis Suarez and Michael Levitt provide an excellent review of intestinal gases including flatulence, and give normal figures for farting at "400 to 2500 mL of gas per day ... with a frequency of ten passages per day (upper limit of normal is 22 times day)" (Suarez and Levitt, 2000, p. 416). They argue that many people are unaware of the normal rate; some present clinically with self-perceived excess but can be effectively counseled that 22 times or less a day is within normal limits. For some it is intimately associated with hygiene, and thoughts of uncleanliness can become a ruminative concern. Reassurance is not always helpful but there are case studies showing success with "paradoxical intentions," a psychotherapeutic technique in which one attends very closely to the source of anxiety until one habituates to it (Milan and Kolko, 1982). Studies of exposure to the fearful thoughts (such as "I am going to fart") and the places where the thoughts occur are also promising (Ladouceur et al., 1993). Just as fear of flatulence can be concerning, so can excessive flatulence. In the palliative care context, flatulence is a very common complaint, more so than hiccup and burp. In one study of home vs. hospital palliative care for advanced cancer, flatulence was the third most common complaint for those at home, after pain and fatigue (Peters and Sellick, 2006).

The public display of flatulence is formed of sound and smell. All of the removal senses operate across a divide of the private and the public. Like burp, but perhaps even more than burping, public flatulence also functions to remind people of their physicality. In his book on curious human behavior, Robert Provine reports an analysis of the sound of flatulence and explores how controllable that might be (Provine, 2012). There are cases of people reporting high levels of control over flatulence. Provine discusses the famous case of Le Pétomane who was a professional farting entertainer, able to play wind instruments with his flatus.

Although farting can be a form of entertainment, for the vast majority of us it is a fairly mundane and uninteresting act. One is supposed to control flatulence. Failure to control it can, however, cause social unease or challenge. Two studies explored this failure of control. In a large study of adult fecal habits including flatulence, Martin Weinberg and Colin Williams from Indiana interviewed people about the sudden loss of control when farting. Typically people expected to be judged for a failure of control or for lacking social manners. One interviewee said:

> It's not so much the action itself, as it is the reaction that passing gas gets from people. I guess the most embarrassing thing about it is the loss of control in holding your gas. It just seems like in social situations . . . that you'd be able to hold your gas.[2]

That uncontrolled farting is embarrassing is not very surprising. However, what is unusual about the findings is just how personal people's sense of failure is over something that happens as often as 22 times a day, every day, in all contexts, even when asleep. The power of this everyday form of social control is what makes farting easy to assign other meanings to, for either a strong identity position or as a vehicle for deviance. For example, in the same study, a different male interviewee boasted about what people would say if they were party to his malodorous flatus: "Guys would say it's raunchy and then say 'Nice one,' because if it's strong it's more manly. You know, because women would not try to clear a room with a fart."[3]

Michael Reisig and Travis Pratt took a very different approach to this question of the social uses of flatulence. They were interested in how low social control finds an outlet in the personal deviation of socially controlled manners. They chose three common minor social offenses in American society: telephoning people when drunk, swearing in public, and, relevant here, "publically expelling digestive gases." There are very few studies like this that ask people to disclose social transgressions, perhaps for obvious methodological reasons. As Weinberg and Williams discussed in some detail, we like to control the impression other people have about us in regard to fecal hygiene, including flatulence. They surveyed 502 university students and explored what supported these different minor deviant behaviors. They found that admitting to public flatulence was more likely in men, and more likely in those who generally have low social control, although they also found that "much of the effect of low self-control on public flatulence was mediated by peer flatulence" (Reisig and Pratt, 2011, p. 613). It appears that for men, at least, flatulence made public is gendered and more acceptable in the company of other men.

In terms of our social practices of distancing ourselves from our animalism, all aspects of digestion are subject to great social pressure (Roach, 2014). They are to be hidden, personal, and often denied. However, this private-public dynamic is gendered. Just as sweating is seen to be undesirable and unseemly in women, and by many women themselves (see Chapter 9), so the public display of digestion in the social control of flatulence is equally gendered. Women are held to more demanding standards than men for control over flatulence.

Why is farting funny?

James Spiegel, a professional philosopher, investigated this question in his paper entitled "Why Flatulence Is Funny?" The answer lies in part in its function to disturb. Speigel argues that flatulence has all of the requirements of humor because it operates as different from the norm and it punctuates everyday life with a sudden reminder of the basic. It can make us feel superior by acting as the social transgressor, highlighting pomposity, and at the same time it can provide a relief from the effortful work of being civilized (Spiegel, 2013). Spiegel's philosophical account is erudite but for me does not get to the heart of why farting should be enduringly funny.

To get a different perspective on how and why we find gas escaping or being propelled from our bodies funny, I talked to Arthur Smith. Arthur is a professional comedian (Box 11.1).

Box 11.1. Arthur, the comedian: *"we are hardwired to laugh at farting"*

Arthur and I met for lunch at Café Boheme in Soho and both ordered the artichoke. We sat outside.

Chris: Have farting and burping always been funny?

Arthur: Burping is the younger brother of farting. Not quite up there in the funny stakes. Farting is much funnier than burping. I think we are hardwired to laugh at farting, which is not true of all bodily functions. Spitting isn't funny, but farting definitely is. I wonder if cavemen found each other's farting funny.

Chris: Perhaps. But we seem to have elevated farting to have other functions.

Arthur: Well, there is nothing quite as funny as a fart in an elevator. Especially when no one admits to it. It provides an added mystery, like Farting Cluedo [Clue].

There have been many farting acts across the ages. Henry II had a court jester called Roland the Farter. He was effectively the top comedian in the country. He was given a house and estate and was required to do his farting act for the king. He would come on and do a leap, a whistle, and a fart, which I think would still work now. He and Le Pétomane are by far the most famous farters. At the moment there is a great performing farter called Mr. Methane (http://www.mrmethane.com).

Chris: How does the fart joke work?

Arthur: The best person to do a fart and make you laugh is a proud and important man. Now if the prime minister launched a big fart during his speech at the Conservative

---

Box 11.1. *Continued*

Party conference, that would be funnier than me doing one now. It is like Greek tragedy: a proud man brought low. The greater the man, the bigger the fall, the bigger the drama. The prouder the man, the funnier the fart.

Chris: Why do you think we use bodily functions to challenge the pompous?

Arthur: It announces that in the end you are just an animal. It is a leveller. In a world where we are all pretending to be sophisticated creatures, it tells people that we are animal. We have all of these elaborate rituals and carapace to try and pretend that we are something beyond a belching, farting creature. Also, done properly, farting can be an act of defiance or deliberate challenge. If, for example, as you shook hands with Prince Charles you launched a huge fart, that would be funny. People should consider farting as a tool in politics.

Chris: When is a fart joke not funny?

Arthur: Well, you won't get any fart jokes at the Royal Variety Awards. Farting is a low form of wit. But *low* matters. I can imagine a long-winded setup that leads you to expect a clever punch line, and then you just deliver a fart. Farting can be used to change the story, to throw people off track, and bring them down to earth.

Chris: Do female comedians use farting?

Arthur: I am sure if you watched 50 female comedians and 50 male comedians there would be more fart jokes from the men. Women do tell fart jokes, but it would be a more radical thing to do. Potentially more funny, though, as we are used to men talking about farting. Yes, a woman making a fart joke—that offers more opportunity for comedy. Women have a harder time farting. Imagine you are on a date with a stunningly beautiful woman and she launches a big fart—does that make her less attractive? These are the important questions . . .

Chris: Mmmmm!

Arthur: In the end, we are basic animals. Base is funny, and it does not get more base than farting.

Farting is funny not in and of itself, but because of how it can be used. Compare, for example, the uninvited sharing of mucus by sneezing over someone. That is rarely humorous because of its relationship with disease. Spitting buccal mucus at someone is also socially disturbing (hard to ignore), but spitting is typically a sign of aggression because it is controllable, and therefore a deliberate act of challenge. Both are socially interruptive. However, as Arthur discussed here, well-timed flatulence is socially disruptive because it is a highly effective form of bathos. Farting reminds us of our bestiality and of the flimsiness of the manners and mores that operate to distance us from that reality.

Continence psychology

Normal defecation and micturition should be thought of as continence. We learn to control or respond continently to the urge to defecate or micturate within certain limits. The physiology of continence is relatively well-described, although there are some gaps in our knowledge, such as what should be considered normal (Palit et al., 2012). For example, paradoxically, most people do not consider themselves normal when it comes to bowel function. At least that was the conclusion of researchers who in 1992 explored the regularity of bowel function and found that "only a minority of adults enjoy conventionally normal bowel function and a little more than half pass normal stools" (Heaton et al., 1992, p. 823). In one U.S. survey of over 1,000 adults, a quarter reported loose stools or diarrhea (Sandler et al., 2000). We probably need to let go of the idea that there is a normal when it comes to defecation. Frequency, timing, stool solidity, and the ability to control urge are all highly variable across people, situations, dietary habits, and time.

The psychology of continence will involve the cognitive science of physical mastery and control, and a social science of what governs private behavior in a public context. I find it helpful to think of continence psychology in three broad domains. The first is how we initially achieve continence and respond to the urges to open bowel or bladder with restraint—how we train the developing child to be continent. The second is the experience of incontinence, either through injury, illness, or frailty. And the third is on the temporary disturbance of learned continence in otherwise normal life; in particular, the role of emotion.

Toilet training

Failing to resist the urge to urinate or defecate is socially restrictive. Soiled clothing, discomfort, social disapproval, avoidance, rejection, and an increased risk of infection are just some of the very good reasons why we have a large number of socialized toileting behaviors. Most children are toilet-trained in the second to third year, although there is interesting discussion on why both the manner of training and when one starts seems to have changed. In the last 50 years there has been a trend toward starting children on toilet training later. This has little to do with the child, their physiology or their psychology, and is instead about parental preference (Vermandel et al., 2008).

Starting too early or waiting too long to toilet train are often the causes of major parental anxiety and parental pressure. Sometimes there is also parental punishment or violence due to the misplaced belief that the lack of continence is a willful act of deviance (Alpaslan et al., 2014). Toilet training, however, is more of a social marker of child development and maturity, and a rite of passage for both parent and child. When parents make the decision to toilet train, the judgment of child willingness or readiness may actually be a proxy for parent readiness. In a study of parent experience of toilet training, parents reported exactly this sense. Making the decision and making time were critical factors, as was the desire to avoid being judged as different by peers. The rite of passage was captured well in this study by one parent's enthusiastic and positive display of child development: "If she urinated a little in the potty it was fantastic, we showed it to the whole family, took a picture, and made it a fun thing" (Jansson et al., 2008, p. 474).

Managing incontinence

Inevitably, losing the ability to control the urge to defecate or urinate is distressing. For example, one study of German women with urinary incontinence captures very well the themes that appear frequently across similar studies. The women reported shame and embarrassment not only at possible episodes of incontinence but at even discussing them. Despite how common urinary incontinence is, it remains for many people a private burden. Also interesting was the description of a life altered, and for some people defined, by incontinence. Women discussed having developed a quite comprehensive "city map" of all public and semi-public toilet facilities in their locality. They had memorized the tram timetable and the opening times of cafés with facilities, and had a good understanding of how much they should drink and what they should drink (e.g., coffee) when planning a trip:

> If I go from here into town—when I go by tram—I'm in town in five to seven minutes, so I've reached the first point in a quarter of an hour. Yes and then I go there, I go for a coffee. Because the other toilets aren't open yet, but the cafés are open, so I go there and it's nearest to the tram stop.[4]

This sort of technical planning and organization is the lived reality of those with incontinence. In medicine, one is perhaps more used to describing disability by functional impairment, but disability for the individual is more often defined by the limits imposed by environment, be it the geography, weather, or even town planning. The public provision, or rather lack of provision, of toilets is an interesting challenge to modern living. The lowly public toilet is a site of major social and cultural debate. Clara Greed argues eloquently and comprehensively for why public toilets matter so much (Greed, 2006). In the United Kingdom, as in many other countries, there has been a steady reduction in the provision of nonproprietary toilets. They have also become the site of private, often secret, behaviors (hygiene, cosmetic, sexual, illicit drug use), so much so that public toilets are now widely seen as a necessary evil. Innovation in toilet provision is urgently needed. The psychology of toilet behavior, both use, and planning and provision, is a public policy imperative (Anthony and Dufrense, 2007). A psychology of continence will perhaps be less about training individuals in techniques of control and more about encouraging policy makers, planners, city officials, and business leaders to ensure the adequate provision of toilets.

Emotion and incontinence

Sudden incontinence can be caused by laughter, coughing, lifting a heavy weight, infection, or drug and alcohol poisoning. More curious, however, is the ability of fear—in particular, of extreme fear (terror or panic)—to cause incontinence. It is not clear what the function of this fear response is. The fear of loss of bodily control is a common concern for those with a panic disorder. In an interesting study involving both chart review and patient interview, Sheryl Green and her colleagues in Ontario asked an unusual question. They wanted to know whether what patients fear most has ever happened. Much of the clinical psychology of the body assumes that patients have unrealistic beliefs about potentially catastrophic events. Are such catastrophic fears always unfounded, or is it possible that fainting, vomiting, and incontinence can happen? Nineteen patients were interviewed and four reported incontinence during an attack. The incontinence was described as sudden, involuntary, and without warning. Patients during panic can experience exactly what they fear most (Green et al., 2007).

This relationship of fear and incontinence may also extend beyond the extreme case of panic disorder. There is a well-documented observation in learning psychology that animals defecate and urinate more frequently when stressed. And in popular culture, we recognize that extreme fear is associated with sudden incontinence. Andrew Solomon describes just such an occasion when he was experiencing the onset of severe depression, presaged by panic and terror, when he was having a breakdown:

> On the way home from the store, I suddenly lost control of my lower intestine and soiled myself. I could feel the stain spreading as I hastened home. When I got in, I dropped the grocery bag, rushed to the bathroom, got undressed, and went to bed. (Solomon, 2001, p. 49)

Stress and emotional dysregulation have also been implicated in explanatory models of irritable bowel syndrome, where chronic, broad-spectrum gastrointestinal complaints are the signature feature (Kennedy et al., 2012). But most discussions of the role of emotion and physiological stress markers tend to be gut-focused (Allen et al., 2014). Perhaps a "continence psychology" will allow for the serious study of the possible role of higher-order cognitive and emotional functioning on the specific behaviors involved in defecation and urination, their control, and their control failure.

Vomiting

Swallowing (*deglutition*) involves both voluntary and involuntary components. The primary phase functions to prepare food into a manageable bolus that can be shaped and softened, then moved to the back of the tongue which triggers the involuntary movement of the bolus to the pharynx, including the closure of the nasal passage. The final phase is marked by the passage of the bolus into the esophagus and the involuntary automatic transfer of the bolus to the stomach (Matsuo and Palmer, 2008). Vomiting (*emesis*) is more than the reverse of swallowing. It is often described as having two distinct phases (retch and expulsion), although from a phenomenological perspective it may be better to think of it as three phases. The first is nausea, which acts as a warning of vomit. Nausea may or may not progress to the second phase of retching, characterized by sudden involuntary abdominal and diaphragmatic contractions. Retching may or may not progress to the third phase of expulsion, in which multiple muscle groups are recruited all with one purpose: the projection of stomach contents as far away from the body as one can achieve (Pleuvry, 2012).

Most people have experienced vomiting either from a food-related infection, motion sickness, pregnancy, neurological disturbance (such as migraine), or as a reaction to treatment—in particular, anesthesia- or chemotherapy-induced vomiting. What is common across these settings is the rather complicated phenomenology of vomiting. It is often experienced as unpleasant and distressing, but in some contexts it can be associated with a positive post-vomit feeling of being purged, a relief from retching, and even of euphoria. The incidence of self-induced vomiting in the general population is quite low (Hilbert et al., 2012), but may be disturbingly high in some populations. For example, almost 60 percent of a sample of 107 women, students at a New Zealand university, said they had made themselves vomit after drinking alcohol (Blackmore and Gleaves, 2013). The context of vomiting can change. It could be a method of weight control, a side effect of a leisure pursuit such as sailing, a symptom of a disease, or an adverse effect of a treatment.

Nausea, retching, and expulsion (the vomiting) are typically described as involuntary, uncontrollable, and unpleasant. In the context of palliative care, these are difficult symptoms to manage, and there is rarely anything positive about vomiting (Maguire et al., 2014). In this and other contexts, however, it is the battle for control and the fear of sudden uncontrolled vomiting that can lead to distress and social handicap. Unlike the expelling of air in burp, hiccup, or cough, the expelling of partly digested stomach contents is socially unacceptable and met with disgust and social rejection. For example, patients with *gastroparesis*—a disorder of failed gastric clearance leading to bloating, fluid retention, nausea, and vomiting—often go to great lengths to avoid the shame and distress caused by the public witnessing of a private suffering. In one study, the efforts patients went to in order to conceal vomit was described:

> They put much thought and effort into managing short-term control of symptoms usually by being overly prepared. One participant always carried plastic bags to vomit in; several timed their food intake very carefully so as not to risk vomiting in awkward places; one participant lobbied her boss for just the right desk at work so that she could vomit unobserved.[5]

Shame and self-loathing are often part of the complex experience of vomiting. The physical experiences are relegated behind the social-emotional experience of embarrassment, shame, guilt, failure of bodily control, and beliefs of personal inadequacy—all of which are brought to the fore in the psychopathological expression of vomiting as deliberate purging (Tasca et al., 2012). These beliefs are also prevalent at the other extreme, in the little-researched anxiety disorder *emetophobia*, fear of vomiting. In emetophobia, the dominant drivers are a morbid fear of infection and disease, patterns of avoidance of food and food preparation, worry, and a heightened awareness of normal gustatory sensations (Veale et al., 2013).

Voluntary vomiting

The pathological case is always interesting and useful in thinking about how disordered cognitions can emerge to support abnormal gastrointestinal behavior. One can come to live in fear of a normal bodily function, or have it highjacked for use by other psychological functions. Missing for me, however, is a *psychological* consideration of vomiting that might emerge in normal, everyday contexts. A comprehensive psychology of the body will need to address how changing food environments will affect normal weight control. For example, in specific environments of food plenty—when combined with the almost impossible task of trying to control the abundance of calorie-dense foods discussed in Chapter 10—do new practices of vomiting appear? When Natalie Blackmore and David Gleaves discussed their finding that 60 percent of students reported self-induced vomiting after drinking alcohol, they did so within a context of possible individual psychopathology. Voluntary vomiting, however, is not a new phenomenon; it has been described before. For example, in his study of Mozart, Andrew Steptoe quotes the Baron Riesbeck describing an eighteenth-century Viennese dining practice in which

> it is customary when an entertainment is given, to provide doses of tartar emetic, and set them in an adjoining room; thither the guests retire when they happen to be too full, empty themselves, and return to the company as if nothing had happened. (Riesbeck JC. Travels through Germany, trans Revd Mr Mary (London 1787), quoted in Steptoe (1988, p. 25)

Perhaps what Blackmore and Gleaves have discovered is a modern variant of voluntary vomiting in the context of a twenty-first-century generation. Alcohol and alcohol poisoning are part of many young people's lives in societies where alcohol is cheap, available, and where overuse can become the norm.

To understand the practice of voluntary or deliberate vomiting better, I talked with Connie Webber (Box 11.2).

Box 11.2. Connie, on modern vomiting: *"we are putting more alcohol in so we need to take it out"*

Connie is 21. She studied medical science at a UK university, graduating six months before we met. She described herself as in an "in-between phase" of life. She was happy to talk about voluntary vomiting, or, as it is known in this student vernacular, "tactical chundering" or "TCing."

———————————

Chris: What is tactical about tactical chundering?

Connie: Well, it is when alcohol is involved. It is usually when I am quite drunk and I come home. If I have a dizzy feeling or I think I am going to be sick at some point, or if I can't sleep properly, then I will make myself be sick because I know it will happen anyway and I will feel horrible if I don't. I guess it has become a bit of a habit. Whenever I get a slight dizzy feeling after I have been drinking, I will make myself sick because I know it will make me feel better. I have known people do it while they are on a night out. So if they feel ill during the evening, they will leave and be sick, then come back and carry on. Mine is more when I get home and I want to go to sleep.

Chris: Is it only when drinking? Or do you vomit at other times?

Connie: I would hate to vomit when I wasn't drunk. That is horrible. I hate the feeling of being nauseous and sick. But I haven't been ill for a very long time. It is not about food. I am happy with what I eat and with food. It is only about alcohol. I don't make myself sick at any other time.

Chris: Tell me about drinking too much then. What is normal?

Connie: It is the culture of universities. Going out a lot. People drink a lot before they go out because they do not have money. So the idea is to power through early and have a cheaper evening in the long run.

Chris: Do you eat before drinking?

Connie: No. Most people get food on their way home. People drink a lot, then go out, then eat, and are then sick. We are putting more alcohol in so we need to take it out. I think that is what is happening.

Chris: Would it be easier to put less in?

Connie: Having less would be easier. But I think when you drink you don't process what is going to happen in the future. Alcohol is just very, very available.

Chris: So is it a commonsense strategy?

(Continued)

Box 11.2. *Continued*

Connie: That is what it feels like to me. It is not abnormal to me. I see it as a barrier to remove. I have drunk too much, put myself into this state, and it can make me feel better, then I can sleep it off. Alcohol makes me quite sick anyway, so if I don't do it I will wake up an hour or two later and be sick naturally. So I get in early.

Chris: Is it taboo? Do you talk about vomiting openly?

Connie: I don't think anyone responds in a bad way to it. Not really. I guess it is almost a joke with the friends in my university house. It is not a serious issue or anything. Maybe they see it as unusual because they don't do it, but not unusual in that they wouldn't think of me in a different way or see it as a problem. People can get the wrong idea. They might think that I drink too much and that is a bad thing. I would never talk about it unless somebody asked me about it, but if they asked, I would be happy to talk. I am not embarrassed by it. It is normal.

There are specific settings in which expulsion behaviors take on different meanings: farting as an expression of masculinity was discussed as one, and here vomiting has become a way to manage alcohol poisoning. In Connie's case, the unpleasantness of vomiting and any social disapproval is inhibited, perhaps by the effects of alcohol, replaced by a positive feeling of purge and the promise of sleep and no hangover. How secondary prevention of poisoning through vomiting becomes preferred to primary prevention through avoidance is an important research question. Also needed is research on how expulsion behavior that is specific to one setting can generalize to others. Is voluntary vomiting a student habit or a generational feature—an inevitable consequence of living in an alcohol-plenty environment?

Reproductive removal

The final two physical removal senses are not gustatory but reproductive. The cyclical removal of blood, mucus, and endometrial tissue vaginally is often preceded or accompanied by discomfort and pain caused by muscular contraction of the uterus. Although not only blood, discharging menstrual fluid is often thought of as an act of bleeding. The psychology of blood is itself an important and relatively unexplored field. We have an ambivalent relationship with blood: thought of often as clean even when outside of the body (in comparison with other bodily tissue), it can be lauded and totemized, become the object of fascination and comfort in self-harm (Glenn and Klonsky, 2010), and be symbolic in religious thought and practice (Lucchetti Bingemer, 2014).

For many women, however, the experience of menstruating is anything but fascinating or comforting. For example, Trine Karlsson and her colleagues in Stockholm surveyed over 1,500 Swedish women, 32 percent of whom reported heavy bleeding. They used the Short Form-36, a popular measure of quality of life, and found that menstrual bleeding was for most women associated with widespread negative impact on aspects of life. But, as Figure 11.2 shows, in all domains of quality of life, those with heavy menstrual bleeding reported a greater impact than those with normal blood loss (Karlsson et al., 2014).

Menstrual bleeding is without a dominant primary sense. Its physical impact is borne from its secondary associations with pain, temperature, and pressure sense changes, and, importantly, from the social demands of managing the crossing of blood from body to society. Menstrual blood as public, arguably much more than other respiratory or gastroenterological removal, is highly stigmatized and subject to very restrictive social norms (Johnston-Robledo and Chrisler, 2013).

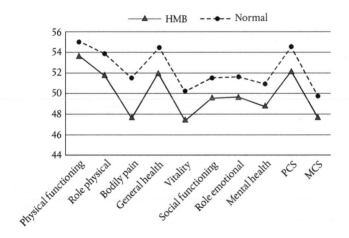

Fig. 11.2. Domains of Quality of Life judged by women with normal menstrual bleeding and heavy menstrual bleeding (HMB).

"Norm-based mean scores for all eight SF-36 domains and physical component score [PCS] and mental component score [MCS]. The scores for heavy menstrual bleeding (HMB)/normal menstrual blood loss (MBL) are shown. The general population norm is 50. Statistical analysis, Student's t-test. The difference between HMB and normal MBL is significant (p < 0.001) for all dimensions."

Ejaculation

The final reproductive removal sense is the experience of ejaculation. Both men and women can ejaculate on orgasm. For men the discharge and propulsion of semen is considered the norm and its absence can be troublesome. For women, the production, discharge, propulsion, and exact composition of ejaculate are all hotly contested. There are likely two forms of female ejaculate, one that is experienced as a gushing and one that has lower motility and volume and is closer to seminal fluid in its biochemistry (Rubio-Casillas and Jannini, 2011). In an interesting study of the medical history of female ejaculation in *The Journal of Sexual Medicine*, Joanna Korda and her colleagues review historical descriptions and observations as well as modern studies. They conclude:

> The phenomenon of female ejaculation has been discovered, described and forgotten in eastern and western culture repeatedly over the last 2,000 years. Today the phenomenon of the female prostate producing female ejaculate is beyond debate, however, future studies are needed to further our knowledge of female ejaculation. (Korda et al., 2010, p. 1974)

Although it is contested it may also be common. In an online survey of 340 women, 163 reported ejaculating, here defined simply as "an emission of fluid during orgasm," at least once a day or "a few times during a week" (Wimpissinger et al., 2013). The lack of precision in their methods means that this survey is likely to overrepresent. However, it is interesting that for women who experience ejaculation, the experience was largely positive:

> For 252 women (78.8%) their ability to ejaculate was an "enrichment of their sexual lives"; 33 women (10.3%) were indifferent; 23 women (7.2%) "sometimes wished they would rather not ejaculate"; 10 women (3.1%) primarily "wished they would not ejaculate," and two participants considered female ejaculation as a "pathological" phenomenon. (Wimpissinger et al., 2013, p. 182)

In some cultures female ejaculation is highly valued and seen as a core part of sexual practice (Larsen, 2010). Considering the importance of menstruation in women's embodiment and physical experience, it was interesting that I could find no discussion of the fate of female ejaculation postmenopausally. Given the common concern with vaginal atrophy, symptoms of dryness, and the prominent place for some of ejaculation in experiencing sexual pleasure, it would be surprising if postmenopausal changes in ejaculation were not part of some women's experience. It has not yet, however, emerged in general research, so may need to be explicitly asked about (Utian and Maamari, 2014).

Male ejaculation occupies a large number of pages in the medical press, although most of these pages are concerned with sexual dysfunction; in particular, with premature ejaculation. But as with many concepts in sexual health, there is a disagreement over measurement making even the capturing of prevalence difficult (Serefoglu and Saitz, 2012). In an interesting review, Alain Giami discusses the problems of what constitutes "premature," whether there is any sense of an objective standard, which he proposes in the heterosexual case as one minute of "intravaginal ejaculation latency time" (Giami, 2013, p. 32). Giami's goals are scientific. How can we measure a phenomenon without agreement or any consensus over its key features? He recognizes, however, that the distress associated with ejaculation, whether premature or delayed, is always personal and always contextual.

Tell no one

The context of reproductive removal is one dominated by social constraint. The public display of both ejaculate and menstrual blood is largely taboo, and discussion is tightly constrained to specific settings and relationships. Two social and psychological determinants largely define the experience of these removal senses. We have seen both before. The first is the public-private dynamic, which makes most removal sensations invisible. The second is the subject-object dynamic, which governs how what is separate from the body stays separate, typically by inducing disgust.

Most people have no sense of what might be considered normal when it comes to male ejaculation. Observation studies place normal ejaculation latencies at an average of about six minutes (Kempeneers and Desseilles, 2014) and the volume of semen produced at about 4 ml (Jørgensen et al., 2012)—but when it comes to measured force of projection there are no data of any quality. However, ignorance of these norms remains common. For example, beliefs about inadequacy dominate the concerns of those seeking sexual therapy, and social comparison nearly always exaggerates others' sexual behavior, allowing individuals to consider their own behavior as abnormal (Scholly et al., 2005).

It is strange that we know so little and that our perceptions are so often wrong. After all, ejaculation is not a new human phenomenon. It seems that when it comes to sexual performance, our propensity to "tell no one" about sexual expectations, desires, or practices means that no one believes themselves average. Sexual behavior is normally distributed, statistically speaking, but perceptions of sexual behavior may actually have an inverted or U-shaped distribution, with the majority of people believing themselves living closer to the extremes. To date, the psychology of ejaculation is largely concerned with perceived problems of timing as the source of personal or relational distress. There is no serious study of the specific beliefs about ejaculation. Psychology appears to be following the cultural norm by staying quiet.

Of course, what keeps us silent about the ejection of reproductive tissue is not a predilection for personal secrecy, but a set of closely observed social practices. One of these is a variant of what we see in defecation, urination, and vomiting. Ensuring distance from ejaculate is a function of hygiene beliefs. Just as menstrual blood is often culturally constructed as disgusting, so semen and vaginal discharges are considered substances to avoid. Once escaped from the body, they enter the world of hygiene management. Disgust can and often does play a role in the experiences of shame and embarrassment in those who avoid sexual contact. These emotions are also behind the stubborn resistance to changing the practice and mistaken belief of there being any benefit to vaginal douching (Ekpenyong et al., 2014). Feminist scholars have convincingly explored the role of hygiene beliefs in subjugating female sexuality, objectifying female sexual practice, and maintaining a disempowering silence around female genital practice, including removal (Fahs, 2014).

Psychology may have a role to play in better understanding how hygiene beliefs operate in both menstruation and ejaculation. In particular, sorely needed is an exploration of how the perception of "normal" has departed so radically from reality, and how any social correction of our misperceptions is culturally resisted.

Summary

Being embodied is an ever-changing reality. We ingest, digest, and divest matter. Operating across all ten expulsion senses is a fascinating, automatic redefinition of subject to object: as matter leaves the body, it becomes other to self. Matter needs to be not only removed but also expelled, and disgust is often the method of ensuring that separation. The way we manage discorporation is socially defined. Some senses, like farting and vomiting, can take on other meanings in particular settings, but typically expulsion is meant to be private, hidden, and silent. Psychology has not really contributed to the embodied senses of expulsion, and there are major opportunities for the development of a "continence psychology." For some people, chronic expulsion—whether in coughing, hiccupping, defecating, or vomiting—is a major source of distress. Needed are effective interventions to reduce the distress and disability caused by the physiological failure of control. Equally important will be to research how and why the expulsion senses are private, sometimes secret. When we "tell no one," unusual beliefs and behaviors are allowed to flourish.

Notes

1. Reproduced from Margaret Vernon, Nancy Kline Leidy, Alise Nacson, and Linda Nelsen, Measuring cough severity: Perspectives from the literature and from patients with chronic cough, *Cough*, 5 (5), p. 6, doi: 10.1186/1745-9974-5-5 © 2009 Vernon et al; licensee BioMed

1. Central Ltd. Quotation used under the terms of the Creative Commons Attribution License (http://creativecommons.org/licenses/by/2.0).
2. Reproduced from Martin S. Weinberg and Colin J. Williams, Fecal matters: habitus, embodiments, and deviance, *Social Problems*, 52 (3), p. 320, http://www.jstor.org/stable/10.1525/sp.2005.52.3.315 © 2005, Society for the Study of Social Problems, Inc.
3. Reproduced from Martin S. Weinberg and Colin J. Williams, Fecal matters: habitus, embodiments, and deviance, *Social Problems*, 52 (3), p. 328, http://www.jstor.org/stable/10.1525/sp.2005.52.3.315 © 2005, Society for the Study of Social Problems, Inc.
4. Reproduced from Daniela Hayder and Wilfried Schnepp, Experiencing and Managing Urinary Incontinence: A Qualitative Study, *Western Journal of Nursing Research*, 32 (4), pp. 486–487, doi: 10.1177/0193945909354903 Copyright © 2010, SAGE Publications. Reprinted by Permission of SAGE Publications.
5. Reproduced from A loss of social eating: the experience of individuals living with gastroparesis, Jose Bennell and Claire Taylor, *Journal of Clinical Nursing*, 22 (19–20), p. 2817, doi:10.1111/jocn.12196 Copyright (c) 2013, John Wiley and Sons.

References

Allahdin, S. (2011). Flatus vaginalis a distressing symptom. *International Journal of Colorectal Disease*, 26, 1493.

Allen, A.P., Kennedy, P.J., Cryan, J.F., Dinan, T.G. and Clarke, G. (2014). Biological and psychological markers of stress in humans: focus on the Trier Social Stress Test. *Neuroscience and Biobehavioral Reviews*, 38, 94–124.

Alpaslan, A.H., Coşkun, K.Ş., Yeşil, A. and Çobanoğlu, C. (2014). A child death as a result of physical violence during toilet training. *Journal of Forensic and Legal Medicine*, 28, 39–41.

Anthony, K.H. and Dufrense, M. (2007). Potty parity in perspective: gender and family issues in planning and designing public restrooms. *Journal of Planning Literature*, 21, 267–294.

Bennell J, and Taylor C. (2013). A loss of social eating: the experience of individuals living with gastroparesis. *Journal of Clinical Nursing*, 22, 2812–2821.

Bhutta, M.F. and Maxwell, H. (2008). Sneezing induced by sexual ideation or orgasm: an under-reported phenomenon. *Journal of the Royal Society of Medicine*, 101, 587–591.

Bhutta, M.F. and Maxwell, H. (2009). Further cases of unusual triggers of sneezing. *Journal of the Royal Society of Medicine*, 102, 49.

Blackmore, N.P.I. and Gleaves, D.H. (2013). Self-induced vomiting after drinking alcohol. *International Journal of Health Addiction*, 11, 453–457.

Bolser, D.C., Poliacek, I., Jakus, J., Fuller, D.D. and Davenport, P.W. (2006). Neurogenesis of cough, other airway defensive behaviors and breathing: a holarchical system? *Respiratory Physiology and Neurobiology*, 152, 255–265.

Burke, W. (2012). Why do we sneeze? *Medical Hypotheses*, 78, 502–504.

Disney, B. and Trudgill, N. (2014). Managing a patient with excessive belching. *Oesphagus and Stomach*, 5, 79–83.

Eccles, R. (2005). Understanding the symptoms of the common cold and influenza. *Lancet Infectious Diseases*, 5, 718–725.

Ekpenyong, C.E., Daniel, N.E. and Akpan, E.E. (2014). Vaginal douching behavior among young adult women and the perceived adverse health effects. *Journal of Public Health and Epidemiology*, 6, 182–191.

Enk, P., Dubois, D. and Marquis, P. (1999). Quality of life in patients with upper gastrointestinal symptoms: results from the Domestic/International Gastroenterology Surveillance Study (DIGEST). *Scandinavian Journal of Gastroenterology*, 231, 48–54.

Fahs, B. (2014). Genital panics: constructing the vagina in women's qualitative narratives about pubic hair, menstrual sex, and vaginal self-image. *Body Image*, 11, 210–218.

Giami, A. (2013). Social epidemiology of premature ejaculation. *Sexologies*, 22, 27–32.

Glenn, C.R. and Klonsky, E.D. (2010). The role of seeing blood in non-suicidal self-injury. *Journal of Clinical Psychology*, 66, 466–473.

Greed, C. (2006). The role of the public toilet: pathogen transmitter or health facilitator? *Building Services Engineering Research and Technology*, 27, 127–139.

Green, S.M., Antony, M.M., McCabe, R.E. and Watling, M.A. (2007). Frequency of fainting, vomiting, and incontinence in panic disorder: a descriptive study. *Clinical Psychology and Psychotherapy*, 14, 189–197.

Hayder, D. and Schnepp, W. (2010). Experiencing and managing urinary incontinence: a qualitative study. *Western Journal of Nursing Research*, 32, 480–496.

Heaton, K.W., Radvan, J., Cripps, H., Mountford, R.A., Braddon, F.E.M. and Hughes, A.O. (1992). Defecation frequency and timing, and stool form in the general population: a prospective study. *Gut*, 33, 818–824.

Hilbert, A., de Zwaan, M. and Braehler, E. (2012). How frequent are eating disturbances in the population? Norms of the eating disorders examination-questionnaire. *PLoS One*, 7, e29125 (1–7).

Hurst, D.F., Purdom, C.L. and Hogan, M.J. (2013). Use of paced respiration to alleviate intractable hiccups (singultus): a case report. *Applied Psychophysiology and Biofeedback*, 38, 157–160.

Jansson, U.-B., Danielson, E. and Hellström, A.-L. (2008). Parent's experiences of their children achieving bladder control. *Journal of Pediatric Nursing*, 23, 471–478.

Johnston-Robledo, I. and Chrisler, J.C. (2013). The menstrual mark: menstruation as social stigma. *Sex Roles*, 68, 9–18.

Jones, W.R. and Morgan, J.F. (2012). Eructophilia in bulimia nervosa: a clinical feature. *International Journal of Eating Disorders*, 45, 298–301.

Jørgensen, N., Nordstrom Joensen, U., Kold Jensen, T., Blomberg Jensen, M., Almstrup, K., Ahlmann Olesen, I., . . . and Skakkabaek, N.E. (2012). Human semen quality in the new millennium: a prospective cross-sectional population-based study of 4867 men. *British Medical Journal Open*, 2, e000990 (1–13).

Kahrilas, P.J. and Shi, G. (1997). Why do we hiccup? *Gut*, 41, 712–713.

Kamolz, T. and Velanovich, V. (2002). Psychological and emotional aspects of gastroesophageal reflux disease. *Diseases of the Esophagus*, 15, 199–203.

Karlsson, T.S., Marions, L.B. and Edlund, M.G. (2014). Heavy menstrual bleeding significantly affects quality of life. *Acta Obsterica Gynecologica Scandinavica*, 93, 52–57.

Kempeneers, P. and Desseilles, M. (2014). The premature ejaculation "disorder": questioning the criterion of one minute of penetration. *Sexologies*, 23, 59–63

Kennedy, P.L., Clarke, G., Quiqley, E.M.M., Groeger, J.A., Dinan, T.G. and Cryan, J.F. (2012). Gut memories: towards a cognitive neurobiology of irritable bowel syndrome. *Neuroscience and Biobehavioral Reviews*, 36, 3210–3340.

Komurcu, S., Nelson, K.A., Walsh, D., Ford, R.B. and Rybicki, L.A. (2002). Gastrointestinal symptoms among inpatients with advanced cancer. *American Journal of Hospice and Palliative Medicine*, 19, 351–355.

Korda, J.B., Goldstein, S.W. and Sommer, F. (2010). The history of female ejaculation. *Journal of Sexual Medicine*, 7, 1965–1975.

Krakauer, E.L., Zhu, A.X., Bounds, B.C., Sahani, D., McDonald, K.R. and Brachtel, E.F. (2005). Case 6-2005—a 58-year-old man with esophageal cancer and nausea, vomiting, and intractable hiccups. *New England Journal of Medicine*, 352, 817–825.

Ladouceur, R., Freeston, M.H., Gagnon, F., Thibodeau, N. and Dumont, J. (1993). Idiographic considerations in the behavioral treatment of obsessional thoughts. *Journal of Behavior Therapy and Experimental Psychiatry*, 24, 301–310.

Larsen, J. (2010). The social vagina: labia elongation and social capital among women in Rwanda. *Culture, Health, and Sexuality*, 12, 813–826.

Leggott, J. (2010). "There's only one way to find out!": Harry Hill's TV burp and the rescue of invisible television. *Critical Studies in Television*, 5, 17–31.

Lucchetti Bingemer, M.C. (2014). The eucharist and the feminine body: real presence, transubstantiation, communion. *Modern Theology*, 30, 366–383.

Maguire, R., Stoddart, K., Flowers, P., McPhelim, J. and Kearney, N. (2014). An interpretative phenomenological analysis of the lived experience of multiple concurrent symptoms in patients with lung cancer: a contribution to the study of symptom clusters. *European Journal of Oncology Nursing*, 18, 310–315.

Matsuo, K. and Palmer, J.B. (2008). Anatomy and physiology of feeding and swallowing—normal and abnormal. *Physical Medicine Rehabilitation Clinics of North America*, 19, 691–707.

Milan, M.A. and Kolko, D.J. (1982). Paradoxical intention in the treatment of obsessional flatulence ruminations. *Journal of Behavior Therapy and Experimental Psychiatry*, 13, 167–172.

Moretto, E.N., Wee, B., Wiffen, P.J. and Murchison, A.G. (2013). Interventions for treating persistent and intractable hiccups in adults. *Cochrane Database of Systematic Reviews*, Issue 1, CD008768. doi:10.1002/14651858.CD008768.pub2

Morice, A.H. and the ERS Task Force Committee Members. (2004). The diagnosis and management of chronic cough. *European Respiratory Journal*, 24, 481–492.

Palese, A., Condolo, G., Dobrina, R. and Skrap, M. (2014). Persistent hiccups in advanced neuro-oncology patients: findings from a descriptive phenomenological study. *Journal of Hospice and Palliative Nursing*, 16, 396–401.

Palit, S., Lunniss, P.J. and Scott, M. (2012). The physiology of human defecation. *Digestive Disease and Sciences*, 57, 1445–1464.

Peters, L and Sellick, K. (2006). Quality of life of cancer patients receiving inpatient and home-based palliative care. *Journal of Advanced Nursing*, 53, 524–533.

Pleuvry, B. (2012). Physiology and pharmacology of nausea and vomiting. *Anaesthesia and Intensive Care Medicine*, 13, 598–602.

Provine, R.R. (2012). Curious behaviour: yawning, laughing, hiccuping, and beyond. Cambridge: The Belknap Press.

Reisig, M. and Pratt, T.C. (2011). Low self-control and imprudent behavior revisited. *Deviant Behavior*, 32, 589–625.

Roach, M. (2014). Gulp: adventures on the alimentary canal. London: Oneworld.

Rubio-Casillas, A. and Jannini, E.A. (2011). New insights from one case of female ejaculation. *Journal of Sexual Medicine*, 8, 3500–3504.

Sandler, R.S., Stewart, W.F., Liberman, J.N., Ricci, J.A. and Zorich, N.L. (2000). Abdominal pain, bloating, and diarrhea in the United States: prevalence and impact. *Digestive Diseases and Sciences*, 45, 1166–1171.

Scholly, K., Katz, A.R., Gascoigne, J. and Holck, P.S. (2005). Using social norms theory to explain perceptions of sexual health behaviors of undergraduate college students: an exploratory study. *Journal of American College Health*, 53, 159–166.

Seepana, S. and Lai, A.C.K. (2012). Experimental and numerical investigation of interpersonal exposure of sneezing in a full-scale chamber. *Aerosol Science and Technology*, 46, 485–493.

Serefoglu, E.C. and Saitz, T.R. (2012). New insights on premature ejaculation: a review of definition, classification, prevalence and treatment. *Asian Journal of Andrology*, 14, 822–829.

Solomon, A. (2001). The noonday demon: an anatomy of depression. London: Vintage Press.

Songu, M. and Cingi, C. (2009). Sneeze reflex: facts and fiction. *Therapeutic Advances in Respiratory Disease*, 3, 131–141.

Spiegel, J.S. (2013). Why flatulence is funny. *Think*, 12, 15–24

Steptoe, A. (1988). The Mozart-Da Ponte operas: the cultural and musical background to *Le Nozze di Figaro, Don Giovanni*, and *Così fan tutte*. Oxford: Clarendon Press.

Suarez, F.L. and Levitt, M.D. (2000). An understanding of excessive intestinal gas. *Current Gastroenterology Reports*, 2, 413–419.

Suess, T., Remschmidt, C., Schinck, S.B., Schweiger, B., Nitsche, A., Schroeder, K. . . . and Buchholz, U. (2012). The role of facemasks and hand hygiene in the prevention of influenza transmission in households: results from a cluster randomised controlled trial; Berlin, Germany, 2009–2011. *BMC Infections Diseases*, 12, 26, 1–16.

Tack, J., Talley, N.J., Camilleri, M., Holtmann, G., Hu, P., Malagelada, J.-R. and Stanghellini, V. (2006). Functional gastroduodenal disorders. *Gastroenterology*, 130, 1466–1479.

Tang, J.W., Nicolle, A.D., Klettner, C.A., Pantelic, J., Wang, L., Bin Suhaimi, A. . . . and Tham, K.W. (2013). Airflow dynamics of human jets: sneezing and breathing—potential sources of infectious aerosols. *PLoS One*, 8, e59970 (1–7).

Tasca, G.A., Maxwell, H., Bone, M., Trineer, A., Balfour, L. and Bissada, H. (2012). Purging disorder: psychopathology and treatment outcomes. *International Journal of Eating Disorders*, 45, 36–42.

Thomas, J.L., Howe, J., Gaudet, A. and Brantley, P.J. (2001). Behavioral treatment of chronic psychogenic polydipsia with hyponatremia: a unique case of polydipsia in a primary care patient with intractable hiccups. *Journal of Behavior Therapy and Experimental Psychiatry*, 32, 241–250.

Utian, W.H. and Maamari, R. (2014). Attitudes and approaches to vaginal atrophy in postmenopausal women: a focus group qualitative study. *Climateric*, 17, 29–36.

Veale, D., Ellison, N., Boschen, M.J., Costa, A., Whelan, C., Muccio, F. and Henry, K. (2013). Development of an inventory to measure specific phobia and vomiting (emetophobia). *Cognitive Therapy and Research*, 37, 595–604.

Vermandel, A., Van Kampen, M., Van Gorp, C. and Wyndaele, J.-J. (2008). How to toilet train healthy children? A review of the literature. *Neurology and Urodynamics*, 27, 162–166.

Vernon, M., Leidy, N.K., Nacson, A. and Nelsen, L. (2009). Measuring cough severity: perspectives from the literature and from patients with chronic cough. *Cough*, 5, 5, 1–8.

Wallander, M.-A, Johansson, S., Ruigómez, A., García Rodríguez, L.A. and Jones, R. (2007). Dyspepsia in general practice: incidence, risk factors, comorbidity and mortality. *Family Practice*, 24, 403–411.

Weinberg, M.C. and Williams, C.J. (2005). Fecal matters: habitus, embodiments, and deviance. *Social Problems*, 52, 315–336.

Welch, D. (2013). Propaganda: power and persuasion. London: The British Library.

Wimpissinger, F., Springer, C. and Stackl, W. (2013). International online survey: female ejaculation has a positive impact on women's and their partners' sexual lives. *British Journal of Urology International*, 1123, 177–185.

CHAPTER 12

EMBODIED AND EMBEDDED

W e exist as bodies operating in context: we are embodied and embedded. It is this tension—of a body that is both experiencing and experienced—that makes physical life so interesting. A psychology of the senses needs to account not only for the individual sensory experiences but also for how they operate together, how they allow action upon the world, and how the world makes action possible (Haugeland, 1998).

In each chapter, I wanted to avoid being distracted by the big five senses of seeing, hearing, smelling, tasting, and touching. I wanted also to treat each of the physical senses separately from each other. Bodies have been carelessly neglected in psychology. For a brief period, I wanted the physical sensations, the experiences that are so important in our everyday lives, to have our undivided attention. Of course, my corralling each sense into its own isolated chapter was artifice, a narrative device. Critics will argue that the senses share many features, and they will be right. There are themes that occur across my exploration of the individual physical senses, themes that emerge to be at the heart of a psychology of the body.

In this final chapter, I dwell on the most prominent of the crosscutting themes. First is *attending*. Always under negotiation in perceptual psychology are the questions of how, when, and under what conditions sensations are made available to conscious awareness: when do we attend and what are the consequences of that attending? Second is what it feels like to be motivated to alter the sensation attended to, the *urge* to change experience. And third is the ability of senses when operating at their limits to challenge the very constructions of physical reality that are essential to embodied cognition and behavior. At the extremes of physical sensation come *derealization* phenomena. In the end—at the extremes, when we are running out of choices—we slip out of our bodies.

My method of reporting the personal experiences of each sense by interview was also a contrivance. People rarely, if ever, experience physical sensations without other sensations. Sometimes one dominates over another, but they often occur together. Take Marni, for example, who lives with lupus and appeared in Chapter 4 to talk about the experience of heaviness; she would have been equally eloquent talking about fatigue, tumescence, imbalance, or temperature. Kerry was superb at discussing fatigue and did so engagingly in Chapter 6, but she could have talked about her experiences of pain at mile 70 of her ultra run. This form of multisensory experience is worth closer consideration and is increasingly important in the context of aging, where it is discussed with a clinical language of "comorbidity."

Transitive and intransitive

Five of our senses operate outside of awareness. Balance, movement, breathing, being at body temperature, and being under normal pressure all operate automatically, without attending. It is only when forced to their limits that the nonconscious emerge as conscious; they become falling, being propelled, not being able to breathe, feeling swollen, or being too hot or cold. The other five of our senses—pain, itch, fatigue, hunger, thirst, and expulsion—exist only on attending; when absent they are typically characterized by relief. The first five are largely proprioceptive (with the exception of temperature) and the last five are largely interoceptive (with the exception of expulsion). I like David Armstrong's original distinction between "transitive" and "intransitive" physical sensations as it captures both the phenomenology and the functionality of physical senses (Armstrong, 1962). My treatment of the ten neglected senses does not map perfectly onto his original scheme, but it comes close. A modern version of this distinction relies more on the role of attending.

Attending

Why attend to one sense rather than another? At any one time aspects of all ten senses are more or less available to be selected into awareness. Run a thought experiment and test it yourself. Am I balanced? (check); moving? (check); itching? (check); etc. At times you might want to do exactly this checking; for example, in deciding whether you should put on a coat, or in being aware of your joint pressure when practicing a yoga exercise. This aspect of choice in attending to bodily sensation is not only a source of pleasure and fascination, but a dominant interest to a psychology of the body; it holds the key to understanding how behavior is altered, how the body limits or enables possibilities.

The limits of possible actions are determined by attention toward or away from physical sensation. But attention is a slippery concept. Traditionally, psychologists have studied attention by reference to its restrictions using metaphors of (limited) resources, (spendable) capacities, (narrowing) bottlenecks, and (straining) filters (Wu, 2011). Perhaps what is most important about attention is not selection for the sake of selection but what Alan Allport (2011) has called "selection-for-action." We attend for a reason, not simply as a response to the most demanding characteristics of the stimulus. We are largely goal-directed creatures, selecting and deselecting information, attending in order to maintain behavioral coherence toward a goal. In this way, Allport argues, "*attention* [better still, *attending*] refers to a state or relationship of the *whole organism* or person" (Allport, 2011, p. 25, his emphasis).

Psychologists often ask the question: under what circumstances can I make one attend toward or away from bodily sensations? Or: what are the consequences of attending toward or away from bodily sensations? And: how stable are patterns of attending over context and over time? The answers to these questions were reviewed across the senses in each of the chapters. Attending is biased toward certain information in our environment when it is meaningful to us. The classic example is in visual attention to something that scares us. People scared of spiders will be more likely to attend to spider-like information in the environment, what we call "cues" for spiders.

Attending toward bodily sensations or their cues has provoked a lot of research interest, discussed in different chapters as attentional bias. There have been attempts to establish attention bias effects for cues of pain, itch, fatigue, and breathlessness. The most interesting findings are in breathlessness, perhaps because of its association with panic. These studies are still at an early phase of development and need methodological innovation. To date, experiments often use cues for sensation that are symbolically coded, either verbally (e.g., the word *itch*) or pictorially (e.g., a facial expression of pain). The most successful studies are those for which the researchers have recreated the physical experience in a controlled environment, as Kim Delbaere did in designing methods of inducing postural instability, and as Omer Van den Bergh did with inducing breathlessness.

Advances will come not only in studying responses to artificially delivered signals of impending sensation, but also in understanding what we preferentially respond to in the natural environment. Again, methodological innovation will help. For example, modern technologies of deliberate falling (the roller coaster, the bungee rope) make movement through space possible to study. And digital recording technology can now capture previously hidden behavior such as how we manage peripersonal space, when and how people scratch, and when changes in body temperature trigger secondary regulation behaviors such as putting on a hat.

Vigilance

Not attending is the blissful norm for most people. Consider the complicated task of remaining upright. We have constant sensory information about our physical position in relation to the ground and to objects around us. However, thankfully, we are unaware of signals of balance in what is largely the noise of constant information. It is only when a change of sufficient magnitude, velocity, or character triggers a shift in attending that we are made aware of an impending trip, slip, or fall. Imagine, though, if every surface in the world was made unstable so that even the most familiar of tasks, like walking down your street, became fraught with danger. Imagine, in other words, that you are trying to walk during an earthquake, or you have had a stroke and are learning to walk again. It would pay to become vigilant for cues of impending instability.

Chronic vigilance is studied under different names, borne from different scientific traditions: chronic preferential attending, hypervigilance, somatic awareness. They differ in specific features but share a presumption of a stable selection of one of the bodily senses over competing demands. Most theorizing about vigilance uses the pathological case as the starting point. If I visit the doctor to complain about being cold, or tired, or itchy, or in pain, both she and I will collude in the idea that my physical complaints are symptoms of an underlying disorder and might indicate an identifiable pathology. If my physical sensation is irrelevant to any pathology, then she might reasonably ask a new question, about why I am attending to that sensation. Throughout I deliberately avoided and will continue to avoid discussion about pathological vigilance. It is well covered in the psychiatric and clinical psychological literature. And, to be fair, the pathological case interests me much less than the nonpathological. Normal vigilance is more common, less investigated, less well understood, and more fascinating. We are only beginning to understand how stable patterns of vigilance emerge and are maintained for specific goals, whether it is in staying continent long enough to reach a public toilet, blocking out high temperature to complete a forging process, or working with an exciting new spider at the zoo.

Delia Cioffi proposed a general model of what matters in awareness that is a good starting point for a normal psychology of bodily sensation (Cioffi, 1991). For Cioffi, preferential selection as a fact of attending is interesting, but is only the beginning of an explanation of behavior. What happens after attending is the *labeling* of sensations. When I become aware of appetite, am I "peckish," "hungry," or "starving"? When I feel pain, is it a "curious sensation," an "annoyance," or a "frightening return of disease"? What governs the labeling, and the variability between people, and within people over time and context, is often what we are studying with the individual senses. The pain example gives a hint of what is often being determined. Interruption by physical sensation, awareness of one's body, and vigilance for that sensation in the future, are affective-motivational phenomena. In other words, when we label something, it is not simply a dry functional cataloging: the labeling is always about feelings and action. When pain or heat or imbalance interrupt me, a specific behavior is not only made possible—it is often urged. I am interested in the phenomenology of the physical senses: what it feels like to be tired, cold, or hungry. But I am just as interested in the behavior that is being promoted: what it feels like to be urged to rest, to seek warmth, or to consume.

Urge

There are at least three related meanings of *urge* that are relevant to the physical senses. First, an urge is a qualia (a unique conscious event) of feeling drawn to act in a specific way, sometimes inexplicably, sometimes overwhelmingly. This urge can easily be seen as either a desire or a craving. This is the common use of *urge* in literatures about addiction. Second, urge is an action done to you. Other people, or other situations, may urge you on, urge you to react, urge you to change. This is the meaning of urge I borrow from ecological psychology in which environments afford behavior. These two senses preserve the dualistic idea of self and other; one is an internal force, the other external. Common to both is the third meaning of urge, which is better understood in its related adjectival form as *urgent*. The behavior being urged has a quality of immediacy, of needing to happen quickly. If it can wait, it is not urgent.

Each of the physical senses is intimately tied to a specific urge function that defines the flow of behavior that follows attending and labeling. One way of understanding the studies reviewed in each chapter is to see them as attempts to explore what it is like to be urged, or to live a life defined by a chronic physical urge. There are studies of the consequences of urge on quality of life, and how we might intervene to treat those who find the urge unpleasant or pernicious. And there are studies of how to promote safety in those who ignore sensations, either naturally or in trying to improve a skill, task, or role. Sometimes researchers have no such practical motivation. They just want to understand. They ask: how is it possible that we manage to achieve coherent and consistent behavior with attention switching repeatedly between multiple physical urges?

Table 12.1 summarizes the specific functions of urge. Each of the physical senses is tied to a functional class of behaviors. Some are specific, like breathing and scratching, and some are more general, like avoiding harm.

Table 12.1: The functions of physical senses

Sense	Function
Imbalance	balance
Movement	control
Pressure	stop
apnea	breathe
Fatigue	switch
Pain	avoid harm
Itch	scratch
temperature	thermoregulate
appetite	consume
expulsion	remove

The transitive senses of balance, movement, pressure, breathing, and temperature all urge when there is a threat to the equilibrium of the whole person, or what Bud Craig has called homeostasis (Craig, 2002). Imbalance urges balance by promoting adjustments in body position in relation to gravity. Moving too fast, too slow, without temporal or spatial fluidity, or without control all urge attempts at direct motor control, either by changing speed, musculoskeletal micro-adjustments, or in close concentration on an otherwise automatic movement. Pressure senses operate in much the same way as movement, but the urge is to stop: they act as a brake on the danger of overextension. Breathing is possibly the purest and simplest form of urge. Halting breathing urges breathing. Finally, temperature urges secondary thermoregulatory behavior. When you are hot you are urged to lose heat, and when you are cold you are urged to seek warmth.

The intransitive senses of pain, itch, fatigue, hunger, thirst, and expulsion come into existence as urge. Like breathing, itch is functionally specific: it promotes scratch. But pain is related to a broad class of avoidance behavior. Pain functions to promote avoidance of perceived harm, so needs to rely on a wide range of perceptual and motor behaviors. In the right context, almost any behavior can be recruited to avoid pain. Fatigue urges switch of attending: to disengage from something old and to engage with something new. Appetite drives the whole organism toward a single goal of consumption. And expulsion urges both symbolic and physical disembodiment. To expel is not only to separate and remove matter from the body, but preferably to project it away from the body, and to keep it away by immediately redefining it as foreign.

Thus the function of physical sensations is to urge change in behavior. In each chapter I discussed the psychology of what happens when we fail to register the need for change, when we try to find ways to master and control the urge for change, or when the context no longer affords change—through illness, decline, or restraint. *Coping* with being embodied is a matter of everyday cognition and behavior: it is how we live. Embracing corporeality could radically enrich the psychology of cognition, motivation, and emotion. Psychology is the study of embodied behavior.

Corporeal derealization

Part of my exploration of the physical senses was an examination of extremes, which at times I called "limit" experiences. What happens when one is at the very edge of apnea? In inescapable pain or itch? So hungry that the category of possible food has expanded to almost everything? So tired, cold, or swollen that taking action becomes unthinkable?

Reading across the physical senses, there are hints of an answer. It was made explicit in Chapter 2 when considering disorders of imbalance and height intolerance. At the extremes of physical experience comes separation from self, a change in the perception of a body as owned. This effect seems to operate across the physical senses but appears as different forms of dissociative experience, all of which have in common a separation from reality. Derealization effects include vague and fleeting feelings of awareness of another's presence and a sense of being watched. Also included are agency alterations ranging from a complete loss in paralysis to autoscopy in which one can elevate out of one's body and observe it from a distance. The ultimate combination is in being out of one's own body watching it watching you (Lopez et al., 2008) (see Chapter 2, Table 2.1).

In clinical neurology and psychiatry, these experiences are narrated as abnormal, brought about largely by the failure of sensory integration through injury, disease, or poisoning. In clinical psychology, dissociative effects are well studied at the extremes of emotion, most extensively in the study of panic and grief. In the clinical literatures, the dissociative experiences of derealization are often called "illusions." But in the normal case, I prefer to think of them simply as limit experiences. Missing is a study of the normal psychology of breakdown in agency and ownership that occurs often at the edges of physical experience. Phenomena of corporeal derealization come in three forms: marionette, immersion, and *unkörperliche* experiences.

Marionette phenomena, or *marionettes* for short, are vivid experiences of disequilibrium in which one's relationship with space alters. These were described by Debbie in Chapter 2, discussing her changed relationship with the properties of the environment, when the rooms seemed near then far away (telescoping); and described as concerning by Luke in Chapter 3 when flying through the air he experiences *knowing* he is in the wrong position in relation to the world. There are changes of agency described by Jeremy in Chapter 3 when he tries to initiate an action but does not complete it, and by Emma in Chapter 4 who has a sense of being moved by gravitational force. Being out of one's space and losing agency come together in the idea of "height intolerance autoscopy," in which one's perception changes radically. Agency is not just lost in paralysis but more accurately surrendered as one is urged to the edge—literally, not metaphorically. Like a marionette, one can feel either totally or partially controlled, as space, time, and will are altered.

Immersive phenomena, *immersions* for short, can usefully be thought of as moments of extreme attending. Immersions are not straightforwardly good or bad: context defines their value. In Chapter 5 Ian described being immersed in the desire for breath at the height of an attack of apnea; in Chapter 6 Sarah talked about not fighting fatigue at the start of a day; and in Chapter 4 Marni talked about an awareness of heaviness that most people will struggle to understand. I am sure that all would happily be free of these immersions, which are unbidden, unwelcome, and often unpleasant.

However, as with Philippe Petit recounting the story of his wire-walk between the twin towers, Luna in Chapter 2 described an immersion in achieving that elusive perfect moment of balance. In Chapter 6 Kerry found an immersion when the whole world seemed to fall away from her when running alone in the jungle. And Jean Christophe (Chapter 10) is easily lost in the complexity of his expert appetite for outstandingly good wine. Finally, some immersions are relational: neither good nor bad, and normally narrated as edifying. Examples are in Chapter 9 when Alex discussed working with iron in his forge as both an escape and a lesson on just how much one can cope with in life, and by Rupert in Chapter 7, who describes pain as having changed his view on how his life can be spent profitably.

There is a third, although rare, form of corporeal derealization, which is neither a pure marionette nor a pure immersion. I call it *das unkörperliche,* "the unbodily." In an essay of 1919, Freud described a class of experiences as *das unheimliche,* "the uncanny," whose root means "unhomely" but translates as "eerie" or "uncanny" (Freud, 1919/2003). For Freud, *das unheimliche* is an expression of repression, like the breaking-through of a faintly recognizable stranger. The original example was the eerie feeling of uncomfortable recognition you have on seeing a lifelike doll or a full-size waxwork figure. The idea has taken on a new life in robotics and computing with the increased use of avatars (Cadeaux, 2013). Unexplored, however, are specific experiences of departures from the bodily senses.

Perhaps the clearest example of *das unkörperliche* was discussed in Chapter 8 with formication. Formication is a paresthesia that is intimately tied to the idea of a perceived cause: in this case, itch feels like insects crawling under the skin. These ripples in the body sensorium, many of which can be artificially created in the laboratory as illusions, may be more than just curious. *Unkörperliche* experiences are derealization as a form of physical departure, experienced at the extremes of sensation. Critically, the sensation becomes inseparable from its cause, and the cause is attributed externally, as arising from outside the body: the itch is due to insects. When pain can no longer be unyoked from the idea of harm, apnea from suffocation, fatigue from oppression, or incontinence from shame, these may be the very situations in which *unkörperliche* derealization will be observed.

In summary, I propose three forms of corporeal derealization that all operate to distance one from sensation: a marionette is a disturbance of embedded agency, an immersion is a disturbance of attending, and *das unkörperliche* are disturbances of attribution. Naming them may make it more possible to study them.

Aging

Some people have lives dominated by a particular sensation: by pain, fatigue, or hunger. As examples, I sought out Sam, who is an expert on holding her breath; Kerry, who can persist through fatigue; and Alex, who works with high temperatures. But many people have lives dominated by not one but multiple sensory experiences. For example, people with chronic pain experience fatigue, and people with chronic fatigue experience pain. There are specific conditions in which multiple senses are involved: for example, patients with rheumatologic conditions can discuss unpleasant changes in balance, movement, pressure, pain, fatigue, and temperature. Injury or disease, and often their treatment, can also bring multiple sensations. In fact, given how long we are now forecast to live, the incidence of multimorbidity is set to increase. "Multimorbidity affects more than half of the elderly population with increasing prevalence in very old persons, women and people from lower social classes" (Marengoni et al., 2011, p. 438). And, for many of us, the last weeks and days of life will be a harsh lesson in embodiment. Many of the examples of specific sensory experiences across the sense chapters came from palliative care; in particular, end-of-life care.

Aging will challenge our assumptions about how far changes in physical sensation can be managed. Psychology does not have a lot to offer yet. There is much unchartered territory. For example, the jury is still out on how best psychology can respond to dizziness and falling in older age: strength building or confidence building? Can we develop an effective treatment for Raynaud's phenomenon? We seem to have given up. And how can the urge to scratch be diminished? In many cases the first questions are still being asked. How on earth did sweating, for example, come to be seen as abnormal and unladylike? And what can we do to change it? Given the taboo over reproductive expulsion, what are the norms for expulsion as we age into our 70s, 80s, and 90s? There is a pressing need for a psychology of the aging body, a need to incorporate embodiment into mainstream psychology.

Hands up

In closing, I am mindful of the unexpected benefits of taking a broad view across terrain normally surveyed tightly within its borders; of exploring the psychology of all of the physical senses together, instead of investigating each within its biomedical context. I will give you one example. How often do adults put their hands above their heads? Infrequently is the answer: perhaps to dust a high shelf or change a light bulb. It emerges that there are many reasons why adults should raise their arms above their heads. In Chapter 3 we saw that children reach for objects often—it is how cognition is enabled, through exploration. And there may be significant benefits to confidence by adopting expansive poses, in literally filling your peripersonal space. In Chapter 4 the consequences of inflexibility and tumescence persuaded me of the benefits of attempting yoga, stretching, exercising. Combine this with the thermoregulatory advantages of moving heat around the body, as discussed in Chapter 9. Add the general cardiovascular benefits of exercise and it is clear: expansive poses that involve raising your hands above your head are highly likely to bring multiple benefits to physical and psychological well-being.

There are other themes, "narrative worms" that travel across the different chapters. For a further example, I was struck by a belief in unitary illness that appeared in a number of interviews. Debbie, for example, in Chapter 2 remarked: "I suppose I look at it that there are people far worse off than me, so it is something you put up with. It is better than having a lot of other things wrong with you." Euphemia said something similar in Chapter 9: "We are all going to get something and if this is it, then that is fine." It was a surprisingly common response to a question about coping. Given the growing challenge of comorbidity, this particular way of isolating and minimizing experience, and the reasoning of having received one's share of illness, will be interesting to explore. It is not clear whether this minimizing strategy will fail when other sensations impinge, or whether it will prove robust and continue to be protective. There will be other worms I have not spotted that work through all of our senses.

A psychology of the body

Psychology has always been too mental, relatively uninterested in the body, treating it sometimes as just the means of transporting the mind from one place to another. The opposite is true. Being embodied makes it possible to experience the world. It is only by acting in and on the world that we are able to construct reality. It is because we are embodied that the limits of our conscious experience are constantly at stake, being defined, challenged, redrawn, exceeded, or surrendered to. You have here a normal psychology of the body that promotes a functional view of physical sensation extended with an appreciation of phenomenological experience. In the end, psychology is better for trying to understand individuals' experiences. If we embrace the corporeal turn in psychological science, we might be able to teach the next generation that there are more than five senses. Being embodied is how we experience, what we experience, and whom we experience.

References

Allport, A. (2011). Attention and integration. In C. Mole, D. Smithies, and W. Wu (Eds.), Attention: philosophical and psychological essays (pp. 24–59). Oxford: Oxford University Press.

Armstrong, D.M. (1962). Bodily sensations. London: Routledge and Kegan Paul.

Cadeaux, L. (2013). Ubiquanny: uncanny perceptions of ubiquitous computing. International Journal of Design in Society, 6, 39–45.

Cioffi, D. (1991). Beyond attentional strategies: a cognitive-perceptual model of somatic interpretation. Psychological Bulletin, 109, 1–25.

Craig, A.D. (2002). How do you feel? Interoception: the sense of the physiological condition of the body. Nature Reviews Neuroscience, 3, 655–666.

Freud, S. (2003). The uncanny. In The uncanny (pp. 122–162). London: Penguin Press. (Original work published 1919)

Haugeland, J. (1998). Having thought: essays in the metaphysics of mind. Cambridge: Harvard University Press.

Lopez, C., Halje, P. and Blanke, O. (2008). Body ownership and embodiment: vestibular and multisensory mechanisms. Neurophysiologie Clinique/Clinical Neurophysiology, 38, 149–161.

Marengoni, A., Angleman, S., Melis, R., Mangialasche, F., Karp, A., Garmen, A., Meinow, B. and Fratiglioni, L. (2011). Aging with multimorbidity: a systematic review of the literature. Ageing Research Reviews, 10, 430–439.

Wu, W. (2011). What is conscious attention? Philosophy and Phenomenological Research, 82, 93–120.

INDEX

Notes: *vs.* indicates a comparison.

A

accidental falling, 14–15
acting, occupational dieting, 218
active engagement of self, vitality, 113
activity avoidance, 37
    fear of falling, 12–13
Adams, Glen, 71
adolescents
    food preferences, 207
    heaviness–lightness continuum, 67
    movement, 36
advertising
    food choice, 210–11, 211f
    hedonic appetite, 208–9
aerophagia, 231
affective touch, 159
aging, 258–9
agoraphobia, panic, 92
alcohol consumption, voluntary vomiting, 240
Allport, Alan, 252
Altenmüller, Eckart, 49
analgesic culture, 140–1
Andersson, Gerhard, 21
animalism, farting (flatulence), 233
annoyance, itch, 164
anorexia, 205
anosognia, 47
anxiety
    farting (flatulence), 232
    pain, responses to, 140
appetite, 6, 201–24
    craving, 217–20
    dietary restriction, 215–16
    food choice, 209–11
    hungry behavior, 216–17
    overeating, 202
    personal responsibility, 214–15
    personal stories, 212–14, 220–1
    pleasures of desire, 205–6
        see also hedonic appetite
    pleasure *vs.* preference, 205–6
    power relationship, 203–4
    priority setting, 204–5
    public understanding, 215
    regulation, 201–3
    unappetizing food, 206–8

    urge, 256
        see also obesity
Arai, Tsuru, 108
Armstrong, David, 5–6, 252
Ashcroft, Howard, 182
assessment tools, itch, 169–70
attending, 251, 252–3
attentional redirection, relearning of breathing, 91
attention-control strategies, 114
attention to threat, pain, 132
Aunger, Robert, 166
autoscopic hallucinations, 27–8t
autoscopy, 27–8t
avoidance of activity *see* activity avoidance
Ayers, Beverley, 189

B

balance, 6, 8–32
    achieving of (equilibrium), 15–16
    biological mechanisms, 9
    loosing of *see* dizziness
    natural awareness, 16–19
    personal stories, 17–19
    urge, 256
        see also falling
ballet, equilibrium, 15
ball-throwing, 36–7
Bardy, Benoît, 35
Bargh, John, 179, 180
baroreceptors, 81
Bastian, Brock, 135
Bath, Anja, 164–5
Baumeister, Roy, 109
behavior
    climate-driven, 181–2
    extinction, 163
    hunger, 216–17
    thermoregulation, 178
Beliefs About Yoga Scale, 58
Berthoud, Hans-Rudolf, 202
biological energy reserves, 202
Blackman, Lisa, 3
Blackmore, Natalie, 240
Blake, Anthony, 210
blood
    flow in Raynaud's phenomenon, 193

blood (*continued*)
  thermoregulation, 178
  viscosity study, overtraining, 65
Blumenthal, Heston, 210
The Body in Pain (Scarry), 132–3
body ownership, height intolerance, 26
body practices, sociology, 4
body temperature
  character judgement, 178, 179
    see also thermoregulation
body weight changes, 65–6
van den Bos, Ruud, 215
brain injury, anosognia, 47
brainstem, nociception, 131
brain-training, fatigue, 113–15
Brandt, Thomas, 25–6
breast cancer, swollen feelings, 68
breathing, 6, 79–100, 256
  to achieve, 82–4
  control of, 81–2
  definition, 79
  diving, 84–5
  dyspnea *see* dyspnea
  endurance sports, 83
  expiration, 82
  fear conditioning, 89–90
  functionalist account, 100–1
  high and low altitude, 84–7, 85f
  lack of *see* dyspnea
  panic *see* panic
  personal stories, 86–7
  physical mechanisms, 80
  physiological monitoring of patterns, 95
  proprioception, 81
  relearning of, 91–2
  respiratory awareness, 88–9
  respiratory variability, 89–90
  terror management, 100–2
  urge, 256
    see also respiration
breathlessness, psychological treatment,
    100
Breivik, Gunner, 40
Bridget Jones effect, 180–1
Brosschot, Joss, 90
Brownell, Kelly, 214
Brown, Judith, 134
Brown, Kathleen, 192–3
Brown, Steve, 4
bruising, 134
Brymer, Eric, 10
built environment, weakness, 63
Buma, Lori, 83
burping (eructation), 225, 230–2
  embarrassment, 231
  gastric self-management, 231
  gastrointestinal disturbances, 231
  humor, 231
Byrne, Susan, 66

C
cachexia, 66–7
California, clothing and temperature, 183
cancers, persistent fatigue, 118
cardiorespiratory inflexibility response, 90
cardiovascular injury, heaviness, 65
Carstens, Earl, 153
CBT *see* cognitive behavioral therapy (CBT)
cerebellum, balance, 9
cerebral palsy, fine motor control, 48
Cervero, Fernando, 130–1
CFS *see* chronic fatigue syndrome (CFS)
Chambers, Lucy, 210
character judgement, body temperature,
    178, 179
children
  behaviour with senses, 3
  dietary studies in development, 207–8
  hand raising, 258
  pain, 129
  self-exploration, 40
    see also infants
China, dietary differences, 206
chronic cough, 227
chronic dizziness, 20
chronic fatigue syndrome (CFS), 118–22
  attentional bias, 120–1
  cognition therapy, 120
  maintenance, 119–20
  social context, 121
  symptoms, 120
chronic hiccup, 229–30
chronic itch, 161–2
chronic obstructive pulmonary disorder (COPD),
    96, 97–9t, 100
chronic vigilance, 254
Cingi, Cemal, 227
Cioffi, Delia
  value in pain, 139
  vigilance, 254
Clark, Andy, 5
classical explanation, fatigue, 108
climate-driven behavior, 181–2
climbing, 84–5
closed social practices, reproductive removal, 246
Closs, José, 133
clothing, temperature, 182–3
clumsiness, 33, 36–7
Cochrane reviews, 147
cognition, embodied, 35–6
cognition therapy, chronic fatigue syndrome, 120
cognitive behavioral model, 119–20
cognitive behavioral therapy (CBT), 122–4
  fatigue beliefs, 122
cognitive enhancement, stimulants, 113–14
Cognitive Intervention Scale, 140
cognitive intrusion, pain, 140
cognitive tasks
  short-term performance, 114

studies of, 114
tests, temperature effects, 183–4
cold, 184
    exposure to, 184
    extreme, 190–1
    mortality, 190, 191f
    Raynaud's phenomenon, 192–3
cold-blooded loneliness, 180–1
cold-hearted character, 179
cold-shoulder of rejection, 181
conditioned behaviors, 163
confusion, dizziness, 20
consequences, fear of falling, 12
constipation, swelling, 69
constricted postures, 44
continuous pain, 141
control development, movement, 34–5
control of breathing, 81–2
COPD (chronic obstructive pulmonary disorder),
    96, 97–9t, 100
coping with pain, 141–2
core body regulation, 178
corporeal derealization, 256–8
cortex, nociception, 131
Costa, Marco, 43
cough (tussis), 80–1, 225, 226–7
    chronic, 227
    disease transmission, 227
    personal distress/social threat, 229
    severity measures, 227–8
'Coughs and Sneezes Spread Diseases,' 227, 228f
courage, 115
courageous engagement, pain, 144
Couture, Roger, 83
Coward, Noel, 182
Craig, Bud, 256
craving, appetite, 217–20
cultural ambiguity, taste, 3
Curtis, Val, 166

D

damage, pain response, 142
dancing
    equilibrium, 15
    flexibility, 58
Das unkörperliche, 258
defecation, 225
    continence, 236
    incontinence, 237
    toilet training, 236–7
deficient hypothesis of overeating, 202
deglutition (swallowing), 238–9
deliberate falling, 10–11
deliberate practice, 38–9
delusional parasitosis, 168
Demain, Jeffrey, 154
depression, persistent fatigue, 118
derealization phenomena, 251
design, strength–weakness continuum, 64

diaphragm, 80
diet
    differences, 206
    insects in, 206
    restriction see dietary restriction
dietary restriction, 215–16
    hungry behavior, 216–17
    see also occupational dieting
dieting, occupational see occupational dieting
disease transmission
    face scratching, 158
    sneezing/coughing, 226, 227
disequilibrium, 19–29
    dizziness, 19–20
    threats of, 20–1
    vertigo see vertigo
disgust
    itch, 165–8
    sweating, 188
    vomiting (emesis), 239
distance swimming, breathing, 83
distraction, pain coping, 142–3
dizziness, 19–22
    chronic, 20
    orthostatic, 19
    treatment, 22
Dolan, Eimer, 218, 220
Domains of Quality of Life, menstruation, 243, 243f
doors, weakness, 63
Dros, Jacqueli, 19–20
Duckworth, Angela, 115
dyspnea, 95–100
    personal stories, 101–2
dystonia, 48
Dzokoto, Vivian, 71

E

Eccles, Jacqueline, 36–7
Edwards, Nicholas, 67
ego depletion model, 109
ego repletion, 109
ejaculation, 225, 244–5
    female, 244
    male, 245
elderly, accidental falling, 14–15
elite sports, equilibrium, 15–16
embarrassment, burping, 231
embodied cognition, movement, 35–6
emesis see vomiting (emesis)
Emmelkamp, Paul, 187
emotions
    dysregulation during incontinence, 238
    heaviness–lightness continuum, 67–8
    incontinence, 238
    respiration vs., 89
endurance sports
    breathing, 83
    pain, 135–6
energy, 112–13

energy reserves, biological, 202
equestrian sports, equilibrium, 15–16
equilibrium, 15–16
Ericsson, Anders, 38, 39
eructation *see* burping (eructation)
Ervin, Claire, 69
eudemonia, 113
Europe
    dietary differences, 206
    historical pandemics, 227
    obesity prevalence, 204
    pain prevalence, 141
event-sampling procedure, respiratory
    monitoring, 93–4
Evers, Andrea
    itch, 163, 169
    scratching, 162–3
exercise avoidance, 36
expansive postures, 44
expertise, value judgement, 39
expulsion, 6, 225–50
    definitions, 225
    releasing gases, 230
    urge, 256
        see also burping (eructation); defecation;
          ejaculation; farting (flatulence); sneeze
          (sternutation); sweating; urination
          (micturition); vomiting (emesis)
extended functionalism, 5
external inhibitions, scratching, 163
extinction, anosognia, 47
extreme cold, 190–1
extreme sports, deliberate falling, 10

F
face, grooming, 154
fairground rides, deliberate falling, 11
falling
    accidental, 14–15
    deliberate, 10–11
    fear of *see* fear of falling
    psychology of, 9–10
    see also balance
Farell, Emma, 85
farting (flatulence), 225, 232–5
    animalism, 233
    anxiety, 232
    humor, 234–5
    hygiene association, 232
    personal stories, 234–5
    prevalence, 232
    public display, 232
    social unease, 232–3
fatigue, 6, 107–28
    brain training, 113–15
    classical explanation, 108
    disengagement in, 111
    indefatigable, 115–18

medical studies, 108
motivational model, 112
motivation to change, 110–11
occupational studies, 107–8
performance measures, 108
persistent, 118–19
personal stories, 116–18, 123–4
popular explanation, 108
prevalence, 107
resource depletion, 109–10
stop emotion, 111
urge, 256
urge to sleep, 112
    see also chronic fatigue syndrome (CFS)
Faulkner, Michael, 95, 101
fear
    avoidance model, 144
    conditioning in breathing, 89–90
    falling *see* fear of falling
    incontinence, 238
    pain from injury/illness, 140
    visual attention, 253
fear of falling, 11–13, 13f
    dizziness, 20
feeling-of-a-presence, 27–8t
felt experience, 114
female ejaculation, 244
feminist theory, 4
Feneran, Ashley, 157
Filevitch, Elisa, 163
fine motor control, movement disorders, 48–9
firefighters, 183–4
flatulence *see* farting (flatulence)
flexibility
    pressure, 56
    see also flexibility–stiffness continuum
flexibility–stiffness continuum, 57–61
    dancing, 58
    personal stories, 60–1
food
    avoidance, 205
    choice, 209–11
    liking *vs.* wanting, 217
    poverty, 201
    regurgitation, 230
    of withholding, 203–4
formication, 168–9
fruit avoidance, 207
Fukuda, Keiji, 118
Fu, Mei, 68–9
funambulism (high-wire-walking), 16
functionalism, extended, 5
functionalist approach, 5
functions of physical senses, 255, 255t

G
gait patterns, 46
Galtrey, Clare, 95–6

Gasser, Michael, 35–6
gastric self-management, burping, 231
gastrointestinal disturbances, burping, 231
gastroparesis, 239
gender, sweating, 189
general distress, pain, 140
genital shrinking epidemic, 71
geography of sweating, 188
Germany, incontinence management, 237
Gibson, Stephen, 141
Gillies, Val, 188
Gladwell, Malcolm, 38–9
Gleaves, David, 240
Glover-Graf, Noreen, 133
glucose hypothesis, 109
gluttony, 202
goals
    control of breathing, 81
    pain, 135–9, 136t
    personal stories, 137–9
Graves, Sue, 188
Green, Sheryl, 238
Greeves, Andrew, 40
grooming, 154–5
    hygiene paradox, 157–8
gustation (taste), 2, 3

H
Hadjistavropolous, Thomas, 12–13, 13f
Haggard, Patrick, 163
hallucinations, autoscopic, 27–8t
Hambrick, David, 38–9
Hammarström, Anne, 216–17
hand raising, 258
hardiness, 115
Harré, Rom, 1
Harrold, Jo, 204–5
Hatano, Taku, 48
head, sensory apparatus, 3
health problems, burping, 231
health-promotion, relearning to breathe, 91
heart rate, perception of, 89
heat loss, sweating, 186–7
heaviness
    heaviness–lightness continuum, 67–8
    pressure, 64–6
    see also lightness
heaviness–lightness continuum, 67–8
hedonic appetite, 202, 205–6
    advertising, 208–9
    food choice, 210
height intolerance, 25–9
    autoscopy, 26, 27–8t
    body ownership, 26
    experience discussion, 25–26
    paralysis, 26
    physical arrest, 26
height loss studies, 69

Helsinki, clothing and temperature, 183
hiccup (singultus), 225, 229–30
high altitude, breathing, 84
high-wire-walking (funambulism), 16
Hill, Andrew, 217–18
Hinckle, Nancy, 168
historical pandemics, Europe, 227
Hockey, Bob, 111
Hollins, Mark, 6
Hormes, Julia, 218
Hot Flush Beliefs Scale, 189
hot flushes, 189
hot-headed character, 179
humanist tradition, vitality, 112
humor
    burping, 231
    farting (flatulence), 234–5
hungry behavior, 216–17
Hunter, Myra, 189
Huta, V, 113
Hutt, Kimberley, 15
hygiene
    farting (flatulence), 232
    grooming, 157–8
    reproductive removal, 246
hypercapnia, 81, 88
hyperhidrosis, 187
hyperventilation, 88–9
    panic, 94
hypocapnia, 88
hypoventilation, 90
    respiratory awareness, 88
hypoxia, 81, 84, 96
    dyspnea, 95

I
illness, chronic fatigue syndrome, 121
immersive phenomena, 257
incontinence, 237
    emotions, 238
indefatigable, 115–18
infants
    accidental falling, 14
    movement, 33, 34–5
    see also children
infections, upper respiratory tract, 228
inflammation, 131
inflammatory pain, 131
insects in diet, 206
inspiration rate, panic, 93
The Integrative Action of the Nervous System
    (Sherrington), 34
intemperate character, 179
intercostal muscles, 80
intermediate goals, control of breathing, 81
internal inhibition, scratching, 163
International Association for the Study of Pain
    (IASP), 130

International Scientific Forum on Home Hygiene, 157–8
interpersonal space, 43
interruption, motivated, 131–2
intransitive sensations, 6, 252, 256
intrinsic cost, tasks, 110
involuntary hyperventilation, 88–9
irritable bowel syndrome (IBS), 238
iStopFalls program, 13
itch, 6, 152–75
    chronic, 161–2
    definitions, 153
    disgust, 165–8
    formication, 168–9
    functions, 153–4
    mechanisms, 152
    personal stories, 159–61, 170–2
    pleasure of, 158–9
    psychodermatology, 169–70
    psychological perception, 163
    shame, 165–8
    social contagion, 155–7
    social emotions, 164–5
    urge, 256
    see also grooming; scratching

J
Jensen, Mark, 146
jockeys, occupational dieting, 218–19
Johnston, Chloe, 16
joints, range of motion, 56
Jütte, Robert, 5

K
Karlsson, Trine, 243
Keays, Glenn, 14
Kelly, Daniel, 2–3
Kindermans, Hanne, 144
kinesthesia, disorders of, 46
King, Sara, 129
Kirby, Amanda, 37
Kirby, Sarah, 20
Klein, Christine, 46
Klein, Donald, 94
Knoop, Hans, 119–20
Krampe, Ralf, 38
Krishna, Aradhna, 208
Kurzban, Robert, 110–11
Kvangarsnes, Marit, 100

L
labeling of sensations, 254
Lacquaniti, Francesco, 34–5
Lang, Peter, 94
language differences, hiccup (singultus), 229
Larson, Jeffrey, 209
LeGear, Mark, 36
Legrain, Valery, 131
Legrans, Dorothée, 43

Leonardelli, Geoffrey, 180
Levitt, Michael, 232
Lewis, CS, 132
Lewis, Glyn, 119
Lewthwaite, Rebecca, 40
Life at the Extremes (Ashcroft), 182
lightness, 66–7
    heaviness–lightness continuum, 67–8
    see also heaviness
linguistic coding, social aspects of
    temperature, 181
Linton, Steven, 144
Lloyd, Donna, 155
location, pain mechanisms, 130
long-term goals, control of breathing, 81
Lumeng, Julie, 207–8
Lussier, David, 141
lymphedema, 68–9

M
Mad Dogs and Englishmen (Coward), 181–2
Magin, Parker, 166
male ejaculation, 245
Man on a Wire (Petit), 16
marionette phenomena, 257
Massey, Anna, 217–18
mastectomy, total, 68
McGill Pain Questionnaire, 162
McNicholas, Fiona, 204
meanings, deliberate falling, 11
mechano-receptors, 34
medical studies, fatigue, 108
Mela, David, 205–6
memory, balance, 9
Ménière's disease, 20, 21
menstruation, 225, 242–3, 243f
mental fatigue, 108
methods of inquiry, 4–5
Meuret, Alicia, 94–5
micturition *see* urination (micturition)
mindfulness
    personal theory of movement, 39–40
    relearning to breathe, 91
mindless, personal theory of movement, 40
mirror neurons, scratching, 157
Morinis, Alan, 134
Morrison, Alan, 14–15
mortality, cold, 190, 191f
Moss-Morris, Rona, 120–1
motivated interruption, pain, 131–2
motivational model of fatigue, 112
motivation to change, fatigue, 110–11
motor control, lack of awareness, 40
motor performance improvement, 37–9
motor problems, clumsiness, 37
movement, 6, 33–54
    adolescents, 36
    clumsiness, 33, 36–7

control development, 34–5
developmental models, 40
disorders *see* movement disorders
embodied cognition, 35–6
infants, 33
lack of, 36
motor performance improvement *see* motor
    performance improvement
personal space, 43
personal stories, 40–2
personal theory *see* personal theory of
    movement
posing, 44–6
space exploring, 35–6
strutting, 44–6
urge, 256
    see also proprioception
movement disorders, 46–50
anosognia, 47
fine motor control, 48–9
personal stories, 49–50
start and stop, 48
tremor, 47–8
Mshana, Gerry, 47–8
Muller, Matthew, 184
muscle disorders, weakness, 63
musician's cramp, 49
myasthenia gravis, dyspnea, 95

N

nasal cavity, 80
Navon, David
disengagement in fatigue, 111
resource depletion, 109
nerve damage, 131
neuroimaging
pain, 131
temperature, 177–8
neurological diseases
heaviness, 65
weakness, 63
neurophysiological studies, thermoregulation, 177
nociceptive pain, 131
nociceptors, peripheral, 131

O

obesity, 36, 204–5
personal responsibility in appetite, 214
prevalence, 204
    see also appetite
O'Brien, Sandra, 56
occupational dieting, 218–19, 219f, 220
personal stories, 220–1
occupations
fatigue studies, 107–8
settings in accidental falling, 14
olfaction (smell), 2–3
opportunity cost, 110

Orbai, Ana-Marie, 57
orgasms, sneeze (sternutation), 226–7
Orloff, Natalia, 218
orthostatic dizziness, 19
Outliers (Gladwell), 38–9
out-of-body experience, 27–8t
overeating, 202
overexposure, food advertising, 209
overtraining, blood viscosity study, 65
Owen, Adrian, 114

P

pain, 6, 129–51
analgesic culture, 140–1
anxiety as response, 140
continuous, 141
coping with, 141–2, 144, 146–7
courageous engagement, 144
damage response, 142
definition, 129–30
fear of from injury/illness, 140
goal pursuit, 135–9, 136t
incidence, 129
mechanisms of, 130–1
motivated interruption, 131–2
neuroimaging, 131
nociceptive, 131
paying attention to, 139–40
personal stories, 137–9, 145–6
psychological interventions, 147
religious aspects, 132–3
rites of passage, 134
self-injury, 134–5
urge, 256
value in, 139–40
vigilance, 142–3
worry, 143
Pain Catastrophizing Scale, 140
Palese, Alvisa, 229–30
panic, 92–5
hyperventilation, 94
panic attacks, 92
Papoiu, Alexandru, 155–6, 157
papular urticaria, 154
paralysis, height intolerance, 26
parasites, grooming cuing, 155
parasitosis, delusional, 168
parents
anxiety in urination/defecation,
    236–7
pressure in urination/defecation, 236–7
Parkinson's disease, 47–8
Park, Lora, 44, 45f, 46
Patterson, Mark, 6
paying attention to pain, 139–40
perception of temperature, 176
peripersonal space, 43
peripheral nociceptors, 131

peripheral sensory mechanisms, appetite
    regulation, 202
perseverance, 112–13
persistent fatigue, 118–19
personal distress, coughs/sneezes, 229
personal responsibility, appetite, 214–15
personal space, movement, 43
personal stories, 5
    appetite, 212–14, 220–1
    balance, 17–19
    breathing, 86–7
    dyspnea, 101–2
    farting (flatulence), 234–5
    fatigue, 116–18, 123–4
    flexibility–stiffness continuum, 60–1
    itch, 159–61, 170–2
    movement, 40–2
    movement disorders, 49–50
    occupational dieting, 220–1
    pain, 137–9, 145–6
    pressure, 72–4
    Raynaud's phenomenon, 194–6
    stroke, 49–50
    swollen–reduced continuum, 72–4
    temperature, 184–6, 194–6
    vertigo, 23–5
    vomiting (emesis), 241–2
personal theory of movement, 39–42
    developmental models, 40
    mindful, 39–40
    mindless, 40
Petit, Philippe, 16–17
physical arrest, height intolerance, 26
physical effects, menstruation, 243
physical experience, respiratory awareness, 88
physical senses, functions of, 255, 255t
physiological monitoring, breathing patterns, 95
pleasure
    of desire appetite, 205–6
    of itch, 158–9
    preference *vs.* in appetite, 205–6
Pope, Janet, 191–2
popular explanation, fatigue, 108
posing, movement, 44–6
postures
    constricted, 44
    control of, 34
power, appetite relationship, 203–4
power poses, 44, 45f
Pratt, Travis, 233
preference, pleasure *vs.* in appetite, 205–6
pre-performance fear, balance, 16
pressure, 6, 55–78, 256
    flexibility, 56
    heaviness, 64–6
    heaviness–lightness continuum, 67–8
    lightness, 66–7
    personal stories, 72–4

    reduction, 69–71
    stiffness, 56–7
    strength, 62
    strength–weakness continuum, 63–4
    swollen, 68–9
    swollen–reduced continuum, 71–4
    urge, 256
    weakness, 62–3
presumed mechanism, pain, 130–1
primary Raynaud's phenomenon, 192
priority setting, appetite, 204–5
The Problem of Pain (Lewis), 132
Prokop, Pavol, 155
proprioception, 6, 34
    balance, 9
    breathing, 81
    disorders of, 46
    training of, 38
    see also movement
psoriasis, 165–6
psychodermatology, itch, 169–70
psychological interventions
    breathlessness, 100
    chronic hiccup (singultus), 230
    itch, 169
    pain, 146, 147
    Raynaud's phenomenon, 193
psychology
    ambiguity in temperature, 189–90
    itch perception, 163
    toilet behavior, 237
The Psychology of Fatigue (Hockey), 111
public display
    farting (flatulence), 232
    thermoregulation, 190
public-private dynamic, reproductive removal,
    245
public understanding, appetite, 215
pulmonary embolism, dyspnea, 95

Q

qualia of feeling, urge, 254
quality of life, chronic itch, 162

R

Rabie, Tamer, 166
Rakhshaee, Zahra, 58
    range of motion of joints, 56
Raynaud, Maurice, 191
Raynaud's phenomenon, 191–4
    attack causes, 192–3
    blood flow, 193
    personal stories, 194–6
    primary, 192
    psychological interventions, 193
    temperature biofeedback therapy, 193–4
recreational swimmers, breathing, 83
Redding, Emma, 15

reduction, 69–71
   swollen–reduced continuum, 71–4
rehabilitation, pain management, 146
Reid, Joanna, 66–7
Reid, Maria, 205
Reisig, Michael, 233
rejection, cold-shoulder of, 181
relaxation protocols, relearning to breathe, 91
relearning to breathe, 91–2
religion, pain aspects, 132–3
reproductive removal, 'normality,' 245
resilience, 115
resource depletion, fatigue, 109–10
respiration
   awareness, 88–9
   emotions vs., 89
   monitoring, 93, 93f
   variability, 89–90
   see also breathing
restless legs syndrome, 65
rheumatologic conditions, diagnosis, 56
de Ridder, Denise, 215–16
   dietary restriction, 215–16
Rigoli, Daniela, 37
rites of passage, pain, 134
Roach, Mary, 206
Rodiek, Susan, 63
room tilt illusion, 27–8t
Rosedale, Mary, 68–9
rumination, 90
running, breathing, 83–4
Russia, cold mortality, 190

S
Sang, Yen Pik, 26
Scarry, Elaine, 132–3
Scholing, Agnes, 187
Schutzer, Karen, 188
Schweitzer, Robert, 10
scratching, 154, 162–3
   mirror neurons, 157
   prevention of, 163–4
   social contagion, 155–7, 156f
   see also itch
secondary Raynaud's phenomenon, 192
secondary thermoregulation, 181–4
secrecy, reproductive removal, 245
Selby, Edward, 135
self, active engagement of, 113
self-contained underwater breathing apparatus
   (SCUBA), 85
self-cutting, 134
self-exploration, children, 40
self-grooming, 157
self-induced vomiting, 239
self-injury, pain, 134–5
self-starvation, as power control, 204
semicircular canals, 9

sensations, labeling of, 254
senses, adult vs. child behaviour, 3
sensorimotor adjustments, fear of falling, 13
sensory apparatus, head, 3
sensory integration, failure of, 257
sensory neurons, thermoregulation, 177
severe morning stiffness, 57
Shalev, Idit, 180
shame, itch, 165–8
Sherrington, Charles, 34
shock, fear of falling, 12
short-term cognitive performance, 114
shrinking waist illusion, 71
Simmons, Roger, 15
singing, breathing control, 82–3
singultus (hiccup), 225, 229–30
skin, thermoregulation, 177
skin disorders
   chronic itch, 165–8
   scratching, 157
skin lesions, disgust tests, 166, 167t, 168
Skinner, Robin, 14
skin weals, 154
Skull, Collen, 82–3
sleep
   disturbance in chronic itch, 162
   onset, 112
Small, Kate, 56
smell (olfaction), 2–3
Smith, Linda, 35–6
sneeze (sternutation), 80–1, 225, 226–7
   disease transmission, 227
   orgasms, 226–7
   personal distress/social threat, 229
sniffing, 80
social behavior
   chronic fatigue syndrome, 121
   coughs/sneezes, 229
   dominance in postures, 44, 45f, 46
   farting (flatulence), 232–3
   itch, 155–7, 164–5
   public display of thermoregulation,
      190
   rejection in vomiting (emesis), 239
   reproductive removal, 245–6
   restriction in urination/defecation,
      236
   scratch, 155–7
   scratching, 156f
   temperature, 176
sociology
   body practices, 4
   temperature, 179–81
Songu, Murat, 227
space exploring, movement, 35–6
spatial impermanence, vertigo, 22
speech, breathing control, 82
Spiegel, James, 234

spinal systems, nociception, 131
sports, breathing control, 82
start and stop, movement disorders, 48
Stephens, Andrew, 240
sternutation *see* sneeze (sternutation)
stiffness
    pressure, 56–7
    see also flexibility–stiffness continuum
stimulants, cognitive enhancement, 113–14
Stoffregren, Thomas, 35
stop emotion, fatigue, 111
strangulation, 134
strength, pressure, 62
strengthening exercises, 64
strength–weakness continuum, 63–4
stress
    breathing, 90
    incontinence, 238
    Raynaud's phenomenon, 192–3
    reduction programs, 91
stretching, 56
stretch receptors, 81
stroke
    anosognosia 47
    persistent fatigue, 118
    personal stories, 49–50
strutting, 44–6
Suarez, Fabrizis, 232
subject-object dynamic, reproductive removal, 245
suffocation
    challenges, 94
    feelings of, 96
Sutanto, Bernadet, 192
swallowing (deglutition), 238–9
sweating, 186–8
    disgust, 188
    gender specificity, 189
    geography of, 188
    heat loss, 186–7
Sweden, menstruation, 243, 243f
swimming, breathing, 83
swollen, 68–9
    personal stories, 72–4
    swollen–reduced continuum, 71–4
Symptom Checklist 90, heaviness, 65
syncope, 19

T
Tai Chi, 114
Tallis, Ray, 203
tasks
    intrinsic cost, 110
    persistence, 110
taste (gustation), 2, 3
temperature, 6, 176–200, 256
    body temperature in character judgement, 178, 179
    climate-driven behavior, 181–2

clothing, 182–3
    cognitive task tests, 183–4
    extremes, 183–4
    mistakes/accidents, 183
    perception of, 176
    personal stories, 184–6, 194–6
    psychological ambiguity, 189–90
    social behavior, 176
    social psychology, 179–81
    sweating *see* sweating
    urge, 256
    working memory, 184
    see also body temperature; cold; Raynaud's phenomenon; thermoregulation
temperature biofeedback therapy, Raynaud's phenomenon, 193–4
tensegral system, 55
terror management, breathing, 100–2
Tesch-Römer, Clemens, 38
thalamus
    balance, 9
    nociception, 131
Thelen, Esther, 34
thermoregulation, 177–8
    behavior, 178
    core body regulation, 178
    public display of, 190
    secondary regulation, 181–4
    see also body temperature
thirst, urge, 256
Thorndike, E, 108
toilet behavior, psychology, 237
toilet training, 236–7
tool use, peripersonal space, 43
To Reach the Clouds (Petit), 16
total cognitive disengagement, 112
total mastectomy, 68
touch, 4
    balance, 9
trachea, 80
transdisciplinary inquiries, 4–5
transitive sensations, 5–6, 252
tremor, 47–8
tussis *see* cough (tussis)

U
unappetizing food, 206–8
United Kingdom
    cold mortality, 190, 191f
    incontinence management, 237
United Nations World Food Programme, 201
upper respiratory tract, 80
    infections, 228f
urge, 254–6
    to change experience, 251
    physical senses, 255
urination (micturition), 225
    continence, 236

incontinence, 237
toilet training, 236–7
USA
adolescent food preferences, 207
child development, 207–8
clothing and temperature, 183
dietary differences, 206
farting (flatulence), 233
obesity prevalence, 204

V
value in pain, 139–40
value judgement, expertise, 39
Van Damme, Stefaan, 144
Van den Bergh, Omer, 88, 89–90
Varlet-Marie, Emmanuele, 65
vegetable avoidance, 207
Verhoeven, EWM, 163
vertigo, 22–5
classification, 22
definition, 22
height intolerance, 25–6
personal stories, 23–5
vestibular system
balance, 9
dysfunction, 21
vigilance, 253–4
chronic, 254
visible skin disorders, 166
vision, 2
balance, 9
equilibrium, 15
vitality, 112–13
humanist tradition, 112
Vlaeyen, Johan, 144
Vlemincx, Elke, 89
voluntary hyperventilation, 88
voluntary vomiting, 240
vomiting (emesis), 225, 238–42
causes, 239
disgust, 239
personal stories, 241–2

self-induced, 239
social rejection, 239
voluntary, 240
Vriens, Joris, 177

W
Waitt, Gordon, 188
Wansink, Brian, 210
Waterman, AS, 113
weakness
pressure, 62–3
strength–weakness continuum, 63–4
weightlessness, 66
weight loss, 69, 70–1f
Weinberg, Martin, 233
Wessely, Simon, 119
Williams, Colin, 233
Williams, Lawrence, 179
Williams, Sarah, 205
Wilson, Geoff, 84–5
Wilson, Margaret, 35
wind instrument playing, breathing control, 82
withholding food, 203–4
Wojcik, Wojtek, 120
women, sweating, 189
Woodcock, Katherine, 11
working memory, temperature, 184
worry, 89
itch, 164
pain, 143
Wren, Damian, 95–6
Wulf, Gabriele, 40
Wundt, Wilhelm, 1

Y
Yardley, Lucy, 20
Yen, Alan, 206
Yeoman, Martin, 210
yoga, 58, 59f, 60

Z
Zhong, Chen-Bo, 180